OPUS DEI

LIFE AND WORK OF ITS FOUNDER

JOSEMARIA ESCRIVA

PETER BERGLAR

OPUS DEI

LIFE AND WORK OF ITS FOUNDER

JOSEMARIA ESCRIVA

SCEPTER PUBLISHERS
Princeton, NJ

Nihil Obstat: John J. Quinn, M.A., *Censor Librorum; Imprimatur:* ✠Patrick Sheridan, DD, Vicar General, Archdiocese of New York, *February 3, 1993.* The *Nihil Obstat* and *Imprimatur* are official declarations that a book or pamphlet is free of doctrinal or moral error. No implication is contained therein that those who have granted the *Nihil Obstat* and *Imprimatur* agree with the contents, opinions or statements expressed.

Library of Congress Cataloging-in-Publication Data
Berglar, Peter, 1919-1989
 [Opus Dei. English]
 Opus Dei: Life and work of its founder, Josemaría Escrivá / Peter Berglar.
 381 p. 22 x 14 cm.
 Translation of: *Opus Dei: Leben und Werk des Gründers, Josemaría Escrivá.*
 Includes bibliographical references and index.
 ISBN 0-933932-64-2. — ISBN 0-933932-65-0 (pbk.)
 1. Escrivá de Balaguer, Josemaría, 1902-1975. 2. Catholic Church—Spain—Clergy—Biography. 3. Opus Dei (Society) I. Title.
 BX4705.E676B4513 1993
 267' . 182' 092—dc20
 [B]
 92-46088
                                                                CIP

Second paperback printing: September, 2000

German original © 1983 Otto Müller Verlag Salzburg
English edition © 1994 Scepter Publishers, Inc.
Printed in the United States of America

Translator's Note

The English language edition of this book is dedicated to the memory of its author, Peter Berglar, who died while this edition was in preparation, but not before he had a chance to review and approve the translation. A number of people joined me in the translation and editing of the book. I would like to mention especially Stuart Chessman, who translated the largest number of chapters, the late John Junge, who volunteered his efforts to translate and review the translation of a number of chapters, and Mary Gottschalk who deserves a large part of the credit for the readability of the final version of the text.

—Bernard Browne

Contents

Introduction

A LTHOUGH OPUS DEI has been active in Europe and North America for the last four decades, information about it tends to be both scarce and unreliable. The information that does surface occasionally in press reports, newspapers, magazines, and conversation often gives a false impression of Opus Dei and its founder, Msgr. Josemaría Escrivá.

Escrivá and Opus Dei (Latin for "The Work of God") deserve to be better known. I hope to introduce them to those who know little or nothing of either. And I hope that those already acquainted with Opus Dei will grow in their understanding of and affection for it. Finally, I want to dispel the doubts and misunderstandings that shroud the man and his Work.

Though a book such as this can only serve as a modest contribution, a forerunner of more comprehensive and definitive critical biographies to come, I felt the need to write it because of a conviction that grew with my research. It is this: in Josemaría Escrivá, we find the sort of great reformer of Christian spiritual life that God gives the Church at critical points in history to help people find their way to salvation.

When on October 2, 1928, Escrivá founded Opus Dei in Madrid, he had no blueprint, no strategic master plan. He understood the idea that God had placed before his eyes, but he had no five-year plan to implement, and no past models to imitate. He simply felt God's call deep in his soul — a clearly recognizable command of love, a divine request. He followed this call until his death on June 26, 1975. When asked about the birth of Opus Dei, he always insisted that he had begun with nothing but his youth,

1

God's grace, and a good sense of humor. Apparently this grace, like a flash of lightning, gave Escrivá not only a clear vision of God's will but also the spiritual energy to do it. Something that had long remained hidden in darkness was now bathed in light: the fact that the life of Christ embraced more than just his three years of public life. The thirty years of quiet, ordinary life in Nazareth, the daily toil as a carpenter, family life with Mary and Joseph — these too were part of the revelation and redemption he wrought. The work of salvation did not consist solely of Christ's teaching, miracles, sacraments, suffering and death, and resurrection. From the annunciation of the angel to the empty tomb on Easter Day, Christ's life was a single work of redemption, a mystery both human and divine. Quantitatively considered, Christ's thirty years of more ordinary, even hidden life are rather impressive. For Escrivá, there was a lesson in this.

In his own life, Jesus Christ, perfect God and perfect Man, had shown all men and women, his brothers and sisters, what their role is: to work. "We have come," explained Escrivá in 1966, "to call attention once again to the example of Jesus, who spent thirty years in Nazareth, working as a carpenter. In his hands, a professional occupation, similar to that carried out by millions of people throughout the world, was turned into a divine task. It became a part of our redemption, a way to salvation."[1]

The underlying spirit of Opus Dei encourages men and women to live the liberating truth — disregarded or forgotten for many centuries by many Christians — that any upright human task done well may become a divine occupation. Thus, for those struggling to correspond to God's love, work is anything but an obstacle. "Sanctity," continues Opus Dei's founder, "for the vast majority of men and women, implies sanctifying their work, sanctifying themselves in it, and sanctifying others through it. Thus they can encounter God in the course of their daily lives."[2]

For many centuries the laity, busy earning livings and raising families, were set apart from priests, monks, and nuns, who devoted themselves "entirely" to Christ. This dichotomy created the impression that full-time and part-time Christians existed. Secular living and spiritual life were seen as being in conflict with each other; and the resulting tensions often found unfortunate outlets. Because they were not called to follow Christ "professionally" in the priesthood or contemplative life, many lay Christians were discouraged from aspiring to an intimate union with God. On the one hand, Christian laity pursued, at best, a partial spiritual development in a pseudoclerical mold. On the other hand, diocesan priests and members of religious orders felt obligated to engage in secular activities, and to adopt the ways of lay people.

Undoubtedly, the division of Christians into first-class and second-class citizens, the former pledging their lives to Christ in consecrated life and the latter seldom entertaining ambitions of personal intimacy with God, has marred the history of Christendom. This impoverishment contributed, for instance, to the violent resentment towards the monastic ideal during the Reformation and the corresponding Protestant emphasis on the priesthood of all believers. Today the Catholic Church is aware of the need for a profound revolution in life and thought to overcome this dangerous duality. I submit that this revolution will forever be linked to the name "Escrivá." This revolution, like all other truly radical ideas, is thoroughly traditional. It involves a return to the lifestyle of the early Christians; even further, to the life of the Holy Family.

What Escrivá had taught and practiced for years, the Second Vatican Council authoritatively proclaimed: all the faithful, including the laity, are called to live the fullness of the Christian vocation. Without prejudice to the Church's hierarchical structure and the various qualities that define the respective states of priests, religious, and laity, Vatican II called all to holiness. To most lay people, this teaching sounded new, if not a bit heretical. Its realization in our time is intimately connected to the establishment and subsequent rapid growth of Opus Dei.

The best ideas are often the simplest, and the message of Opus Dei is no exception. All men and women are called to join in Christ's saving work. They do this to the degree in which they resemble Christ. This *imitatio Christi* is nothing if it is not voluntary. Christians must freely answer the invitation to sanctity, but they will have help: God's never-failing grace and the assistance of fellow Christians. This challenge is the essence of Christian life, as pertinent to the cab driver as to the Carthusian monk. The distinctive, revolutionary feature of Opus Dei is the setting where this identification with Christ takes place. A person involved in the daily round of work, family cares, and duties can be following God's call. Must we decide between imitating Martha and imitating Mary, or divide our time between the two? Escrivá rejected this division and boldly called for unity of life. This unity is achieved when one does Martha's work with Mary's spirit, working conscientiously and at the same time conversing with God in one's soul, for he is present with us when we work.

Escrivá taught and demonstrated that this marriage of active and contemplative life is feasible. How could devotion to God and the routines of everyday life be incompatible when both duties are enjoined upon us by our Father God? We are called to weave these strands of life into a whole. We can understand the possibility and desirability of combining total Christian commitment with our ordinary work, but this happy union does not come easily. Unity of life according to the divine plan may be a duty and an ideal, but something more than a vibrant faith is required. Between the goal and its achievement lie many pitfalls. Perhaps that is why God not only gave Josemaría the insight to communicate with others through his priestly work and writings, but also commissioned him to found a spiritual family that would teach its members how to lead such lives.

It was fortunate that Opus Dei's founder was a lawyer as well as a priest. Josemaría Escrivá knew that Opus Dei was not to be a transitory, amorphous movement of pious souls with similar sentiments and views. It would be a corporate body within the Church, with a legal status enabling it to fulfill its universal mission. What he saw on October 2, 1928, extended to the essential features of the legal form Opus Dei would need. No juridical model existed to govern a way of life that, through a specific vocation, was to lead lay Christians to sanctification in and through their everyday work. What was needed was a juridical framework that would respect and complement the constitutional structure of the Church, while allowing Opus Dei to carry out its mission within the Mystical Body.

The process of clarifying Opus Dei's legal status lasted fifty-five years. It ran through several stages, finally ending on November 28, 1982, when Opus Dei was raised to the status of a "personal prelature." The term is unusual. Its origin is Vatican II's Decree on the Ministry and Life of Priests (*Presbyterorum Ordinis*).[3] Article 10 of this document, which was proclaimed by Pope Paul VI on December 10, 1965, reads: "Where the nature of the apostolate demands this, not only should the proper distribution of priests be made easier, but also the carrying out of special pastoral projects for the benefit of different social groups in any region or among any race in any part of the world. For this purpose, there can with advantage be set up some international seminaries, special dioceses or personal prelatures and other institutions to which, with methods to be decided for the individual undertaking and always without prejudice to the rights of local ordinaries, priests can be attached or incardinated for the common good of the whole Church."

The Latin Church is organized and divided along territorial lines.[4] Its members live in territories called dioceses, each under a bishop. The growth of the Church brought with it the flowering of religious orders as well; as they spread over several regions, the orders found it awkward to function under the autonomous jurisdiction of various local bishops, and friction occurred frequently. Most orders eventually achieved canonical independence, or "exemption," whereby they were responsible directly to Rome in most matters. Other Church structures were also created to provide customized pastoral care for those who were somehow linked, yet spread over many geographical regions or dioceses: the armed forces, immigrants, exiles. But where did Opus Dei fit in? It is the essence of its spirit to believe that ordinary Christians can and should strive toward holiness in the ordinary circumstances of home and work. It is not necessary — indeed, it would be counterproductive — for them to have a special ecclesiastical status. It would be absurd to promote sanctification through normal Christian life if Opus Dei members segregated themselves from their peers by assuming a special state or condition of life. Thus Escrivá did not seek to withdraw members of Opus Dei from the jurisdiction of their local bishops.

Maintenance of the lay status is one indispensable aspect of Opus Dei's canonical configuration. Linked to it is another, equally important, characteristic. Members of Opus Dei must be able to carry out their apostolic activity among their peers. They are loyal members of the faithful in their own dioceses, subject to their own bishops, but they subject themselves freely to the demands of their specific vocation: prayer and other devotions, doctrinal instruction, spiritual guidance, and apostolic training. From diocesan sources they receive ordinary pastoral attention; from Opus Dei they receive whatever further pastoral care they need. In this extra pastoral attention, priests of Opus Dei play a large part. They are responsible to the prelate of Opus Dei, whose jurisdiction is limited to the purposes of the prelature.[5] Membership in Opus Dei requires, on the one hand, an affirmative response to the call to dedicate oneself completely to Christ by trying to live all the Christian virtues and, on the other, a commitment to use the means that Opus Dei supplies to that end. A member takes no vows, but enters into a contractual agreement with the prelature. On their honor, members agree to receive the spiritual and apostolic guidance that Opus Dei, on its side, agrees to offer them.

Lay members of Opus Dei are simultaneously under the jurisdiction of both their local bishop and the prelate of Opus Dei. In the juridical eyes of the Church, this is what a vocation to Opus Dei means. When a diocesan priest affiliates himself with Opus Dei, he remains completely under the authority and direction of the local bishop. At the same time, he becomes a member of the Priestly Society of the Holy Cross, an association which is inseparably linked to the prelature of Opus Dei, and from which these members receive pertinent spiritual formation.

These arrangements represent an innovation in Church law. Now, for the first time, it is possible for the faithful in the Church, ordinary lay Christians, to follow explicitly and formally a vocation of full dedication within the Church. A legal category has been established that gives them a specific spiritual formation, without changing their place or lay status within the Church. For the history of the Church, November 28, 1982, is an important date. It marks a decisive step towards the third Christian millennium, for it was on that day that Opus Dei became the Church's first personal prelature. In 1962, Msgr. Escrivá had requested from the Holy See the very solution that was now to become a reality. Pope Paul VI understood Opus Dei well; in 1963, he wrote to Escrivá that he saw in Opus Dei "a living sign of the eternal youth of the Church," a sign which "opened to her a fuller understanding of the requirements of a modern apostolate."[6] But another two decades were to pass before the new theological and pastoral phenomenon of Opus Dei could be given its necessary canonical form.

The Vatican was keenly aware that this unprecedented case needed a canonical solution to ensure a firm grounding for its future development. Veritable mountains of paperwork were accumulated during those years when the nature and implications of the problem were being exhaustively considered. Throughout this process, bishops from around the world were involved. Over two thousand bishops were consulted from those countries where Opus Dei was active. Most responded enthusiastically. Thirty-eight bishops submitted amendments and suggestions for careful consideration before the final pronouncement was made by Pope John Paul II on August 23, 1982. On the first Sunday of Advent, the beginning of the Church's new year, the pope formally promulgated the establishment of the personal prelature of Opus Dei.

Any biography of Escrivá, no matter how rudimentary, must delve into the spiritual family of Opus Dei. The establishment and growth of Opus Dei constitute the meaning and content of his biography. He lived and died for Opus Dei. Opus Dei was called into being as a new instrument for the Church to further her salvific mission: to permeate the whole world with the love of Christ until the end of time. As the human instrument for the founding of Opus Dei, God chose a young man from northern Spain, Josemaría Escrivá, and endowed him with abundant natural and supernatural gifts. Escrivá spent this endowment to found and nurture God's work.

Escrivá did not found Opus Dei only as a way and home for others; Opus Dei was first personified in himself. On October 2, 1928, the young priest saw that God wanted him not only to begin but also to *be* Opus Dei for the Church. If Opus Dei was to raise up saints for the modern world, they would have to be chips off the old block. If Escrivá wanted to do the work of God, he would first have to *become* a work of God.

From the start, this book has faced two considerable limitations. First, I never met Msgr. Escrivá. Second, his life ended only a short time ago — in 1975 — too short a time for one to research the nooks and crannies of such a prodigious life and put it in proper perspective. Initially, these circumstances led me to doubt the viability of the undertaking, but talking with members of Opus Dei and receiving the encouragement of the prelate of Opus Dei, Bishop Alvaro del Portillo, dispelled my doubts.

Since Escrivá's process of beatification is now in progress,* many documents, such as his personal correspondence and the internal records of his administration of Opus Dei, are unavailable. Nevertheless, rich sources remain for the purposes of a general biography, especially his books and articles, and the many publications of Opus Dei. These publications include general letters from Escrivá to the members of Opus Dei, over a period of forty-seven years, and Opus Dei's internal journals, *Crónica*, *Noticias*, and *Obras*, which span more than twenty-five years. I also studied the extensive writings connected with the introduction of the beatification process. There were some personal accounts as well. I enjoyed lengthy interviews with many of the earliest members of Opus Dei, people who had known Escrivá as a young man.

This book, however, cannot pretend to be a definitive history of Josemaría Escrivá and Opus Dei. Such a book will have to wait many years. My book is both a biography and an echo of the message of Opus Dei. It is about the Christian vocation in the twentieth century. My sole intention has been to make the founder of Opus Dei better known, more fully understood, and more justly appraised. I hope to show that Escrivá blazed a trail for Christians seeking God amid everyday life, and thus ushered in a new era of Christian discipleship.

---

* The original German-language edition of this book was published before the beatification of Msgr. Escrivá on May 17, 1992.

Chapter One

Family history

The town of Barbastro lies quietly between the main provincial towns of Huesca, Lérida, and Saragossa, the capital of Aragon. In the centuries since 1065, when Pedro I of Aragon recaptured it from the Arabs, Barbastro has grown in regional and commercial stature. Sometime before 1300, a Franciscan monastery was built there; so also was an impressive cathedral, because Barbastro occasionally served as the see of the local bishop.[1] Visiting Barbastro in 1981, I saw this cathedral being decorated for the Corpus Christi procession, with banners, red carpeting, and flowers galore. As I watched young and old pitching in, I was struck by the town's modernity: its traffic, Coca-Cola advertisements, and blue jeans. Seventy or eighty years ago, it must have presented a markedly different face.

What would it have been like to live in an Aragonese town back in 1902? No trucks or cars, no aircraft, no telephones, radios, or TV sets; nothing but the ordinary sights and sounds of people and animals going about their daily business. The odors would be simpler too. More smells of cooking and farming, tobacco and wood smoke, more sweat, and consequently more cologne and perfume. Men's clothing would be more severe and formal: hats and walking sticks were in their heyday. The women would go about in darker, longer dresses with laced bodices. The children of that time, while no strangers to play and pranks, would readily obey their parents, teachers, and priests. All in all, the people of Barbastro at the turn of the century practiced a more formal social decorum, particularly in manners and dress.

Here, in the center of this town of some seven thousand inhabitants, Josemaría Escrivá was born, on January 9, 1902. The house of his birth, which was situated on the narrow side of Barbastro's market square, no longer stands. In the sixties, it was replaced by a new building that houses a center of Opus Dei. Nevertheless, it is easy to imagine the home and shop belonging to Escrivá's parents; many of the houses and shops on the square today date from the turn of the century.

The Escrivá family originally came from the little town of Balaguer, some twenty miles northeast of Lérida. Josemaría's great-grandfather, José Escrivá, was born there; he became a physician and married Victoria Zaydín, a landowner's daughter from nearby Perarrua. José Escrivá Zaydín was born of that union. In 1854 he married Constancia Corzán, who was from the village of Fonz, near Barbastro. They were to be the paternal grandparents of Opus Dei's founder.

Little is known of the Corzán family. They were medium-scale landowners in Aragon. Grandmother Constancia, whom Josemaría knew, was a devout lady, active in doing good works. She died in 1912, leaving six children: two daughters and four sons. Of the sons, the eldest died as a child. The second, Teodoro, became a priest, lived in Fonz, and died there in 1933. The third, Jorge, died in 1885 while studying medicine. The youngest child was José, born in 1867. In 1898 he married Dolores Albás, from Barbastro. They were to be the parents of Josemaría Escrivá de Balaguer y Albás.

The maternal branches of the family tree exhibit remarkable vitality and vigor: prolific families and more than a few members choosing priestly vocations. Although most of them were land-owners involved with farming, they never earned enough to make this a viable livelihood for all of their children. Many of the sons, therefore, entered business and commerce in the surrounding cities and towns. Some of them pursued university degrees. Others, the pride of the family, became priests and entered religious orders. Dolores Albás had twelve brothers and sisters. She and her twin sister were twenty years younger than the first-born girl. The youngest Albás was her brother Florencio.

The Albás family had lived in Barbastro for three generations, ever since Josemaría's maternal great-grandfather, Manuel Albás, married Simona Navarro, who had lived there all her life. Their son Pascual, Josemaría's grandfather, ran a prosperous business in Barbastro.[2] His was the life of an honorable citizen, with a large family and an elegant townhouse. Pascual's elder brother, Simon, became a priest. The next brother, Juan, had nine children, including Mariano, who when his wife died in middle age was also ordained a priest. (When he was baptized, the future founder of Opus Dei received the name of this uncle-priest, who was also one of his godparents. He proudly used this name for a long time, out of love for the Mother of God.) Another of Juan's children, Rosario, became a nun.

Josemaría's maternal grandmother, Florencia Blanc, whose brother (also named Josemaría) became the bishop of Avila, also came from Barbastro. Among the thirteen children of this marriage, we once again find two clerics, Vicente and Carlos Albás, both of whom died in the middle of this century. There were also two nuns in this family. In the maternal line alone, including the bishop Josemaría, there were nine priests. There was a striking similarity, beyond name and appearance, between Escrivá and his great-uncle, the bishop of Avila. Both brought to their respective positions a broad education, literary and oratorical skill, and a legal cast of mind.

Childhood in Barbastro

What we know of Escrivá's parents, José and Dolores, comes largely from their son. Escrivá never described his family in any systematic way. Now and then throughout his life, however, he did refer to his parents to illustrate a point or to voice his filial gratitude. When such remarks are compiled, the parents' portraits emerge like tinted pen-and-ink sketches — general outlines with splashes of color here and there.

José and Dolores were married in September 1898; he was thirty, she was twenty. Their first child, a daughter named Carmen, was born a year later. In 1902, Josemaría (actually baptized José María Julian Mariano) arrived. Three daughters followed: María Asunción in 1905, María Dolores in 1907, and María del Rosario in

1909. Between 1910 and 1913, the three Marías died, starting with the youngest. "Because the three daughters had died in inverse order of age, the eldest last," writes Salvador Bernal in *Profile*, "Josemaría once said that it would be his turn next."[3] An understandable remark, perhaps, from an eleven-year-old, but one that must have cut his mother's heart.

She later told him that when he was two, he had been taken seriously ill — so seriously, in fact, that the doctors had given up all hope of saving him. In their desperation, his parents begged the Blessed Virgin to intercede for him, and he recovered. To repay their debt to the Virgin, they took Josemaría on a pilgrimage to the ancient shrine of Our Lady of Torreciudad. "The Virgin," Dolores once told her son, "must have left you in the world for some great purpose, because you were by then more dead than alive."[4]

Escrivá's father was a merchant, a partner in the textile firm of Cirilo, Latorre and Co. The three-man partnership prospered for quite a while. In 1902, however, Latorre withdrew, leaving the remaining partners, Juan Juncosa and José Escrivá, with considerably reduced capital. Their textile business, now reduced to one outlet, was unable to support the two families indefinitely. After a decade, it was practically bankrupt. José Escrivá was hit by this failure very forcefully — apparently more so than his partner.

Photographs of José from this time show a well-dressed man of medium height, with a strikingly high forehead and a fine, straight nose. The dashing full-lip moustache, along with the faint lines of kindness and good humor around his eyes and mouth, gives his face an air of youthful openness. "He was," his son said, "a man of enterprise, a hard worker, honorable, full of goodness, patience, and honesty, very cheerful, elegant, sincere, generous, lavish in almsgiving, friendly and attentive to all, especially to his subordinates ... filled with a great love for the Eucharist, Christ on the cross, the Mother of God, and the holy rosary."[5]

José's own rectitude, coupled with an innate confidence in others' decency, made him vulnerable to clever accountants and unscrupulous traders. Although he was a dexterous businessman, Señor Escrivá suffered losses at their hands. Those setbacks, along

Josemaría's parents: José and Dolores Escrivá, about the year 1905.

with diminishing profits and liquidity, portended financial catastrophe. Between 1913 and 1914, the firm went bankrupt.

Josemaría's parents were forced to bear no few humiliations as a result. Poverty never far away, they found themselves having to dismiss their servants and business employees. Eventually they resolved to leave Barbastro and make a new start elsewhere. The half-decade between the death of the infant María del Rosario in 1910 and the uprooting of the now smaller family in 1915 was an especially unhappy time.

The Escrivá children grew up in a household where piety suffused everything without suffocating anything. God, Christ, Mary, and the saints might be invisible, but they were certainly present. They cared for the children just as their parents did; in fact, the parents and the blessed spirits seemed to engage in a joint venture. Dolores taught her children appropriate prayers and devotions. Now and then, with his sister Carmen, Josemaría would accompany his parents to Mass. At the age of six or seven, he made his First Confession. His mother prepared him and took him to her own confessor, a Piarist father.[6] She literally escorted him to the confessional. "It made me very happy, and it always gives me joy to recall it," said

Escrivá more than sixty years later. The year before he died, he again voiced his gratitude: "Bring children to God before the devil gets to them. Believe me, you will do them a lot of good. I speak from the experience of thousands of souls, my own included."[7]

In 1912, amid dire family straits, Josemaría received his First Communion. Only ten years old, he was the youngest of the communicants. His parents considered him ready, and eagerly availed themselves of the new directives of Pope Pius X lowering the age for reception of the sacrament — regulations that were implemented slowly in Barbastro, as elsewhere. Immediate preparation was handled by a Piarist priest — "a pious, good, simple man," in Escrivá's words. The priest taught the boy a formula for making a spiritual communion: "I wish, my Lord, to receive you with the purity, humility, and devotion with which your most holy Mother received you, with the spirit and the fervor of the saints."[8] Escrivá later taught this prayer to his children in Opus Dei.

From all available accounts, young Josemaría was a happy, well-balanced, normal child: neither spoiled nor sheltered. But he was not spared suffering. What goes on in the mind of a boy who experiences within three years the ruin of the family business, the deaths of three sisters, the grief of his parents, and heart-rending trips to the cemetery? An episode described by Bernal allows us a glimpse into Josemaría's soul. The Escrivá children liked to build castles out of playing cards. One afternoon — it must have been between July 1912 and October 1913, because the two younger sisters were already dead — they gathered around the table and held their breath while the last card was being placed on that day's castle. Suddenly and uncharacteristically, Josemaría toppled it with a swipe of his hand. On the verge of tears, he said to them very seriously, "That is exactly what God does with people: you build a castle, and when it is nearly finished, God pulls it down."[9] The boy, at ten or eleven years old, had already experienced the inscrutable ways of God, and was trembling at the brink. But he rejected the temptation to doubt God's mercy, and thus strengthened his love for God. One might compare Josemaría's reaction to that of the seventeen-year-old Vladimir Lenin when his brother was executed for plotting the assassination of Czar Alexander III. "When he concluded therefrom that there was no God," writes his friend Lepeshinski, "he tore the crucifix from around his neck, spat on it, and contemptuously threw it away."[10] Under the weight of a heavy blow, Lenin plunged onto the path of hate. Perhaps it was the strong Christian spirit of the Escrivá home that buoyed Josemaría's soul up from such despair.

Josemaría received his earliest schooling from the Piarist fathers, who ran a small school near his home. These private schools were under state supervision, which meant that the year-end examinations were administered by public officials in Huesca, and later in Lérida. Young Escrivá completed the first three years of schooling in Barbastro. Teachers described him as "neither noisy nor rough, but studious and pensive; neither loud nor surly, but well-mannered."[11] He did especially well in the subjects of arithmetic, geometry, Spanish geography, Latin, and religion. He felt particularly inclined to mathematics and technical drawing, and thought of becoming an architect.[12]

The priesthood

The Escrivá family moved in 1915, when Josemaría was thirteen. They settled in Logroño — quite a change from Barbastro. (Today, Logroño claims eighty thousand inhabitants and is the capital city of the province of Rioja. It lies in the upper reaches of the Ebro River, in the center of the Rioja wine-growing region.) The father, José, associated himself with the textile firm of Antonio Garrigosa y Borrell. After the financial collapse in Barbastro, the forty-eight-year-old merchant made a fresh start with this Logroño firm.

At first, life in Logroño was difficult. The Escrivás knew hardly anyone in town. For months they lived in a very modest walk-up apartment that was hot in the summer and cold in the winter. Then they moved to another rented fourth-floor apartment that was only slightly more comfortable. Despite the hardships, Escrivá always spoke in later years of his "bright and cheerful home." His parents showed him an example of Christian dignity and hidden heroism, always accompanied by a smile.[13] Such was the environment he later sought to duplicate in centers of Opus Dei.

Now enrolled at a public school, Escrivá continued to do well in his studies. He had a considerable amount of natural ability, and this was enhanced by his habitual diligence and concentration. He read extensively, especially in history and the classics. (This education served him well; later in life he demonstrated a great facility for quoting texts and authors.) Meanwhile he was acquiring a keen mastery of Spanish, which made his written and spoken style clear, logical, and persuasive.[14]

For many young people, puberty brings in its wake emotional upheavals and often an aversion to religion, which begins to seem childish. But adolescence can also have the opposite effect: dramatic conversions sometimes occur, leaving the young person desirous of following God more closely. Josemaría did not distance himself from God as he entered his teens. We know, for instance, that on more than one occasion he had to battle drowsiness all day after having prayed into the night for classmates who unthinkingly spread off-color jokes.

The tall, good-looking youth (so he was described to me by an elderly lady in Logroño) was known for his good sense of humor.[15] But the same could be said — and was said — about all the Escrivás. Theirs was a home with a distinctly attractive Christian tone, neither opinionated nor sanctimonious.

In June 1918, Josemaría eagerly awaited graduation from secondary school. But six months earlier, something had happened. One particularly cold morning between Christmas, 1917, and the Feast of the Epiphany, 1918, he noticed, in some freshly fallen snow, the prints of a Carmelite's bare feet.[16] The sight of these footprints of a humble follower of Christ forcibly moved the young man and set his heart on fire. He was filled with a burning desire for a great love: the love of God.

Bare footprints in the snow may not mean much to some people. They may just seem representative of a quaint and rather extravagant asceticism. After all, what is wrong with wearing shoes? Such "excesses" can only be understood as the efforts of a restless soul casting about for ways to manifest its love for God. The young man destined to found Opus Dei did not, as we know, join a religious order, but the Carmelite's foot-

Student days: Josemaría during the school year 1918–1919.

prints did lead him to Christ; in them, he saw the footprints of Christ himself.

From then on, Escrivá felt himself drawn to a more intense life of piety. The sixteen-year-old began going to daily Mass and Communion. He went to confession more regularly, and tried to weave prayers of reparation and thanksgiving into each day.

He sought out a spiritual director "who would guide or help him to give himself even more fully."[17] During the early months of 1918, he discussed his future from time to time with a Carmelite. The priest advised him to enter Carmel, but Josemaría distinctly felt — and in prayer the feeling became a certainty — that God had a different way in store for him. Exactly what, he did not know. He no longer considered his calling to be architecture, but what would it be? Though he did not know the ultimate extent of his vocation, he did feel that the priesthood would be a necessary component. "I can distinguish two callings from God," Opus Dei's founder later admitted, "one at the beginning when I did not know what it was for, which I resisted. Later on, I resisted no longer, when I knew what it was for."[18]

Tears came to his father's eyes when Josemaría told him that he wanted to become a priest. Tears of joy? Perhaps, but not entirely. The father was fully aware that a vocation to the priesthood is a great grace. On the other hand, he was equally aware of what such a vocation entails. "A priest has to be a saint," his father warned. "It is very hard to have no house, no home, to have no love on earth."[19] José was asking his son, in effect: Will you be able to see it through? Are you certain that this is what you really want to do?

Perhaps the father was thinking also of something else. Josemaría's decision would mean the end of the Escrivá family name. At that time, the extinction of the male line was considered, at the very least, a serious misfortune. Josemaría understood this disappointment. So he set about begging God to send his parents another son.[20] Nearly a year later, Santiago Escrivá came into the world. His brother was seventeen; his father, fifty; his mother, forty. (Today Santiago is a lawyer, the father of a large family.) For the elder brother, the arrival of a male heir confirmed his own decision.

Far from opposing his son's vocation, José Escrivá arranged for Josemaría to discuss the matter with some priests in Logroño — not only so that he could receive some advice, but also to test, strengthen, and deepen his resolve. They encouraged him to follow his call to the priesthood. They also tutored him in philosophy and Latin. Thus they helped him, as an "extern" (non-boarding) student, to complete the first two academic years at the Logroño seminary. In September 1920, he transferred to the pontifical university in Saragossa. By then he was eighteen years old; his childhood lay behind him.

Chapter Two

PRAYER IN THE NIGHT

The seminarian in Saragossa

The changes in lifestyle wrought in the last seventy years are nowhere more apparent than in the lives of seminarians. This is true not only in Spain, but also in other Western countries with Catholic seminaries. In 1920, a candidate for the priesthood would have been quarantined from the secular life of the "outside world," from its comforts, freedoms, cares, and dangers, on the grounds that the priestly vocation is a special divine seal — the sacrament of Holy Orders — a license to work *in persona Christi*. At the center of this work is the renewal, in an unbloody manner, of Christ's sacrifice on Calvary, the celebration of the Mass. A priest's destiny is a personal identification with Christ, the High Priest. During their time of formation, seminarians were given great protection to enable them to develop their prayer life, ascetical spirit, and identification with Christ. They were schooled in order, self-discipline, and professional religious studies. Seminarians received their pastoral, ascetical, and liturgical formation at the seminary where they lived, and their academic training in philosophy, theology, and canon law at a university.

Josemaría lived in the seminary of San Francisco de Paula.[1] Every day he walked to class at the Pontifical University of San Valero and San Braulio. Salvador Bernal draws a vivid picture of the daily routine: "The seminarians wore sleeveless black tunics, with red sashes, and metal badges emblazoned with the sun and the logo *caritas*. From San Francisco de Paula they walked along El Coso to classes in the La Seo Square. They walked in double file, accompanied by a prefect. At San Francisco de Paula, they did half an hour of meditation and attended Mass before breakfast. After morning lectures (normally three periods), they returned to San Francisco for lunch. Afternoon classes at the university were followed by recreation, study, and rosary at the seminary. Between supper and bedtime, they said prayers and listened to a short talk outlining some points for the following day's meditation. On Thursday afternoons they went for walks, in single file, through the quiet districts of the countryside. On Sundays, those who had relatives in Saragossa could go out and spend the day with them."[2]

Such respite should have been available to Josemaría, because his mother's brother, Carlos Albás, was the archdeacon of La Seo Cathedral. Albás, however, kept his distance — perhaps because he misinterpreted the business failure of his brother-in-law. He did not attend José's funeral; nor did he attend his nephew's first Mass the following year, 1925.

Most of the seminarians were from large, peasant families of simple Aragonese farmers. They came from villages and small country towns. On the one hand, they were healthy and hardworking, with a simple piety and an uncomplicated faith. On the other hand, they were poorly educated and bereft of sophistication and refinement. They had only the most basic notions of the clerical life, and they were often unkempt. Josemaría was quite different. Without cultivating idiosyncrasies, he had a style of his own. To the surprise of many, he washed himself from head to toe every day. Unusual for a seminarian, his concern for hygiene caused some of his fellow students to doubt that he would become a priest; he appeared to have the makings of a "better" career.[3]

The young Escrivá was well educated. Clever in speech, he amused his classmates with serious and satirical epigrams. His combination of wit, piety, and human warmth lent him an easy confidence that later enabled him to move naturally among high-ranking representatives of church and state. "I take it as a special privilege," wrote King Juan Carlos I of Spain to Pope Paul VI, "to have known Msgr. Escrivá de Balaguer ever since my childhood and to have had personal contact with him. Because of this, I have been able to appreciate his spiritual good works and the renewal of Christian life which his priestly work, as well as the influence of his extraordinary personality, so full of the love of God, has called forth."[4]

This strength of personality was already in evidence when Escrivá was only twenty years old, and so it came as no surprise when later in life he displayed a knack for provoking instantaneous conversions. After meeting Msgr. Escrivá, many people dedicated their whole lives to God. Others, inevitably, turned away, but no one remained indifferent or neutral.[5] As Escrivá wrote in *The Way*, "You clash with the character of one person or another.... It has to be that way.... You are not a dollar bill to be loved by everyone."[6] Josemaría was no dollar bill.

The seminarian at Saragossa.

His university grades were similar to those he had received while in grammar school. Most of the professors assessed him as "excellent," and his classmates enjoyed his company. They remember him as a sincere young man with a helping hand and a good sense of humor. No doubt, his popularity caused envy and irritation at times. On one occasion, Josemaría became involved in a quarrel with a fellow seminarian who had insulted him. The confrontation came to blows when the other seminarian struck him. The details of the fight are unknown. Escrivá accepted the punishment meted out to him, but the incident failed to diminish the esteem in which he was held. (Thirty years later, his opponent, by then a hospital chaplain in Jaen, wrote a moving letter of apology to him.)

During the autumn of 1922, at the beginning of his third year of studies at Saragossa, Josemaría was appointed a seminarian-superior. This involved a change in lifestyle. He was given a room of his own with a servant, like an orderly in the army. He was free to come and go as he pleased. Although he was still a student, as a superior he had the authority to give orders, supervise the work of other seminarians, escort them to and from the university, and lead them on their outdoor walks. It was also his duty to preserve discipline in the seminary. Suddenly the young student was a member of the establishment. He ate, and was served, at a special table; his room was cleaned, his bed was made for him. He had to command the seminarians' respect without ceasing to be their classmate. Naturally, such a position presented problems that required considerable tact and prudence. Indeed, at Saragossa Josemaría learned not only theology and law, but also the art of leadership. From the beginning, he recognized that the exercise of authority requires honesty, impartiality, persuasiveness, and a continual balancing act between inflexibility and indulgence. Moreover, he had to learn to present himself with humility as a model for others. Instead of becoming haughty, "he neither overestimated the importance of his duties nor boasted about his appointment, but took pains to be unobtrusive and inconspicuous."[7]

Death of a prince of the Church

His years in Saragossa offered Josemaría another lesson in subordinating his own inclinations to the demands of office and apostolate. Saragossa was Josemaría's first acquaintance with big-city life. Equally important to the Romans, the Visigoths, and the Moors, it was one of the focal points of Spanish history, a center of commerce and culture. A bishopric since 1118, and an archbishopric since 1318, Saragossa is the metropolitan diocese of the Church province of Aragon. It features an ecclesiastical curiosity: two cathedrals. One is the cathedral and shrine of Our Lady of Pilar, a superb baroque structure whose silhouette, with its four corner towers and a central dome, is world famous. The other is the twelfth-century Gothic cathedral La Seo, which was built on the former site of the principal mosque of the region. Escrivá spent many hours in prayer at both cathedrals, but he had a special devotion to the shrine of Our Lady of Pilar, the Patroness of Aragon and of all of Spain. He dedicated himself to her when he set off for Rome in 1946 to seek papal approval of Opus Dei, and he returned to the shrine time and again. Notably in 1951, when the continuation of Opus Dei appeared to be in danger and the founder was almost in despair, he placed all his hope in the Mother of God, in whom he had already taken refuge at the shrines of Lourdes and Loreto.

We know neither how nor when Josemaría was first introduced to the archbishop of Saragossa, Cardinal Juan Soldevilla y Romero. Presumably the rector of the seminary saw how the newcomer from Logroño stood out among his fellow seminarians. In his report to the archbishop, he would mention the natural qualities of this seminarian — his piety and intelligence, his good influence on the other seminarians. When the cardinal visited the seminary, or came across him at the cathedral, he spoke to Josemaría and inquired about his health and work. Occasionally he invited Escrivá to visit him — an unusual honor.[8] Moreover, Josemaría was appointed to the post of seminary-superior before he received minor orders;[9] but only clerics can be superiors, so the prelate personally conferred the tonsure upon the young student on September 29, 1922, in his private chapel.[10]

This eighty-year-old prince of the Church, Juan Soldevilla y Romero, is one of the great figures in the history of Spanish Catholicism.[11] Born in 1843, ordained in 1867, and having served as secretary to several bishops of Valladolid, he attended the funeral of the Dowager Queen María Cristina in 1878. There the dead queen's grandson King Alfonso XII noticed him, and appointed him court chaplain that same year. In 1889 he became bishop of Taragona, and twelve years later, bishop of Saragossa. His elevation to the rank of cardinal followed in 1919. As the head of the Aragonese Church province for more than two decades, he became one of the most important members of the Spanish hierarchy. He had two great loves. The first was his homeland, Aragon; he researched and promoted its history, art, and literature. The other, inseparable from the first, was Our Lady of Pilar; he strove to spread devotion to her throughout the whole country. Through his efforts, the shrine of Pilar was declared a national monument and became a place of worship for the entire nation.

The anarchists' bullets that struck the cardinal out on the street on the afternoon of June 4, 1923, killed a man who, as a bishop of the Church and member of the Spanish Senate for well

over twenty years, had tirelessly defended the rights of the episcopacy and of religious education. Fighting against anarchy, terrorism, and weak government, he had earned the hatred of the
militantly anti-Catholic socialist camp. His murder was not an
isolated act of terrorism, but stands in the long line of political
and ideological attacks that led to the Spanish Civil War.

Regarding the political background of these bloody years,
Escrivá kept a consistent silence, a manner of behavior that he
exhibited throughout his adult life. When I asked his successor,
Alvaro del Portillo, about this silence, which in the face of the
problems and conflicts of those turbulent days appeared almost
apathetic, he replied that no one could say Escrivá was indifferent
to the historical-political developments in the world. "Msgr.
Escrivá de Balaguer was a man of great depth of feeling who
always concerned himself with world events. He was not merely
interested in such matters, but participated in them with joy or sorrow, and even passionately in things relating to the Church.
However, so far as the actual events themselves were concerned,
he took no public stand with regard to the temporal aspect of
them, not because he was not interested, but because it would have
destroyed Opus Dei, whose nature is purely spiritual."[12] Concerning the essence of events, whenever principles of justice were
at stake, he always spoke out. He kept silent about particular political incidents out of regard for the freedom of his spiritual children
to judge for themselves in temporal affairs. He did not want anyone to accuse the members of Opus Dei of adopting any specific
political stance, certainly not his own.[13] Escrivá often referred to
himself as "just a poor priest who wanted — and was only able —
to speak of nothing but God." Even while still a seminarian,
Josemaría followed this principle of priestly discretion.

Love for the priesthood

I felt strangely moved when on June 19, 1981, in the chapel at the
San Carlos Seminary, I stood and looked past the altar to the corner
of the right-hand side gallery where Josemaría used to pray. There
he spent many night hours praying before the tabernacle.[14] Again
and again he turned to Our Lord in the Blessed Sacrament, asking

for the understanding and the grace to do God's will. He asked God to prepare him for service "how, when, and where he would."[15] This was the continual refrain of his prayers.

No one knows the silent words of a soul's dialogue with God. And yet, the content of that nightly communion of Josemaría with the Lord in the Blessed Sacrament, in the chapel of the San Carlos Seminary, we need not guess. What does a future priest talk about with God, with Christ? Naturally, about the significance of his priestly vocation. In order to found Opus Dei, it was necessary for Escrivá to be a priest. And for Opus Dei to be born, to grow and to take root in many men and women in all future ages, he himself had to *be* Opus Dei. But Opus Dei is not an organization of priests alone. While priests may be members, Opus Dei is also an organization of lay people, both married and single. It is therefore understandable that these three states should have found an echo in the person of the founder. It characterizes the nature of his greatness and the secret of his achievement that he was a priest through and through, but with a lay mentality and the outlook of a typical family man. This union of priestly soul and lay mentality, so characteristic of Opus Dei, needs to be properly understood.

What did it mean for Escrivá to be "a priest through and through?" We cannot go far wrong if we seek the answer in the prayer of his student days in Saragossa. "What is the identity of a priest?" Escrivá asked during a meditation in 1973, and then he gave this answer: "Identity with Christ.... Every Christian can and should be not only *alter Christus* (another Christ) but also *ipse Christus* (Christ himself). Indeed, in the priest, this actually occurs sacramentally."[16] Here lies the incomparable dignity of the priest. "Every day he is the direct instrument of that saving grace which Christ earned for us. If one can grasp this, if one has closely considered it in the loving, attentive silence of prayer, how can one still regard the priesthood as a renunciation?"[17] To a question about the purpose of the priest, Escrivá responded, looking back over his forty-eight years in the priesthood, "I don't understand the enthusiasm of some priests who want to go out among other Christians and to put aside or to neglect their own special role in the Church, that role which they have been called to fulfill. They permit themselves to be led by the thought that Christians want a priest to be just like anyone else. But that is wrong. They do, in fact, want to see in a priest the virtues which should be seen in every Christian, and in every good man: understanding, justice, industriousness (which in the case of a priest refers to specifically priestly work), brotherly love, propriety, politeness. But apart from this, the faithful expect the priestly character to stand out clearly.

"The priest should be recognized as a man of prayer who does not spare himself in the administration of the sacraments, a man who is ready to take everything on his own shoulders but never allows himself to be tempted into becoming a militant champion of one human interest or another. People expect the priest to celebrate Mass with love and devotion, to hear confessions, console the sick and the distressed, support the needy with advice and love, teach children and adults the doctrines of the faith, and preach the word of God. They do not expect him, however, to become involved in secular science, but only in the science of salvation and eternal life. In a word: one expects a priest not to be an obstacle to the presence of Christ within himself, especially when he celebrates the holy sacrifice of the Body and Blood of Jesus Christ, and when in the sacrament of Penance — in individual, auricular confession — he forgives sinners in the name of God. The administration of these two sacraments takes such an important place in the work of a priest that all else must revolve around them."[18]

This quotation might be called a Magna Carta of the Catholic priesthood. This doctrine of the priesthood was communicated by Christ, through the operation of the Holy Spirit, to the Church, which has always taught and authentically interpreted it. For Escrivá this was beyond question. This conviction, however, is today neither self-evident nor commonly held. Like so many other truths of the faith, it has fallen into theological, journalistic, and often public controversy. For this reason, Josemaría Escrivá stressed this fundamental teaching all the more.

If, as the Catholic faith teaches, the sacrament of Holy Orders imprints a special character on the soul, forging in it an identity with Christ beyond that of the common priesthood of all believers, then a priest must not knowingly and willingly set aside or distort the model of the Eternal High Priest. He cannot live as if he were an official bureaucrat, a civil servant. He will practice a more intense poverty, chastity, and obedience than his lay brothers do, because Christ, his alter ego, lived in poverty and chastity and surrendered himself, "obedient unto death," as a sacrifice of love. True, the priest is a sinful man, and through his weakness he will fall short of the standard required by his vocation. This sober truth is a reason for humility on his part, and a cause for prayer on the part of both himself and his fellow Christians. Such weakness, however, cannot be an excuse for lowering the demands of the vocation. A compromise here would inevitably diminish the priesthood and those sacerdotal sacraments that are vital to the whole Church.

The country priest

In June 1923, Josemaría completed the fourth year of his theological studies, and twelve months later, the fifth year necessary for his doctorate.[19] (Because of frequent interruptions and the founding of Opus Dei, Escrivá was unable to complete his theological doctorate until 1955, when he received it at the Lateran University in Rome.) On December 20, 1924, Cardinal Soldevilla's interim successor, Miguel de los Santos Díaz Gómara, conferred the diaconate upon Josemaría. According to the documents submitted for Escrivá's beatification process, on that day "the Servant of God held, as he gave Holy Communion to his mother, the Body of the Lord in his own hands for the first time."[20] It must have been a moving moment; only three weeks earlier, on November 27th, his father had died. José had suffered a heart attack, and his son had been called by telegraph to his deathbed. With composure despite the pain, and with courage in the conviction that his father was now with God forever, Josemaría accepted the sorrow of this farewell. In 1975 he told a group of husbands and wives in Argentina, "I have a wonderful memory of my father, who had become a friend to me. I recommend to you, therefore, what I myself experienced: be friends to your children."[21] Escrivá never tired of emphasizing that he had learned inner composure, courage in misfortune, joy in the cross, and, not least of all, the spirit of poverty from his parents, especially from his father.

If one assumes that Escrivá did indeed have a divine mission to fulfill, then all the events of his life can be seen as bricks for the building that God planned, Opus Dei. Everything that affected his person, the seemingly bad as well as the good, directly or indirectly served to provide the optimum conditions for the development of Opus Dei. His father's sudden death not only crowned a life of hard work, but also enabled his mother to play an important role in the history of Opus Dei. Dolores Escrivá was to help shape one of the chief characteristics of the spiritual physiognomy of Opus Dei: its family spirit. But first she had to find a home for her priest-son, Josemaría, her daughter Carmen, and little Santiago.

Early in 1925, at forty-seven years of age, Dolores moved the family to Saragossa. They rented a modest flat, in a modest house, on a modest street. On March 28th, Josemaría Escrivá de Balaguer was ordained to the priesthood in the San Carlos Seminary, again at the hands of Don Miguel. Two days later, the new priest celebrated his first public Mass in the Lady Chapel of the Cathedral of Our Lady of Pilar. Only a dozen people were present, including his mother, sister, and younger brother. The Gospel of the day contained the following passage: "If anyone is thirsty, let him come to me, and drink; yes, if anyone believes in me, as the Scripture says, 'Fountains of living water shall flow from his bosom'" (Jn 7:37-38). Escrivá accepted the invitation to drink from the source of salvation, and his thirst was followed by more thirst — the thirst of love. The young priest from Aragon had an unquenchable belief, and from his heart streams of living water certainly did flow, for on his golden jubilee as a priest, he was able to look out upon a worldwide spiritual family of some sixty thousand souls, including nearly a thousand priests.

On the day after his first Mass, he traveled to the village of Perdiguera, about two hours from Saragossa, to replace temporarily the ailing parish priest. The extreme poverty of these peasant communities is barely imaginable today. For seven weeks Josemaría lived there with a farming family: a father, mother, and son (none of whom is still alive). These people smothered him with love and let him have the best room of the house. Years later, the founder of Opus Dei occasionally spoke of this family and especially of the boy, who spent his days tending the goats, and whose ignorance saddened him. Josemaría managed to teach the boy a little catechism in preparation for his First Communion. When he asked the youngster what he would do if he were rich (and after he explained what "rich" meant), the boy answered, "I would have wine soup [a local specialty] every day." Escrivá was struck by the universality of the age-old, materialistic criterion for a paltry happiness. The goatherd's wine soup, our dreams of grand slams, beautiful women, world cruises — was there really much difference? "I became," he recalled, "very serious, and I thought, *Josemaría, the Holy Spirit is speaking to you*. The wisdom of God confronted me: how little, in the end, worldly goods matter."[22]

His short stay in Perdiguera was of great significance for Josemaría Escrivá. There he saw the hard and wretched life of the peasant farmers — and that of their country priests. The conviction became rooted in him that these country people needed help to improve their working lives. They needed new agricultural techniques, and a sound moral and religious education. The country clergy, so often left to their own devices, needed spiritual and academic training. Many schools for the professional, religious, and cultural education of peasant families in the poorest, most isolated places of Spain and Latin America were inspired by the teaching of the founder of Opus Dei. Opus Dei members used the spirituality of daily work and family life to help the needy. The earliest impulse for this apostolate lies in those weeks, during the spring of 1925, when the twenty-three-year-old priest completed his first pastoral assignment on the ground floor of Spanish society. Later, in Madrid, he would learn about the basement of this society.

Law studies in Saragossa

On May 18th, Josemaría returned to Saragossa and resumed his law studies. He had begun studying law in 1923, with the approval of his father, who saw additional security in such study. The same thought struck the son, but from a different angle. Before he knew the exact content of his life's work, he sensed instinctively the qualifications that its fulfillment would require: an interior life of intimacy with God was taken for granted; the priesthood — that was not hard to see; and finally, a legal education. What his father saw as useful, Josemaría recognized as necessary. This is astounding, since in 1923 he could hardly have foreseen that one day the juridical nature of Opus Dei — its status vis-à-vis canon law and the universal Church — would become a critical issue.

"Although I do not know what it is, may your will be done," he prayed night and day.[23] Yet he knew clearly what God did *not* want of him. Escrivá had no intention of becoming a bishop or of embarking on a hierarchical career. During his law studies, he did, however, become convinced that God's plan for him would have important implications in Church law. As preparation he studied not only Church law, but also all the branches of civil law. He passed his examinations, and in January 1927 he received the licentiate in law. When I was in Saragossa in 1981, I met a lawyer, a retired government official who in 1925, at the age of fifteen, had met Josemaría Escrivá. Escrivá usually celebrated Mass at the Jesuit Church of St. Peter Nolasco, and it was there that he first met Juan Antonio Cremades Royó. Soon Juan Antonio was attending the catechism classes that the good-natured priest held for children and youths in the suburbs of Saragossa.[24]

"He made a strong impression on young people," Cremades remembered. "He had a keen sense of humor, and adapted to others easily." Cremades related the following anecdote: "Among the Saragossa law faculty there were some eccentric professors, real characters — indeed, sometimes caricatures. One of these insisted that everybody had to learn the whole code by heart. He had a habit of waving his thick, long index finger right in front of students' faces, until one day Escrivá grabbed hold of it. The professor showed no ill reaction, but simply waited for it to be released."[25]

According to Cremades, Escrivá, who had to support his mother, sister, and brother, had become poor. He gave Latin lessons for twenty-five pesetas a month, and he lectured at the Amado Institute, where he taught Roman and canon law. Housed in an imposing building, the Amado Institute was the type of private academy that used to be found in every large Spanish town. In these academies, one could acquire a high-school education and prepare for the state-administered exams. More importantly, one could prepare for university studies and for entrance exams to the military, naval, and forestry academies. The founder and principal of the Amado Institute was a former infantry captain. He held a licentiate in mathematics and natural science and was well respected for his teaching ability.

A copy of the March 1927 Institute magazine *Alpha-Beta* advertises preparatory courses for army and navy cadets. On the back cover, all thirty-three lecturers are named. The list includes management experts,[26] natural scientists, engineers, and one solitary priest, Josemaría Escrivá. All in all, some fifty preparatory courses were offered by the Institute. The same issue of *Alpha-Beta* also contains a historical treasure: the first published work by Josemaría Escrivá, entitled "The Form of Marriage in Present-Day Spanish Legislation."[27] The article is signed "José María Escrivá y Albás, priest and lawyer."* Drawn from lectures for students of canon and Roman law, it deals with the licensing, validity, and use of civil marriage in contemporary Spain. Throughout the nineteenth century, attempts had been made to strip marriage of its divine and sacramental character. Even such countries as Italy, Spain, and Belgium, where the Catholic Church was explicitly established in national law, could not escape this trend for long. Demonstrating dogmatic and legal precision, as well as a thorough knowledge of ecclesiastical and civil legal requirements, Escrivá offers in this essay a significant contribution to the debate. He does not refrain from deploring the multiplication of Registry Office marriages facilitated by laws changed on the sly — through the legislative back door, as it were. He emphasizes the fact that marriage is rooted in the natural law established by God for all human beings, Christians and non-Christians alike. He concludes, "Civil marriage must remain available in Spain for the unbaptized who wish to form a family according to the divine law and for whom such marriages provide a legitimate union with legitimate effect."[28]

Immediately after receiving his licentiate in law, Escrivá presented a petition to the new archbishop of Saragossa requesting a

---

*It was some time later that the founder of Opus Dei began to write his first two names as the single word Josemaría to express his feeling that Joseph and Mary should not be separated.

transfer to Madrid, because only at Madrid's central university could one complete a doctorate in civil law. On March 17, 1927, permission to transfer was granted; for a period of two years, Josemaría could study in the capital in order to finish his dissertation and receive his doctorate. Soon after he enrolled in the law school at Madrid, in April 1927, the growth of Opus Dei began to dominate his whole life, demanding all his energies. Nevertheless, he remained determined to complete his doctorate. It was characteristic of him that once he made up his mind to accomplish something, he would complete it no matter how long it took. José López Ortiz, later the bishop of the Spanish Armed Forces, reports that when he met Escrivá after the Spanish Civil War (in Madrid, 1939), Escrivá was still busy with, among other things, his doctoral thesis, entitled "The Abbess of Las Huelgas."[29] Twelve years had passed since he earned his licentiate. He had been forced to abandon his original thesis topic (concerning the ordination of mestizos in Spanish colonies during the Renaissance), because his research notes and personal library were lost in the war. Nevertheless, he persevered in his resolve and completed his doctoral dissertation in December 1939. Another five years were to pass before this extensive theological-legal study would appear in book form, but appear it did — the fruit of perseverance.[30]

Escrivá dedicated the last chapter of *The Way* to the theme of perseverance. I believe that the importance of this virtue can hardly be exaggerated. Perseverance is the modest daughter of love, the little sister of fidelity, and the long-distance runner among the virtues. Without perseverance, the fields of human endeavor will never yield a harvest, either from the soil of the countryside or from individual souls. Without perseverance, nothing of worth is won, and nothing won is kept. Opus Dei could easily have disintegrated in the Spanish Civil War; Escrivá's book need not have been published. But the spirit of Opus Dei, the spirit of persevering in the fulfillment of secular duties for the love of Christ, demands that a job begun be finished. "To begin," wrote Escrivá in *The Way*, "is for everyone; to persevere is for saints."[31] And that goes for authors as well.

Chapter Three

THE BELLS

A brother to the poor of Madrid

What began as a two-year stay in Madrid stretched, in the end, to eighteen years. Josemaría Escrivá lived and worked in the Spanish capital from April 1927 until October 1937, when he fled from Republican Madrid to the Nationalist Zone,[1] and from March 1939 until November 1946, when he moved to Rome for good. This period in his life corresponds to the birth and infancy of Opus Dei. Msgr. Escrivá *was* Opus Dei — I have said it before, but it bears repeating — and in the beginning, Opus Dei was only himself. In the fullest sense of the words, he was the father, priest, and teacher of this new spiritual family.

For the sake of description and analysis, every biography must break down what is in fact an unbroken unity: a person's life. The student taught classes, the scholar prayed, and the priest moved in academic circles. At the same time, as a priest who had been assigned by his bishop to another diocese, he had to take all the preliminary exams for extra-diocesan priests in the diocese of Madrid-Alcalá, in order to celebrate Mass, administer the other sacraments, and preach.[2] All this constituted the "raw material" of his priesthood.

And when he had finished teaching his classes, the scholar set out, almost always on foot, to attend to *les miserables* in the vast and distant suburbs of the city. He gave them the sacrament of the Anointing of the Sick as well as Holy Communion, and attended to their various needs, staying with many who were on their deathbeds. From there he went to teach catechism to the children he was preparing for their First Confession and Holy Communion. Then he went to one of the several hospitals where he lent his services as a priest. All this done, there still remained the long trip home, where he bent over his books, continuing to work on his doctoral thesis or preparing classes for the next day. He could switch the order of his activities, but because there were so many, they were never finished by the end of the day.

In the previous chapter, I noted that in Perdiguera Escrivá had encountered the ground floor of Spanish society, but the basement still awaited him. The material poverty of the peasants in Perdiguera and their lack of ordinary culture were staggering, but they still had hope; normally they did not go hungry, and the bonds of kith and kin survived. Their closeness to nature, austere and hostile though it could be, sheltered them from total misery. From a sociological point of view, it was fairly easy to formulate a profile of the proletarian peasant; it could also be hoped that reforms would have the desired effect. The needs were obvious, tangible, and, if someone initiated a program and the state supported it, manageable. These poverty-stricken peasants lived in the light of day; they were within the focus of a society that knew them, a media that paid attention to their plight, and an administration disposed to help them.

The situation in the suburbs of Madrid, as in most of the world's other big cities, was totally different, for there the darkness of night still reigned. Those born or ending up there were condemned to a subterranean existence: a life whose violent convulsions registered no signal on the seismographs of society, a life touched by neither sociologists nor civil registrars, nor even the police; and, of course, they lay outside the parish system of the Church. This underworld was dead even to statistics — the most complete death possible in civilized society.

All generalizations, of course, need qualification. Just as a clearly defined "nobility" or "bourgeoisie" has never existed, neither has there ever been a permanent lower-class "proletariat," if this is taken to mean a homogeneous, immobile mass. What there has always been is a more or less stable nucleus with marginal groupings in a constant state of flux.

Take Madrid, for example. Between 1860, when industrialization began in Spain, and 1970, the population multiplied tenfold, from three hundred thousand to three million inhabitants. In 1900, a little over half a million people lived in Madrid. In the 1920s (when Escrivá arrived), the population had grown to eight hundred thousand, and by 1940 (just after the Spanish Civil War), to almost one and a half million. The working class that had arisen from the proletariat of the previous century lived in outlying neighborhoods or sprawling suburbs. These people maintained a low standard of living that depended on the job market; they were constantly at the mercy of work stoppages and unemployment, and their wages were at a subsistence level or below. And yet, in spite of everything, workers continued to pour in from the countryside.

From the beginning of the century, this migratory flow had persisted, and all around the city there were areas with shanties or hovels where the refuse and overflow of society were settling.

Although Madrid then had only a quarter of its present population, the destitution of its outcasts was greater than it is today. Here Escrivá saw the extremes of human misery, the degradation and the blotting out of the divine image of man and woman. And in this human wasteland he was a good shepherd, in search not of a single lost sheep but of a whole wayward flock.

His position as chaplain of the Foundation for the Sick, a charitable institution run by a women's congregation called the Apostolic Ladies (Damas Apostólicas) of the Sacred Heart, facilitated his task. The congregation had been founded a few years earlier to tend to the sick and poor, especially in the suburbs of Madrid. In 1927 it was approved by the Holy See. The Foundation treated some four thousand sick people every year; it brought food, medication, clothing, and pastoral care to their homes. This was only one of the many social and charitable projects of the Foundation, which by 1928 already managed sixty-one schools and soup kitchens. It also provided a residence for priests, where Escrivá lived during his first months in Madrid.

Though Escrivá had been named chaplain of the Foundation for the Sick, his work did not stop there. Driven by apostolic zeal, he set about helping, on his own time, in the various urgent projects of the Apostolic Ladies. This was not part of his duties as a chaplain; this was his interpretation of fraternal charity as it should be lived by a priest.

The importance of his priestly work in Madrid cannot be stressed enough, for it was closely linked to the birth and infancy of Opus Dei. The Work had no better luck than did the Lord who gave it life. It was born and it grew up in poverty and danger. Escrivá never denied (and toward the end of his life, he especially liked to remind people) that the poor, the wretched, the abandoned, the sick, and the dying whom he visited — or rather, whom he sought as one seeks treasures — had been the "midwives" of Opus Dei.

Among the beggars, he begged for the alms of prayer; and they, who had nothing, gave him all they had: their prayers and sufferings. They did so not because they knew and understood his intentions, but for one simple reason: they loved this young priest and trusted him, even though some had not gone to a priest or let one come near them for many years.

In 1975, a few months before his death, Escrivá spoke of those days. "I went to seek strength," he recalled, "in the poorest neighborhoods of Madrid. Hours and hours, back and forth, every day, on foot from one part to another, among the wretched poor who owned absolutely nothing; among children with runny noses and coughing spells — all filthy, but still God's children, still souls that were pleasing to him. And in the hospitals, and in the houses of the sick (if one can call those hovels houses), the people were forsaken and sick. Some had a disease that was incurable then — tuberculosis. And so I went in search of the means to do the Work of God in all these places. The sick constituted the human strength of the Work. The most wretched, those for whom the faintest human hope was dead, the most ignorant people of those outlying districts, these were the treasures of Opus Dei, the human means we used: the incurably ill, the forsaken poor, children without families or education, living in homes without fire, without heat, without love."[3]

It had been eleven years since Josemaría, while still in high school, had discovered that those footprints in the snow were the footprints of Jesus Christ, and had begun to sense that they implied a personal call. It had been a gentle, quiet call at first, a call to keep him alert for — what? something he still did not know. To succumb to the temptation of imagining something on his own initiative would have meant losing the guidance of the Divine Teacher. But Escrivá had traveled the long years of uncertainty on his own road.

He had a humble and unshakable confidence that God was preparing him, step by step, for the hour of clarity in which the veil would fall from his eyes and the clear picture of his vocation would stand bathed in clear light. It is of capital importance to the natural development of Opus Dei that Christ, in the time immediately surrounding the birth of Opus Dei, showed himself to Escrivá as crucified and suffering.

When that twenty-six-year-old priest began to see Christ on the cross in those souls who were eking out a miserable existence, and in those who were dying in the hovels of the outlying districts, and in those lying sick in the rooms and corridors of Madrid's hospitals, his apprenticeship was over. Kneeling next to the sick and dying, he was kneeling on the foundations of Opus Dei, the beams of which had already taken the shape of the cross.

It is impossible to be Christian and at the same time to hate the cross — that is, to flee all types of suffering and pain — for it is a central tenet of the Christian faith that only through the cross can we reach God, beatitude, and salvation. This path, which our human nature resists, is the road to the happiness toward which every soul, without necessarily knowing it, is attracted. Escrivá said that for some, this love for the cross had been a source of scandal. "This is because they do not know that when the soul walks where Christ walks, when it feels no reluctance, but rather conforms to the cross, it takes the shape of the cross. When we love the will of God and the cross, then it is no longer a burden; it is not mine but his, and he carries it with me .... To find the cross is to find Christ."[4]

In 1935 he repeated the same thought: "There is no surer sign that you have found Christ than to feel yourself shouldering his blessed cross."[5] Even when the cross causes pain, it is a fount of joy, because God chose it as the instrument of salvation. When Escrivá thought back to the bitter days in the 1930s when death had struck the first members of Opus Dei, and others who had heard the call had "slipped away like eels," he claimed that at the time he had not understood what meaning those sufferings could possibly have. But then he added, "Now I see things in a new light. Lord, you have made me understand that to carry the cross is to find happiness and joy. And the reason — I see it more than ever — is this: Carrying the cross is identification with Christ."

Escrivá never tired of repeating this idea. "The cross: that is where Christ is, and you must lose yourself in him! No more sorrow, and no more fatigue. You must never say, 'Lord, I can do no more, for I am a wretch.' No! That's not true! On the cross, you will be Christ."[6] Transmitting this conviction was precisely how he consoled the living dead in Madrid. His priestly love, given in the name of Christ, raised the desolate and disinherited, the poorest of the poor, to the incomparable dignity of the suffering Christ.[7]

The words that he whispered in the ears of the dying, as he asked them to offer their sufferings for the growth of the Work of God, are recalled in point 208 of *The Way*: "Blessed be pain. Beloved be pain. Sanctified be pain. Glorified be pain!" I know of no thought more at odds with the spirit of our century, especially in the last three decades, than this blessedness of pain. It is easy to denounce this idea as masochistic, scandalous, or simply abnormal. What we might call the sound-body principle has always been allied with rejection and contempt for that cross that St. Paul called "a scandal to the Jews, and foolishness to the gentiles"(1 Cor 1:23). The mystery of the cross is the mystery of the love of God for humankind; and this mystery includes the mystery of freedom, without which we could not respond to the love of God and thus achieve the purpose of creation.

Now to suppose that a purpose of creation could exist that is unattainable makes little sense. Thus the only possible explanation is that the cross is the path to the love of God, the path that brings freedom and happiness to people. Only in the light of this love does the cross make sense. On this point there can be no debate. Jesus Christ did not say, "Come, let's talk this over." He said, "If anyone wishes to come after me, let him deny himself and take up his cross and follow me" (Mt 16:24). The founder of Opus Dei listed the things a person could expect to encounter in following the call of God: "I am going to tell you what are the real treasures on earth, so you don't despise them: hunger, heat, cold, pain, disgrace, poverty, loneliness, betrayal, slander, prison...."[8] He experienced many of these things personally, and never forgot that when one loves, suffering disappears in the face of what one is willing to do for the beloved. Escrivá used to say that knowing how to suffer was proof that someone knew how to love — proof that that person had a heart.

The birth of Opus Dei

Along with his writings, letters, and informal pronouncements (quoted in the internal magazines of Opus Dei), and in addition to the films of the last years of his life, still another rich source of material exists for Escrivá's biography: the voluminous document prepared for the postulation of Escrivá's beatification, which contains all of the above, as well as ample testimony by many witnesses.

This document begins with a brief sketch of Escrivá's life. The account confines itself to a summary of those facts that are known with complete certainty. For this reason, I am relying on this document in order to speak about the founding of Opus Dei. This is what it says: "On October 2, 1928, while the Servant of God[9] was alone in his room, participating in a retreat in the residence of the Vincentian Fathers[10] of Madrid, on García de Paredes St., God deigned to illuminate him.[11] He saw Opus Dei, as the Lord wanted it and as it would be, down through the centuries."[12]

For eleven years, ever since that winter day in Logroño, Escrivá had asked for light to see. One day, the scene in Mark's Gospel involving the blind man Bartimeus caught his attention. It was his habit to meditate on a passage of the Gospel by participating mentally as a spectator on the scene. In this spirit, he relived the moving scene in which Jesus asks this blind man, "What do you want of me?" and Bartimeus responds, "Lord, that I may see."

In a homily in 1947, Escrivá remarked, "This is something I cannot forget. Many years ago, after meditating upon this passage, knowing that Jesus wanted something of me — something unknown to me — I made my silent spontaneous prayer: 'Lord, what do you want? What are you asking of me?' It occurred to me that I was looking for something new, and this *rabboni ut videam* — Lord, that I may see — moved me to beseech Christ in a continuous prayer: 'Lord, whatever it is you want, may it be fulfilled.'"[13]

This aspiration (repeated innumerable times, with an ever greater urgency), his continuous living in the presence of God, his spirit of penance and reparation, the intense pastoral work that he carried out, and his many works of mercy all flowed into his offering of the Eucharist. The holy sacrifice of the Mass became a daily surrender of his whole being, and the root of all his activity. All this filled the three years between his ordination and his discovery of the specific vocation that Divine Providence had reserved for him: the founding of Opus Dei, which began on October 2, 1928. In those three years, God prepared Escrivá both to understand the mission he was to reveal to him and to accomplish it with his help.

On October 2, 1928, Escrivá's apprenticeship ended. His mission was entrusted to him, and its fulfillment began. Of the founding, or birth, of Opus Dei we know little more than the few finely chiseled sentences already quoted. And yet this "little more" merits our attention. For in the silence of his room during that retreat, he heard — "in the distance" — the bells of the church, Our Lady of the Angels.[14] That the bells were heard "in the distance," while the church is actually quite close to the Vincentian residence, seems contradictory. But the truth is that even when a church is less than a mile away, bells do sound far away at that distance, though they can still be heard clearly if the land is not developed. At that time it was not, and so the bells were heard perfectly. (Today, if one is standing in the middle of García de Paredes St., the bells cannot be heard.)

I feel a need to dwell on these bells which, on that Feast of the Guardian Angels, rang in the church dedicated to the Queen of the Angels. The present prelate of Opus Dei, Bishop Alvaro del Portillo, supports my hunch about the mystical character of the founding of Opus Dei, even though neither he nor Escrivá ever used the word "mystical" in this regard.[15] Escrivá always insisted that Opus Dei was not his own invention, that it was not the consequence of a series of speculations, analyses, discussions, or experiments, and

The Vincentian residence in Madrid where Msgr. Escrivá was making a retreat when he saw Opus Dei on October 2, 1928.

that it was not the result of good and pious intentions. He clearly implied that the actual founder was God himself and that the commission of the task to a young priest was a supernatural act, a unique grace. And so when he said many years later that he had never ceased hearing those bells,[16] he was not just speaking metaphorically; he was describing the permanent state of a person who has really perceived a vocation, a call.

Out of humility and prudence, Msgr. Escrivá remained silent throughout his life about what he had received on that special day in 1928; he was extremely cautious in speaking about mystical graces or charisms he received from the Lord. (Those of October 2, 1928, were not the only ones.) For one thing, any disclosure of such an extraordinary or mystical encounter with God automatically raises doubts about its authenticity. We know that many saints, from Francis of Assisi to the Curé of Ars, received mystical graces, but we know of none who did not refrain from making such graces the theme of their conversation, either out of charity or so as not to satisfy others' curiosity. Regarding special displays of divine affection, intimacies between the soul and its Creator, modesty (as in human affairs) forbids any sort of spectacle or publicity.

In 1968, on the fortieth anniversary of the founding of Opus Dei, Escrivá was visiting a retreat house near Jerez de la Frontera. When someone asked what exactly had happened that day and why so little was known of it, Escrivá said he had kept quiet so that no one in Opus Dei would think that their founder, a poor sinner, was someone special. Another reason he did not want to talk too much about such things was because although there really had been extraordinary events in the life of Opus Dei, "ours is the sanctification of ordinary things."[17]

Those events that the Church calls miracles, and whose existence in his life Escrivá was not denying, are special graces from God. They are granted not so that the person who receives them can be admired, but to strengthen that person in the service of God. Whoever would draw near to Escrivá, or to Opus Dei, would do so in order to follow Christ in their daily life, the life of job and family, with complete naturalness and the sincere desire to identify themselves with Christ according to the spirit of Opus Dei. On that day, Escrivá saw not only the field that would yield so much fruit in the future, but also the way to plow this field forever.

The Feast of the Guardian Angels ... a young priest making a retreat, praying in his room ... a peal of bells ringing in his ears from a nearby church dedicated to Our Lady of the Angels ... before his eyes, the sudden revelation of Opus Dei — the whole situation becomes a unity. Nothing is without meaning, and nothing happens by chance — neither the time nor the place nor the other circumstances; it all adds up to the mysterious unity of a divine inspiration. Josemaría Escrivá, unable to see clearly, able only to guess in the dark, had already handed God a blank check out of love, a commitment to total self-surrender and dedication. Only now did he realize what it was that he had signed, and for what purpose the check was about to be cashed.

The birth of Opus Dei on the Feast of the Guardian Angels is noteworthy in an age when so many rooms in the mansion of Catholic doctrine are dark, dilapidated, or even deserted. Among the dimensions of our religious and devotional life that we have neglected, we find the lively awareness of the guardian angels. Many Catholics would be surprised to read, in the Roman Catechism of Popes St. Pius V and Clement XIII, the official teaching of the Church concerning guardian angels.[18] There we read, "Out of nothing, God created the spiritual nature of the countless angels who serve and attend him. Then he enriched and beautified them with the wonderful gift of his grace and might."[19] The Catechism goes on to affirm that "even though we do not see them, we are rescued daily by their protection from many great dangers, spiritual as well as physical...."[20] Then it speaks of the "charity with which angels love us and which moves them to intercede for us by offering our prayers and tears to God."[21] The archangel Raphael protected and guided the young Tobias,[22] an angel freed Peter from jail in Jerusalem,[23] and Christ himself spoke of the angels on numerous occasions, perhaps most forcefully when he warned against scandalizing little children: "For I tell you, their angels in heaven constantly behold the face of my Father, who is in heaven."[24] If, by the will of God, Opus Dei was placed in the soul of Josemaría Escrivá on the Feast of the Guardian Angels, to begin on that day its journey as a living force in the world, we can deduce three things:

1. Not only Escrivá but also the whole of Opus Dei would be under the protection of angels, as are all human beings. "Increase your friendship," said Escrivá, "with the holy guardian angels. We all need lots of company: friends in heaven and on earth. Be devoted to the holy angels!"[25] We shall see later how Opus Dei, in its diverse apostolic activities with young people and adults, has been put under the protection of the holy archangels Michael, Gabriel, and Raphael.

2. The birth of Opus Dei on the feast of the angels, coinciding with the sound of the bells from the church of Our Lady of the Angels, shows the profoundly Marian spirit of Opus Dei even at its origin.

3. The Feast of the Guardian Angels is a feast that teaches us humility. Angels fulfill the will of God with loving humility, and only a similar humility can bring one to confide in them. Therefore, it can be said that Opus Dei came into the world on October 2, 1928, branded with a collective humility.

In his first letter to the members of Opus Dei, its founder wrote, "This has been and will always be the ambition of the Work: to live without human glory; and do not forget that at the outset, I would have been pleased if the Work had had no name, so that its history would have been known only to God."[26] Two years later he wrote, "You should work with a personal humility so deep that it forces you to live collective, corporate humility, never seeking to receive individually the praise and admiration that the Work of God and the holy lives of your brothers and sisters merit."[27]

On October 2, 1977, when the Work was beginning its fiftieth year, Alvaro del Portillo, Escrivá's successor, told some members in Rome that the birth of Opus Dei in 1928 had been preceded by many premonitions in the soul of the Father (as his spiritual children called him)[28] — divine lights and inspirations that he had noticed and recognized.

On that morning of October 2, 1928, after Mass, Escrivá withdrew to his room to organize, reread, and pray about the notes he had been jotting down. "And that day he did not see the notes he held before his eyes, for the Lord our God wanted him to see the Work, as it would be until the end of time."[29] As the bells began to chime, the veil, which had been growing ever thinner and more transparent, was ripped. It vanished without a trace.

What did Escrivá see in his prayer? I do not know. The mystical vision which God grants can embrace places and times without regard to maps or calendars. God provides a vantage point from which the course of centuries can be seen concentrated in the vision of a single second. The eye of the soul can miraculously see the abstract — concepts, qualities, and destinies — as the breath of the Holy Spirit. All this is seen in images which do not capture photographically but reproduce subjectively, with accurate fidelity, what is objectively produced in eternity.

In 1928 Escrivá did not yet see the women's branch of Opus Dei, nor the Priestly Society of the Holy Cross, and I do not suppose he saw the faces of future members or centers of Opus Dei throughout the world; but he saw the sanctity of ordinary Christians, the sanctification of work, and the ways, means, and fruits of a personal apostolate everywhere and forever. He saw the essence of the vocation to this divine Work; he saw its universality and the unbounded "field of wheat" made up of those who could form this Work; and he saw, above all, that Opus Dei was the indefatigable march of Christ through the world.

"From that moment on," Escrivá would say later, "I never knew peace, and I began to work — unwillingly, because I did not want to be the founder of anything."[30] This is a perplexing statement. When

God showed him what he wanted — the sanctity of ordinary Christians in their daily lives — did he not impose the duty of fulfilling this will by means of an organization now called Opus Dei? But we are thinking simplistically, and in merely human terms. When God wishes to accomplish something, he does not publish a celestial decree or issue an official bulletin, for God is Love and he takes each soul individually, respecting its freedom even while he asks for total self-surrender. We see in saints individuals who surrender their freedom to serve God, forsaking, with a childlike humility, any attempt to put their own plans first. Because of their love for God, they are sometimes led to do certain things that to others might seem crazy or incomprehensible. For example, when St. Francis of Assisi heard the voice of God instructing him to reform the Church through the mendicant order he was going to found, he started by rebuilding a ruined church in his hometown.

The humility of Escrivá was such that without doubting the truth of what he had seen, and without doubting his call to accomplish the Work of God as he had seen it, he tried to fulfill his mission without drawing attention to himself. He wanted to pass unnoticed. Such an attitude seems impractical from a logical point of view, but it certifies the truth of his vocation. He set about checking to see whether an organization or movement like the one he had in mind already existed somewhere in Europe. If he had found one, he would have sought admission immediately, "to take the last place and to serve."[31]

Escrivá's whole life was bound up with his mission, and as Opus Dei grew, the figure of Escrivá gradually came into the public eye. This does not mean that his motto "To hide and disappear," which he had originally intended to practice to the letter, eventually lost its force or meaning. The complete phrase was, "My duty is to hide and disappear, so that only Jesus shines forth."[32] The founder of Opus Dei learned gradually the profound significance of his own words, and only toward the end of his life did he fully grasp it. This oft-repeated phrase implies a total dedication of the whole personality, of the self, to God the Father through Christ; it presupposes a surrender of all personal plans, projects, desires, and inclinations.

"To hide and disappear!" — a motto of humility. As Escrivá demonstrated during his lifetime, this simple saying has many ramifications. For Opus Dei members, it means subjecting personal desire, which can insinuate itself ever so subtly into the heart, to the divine command to do Opus Dei. It also has an ascetical meaning. It means avoiding publicity, refusing to attract attention even when it seems necessary.

"After 1946, when the headquarters of Opus Dei moved to Rome," I was told by a Spanish colleague who had known Escrivá, "the Father remained in Rome for long periods of time (especially between 1950 and 1954), working silently and alone. In the 1960s, the number of people who visited him grew remarkably."[33] When in 1944 the first three priests of Opus Dei were ordained, their spiritual father — for it was through him that each of them had received his call not only to Opus Dei but to the priesthood — chose to be absent from the ceremony. He did not want to receive any congratulations.

In the early 1950s, when the work of the Priestly Society of the Holy Cross began, some of the first diocesan priests in Opus Dei attended a workshop at the retreat house Molinoviejo, near Segovia. "Despite our urgings, the Father chose not to come," one of them had told this professor. "He sent us some messages, which we read and discussed carefully. But he deliberately did not participate, so that we would be forced to overcome our timidity and get along on our own. He was putting into practice a principle of formation his followers often still use: 'Throw the ducks in the water, and they have to swim.' Since he was naturally gregarious and his interest in people was as great as his facility in dealing with them, he could have enjoyed many opportunities to use this ability. But he deliberately put himself in second place. This was his personal *modus operandi,* and he taught it to his spiritual children."[34]

The catechetical trips that Escrivá undertook in Europe and Latin America were also acts of humility reflecting his selfless concern for the Church. "He had to give witness," comments the professor. "That was his job. The same humility that kept him silent when others fulminated — when the Work was being persecuted, for instance — now made *him* speak while many remained silent about the internal and external afflictions of the Church."[35]

The less he was able to avoid cameras, microphones, and loud-speakers, the more honors and distinctions he received. But the more the media's curiosity was stirred, the more he took refuge deep in the shadows of Christ's cross, so that he himself all but disappeared. Christ rewarded him by speaking through his mouth, blessing through his hands, and working through his labors. Escrivá appeared that way to everyone, to those closest to him and to those who met him only in passing; his humility shows even in those movies filmed during the trips he made in the last years of his life.

Invisible to human eyes

On the afternoon of October 2, 1928, Opus Dei consisted of just one man: a twenty-six-year-old priest who had been given a light which would never fail and a zeal for building that would never lose its vigor. In a strict sense, one might say that Msgr. Escrivá did not actually found Opus Dei until the first vocations had persevered at his side; he had first to transmit to others what he had received.

And what was it that he had received? It is impossible to express this with more clarity, force, and succinctness than we find in these phrases from the postulation document: "God asked him to devote his entire life to promoting, in the service of the Church, this supernatural task which would later be called Opus Dei. Its end was that persons of every social condition would strive to seek sanctity and exercise their apostolate among their colleagues and friends. This apostolate would start with intellectuals in order to reach the rest. These Christians, conscious of the grandeur of the Christian vocation, would receive a specific call from God. They would each remain in their own profession and social situation in the world, without changing their lay status."[36]

This concise definition of Opus Dei contains the golden nugget that Escrivá's successor, Alvaro del Portillo, brought out on the first anniversary of his death: "The basic conviction, the root of the whole spiritual message of Msgr. Escrivá, was the urgent need to seek personal sanctity in the midst of the world."[37] From the very beginning and to our own day, an inability to comprehend the validity of this conviction has been the principal obstacle not only to a fair assessment of Opus Dei, but also to the spiritual renewal of many lives.

This incomprehension occurs quite often. For some complacent Christians, the word "sanctity" belongs to a passé ecclesiastical vocabulary. Others may answer, "But this is nothing new! It is totally normal and ordinary." Indeed, the demand that baptized Christians be saints is not something new; or rather, it is as old and as new as Christ's challenge, "Be perfect, as your heavenly Father is perfect" (Mt. 5:48), or St. Paul's affirmation in his first letter to the Thessalonians (4:3), "This is the will of God: your sanctification."

When ordinary Christians, the infantry of Christ's army, take seriously the call to sanctity and identification with Christ in the midst of the world, then this familiar truth has the force to change individuals and the world. The pulse of God's presence in our lives is transmitted through the work that unites us, a work that is simultaneously a means and an expression of personal sanctity. "I believe holiness attracts holiness," Escrivá said in 1968 to two Italian journalists. "My only formula is this: Be a saint, want to become a saint, with personal sanctity."[38]

For ordinary Christians, this personal sanctity is realized in and through professional work. Work that is thus sanctified also sanctifies; it creates a glowing and growing presence of Christ in the world, a spirit that is contagious. Work then becomes the way to bring others into contact with God; it is, in a word, apostolic.

"Renew the world in the spirit of Jesus Christ," wrote Escrivá in 1932. "Place Christ on high and in the heart of the world. We come to sanctify all honest human labor, our daily work in the midst of the world. And we do this in a completely lay and secular manner, in the service of the holy Church, of the Roman pontiff, and of all souls."[39] Eight years later he told the members of Opus Dei, "The Lord wants every single one of you, in your personal apostolate or in working with others — perhaps even with those who are far from God, Catholicism, or Christianity — to establish and carry out all sorts of honest and beautiful initiatives. These undertakings should be as diverse as the face of the earth and the yearnings of the men and women who inhabit it. You must contribute to the spiritual and material well-being of society, transforming these initiatives into opportunities for all to encounter Christ, and thus becoming occasions of sanctity. This is why I have reminded you so many times that your professional vocation is an important part of your divine vocation. For this reason too, the apostolate that the Work carries out in the world will always be up-to-date, relevant, and in demand. As long as there are people on earth, there will be men and women who have a particular profession or task — whether intellectual or manual — that they will be called to sanctify. And they will use their work to sanctify themselves and to bring others naturally to God."[40]

Time and again throughout his life, Escrivá called attention to the need for a unity of sanctity, work, and apostolate. For a Christian, this unity expresses the fundamental oneness of the world, a situation that Christ himself has ordained to be that way. Awareness of this unity protects Christians from a ghetto mentality, a defensive isolation, and ensures their effective presence in the world.

Escrivá expressed this energetically: "To think that this spiritual awakening means leaving one's normal existence and is intended only for those to whom God has given a religious vocation with its *contemptus mundi* is untrue! To make this abandonment and shunning of the world the essence or culmination of Christianity is absolutely erroneous!"[41]

At the time he said this, Opus Dei was forty years old. It was present in dozens of countries, had overcome grave dangers, and was now finding itself in a period of irrepressible expansion. The denigration and persecution of the Work, as well as its showering of apostolic sparks throughout the world, were direct consequences of Escrivá's central thesis: for the vast majority of Christians, the place for sanctity and sanctification *is* the world. All baptized Christians are integrated into the world; when they try to imitate Christ, they fashion the world from within, according to God's plan. This is the vocation of the laity.

To remove oneself from the complexity of worldly affairs and their sanctification requires the special vocation traditionally referred to as a vocation to the religious life. It is reserved for a few chosen ones, and it enjoys its own graces and spirituality. To use a metaphor, the religious vocation can be envisioned as covering the body of humankind with a fine net of blood vessels through which the grace of God can circulate even when the body suffers from hypothermia or some circulatory disorder. The religious state is a pillar of the Church. It guarantees that total dedication to Christ will never cease, even when human frailty spreads throughout the common faithful, and no matter how many people are worshiping the golden calf, in any of its many guises. The religious orders must remain strong, or regain their strength where they have lost it, for they have often been the source of desperately needed renewal for the whole Church.

Escrivá realized, through the light that Jesus Christ granted him, that the Church stood on the threshold of a new era. This would be an age characterized by the Christianization of the world from within; and so a different type of renewal began. Opus Dei was the first great step in crossing this threshold.

If Escrivá had limited himself to putting his thoughts in writing, perhaps in a book he could have called *Secularity and Sanctity*, he would surely have achieved considerable fame as a theological and ascetical author; other authors would then have come forward to comment, agree, and qualify. An "intriguing controversy" or a "noteworthy discussion" might have begun; but the true originality of Opus Dei would have been missed.

It was only a corollary novelty to change the concession, "Even though you are a lay person, you can sanctify yourself," to the challenge, "Because you are a lay person in the midst of the world, you can and should sanctify the world and sanctify yourself in the world." The real novelty consisted in joining arms with one's neighbors, teaching them in a practical way — by one's own life — how to be saints.

One more point must be made clear: the existence of Opus Dei, the light that Escrivá saw on October 2, 1928, was at first unknown.[42] It was nothing but an interior stimulus in the soul of a priest, a spiritual seed that took root only in him who received it.

In the beginning, not even Escrivá knew the name of this phenomenon. It grew inside him in preparation for the sowing of more seeds and the search for the first vocations. All this took place, without calling attention to itself, in Escrivá's daily life and work.

It took place in a womb of anonymity, far below the level necessary to arouse public scrutiny.

In the beginning, there was no external change whatsoever. Josemaría Escrivá did not act as would most founders of human projects. Such people usually make declarations and present proposals explaining their motives, means, goals, and immediate plans. Constantly concerned about their public image, they try to stir up interest with press releases. The birth and development of Opus Dei was nothing like this. Its founder did not promulgate any written document in which he expounded, for example, upon the general situation of Spain's Christianity, current problems in the Roman Catholic Church, or the steps that he believed should be taken to promote full Christian dedication among the laity.

He did not found an association to put these principles into practice, nor did he draw up statutes for a proposed organization. Although there have always been and always will be founders and foundations that follow this conventional path of development, the founder of Opus Dei did not proceed in this way. Opus Dei grew as all living things grow, as all things that are not built according to a blueprint are built: it grew silently and slowly, as a plant first breaks through from a seed.

"The Lord," Escrivá said many years later, "wanted to plant this marvelous seed of his work in the heart of that poor priest, so that it might grow quietly, without any noise, slowly but surely."[43]

Besides attending to the Foundation for the Sick of the Damas Apostólicas, Escrivá directed dozens of activities at the Cicuéndez Academy. There he gave courses in Roman and canon law from 1927 to 1931. This type of institution, unknown in America, is comparable to the English Inns of Court that first appeared in the fifteenth century. The Academy complemented university courses and offered the opportunity to pursue certain subjects in more detail. It had been founded by a priest who was also a lawyer and theologian, Fr. José Cicuéndez; he remained its director until 1930.

The professors, mostly laymen, held doctorates in law or philosophy and letters. Normally the classes were in the afternoon. Although some pursued other degrees, most of the students were law students who wanted to take university exams. The average class had ten to fifteen students. (Most of the graduates from this institution achieved prominence in their professions.) In *Profile*, Salvador Bernal relates the surprise of some students on discovering that the priest who taught them and impressed them with his elegance, culture, and intellectual gifts was also working tirelessly among the poor. It seemed so strange that they decided to find out for themselves if he was really doing this, and so one day they followed him.[44] That his behavior came as such a surprise and caused such a sensation suggests just how arthritic the prevalent view of Christian life was at that time.

What seemed extraordinary to his students, Escrivá thought perfectly normal for a priest and absolutely necessary for the development of Opus Dei as God had shown and entrusted it to him. Years later, when he spoke of the "foundations" he had started with, he referred particularly to his priestly work among the poor and the sick of Madrid, a service he continued to perform with an even greater intensity after October 2, 1928. It was this service of love that gave Opus Dei the spiritual nourishment it needed while it was still teething: a nourishment consisting of the prayers of those who were suffering, and their offering of sorrows and pains for a "work of God" that they did not yet know. Their generous offering was a response to the tireless dedication of the priest who asked for their prayers and sacrifices.

According to the records of the Damas Apostólicas, members of the organization visited about five thousand sick people in 1927. More than three thousand of these received the sacraments of Penance and the Eucharist, and some fifteen hundred received the sacrament of the Anointing of the Sick. About a hundred people were baptized, and there were almost eight hundred weddings.[45] Whenever Escrivá came to the Foundation, he was sure to find mountains of notes on his desk directing him to particular parts of the outlying neighborhoods where he had to visit sick people or assist them in their last hours. Hundreds of these notes have been saved; on some can still be read the numbers that Escrivá jotted down as he planned his itineraries.[46]

The roads were not comfortable, and the visits were often anything but pleasant. Spain in the 1920s and 1930s, especially in the industrial cities, showed a growing loss of faith, disrespect for the Church, and hatred for priests.

Priests and members of religious orders, easily recognized by their attire, were frequently insulted and threatened. Sometimes they were spat upon or bombarded with rocks. The most tremendous blasphemies were the order of the day. The virulence of this anticlericalism grew steadily until the Spanish Civil War. It took great courage to run a charitable organization in the blue-collar neighborhoods and in the poor sections of Madrid.[47]

Those who did work there did not go because the sick person had called them; they almost always went against the will of the person who was sick, dying, or impoverished. They came on their own initiative or because some merciful soul — perhaps a pious grandmother, or some woman in whom there remained just a glimmer of faith — had interceded. But often they were received the same way they were generally viewed — as enemies.

Escrivá almost always managed to overcome the mistrust. Even the hardest hearts opened themselves to him. Very few were able to resist his naturally affectionate manner. "When we had a sick person who was going to die far from God's grace," says one of the first Apostolic Ladies, recalling this fifty years later, "we entrusted him to Fr. Josemaría, certain that he would be cared for. I do not remember a single case in which we were disappointed."[48]

Even as the founder of Opus Dei was dedicating himself completely to God, he was sacrificing himself completely for other people. He did not want to keep anything for himself, but shared everything he received. This generosity typified his entire life. Moreover, he was humble. He was constantly begging for alms; for begging is a part of humility, just as giving is a part of joy. Both acts are typical of children and pleasing in the eyes of God. He received many alms — above all, the alms of prayer, which were what interested him most. Fr. Casimiro Morcillo, then a young priest who would later have a brilliant ecclesiastical career as archbishop of Madrid, recounts that one fine day in 1929, at the break of dawn, as he was walking down the street, a young cleric stopped him. He had seen him several times before. "Are you on your way to say Mass?" this young cleric asked. "Could you pray for an intention of mine?" Needless to say, Fr. Morcillo was somewhat taken aback, especially since the priest did not tell him what the intention was. But Fr. Morcillo promised to pray for it, and he did. Afterwards, in the course of time, he and Escrivá became good friends.[49]

This was not an isolated case. Escrivá often approached people he did not know, but whose expression made it clear to him that they were leading a decent life and striving to live their Christian principles. In this matter, he enjoyed a special intuitive sense that grew with the years: he was able to see souls in all their profundity, and he was almost never wrong. People might have been shocked when he asked them to pray for an intention that would give great glory to God. But something about Escrivá made such people pray, their surprise notwithstanding. "Child, when you are sincere," reads point 863 of *The Way*, "you will be omnipotent." Those who gave him the alms of their prayers seemed to realize that in his life these prophetic words would come true.

God wants women in Opus Dei

"I did not want to found the men's branch *or* the women's branch of Opus Dei. I had never thought of the women's branch. I assure you with a physical certainty, and I do mean physical, that you are daughters of God."[50] Elsewhere he said, "The foundation of the Work took place without me; the women's branch, against my personal opinion."[51] Over the years, with these and similar words, Josemaría Escrivá testified that Opus Dei is neither a human organization nor an initiative of the Church, but rather an instrument in and for the Church, an instrument that came directly from God.

It is certain that Escrivá, on that day in October 1928, "saw" Opus Dei. He saw it in accordance with what he could understand at that time. (This is, in fact, what happens when we see anything — we recognize what it is, even though it may be impossible to notice all its details in a single glance.) What is more, he saw quite clearly that in order to gradually understand all the dimensions of what God had made him see, he would need further inspiration and supernatural illumination.

When he tried to make a decision on his own, without asking God's help — especially with regard to the beginnings of Opus Dei — he found himself groping in the dark. God had to show him what to do. "There will never be women — not even in jest — in Opus Dei," he wrote at the beginning of February 1930.[52] But on February 14, 1930, God corrected Escrivá, making him see that he wanted women to take part in his Work.

It happened during Mass, a Mass which he celebrated in the little chapel of the Marchioness de Onteiro,[53] on Alcalá Galiano St. in Madrid. After Communion, the women's branch of Opus Dei stood before his eyes, just as the Work had appeared sixteen months earlier. That was what he meant when he spoke of "physical certainty." It was not a question of Escrivá's adding a women's branch; it was God, with whom he had united himself sacramentally in Communion, who decreed it and placed it before his eyes. "By God's will," he wrote in 1965, "Opus Dei is made up of two different branches which are completely separate, as in two distinct works, one for men and another for women.[54] There is no interaction whatsoever in terms of government, or financial affairs, or apostolate, or day-to-day activities."[55]

This point has at times given rise to questions, and even misunderstandings and criticism, but the founder explained it very well. "In the Work," he said, "the two branches are like two little donkeys pulling the same cart in the same direction."[56] They are not two opposed forces, but rather two forces that work together precisely because they are parallel. The two forces unite in the heart of the Father [the prelate, who heads both branches], and in the love of God.[57]

In a time such as ours, when partially mistaken notions about the nature, mission, and cooperation of the sexes are prevalent, it is necessary to examine the clear, basic convictions of Josemaría Escrivá on this subject. Otherwise, it may well happen that one approaching Opus Dei and seeking to understand it will stumble over obstacles that do not in fact exist.

The founder of Opus Dei had grown up in a normal Christian family. In his parents' home, the young Escrivá had seen the faithful fulfillment of what Christ demanded of men and women as spouses and parents. This faithful fulfillment of the divine will is based on a recognition of the division of labor between man and woman, as established at the very beginning of the human race. Men and women are equal in their human nature; they are equally created, loved, and redeemed by God. There are, however, some clear differences between them. Men and women collaborate fully and with equal dignity in the conservation and progress of humanity, in the building up of the world, and in the fulfillment of God's plan of salvation. They do not, however, collaborate in exactly the same way, but rather in ways which, while intimately related, are quite different.

Escrivá had seen, in the example set by his parents, how married couples should follow Jesus Christ in daily life and in their professional and social affairs. He had seen how they should strive to reach sanctity and be always mindful that marriage is a divine call to the sanctification of children and of the world. He knew quite well that permeating society with this spirit, with the possibility of sanctification of and through ordinary life and work, is impossible without relying on parents, both as individuals and as couples, to travel this road and direct their families along it.

Someone once asked me why Escrivá did not immediately realize that the renewal of the Christian laity, the sanctification of daily life, would be impossible without women or married couples. I answered in this way: I believe that Msgr. Escrivá, for all his greatness, was a man of his times; and that to whatever extent his understanding was raised above the mentality of his contemporaries, this was only by the grace of God, as he himself stated on many occasions. Another reason is that the fullness of what Opus Dei would eventually be could only take shape little by little. God entrusted to him, moment by moment, a particular direction — the exact step at the exact time necessary for the development of the Work.

Let us take the example of women in Opus Dei. Why was the founder convinced, for more than a year, that there was no place for them in Opus Dei? In 1928 God had made him see that Opus Dei meant the sanctification of the world from within. God had presented Opus Dei to him as an entity made up of those who would travel this road and form a spiritual family united around him as its father and founder.

Then God had showed him the first nucleus of this big family that was coming into being: a group of men, mostly laymen, who would live and work as the ordinary citizens that they are in secular society; a group we might call pioneers, because they would be the first to accept the divine call to blaze this trail of sanctity throughout the world — a path that would sanctify all human activities. To fulfill this ideal, people would be needed — people who could give up marriage and a human family for the love of Christ and other people, in order to be more available for the needs of the Work. Escrivá was still young; the Work was like a tiny plant whose first green shoots have barely sprouted. Is it strange, then, given the circumstances, that he should have found those first pioneers among students and young workers disposed to total dedication and to an absolute availability that included celibacy?

This first nucleus of the family of Opus Dei, to which others would later be added, was and will continue to be, in the words of Escrivá, "the foundation, the force that sustains our whole family, the force that pushes many other people to live Christian lives: young people we meet, our parents, our colleagues and officemates, and all our friends, each of whom we try to draw closer to Opus Dei."[58]

The reason Escrivá thought, until God corrected him, that this foundation would be exclusively male was that the idea of a celibate dedication outside of religious consecration — a 100 percent lay and secular dedication — was already something new and revolutionary with regard to men, and for women it seemed impossible. One must recall that in those times very few women pursued professional careers; in general, they were absent from public life. The general view at that time was that women who were not married and raising families had only two options: they could join a religious community or resign themselves to being the maiden aunts of their families. This made the vocation of lay women to dedicated virginity look like an act of incomprehensible daring, something much less feasible than a similar vocation for men.

It takes some effort to imagine the situation of Escrivá after February 14, 1930. There was no one but himself in Opus Dei; he had to find ways by himself to meet people, pursue contacts, and find those who could understand his message. Moreover, he had to learn, starting from scratch, how to transmit clearly and unambiguously, by word and example, the content of that message. He needed to speak to people in such a way that they would begin to think, and perhaps be attracted and disposed to follow his path.

"The souls slipped away as eels escape in water," he recalled in the early 1970s. "What's more, there were brutal misunderstandings, because the teaching spread throughout the world today was not so then. And anyone who says otherwise is mistaken."[59]

The men's branch in 1928; the women's branch in 1930. It was nothing more than a dream, a light, a divine proposal. This proposal included the notion of the unity of the Work — a concept that at that time only Escrivá himself knew and understood; something so simple that many people still have trouble understanding it. All the members of Opus Dei receive the same spiritual vocation. They bind themselves to Christ in the world and try to lead others to God. From within, they offer the world as a sacrifice that Christ presents to his Father God. It is part of this vocation to live closely united to the head of Opus Dei (called the President General until November 1982, when Opus Dei was raised to a personal prelature and his title became Prelate), whom the members call and respect as "the Father." In his person the unity and authenticity of Opus Dei take flesh. Inasmuch as the priests of Opus Dei are at the disposal of both the men's and the women's branches, they constitute an essential element in the unity of the Work. The vocation to Opus Dei — the call of God and the soul's response — is always something personal. Equally personal is the fight to be faithful to one's vocation, a fight that can only be personal, never collective, because it pertains to the spiritual life of each soul. A married couple, as harmonious and full of love as they may be for each other, cannot, for example, be operated upon together if one of them suffers an attack of appendicitis; neither can they give a joint accounting of their souls to God. Each eventually dies in his or her own particular time and way. A disregard for this quality of individuality would destroy the unity of love lived by that couple.

This is how we must understand the exhortation of Escrivá: "Do not break the unity of the Work! Love it, defend it, foster it!

Not in vain did the Lord plan for these two manifestations of his kindness to occur on the same date.[60] While they always live five thousand miles apart, my sons and daughters feel themselves forming part of a single home.... Ask the Lord to teach us to love the unity of the Work as he wanted it from the beginning."[61]

Those "five thousand miles" that separate the men's branch from the women's branch have shocked people from time to time, especially those who confuse being equal with being interchangeable. They argue that in the technological society of our day, men and women do everything together — in work, in sports, in politics, and in the Church. And they ask: Why must they be separate in Opus Dei? The answer is that Opus Dei is a spiritual family with exclusively spiritual goals; that is the basis for its unity. Its path through the world and across time is a road of salvation and joy, but it is not easy or comfortable. In the two branches, those who are called to the Work through a celibate vocation, those who can give up marriage "for the sake of the kingdom of God" (Mt 19:12), form the backbone. In today's sexually charged environment, the celibate members of Opus Dei, who are not at all sheltered by the walls of a convent or by a religious habit, need considerable grace, fortitude, and fidelity to stand firm in their vocations. It is a demand of charity and prudence to make this as easy as possible. It is natural for a family to help its members instead of creating extra burdens for them through questionable or imprudent internal relations.

Msgr. Escrivá drew his spiritual daughters to Opus Dei with the same spirit of prayer and self-sacrifice that attracted his spiritual sons. He formed and looked after them with the same unstinting fatherly affection. He set before them the whole gamut of women's professions, so that they might see them as fields in which to serve Christ and other people.

The separation of the two branches of Opus Dei does not prevent them from complementing and helping each other in the carrying out of Opus Dei's apostolic task in the world. On the one hand, certain members of the women's branch handle the material care of the centers, including many of the men's centers, thus helping to transform them into comfortable homes. On the other hand, the men's branch supplies the priests who preach, say Mass, give days of recollection and retreats, teach theology courses, and otherwise make themselves available for the needs of the women's centers, as well as the men's. And when the women of Opus Dei begin their work in a new country, they usually find the ground already broken. "My daughters," Escrivá addressed them in 1964, "because of the unity of the Work, you have great good fortune, because when you go to a new country, your brothers have already picked up the cross from the ground; they have already carried it on their shoulders for a while, and they have already raised it over the earth."[62]

From the book *Conversations with Monsignor Escrivá*, we know the clarity and force with which in his later years Escrivá expressed himself on the issue of woman's role in the modern world and in the society of the future. He never let himself be deceived by popular caricatures of women; he did not use clichés and slogans such as "self-realization" or "emancipation." His opinions came from a deeper base.

In a 1968 interview with one of the major women's magazines in Spain, he was asked about the increasing separation between the woman and the family, and the corresponding growth of woman's role in social life.[63] The journalist wanted to know what Escrivá considered to be the general norms that women should keep in mind to fulfill their mission. Escrivá answered that in the first place, he would like to see the supposed dichotomy between home and professional work defined more carefully. He warned that "simply by changing the emphasis," such a "systematic contraposition might lead, from the sociological point of view, to a greater confusion than the one being corrected." Care and affection for her husband and children; the creation of a warm, Christian family life — all this will always be the primary task of woman and will occupy a most important place in her life. But, he added, "this is not in opposition to her participation in other aspects of social life — even of politics, for example. In those sectors too, women can make valuable contributions. And they will always do this by means of the special characteristics of their feminine nature." A woman's contributions are something society needs as much as each family does. The life and work of a woman "should be truly constructive and fruitful, full of meaning. It should produce results — whether she spends the day dedicated to husband and children, or whether having renounced marriage for some noble reason, she is fully dedicated to other tasks. Each one in her own way, by being faithful to her natural and supernatural vocation, can realize the fullness of the feminine personality."[64]

Obedience, the stamp of authenticity

The youthfulness of Escrivá was a necessary gift from God in the face of the magnitude of the task before him. Throughout his life he retained that youthfulness: a supple interior flexibility, a capacity of the soul to love. And he saw this kind of youthfulness as an almost indispensable criterion for the vocation to Opus Dei.

At the same time, however, he had received from God the task of setting in motion within the Church a work of huge dimensions, and for this he needed to radiate dignity and authority. These qualities, which he already had in his youth, called for expression in corresponding forms of behavior. For this reason, he used to ask in his prayer for "the gravity of eighty years." For this reason also, he used to wear a full black skullcap, a *calotte*, which covered almost his whole head, and of which he later joked, "It was like a hair shirt." He even tried to make sure he walked slowly, and with due dignity. Since he had a lively temperament, this surely required considerable effort. The present prelate of Opus Dei remembers being greatly surprised one day in 1935, at seeing him "hurrying along, with a light step," down the long hallway of the first university residence of Opus Dei in Madrid.[65] Here he was at home and did not need to hide his natural impulses. Almost thirty years later, during a trip to the Americas in 1974, Escrivá explained why he had acted in this manner: "I was twenty-six years old, and I had to ask Our Lord ... for the dignity that was typical of the priests of that time. Moreover, I was afraid of myself, and I asked the Lord for something else: that I might hide and disappear.... I needed age, years. Then the Lord made me understand: 'Look, you should seek age in another way. *Super senes intellexi quia mandata tua quaesivi* (Ps

118:100). Seek out my will, fulfill my commandments, be faithful to my inspirations; I will give you the maturity and gravity you desire.' For if it took age to make one learned, wise, and prudent, the seven sages of Greece would have had to have been decrepit old fellows. So how was a *calotte* going to make me look like an older priest and of great respectability? It was foolishness."[66]

One may laugh at such trifles, but they do have their importance. Whoever wants to win souls for Christ should take care not to make them stumble in their first steps over something that is not essential; this would violate the basic laws of charity and prudence. If the customs in a particular time and place demand that a priest, even outside of liturgical functions, should carry himself with formality, why not carry yourself with formality? In the final analysis, what matters is a sincere humility which, through love, enables us to cheerfully avoid seeing ourselves as the norm, and our own opinions as the measure of all things. In both the big and the small things, Escrivá allowed himself to be guided by this humility. "Our life of dedication," he wrote in 1930, "silent and hidden, should be a constant manifestation of humility. Pride and vanity can make one look for holiday fireworks in one's vocation. Much better to aspire to remain in a corner, like those candles that accompany the Blessed Sacrament in the shadows of an oratory ... and without making a commotion, inspire your neighbors — your friends, your colleagues, your relatives, your companions in the Work! — with your example, with your teaching, with your work, with your serenity, and with your joy."[67] Escrivá not only preached this, he also lived it.

Fr. Pedro Casciaro, who is now working in Mexico, remembers how he met Escrivá in the first center of Opus Dei, a student residence in Madrid. This was in 1935, when he was a young architecture student. "I remember," he says, "having seen the Father ... preparing breakfast for the residents in the kitchen, washing plates, shining the apples with a rag, and doing many other humble services, but the residents never guessed who was doing these jobs."[68] And another former student recalls that Escrivá cleaned the floors (there were twelve rooms), made all the beds (about twenty), and busied himself preparing meals, all without the students' knowing it.[69]

Humility has a twin sister: obedience. And the way one can tell when these twin virtues are genuine is by the yielding of practical results. It is the person lost in useless introspection who sighs, "Oh, how tiny is one mere mortal, compared to the starry heavens!" Such a one proclaims not humility but affectation. And anyone who stoically says, "I follow only my God and Lord" (or to use the more popular phrase, "I only follow my conscience") is not submitting to obedience, but rather fleeing from it.

In a letter written in 1954, Escrivá said, "In the spirit of Opus Dei, we feel free and understand perfectly at the moment of obedience why our directors order us. They realize that we are intelligent people, with maturity and personal responsibility, who actively put to work our understanding and our will in obeying, and who accept the consequent responsibility in each act of obedience."[70] Nine years earlier he had written, "Obedience in the Work fosters the development of your individual strengths, so that without losing your personality — remaining basically the same person at eighty-two that you were at the age of two — you live and grow, and acquire maturity."[71]

A sure sign that people are living a life of sanctity is their humility and obedience with regard to matters that from a natural point of view are not strictly necessary and may seem unimportant. In matters of discipline and doctrine, all the saints of the Church were subject to the directives of their pastors, sometimes in spite of fierce interior struggles and bitter sufferings. Often they have greatly surpassed their superiors or spiritual directors in grace, wisdom, and virtue, but precisely for this reason, their humility and obedience have been especially pleasing to God.

Undoubtedly, Escrivá knew that he was an instrument of God, for on many occasions the Lord granted him his light directly. But at no point in his life was he without a spiritual director. In making his personal decisions, he always strove to have the backing of the Church hierarchy.[72]

Escrivá entrusted himself to the spiritual direction of a priest first in Logroño, when he was still a high-school student, and later in Saragossa and Madrid. Not only did he make his confession regularly, but he also spoke to these counselors in confidential conversation, hiding from them nothing of the mystical graces and divine inspirations he received. He subjected them all to his confessor's judgment. There were no hidden corners in his heart. A religious-order priest was the first to know of the birth of Opus Dei, and he recognized and confirmed that it was from God. On February 14, 1930, when Escrivá told his confessor that the Lord had entrusted him with founding the women's branch, he responded, "This is also from God, just like the rest."[73]

It was also in 1930 that his confessor, referring to Escrivá's priestly activities, asked, "How goes that work of God?" Work of God! That shortest and most accurate of all possible names was neither sought nor imagined, but came as an unintended gift. The good confessor had no idea that with his question, he had casually introduced into the history of the Church and Christianity a name that would not disappear — two words that with the strong peal of a bell would never stop ringing throughout the world, calling to mind the bell inscription immortalized by the German poet Schiller: "Vivos voco. Mortuos plango. Fulgura frango." "The living I call; the dead I mourn; the thunderbolts I break!"[74]

The first letter

Two years old at that point, Opus Dei received its name; with that, it truly entered the pages of history. The sprout that had appeared on October 2, 1928, was already beginning to bud. It was still small, but it was visible. One could point to it and say: "This is Opus Dei." Since God had shown Escrivá the vast harvest of the future, he was not troubled that no more than a few seedlings were to be seen in the field. Quantitatively speaking, Opus Dei barely existed, but its founder pushed it forward by the same means he would use later, when tens of thousands of people around the world belonged to Opus Dei. These means would continue to be used after his death, and will never lose their validity.

One of the means he used from the beginning was the explanation, in the spoken word and in writing, of what Opus Dei was, as well as directions on how it should be carried out. Many of the innumerable explanations he gave in homilies, conversations, family gatherings both big and small, catechetical journeys, and so forth, have also been set in writing, and some have been published. Many others still await publication. We also have letters, full of fatherly affection, which I would venture to call "foundational letters": letters he wrote to teach his followers in Opus Dei the path of "sanctification of ordinary life" they should walk. These letters exhorted, encouraged, consoled, and strengthened them, filling them with optimism and joy. The first of these foundational letters is dated March 24, 1930 — the Feast of the Archangel Gabriel. The last is dated February 14, 1974 — the birthday of the women's branch. From a strictly natural perspective, the former is a magnificent, pious fantasy worthy of Don Quixote, for it was addressed to people who were not there yet. The latter was addressed to more than sixty thousand actual members of Opus Dei.

So that these letters could be preserved in archives, because they are of such great importance to Christian spirituality and to the history of the Church, most of them have been translated into Latin, the basic language of the Church. As is the custom in such cases, they are referred to by their first two words. For example, the first letter, addressed to those whom only God had in mind, is called *Singuli Dies*. This letter has special importance for an understanding of Msgr. Escrivá and Opus Dei: it is the first historical record of that vocational charism granted Escrivá in 1928. Reading it, one is immediately struck by its clear and cogent presentation. Anyone can understand it, from a poor peasant with a meager education to the most erudite scientist. The peasant might understand it more easily, being (probably) more down to earth. But the intellectual too, if well-disposed, will grasp the great profundity of these simple phrases.

"Our dedication to the service of souls," the letter begins, "is a manifestation of the Lord's mercy towards us — and not only towards us, but towards all of humanity. For he has called us to sanctify ourselves in ordinary, daily life, and to teach the others 'providentes, non coacte, sed spontane secundum Deum' (1 Pt 5:2 — 'prudently, without coercion; spontaneously, according to the will of God') the way to sanctify themselves within their own state, in the midst of the world.[75] We are concerned with everyone, for everyone has a soul to be saved in God's name. We carry an invitation to everyone — an invitation to seek Christian perfection in the world — by repeating these words to them: 'Estote ergo vos perfecti, sicut et Pater vester caelestis perfectus est' (Mt 5:48 — 'Be perfect, as your heavenly Father is perfect')."[76]

From time to time, one may read or hear that Opus Dei has an "elitist spirit." Let us set aside the inaccuracy of the expression itself and simply say this: If we label as elitist any association whose members are personally nominated and accepted, then we must consider, for example, the French Academy or Rotary International to be elitist.

In religious language, such terms as "election," "the elect," and so forth are used to indicate that someone has been called to serve by a divine appointment, by a gift and a grace that always require a personal affirmation. This is the case with the patriarchs and prophets, judges and kings of the Old Testament, the Blessed Virgin Mary, the apostles and their successors, priests and religious, and ultimately every baptized person. In this sense, Opus Dei *is* elitist: the road to the Work begins with a personal vocation. But that is all there is to Opus Dei's elitism. I know of no association of Christians more egalitarian than Opus Dei; the elitism of Opus Dei is based on the equality of the children of God.

"The supernatural mission that we have received," writes Escrivá in *Singuli Dies*, "does not lead us to distinguish or separate ourselves from others; it leads us to unite ourselves to everyone, because we are the equals of the other citizens in our country. We are, I repeat, equal to everyone else, though not *like* everyone else. We live in the same general environment, wear regular clothes, have no distinctive mannerisms. We share all the ordinary civic concerns, and those pertaining to professional work and other activities. We are ordinary men and women who in no way differentiate ourselves from our companions and colleagues, from those who live within our everyday environment and circumstances."[77]

Opus Dei was born in the world to sanctify it from within; members lead other ordinary Christians to sanctify their daily life and to sanctify themselves in and through it. Each of them thus responds, as an everyday Christian, to the standard set by Christ. It is crucial to understand the significance of this radical equality. It is an attitude of not discriminating against anyone or separating oneself from others. The normal living arrangement for the Christian in the midst of the world is that of one among equals. "Our way," writes Escrivá, "is not that of the martyr (though if martyrdom comes, we will receive it as a treasure), but rather of confessors of the faith — confessing our faith, manifesting our faith in our daily life.... In our daily work we should always manifest an ordered charity, the desire and the fact of making our work perfect through love. This means getting along with our neighbors, to bring them *opportune et importune*, with the help of the Lord and with human tact, to the Christian life, and even to Christian perfection in the world. It also means detachment from the things of this earth, a personal poverty that is loved and lived."[78]

Perhaps it is necessary to read these phrases several times to truly understand them. They seem innocuous enough, but they imply the beginning of a new era in Christian life. Be of the world, yes; but do not be worldly. Do not be children of this world; rather, be children of God *in* this world. Love the world as the work of God, and work in it as his collaborators, but without wanting to hoard the fruit of that work. Present it, as Abel presented his yield, to the Lord of the earth, the divine source of all life and growth. This is the only way to really possess and enjoy the fruit of one's labors, satisfying at once both the hunger and the thirst of the soul.

Escrivá then took a really decisive step. The discovery that God wants men and women, especially Christians, to identify themselves with Christ in their daily lives was a rather nebulous concept; it needed to be made more specific. A "daily life in the midst of the world," explained Escrivá, was what Jesus Christ spent in Nazareth — those decades of ordinary professional work, neither brilliant nor ostensibly important. It would be absurd, however, to assume that those years lacked actual importance for his messianic task, for the history of salvation, for our redemption.

The earthly life of Jesus Christ affords us a model for sanctity. For most of his life, all of which he spent in ineffably intimate correspondence to the will of God, he was a simple artisan in a

Palestinian village, busy with the hundred thousand banalities in the life of a carpenter who must look after his mother, finish the jobs his clients send him, be a good neighbor to the other villagers, and so forth. In those years he neither performed miracles nor preached a new doctrine. He drew no attention to himself.

It takes little imagination to picture him as an excellent, capable artisan, both industrious and patient. Christ was an affectionate son and cousin, and a neighbor held in high esteem, especially by the local children. Perhaps there were those in the village who did not like him, who laughed at him or otherwise tried to make life difficult for him. But in those thirty years of absolutely normal existence, of quiet, unobtrusive living, he was planting in the world the cross that he would eventually make visible to everyone on Calvary.

The bloody sacrifice of Calvary was not an isolated incident in Christ's life, but rather one part of an organic whole, the culmination of a greater sacrifice that had begun with the Incarnation, his conception in the womb of Mary. It continued through the years he worked in Nazareth and in his public life, and ended with his Passion and death. The child in the manger, the carpenter in Nazareth, the teacher of salvation, and the crucified God are all the same victim offered on the altar of this world. Just as the sacrifice was accomplished once and for all in a sacramental manner at the Last Supper, instituted forever as a fountain of grace and sanctification and a remedy for human weakness, so also was that same sacrifice prepared during the thirty years in Nazareth, so that the way of salvation could be made clear to us both individually and collectively. In principle, nobody who wants to follow Christ in this world can travel a different route from the one Christ followed.

This, then, is the heart of Escrivá's message, "Sanctify your daily life, and sanctify yourself in and through that daily life": Try to live in the world just as Jesus lived in Nazareth. The Nazareth of any Christian is the whole earth.

That is why Escrivá called Opus Dei "a corner of the home in Nazareth." In this home, pomp and splendor do not reign; no sensational or spectacular feats are performed. Life consists chiefly of the fulfillment of little, everyday things which can sometimes seem trivial and tiresome. But to flee from them, to follow the fanfare of what is perceived as the great theater of the world, is to distance oneself from the carpenter of Nazareth, Our Lord. "If the temptation to do amazing, extraordinary deeds should come along," writes Escrivá, "conquer it; because, for us, that way of working is mistaken, the wrong track."[79] He explains this warning with an anecdote. A customer at a restaurant asks for fish, but the waiter brings him a snake. What should the customer do? Escrivá outlines the possibilities with his typical flair for humor: "One of those great miracle-workers of old, one of those classic saints whom I admire and whose lives were full of marvels, might have reacted by bestowing a blessing and transforming the reptile into a well-cooked haddock. That approach merits all my respect, but it is not ours. Our way is simply to call the waiter and say, 'This is junk; take it away and bring me what I asked for.' Or perhaps, if there are reasons that make it advisable, one could make an act of mortification and eat the snake, well aware that it is a snake, offering this to God. There is, in fact, a third alternative: call the waiter over and flatten his nose; but this is not our solution either, because it would show, shall we say, a certain lack of charity."[80]

In the course of conversation, I sometimes encounter the mistaken notion — which I myself shared for a time — that Escrivá's assiduous rejection of "amazing, extraordinary deeds" amounted to a proposing of mediocrity as the Christian ideal. In the summer of 1981, I spoke about this with an Opus Dei priest who had known Escrivá since 1939. His answer is of great importance to me. "The Father," he explained, "used the expression 'amazing deeds' to suggest behavior that was strange or eccentric, the opposite of normal, genuine, natural behavior. 'Extraordinary' refers to the opposite of daily life, of ordinary living. Escrivá meant that the search for the extraordinary must not become an obstacle to our fulfilling and taking seriously what is ordinary and normal. Now, what is normal for a particular person can be, if we distinguish a norm from a mere average, something extraordinary, because it may be above average. Whoever can give ten should not give only five. I mean, the fruits should correspond to the gifts received. If the gifts are extraordinary, the fruits should be extraordinary too. In this sense, Opus Dei recognizes only one equal vocation for everyone, regardless of whether a particular person has received one, three, five, or ten talents."[81]

Singuli Dies is, for all practical purposes, the Magna Carta of Opus Dei. All of Escrivá's subsequent writings develop, amplify, explain, and refine this first letter. The letter is full of youthful freshness. It is written with strong words: words that are neither sticky-sweet nor laden with pious jargon, but clear and illuminating like the words of the evangelists; words as crystal clear and, for those who enter into them, as deep as the sea. "The Lord has called us to his Work to be saints; but we will not be saints if we do not unite ourselves to Christ on the cross. There is no sanctity without the cross, without mortification. And we will find mortification most easily in ordinary, everyday matters — our orderly, unstinting, hard work. We must know that the best spirit of sacrifice is shown in perseverance; in finishing well the work we have begun; in being punctual and filling the day with 'heroic minutes';[82] in our care for the material things we have and use; in our zeal to serve, which makes us fulfill with care our smallest duties; and in our little acts of charity, which make the path of sanctity in the world pleasant for everyone. At times, a smile can be the greatest manifestation of our spirit of penance. On the other hand, my sons and daughters, it is not the true spirit of penance to make great sacrifices one day, and completely abandon mortification the next. You will have the spirit of penance when you know how to conquer yourself every day, without any spectacular show, offering the Lord a thousand little things. That is the sacrificial love that God expects of us."[83]

That twenty-eight-year-old priest, who was speaking in the face of history and the future, knew that to walk this humble road, a road devoid of ballyhoo, requires some very specific forms of spiritual assistance. "Each day," he said, "should include some time that we have dedicated especially to dealing with God, but never forgetting that our prayer has to be as constant as the beating of our hearts: offering to God our aspirations, acts of love, acts of thanksgiving, acts of reparation, spiritual communions. When walking down the street, opening or closing a door, spying in the distance the bell tower of a church, beginning our work, doing it, finishing it — we should refer everything to our Lord."[84]

"My children, I repeat once more: We have lost the way if we despise little things. In this world, everything great is an accumulation of little things.... This is not an obsession, it is not a mania. It is charity, pure love, a constant supernatural outlook — love. Always be faithful in little things for love, with an upright intention, without expecting from the world a smile or even a glance of appreciation.[85]

"My sons and daughters, we have a lot to do in this world. The Lord has given us a divine mission. From the very first day, I have invited you to give thanks for this show of divine predilection, this divine call to serve all men and women. God asks us to fill our hearts with apostolic zeal, to forget ourselves, to busy ourselves — in a joyous sacrifice — for the whole human race. Most people with personal problems have them because their egoism makes them think only about themselves. Give yourself, give yourself, give yourself! Give yourself to the others, serving them for the love of God. That is the way!"[86]

The last letter

It was the bells of October 2, 1928, that moved Escrivá to set his face toward the future, toward a new epoch of grace in the Church. And it was at the sound of bells that he ended his journey. This can be taken both literally and metaphorically. It was at noon (when the bells chime for the Angelus) on June 26, 1975, that he suffered the heart attack that took his life, despite the doctors' hour-and-a-half struggle to save him.

But he had also expressly stated that he wanted his last three letters, written to the members of Opus Dei between March 1973 and February 1974, to be "three peals" whose ringing would awake, invite, gather, and encourage all men and women. "Upon hearing that familiar bell," Escrivá wrote in his last letter (dated February 14, 1974), "people definitely picked up the pace. And when they heard the third peal, they literally ran toward the house of the Lord. This letter is, as it were, the third invitation I am sending in less than a year, in the midst of the difficult trials now facing the Church, to impress upon your souls the demands of our vocation.

"I hope that this bell will place in your hearts the same joy and vigilance of spirit that were left in my soul, almost half a century ago, by those bells of the church of Our Lady of the Angels. Surely a bell of divine jubilation, the ringing of a good shepherd, cannot upset anyone. Nevertheless, my sons and daughters, it should move you to contrition, and, if necessary, it should stir up a desire for a profound interior conversion. It should call you to a new uplifting of soul, more prayer, more mortification, more spirit of penance, and — if this is possible — a greater determination to be good sons and daughters of the Church."[87]

For forty-six years, Escrivá had worked hard to make not only the whole Church but the whole world hear those bells of the Feast of the Guardian Angels. And that call had not gone unanswered. Awakened from their slumber, many Christians set aside their sleepiness and discovered the fullness of the Christian vocation. The Church universal, in the Second Vatican Council, then embraced this discovery, making it the nucleus of that most recent of the many renewals Christ has given her throughout her history.

This theme is taken up in various constitutions and decrees of the Council, such as *Lumen Gentium, Gaudium et Spes, Apostolicam Actuositatem,* and *Presbyterorum Ordinis.*[88] These documents affirmed, as a valid road for the Church in the future, a trail that Escrivá had blazed some thirty years before and that thousands of Christians were already traveling.

The nucleus of this renewal has always been and always will be the same: sanctity for everyone in the Church. The focus is not the "emancipation" of the laity, but rather their sanctification, which is born of liberty and presupposes it. So that the laity, for the good of all people, can realize their duty to be bearers of Christ, they must first of all be pious, not pushy, and they must pray, not prattle. They must lead lives that are humble, obedient, and pure, which means that they must receive the sacrament of Reconciliation. They must obey the pope and the bishops in matters of faith and morals, shunning the pervasive climate of sexual license and greed. The rediscovery of the common priesthood of all Christians does not mean either that the laity should storm the sacristies, taking upon themselves priestly duties, or that priests should hand over such duties to them, like consolation prizes, while they themselves aspire to become secularized by behaving like lay people.

It is impossible to give marriage and the Christian family a new dignity and beauty while ridiculing and trying to tear down evangelical celibacy. There is no more intimate a relation than that between the sacraments of Matrimony and Holy Orders. Because "the Enemy" (as Escrivá used to call the devil) never sleeps or takes a vacation, he gathers his greatest harvest precisely in those epochs that deny his existence, whether in theory or in practice. In the years after the Second Vatican Council, there arose a series of perversions of the Council's good intentions, including a scorn for priestly celibacy. Blight and pestilence made severe inroads on the wheat. Once again, at the age of seventy-two (just one year before his death), Escrivá had to toll the bell of alarm. The danger was imminent, for the enemy was at the gates, and even *within* the City of God. And so "fulgura frango" — this bell would break the thunderbolts!

The founder of Opus Dei suffered a lot, seeing the new dawn of Catholicism clouding over, that dawn in which he had grown up and which for so many years he had advanced with all his strength, through the dedication of a whole lifetime. But though he suffered intensely, he never lost his hope and his joy. He did not know the meaning of the word "resignation"; that was something only for the weak in faith, for those who had lost their trust in God.

The letter of February 14, 1974, did not toll for a death. It was a militant chime, a confident call to arms. And its ringing mingled with the echoes of the bells Escrivá had first heard almost fifty years before: the bells of Our Lady of the Angels. "God needs us for a bold apostolic undertaking," he wrote. "We must speak about him to the nations." We are not, however, to preach as from a pulpit, but simply as ordinary citizens. This down-to-earth approach "enables us to weave apostolate throughout our professional affairs, throughout the ordinary tasks of each day, without gimmicks or false discretion. Years ago I buried that word 'discretion,' so that there would be no room for ambiguity."[89]

Escrivá's final letter concludes with these words: "Christians should overcome any fear that their faith may be in conflict with the ideologies or values currently being imposed on people.... My sons and daughters, now is the time to live more piously than ever, more sincerely than ever, more obediently than ever, more apostolically than ever. God has blessed us greatly: thank him with all your heart. May we feel, despite our personal wretchedness, an immense confidence in the mercy of his most Sacred Heart, a confidence encouraged by the most sweet heart of our Mother Mary. With this trusting piety, we will never stop carrying ourselves in accord with the Lord, his Church, and the Roman pontiff, and we will savor the joy of being strong children of his holy Church."[90]

A thousand times over, Josemaría Escrivá multiplied the sound of those bells of 1928. The reverberations have spread around the globe, and today every Christian willing to listen can hear them. The bells will not stop ringing out the call of God.

Chapter 4

Conquistadors and Grains of Wheat

A young priest of Opus Dei was preaching in one of the organization's centers. Unnoticed, the founder entered and sat in the last pew. When the priest said that the key to following Christ in Opus Dei was humility, everyone was doubly surprised to hear Escrivá call out, "No, my son; it is divine filiation!" But this truth should not be surprising. All human beings are creatures and *children* of God. Christians should know this, and it should make an impact on their daily lives. Jesus Christ revealed himself not only as a logos or idea, but in flesh and blood. And in the four Gospels, he refers to God as a father a total of 131 times.[1] In his fatherly love, God our Creator has actually adopted us as his children, as brothers and sisters of his only begotten Son. God is Love. That is the foundation of the Christian religion, and the essence of Opus Dei. Of course, to acknowledge one's divine filiation as a younger brother or sister of Christ is one thing; to live accordingly is quite another. "Divine filiation" is the sort of religious expression that rolls all too easily off the tongue. It seems easy, self-evident, perhaps too simple. Yet what is simplest is often most challenging. The spiritual life of filiation to God is a gift of baptism, but since men and women are free, this new life does not mature automatically; it is the freely chosen way of love.

Josemaría did not invent these truths; they are, as we know, the essence of the Christian vocation. But he announced them anew and lived them in a way that infectiously spread this sense of the supernatural reality of divine filiation in the ordinary circumstances of life in the world. The young priest discovered that living as God's child encompasses and explains everything else: humility, faith, joy, detachment, purity, generosity, charity, sacrifice. From divine filiation springs unity of life.

75

That was the message of Msgr. Escrivá. Opus Dei is nothing if not a way to achieve this unity. In Josemaría Escrivá, God chose a model to demonstrate this unity and a means to make it accessible to countless souls. The first members of this new Christian family were attracted by Josemaría's keen sense of divine filiation. God called them through Josemaría: through his prayer, work, and mortification; in a word, through his love, which inspired love in many others.

Christopher Columbus and Escrivá

This apostolic activity served as the framework of Escrivá's daily work as a priest after October 2, 1928. To consider the way he spent his days is to learn firsthand what Opus Dei means in practice. It is ordinary life — ordinary life lived extraordinarily for Jesus Christ. Escrivá just went about his priestly duties, and here and there he got to know many people. But to meet him was to be introduced to affection and infectious optimism. He inspired a trust that put people at ease. Getting acquainted led to conversation; conversation led to confidence; both led to spiritual guidance. And little by little, those who entrusted themselves to him discovered the splendid fullness of the Christian vocation for a lay person. Of course, he had to show them, step by step, how to reach that fullness. He could not hand them an instruction booklet and say, "Here, read what Opus Dei is all about, and how one does it...." He could only communicate it through his own life. As he explained in 1932, "After so many centuries, the Lord wants to employ us so that all Christians will finally learn the sanctifying value of ordinary life — of professional work: what it is to practice the apostolate of teaching and example, of friendship and confidence...."[2]

Josemaría and his first followers remind me of the conquistadors. They were young; they were enthusiastic, fresh, tireless, and enamored of spiritual adventure. Eager for a voyage of discovery, they gathered around a leader they called simply "the Father." There would be dangers in the waters ahead, but so what? There were uncharted lands to discover. Paradoxically, however, their destination turned out to be the very ground they had started from. Through a simple journey, the familiar scenes of family, work, and friendship had become a new world. For nineteen centuries the Church had inhabited the world. It had always sought to saturate the world with the mystery of Christ, the God who had become man, and now Opus Dei had given a new impulse to this divine project. Such renewal is a perennial phenomenon in the Church. What a multitude of great saints populate the Counter-Reformation, not to mention the eighteenth and nineteenth centuries! And was not the Romantic Era in Europe to some extent a Catholic renewal?

Nevertheless, we must face a hard truth. The last five hundred years of Renaissance, Humanism, Reformation, Enlightenment, and Socialism — regardless of their significance in God's providence — have shown the roots of Christianity to have less depth than one might have hoped. Our own age has shattered many false and comforting illusions, awakened many sleeping Christians. We are forced to see that Christian culture, with its cathedrals, monasteries, sculpture, paintings, literature, customs, and habits is one thing, while personal friendship with God is quite another. Culture can eclipse holiness. The splendor of Christian culture can at times blind the faithful to the need to strive for sanctity. But no amount of Christian culture can actually substitute for Christian virtue.

Time and again, the Church has been graced and adorned by men and women of extraordinary virtue, talent, and sanctity. These luminaries are loved and applauded by pontiff and peasant alike. Most Christians, admittedly, are not called to these "supernatural Olympics." But in their own unspectacular way, might they not strive to be salt and light to the world, to leaven it from within? St. Paul did not exclude anyone when he told the Thessalonians, "This is the will of God: your sanctification"(1 Th 4:3). This was one of Escrivá's favorite passages in Scripture. In 1967, in a sermon at the University of Navarre, he said, "Be clear about this: God has called you precisely to serve him in and through the material, worldly tasks of human life. In the laboratory, in the hospital operating room, in military camps, in the university classroom, in the workshop, in the fields, in the household — in the whole limitless arena of human endeavor, God is waiting for us day after day. Be convinced of this: Every situation, no matter how ordinary, has something divine hidden in it, and it is your job to discover it."[3] If we fail to discover it, says Escrivá, then "the church becomes the only true place of Christian life. Then being a Christian means just going to church and participating in services — isolating oneself in a religious environment, a secluded world that presents itself as an antechamber of heaven, while the ordinary world outside goes its own way. The truths of Christianity and the life of grace, in that case, might just touch the edges of the arduous path of human history, but they would never really meet it."[4]

It was this fusion of the human and the divine that Escrivá preached to the young people who first followed him. "I used to tell the students and workers who joined me in the thirties that they had to materialize their spiritual life. I wanted to free them from the temptation, as common then as now, of leading a double life: an interior life for God, and a separate life for family, work, and society, full of little daily duties. No, my children. If we want to be Christian, we cannot lead a double life, we cannot be schizophrenics. There is only one life, composed of flesh and spirit, and it has to be — both body and soul — holy and full of God, that invisible God whom we find in the most visible and material things. There is no other way, my children. Either we find God in our daily life, or we will never find him."[5]

This is not a discovery that can be passed along by way of books and lectures; one must discover it for oneself. When Columbus, searching for a western route to India, chanced upon America, he made a lasting discovery for himself and for everyone else. America need not be discovered again; it was on the map, once and for all. But if other people were to share Escrivá's discovery, they would have to set sail themselves; for a discovery of the soul happens only when the soul experiences new territory. To know that spiritual land, one must live in it. Unless one tries to seek, find, and love Jesus Christ in the little things of every day, Escrivá's message simply does not come across. To the detached spectator, Opus Dei is a spiritual pie in the sky.

This comparing of Escrivá with Columbus, initially a passing fancy, has yielded some surprising parallels. Pardon me if I indulge in a little digression here. It is said that Vikings had visited America long before Columbus discovered it, but their trips in the tenth and eleventh centuries had led nowhere. The level of consciousness of those sailors, along with their whole intellectual, religious, economic, and social milieu, worked against the transformation of this local event into a universal accomplishment. Neither Christendom nor society in general felt the need for a new world. Its historical hour had not yet come. So the discovery was forgotten; it sank into a legendary twilight, there to join the ancient belief, once commonly held, that the world was round.

By the time America was discovered by Columbus, Europeans were busy exploring and populating the world, but their attention was focused elsewhere: Northern Europe, the Mediterranean, the Orient, Africa. It was a convergence of historical, political, and economic factors that sent Columbus westward at the end of the fifteenth century. The Moors had been driven from the Iberian peninsula, and the royal marriage between Aragon and Castile had cemented a new spiritual unity. The life story of Columbus, from his birth in 1451 to that morning in October of 1492 when he spotted that first outcropping of the New World, had prepared him for such an achievement. And we now know what Columbus did not: on the western side of the Atlantic, pre-Columbian civilization was on its last legs. The time was ripe.

The are striking similarities between Columbus's geographical and Escrivá's spiritual discoveries. The ideal that Josemaría envisioned on October 2, 1928, had been known before. In fact, in the first three centuries of Christianity it had been taken for granted. Long before there were any desert fathers, hermits, or monks, there were Christians in the far-flung cities and villages of the vast Roman Empire. These people led the lives of normal citizens. Whether they were landowners or artisans, free or in slavery, made no difference. They understood simply that they must be holy and win souls for Christ. And where else but in their day-to-day lives?

The first martyrs and others who encountered persecution were not special Christians. They were ordinary members of the

Christian community. But with the fall of Rome and the growth of the monasteries, a new age was ushered in, an age that was to last until our own time. In the beginning, Christians felt obliged to bring Christ into the everyday haunts they shared with pagans so that they might share him too. Theirs was a supernatural, but utterly natural, form of apostolate. As the Empire crumbled, however, Christianity retreated into monastic enclaves. Soon the monastic exception became the rule for anyone seeking sanctity. People gradually lost sight of the possibility and importance of Christianizing the world from within it.

Certainly there were splendid flowerings of Christian life, invaluable treasures of holiness. We in no way want to underestimate or downgrade the monastic inheritance of fifteen hundred years. But it is precisely those who love and cherish the monastic ideal, and want to see it bloom again in the Church, who must realize that this will happen only when lay sanctity is recognized as the norm for Christians.

Columbus and Escrivá, two discoverers: one in the service of Spain, the other a Spaniard. Neither lacked predecessors. Often enough, men had sailed in a westerly direction; contrary winds and unfortunate circumstances had forced them back. Often enough, men had preached the need for lay apostolate, and urged the sanctification of ordinary life — one thinks of St. Francis de Sales,[6] St. Vincent Pallotti,[7] John Henry Cardinal Newman,[8] and popes from Paul III to St. Pius X.[9] Too often, however, they had offered not a specific spirituality for lay people, but rather a semimonastic spirituality for people living semimonastic lives.

Neither Columbus nor Escrivá was without opposition. The discoverer of the New World returned from his third voyage in chains. In the 1940s, especially in Madrid and Barcelona, Escrivá was fiercely defamed as a freemason and a heretic, so much so that he was threatened with arrest. He even had to keep, and occasionally use, an alias.[10]

But here ends the analogy between the two explorers. Columbus died thinking he had discovered the western passage to India. He did not get to guide or savor the consolidation of his achievement. It remained for others to turn his discovery into "America." Escrivá, on the other hand, not only was first to tread the new land of lay sanctity, but also formed and directed, with the help of God's grace, the people who would live in it, cultivate it, and spread it.

Foundation of granite

In June 1981, I traveled to Spain to complete the preliminary work for this book "on location." I came from Rome, where I had inhaled the atmosphere of the stage on which Escrivá spent nearly thirty years of his life. At Villa Tevere, the central headquarters of Opus Dei, I had sensed his presence everywhere — in the halls and stairways, in his bedroom, at his work table, in his chapel. And now I wanted to return again to his beginnings. From his dimly lit, quiet crypt under the chapel of Our Lady of Peace, I wanted to go back to the nursery of Opus Dei — the bright and lively streets of Madrid where the young priest had worn out so many pairs of shoes. His surviving friends understood my wish, and turned back the clock to take me for a tour in his footsteps.

In the preceding chapter, I spoke of hospitals where Escrivá attended innumerable poor and suffering patients, many of them terminally ill. He visited them not only as a priest — bringing the sacraments, offering comfort, and reconciling them with God — but also as a brother, doing little favors such as cutting their nails and emptying bedpans. He did not do this alone. By the early thirties, he was joined every Sunday afternoon by young men whom he had met through his priestly work — the giving of spiritual direction, catechism classes, simple friendship. Those he "infected" with love of God and neighbor would introduce their own friends to Josemaría.

He did not lecture these youths on "Social Problems in the Hospitals of Madrid" or on "Structural Improvements in the Medical Care of the Lower Classes." Instead he said, "Come along. On Sunday, we will go to the General Hospital and help out. At Station X, the patients need their fingernails and toenails cut, their hair washed and combed, their beds remade; at Station Y it will undoubtedly be necessary to empty and clean bedpans and clean the bathtubs." This sort of volunteer work was, of course, nothing new. Care of the poor and the sick is a basic duty of Christians. Many religious orders devote themselves to these corporal works of mercy. In our day, however, caring for the sick and the poor has become a specialized and professional affair, with eight-hour days and negotiated wages, with a cost explosion and a staff shortage. Though this professionalization has been in many ways a wonderful development, it would be a shame if it were to lead people, especially Christians, to feel dispensed from the cardinal duty of loving their neighbors, especially those in need. The founder of Opus Dei had to bring consistency back into Christian daily life by teaching his first companions the unity of professional work, a life of prayer, and the works of mercy. He taught this unity by living it with them. And to this day, no young man or woman comes to Opus Dei without learning this threefold unity.

Escrivá was always reminding his followers that among the many tasks of the Christian apostolate, "two imperative duties are giving doctrine and visiting the poor."[11] Recalling the early days, he said, "We used to refer to those poor people as 'Our Lady's Poor.' Those who had no strong desire to do apostolate did not like this and would not go along. This by itself resulted in a sort of natural selection."[12] These visits not only helped the poor people, but also had a profound impact on the young people who made the visits. The experience was an indispensable means of formation into the Christian life. Escrivá did not like to use the term "social work" in this connection. He found it pretentious. "We are not trying, by these visits," he wrote in 1942, "to solve any kind of social problem.... Explain this to the young people.... It is only a matter of making a small gift, a little something that will give a poor, sick, or lonely person some strength. We try to brighten somebody's life for a quarter of an hour, perhaps doing that person some small service. That's all.... Those who are beginning to feel some interior life within themselves will understand this right away, particularly when they learn that we are doing this to honor the Mother of God.[13] We don't want to arouse social tension with these visits. We just want to make it clear to the young people of St. Raphael what they owe their neighbor.[14] They must learn, in a practical way, to recognize Jesus Christ in the poor, the sick, the weak, the lonely, and the suffering, and in children."[15] In wholehearted service these young Christians would find their own hungers satisfied. "Contact with misery or human frailty," said Escrivá, "is an opportunity that Our Lord uses to kindle in a soul a longing for magnanimous, divine adventures." (This is what I meant when I spoke of Escrivá's "conquistadors.") "At the same time," he added, "even in the youngest fellows, he plants uprightness and love."[16]

I could not help thinking of these words as I stood in front of the General Hospital on Santa Isabel St. on that dazzlingly bright summer day. Not all of the original building remains, but what does remain of it struck me as a rather desolate and brutal colossus. Few hospitals of this kind remain today, but I remember them well from my childhood and my years as a medical student. Endlessly long corridors, huge wards with as many as a hundred beds each; high, dreary windows, very little sunlight, plain electric bulbs (without shades) hanging from the ceiling, all the patient's belongings on a small night table next to the bed — this is how I pictured the provincial hospital of Madrid in about 1930. Next door was the Hospital del Rey, built in 1925 to house patients with infectious diseases (smallpox, spotted fever, typhus, dysentery, and tuberculosis). After the cancellation of its chaplaincy by the anticlerical laws of 1930, this hospital of more than twenty-five hundred patients had no priest taking care of it. Sensitive to the need, Escrivá took this task upon himself. (In the summer of 1931, he had given up his chaplaincy with the Damas Apostólicas. The extent of that work had become incompatible with the growing demands of his other duties, including the spiritual direction of Opus Dei.)

Escrivá was able to share his heavy workload at the Hospital del Rey with a young cleric from Asturias named José María Somoano Verdasco. Soon they became close friends. Official membership was not yet possible for priests, but Somoano was one of the first to be in some real way associated with Opus Dei. He was filled with a glowing love for Christ and souls, and he loved his coworker deeply. He understood how a secular priest could also follow a vocation to secular holiness in Opus Dei. For the short time granted him, Somoano lived side by side with Escrivá. He died on

July 16, 1932, possibly poisoned by anticlerical fanatics. In a short eulogy for his friend, Escrivá recounted how he had once entered a chapel where Somoano, thinking he was alone, was praying aloud.[17] He had heard Somoano offer himself to Jesus as a sacrificial victim "for this poor Spain," where hatred of God and his Church was spreading. (In that year, there had been persecutions of the clergy and arson attacks on churches and convents.) "Our Lord Jesus Christ," the eulogy continues, "accepted this holocaust, and with a twofold love, for José María himself and for Opus Dei, he made a gift of it to us: so that our brother might perfect his union with God, his heart increasingly aflame with faith and love; and so that the Work might have someone close to the Trinity and the Immaculate Virgin Mary, that they might always accept our service." Escrivá concluded by saying, "I know that when he prays for us crazy ones — crazy as he was and as Our Lord was — his earnest prayers to the all-merciful heart of Jesus will have great power, and we will receive the superabundant grace we need to fulfill the will of God."

Opus Dei began and spread thanks to the grace that came from the patient sufferings of the poor, the sick, and the dying; but that was not all. Its firm roots and remarkable fruitfulness in human society also required the martyrdom of some of its first few members. Without sacrifice, to the point of death if need be, nothing holy can be founded in this world. The joyful and loving martyrdom of this priest chosen by God to accompany Escrivá must be considered part of the foundation of Opus Dei. It should also be noted that in accordance with the spirit of Opus Dei, his death was a quiet, unnoticed, hidden martyrdom, not something fit for the stage.

The second priest who wanted to join Opus Dei also suffered a quiet martyrdom. Fr. Lino Vea-Murguía was murdered during the Civil War in Madrid.[18] And on November 5, 1932, just four months after Somoano's death, Luis Gordon died. An engineer and factory owner, Gordon was one of the first laymen in Opus Dei. He was in the group of friends who helped out at the hospitals, and was about the same age as Escrivá. "We now have two saints," wrote Escrivá, "a priest and a layman...."[19] He then sketched in broad lines a picture of the deceased that could serve as a blueprint of what is expected from any member of Opus Dei. "He was a good model — obedient, very discreet, spending himself in doing good; humble, self-denying, filled with a spirit of mortification...; a Eucharistic and prayerful man who honored from the depths of his heart the Mother of God and 'little Thérèse' [of Lisieux].... He was a father to his workers, and they truly mourned him at his death." In his memorial to "our brother Luis," Escrivá expressed his firm conviction that the deceased members and friends of Opus Dei would help the Work with their loving intercession and would form a supernatural backbone for their brothers and sisters struggling on earth.

Only ten months later (on September 13th, eve of the Feast of the Exaltation of the Holy Cross), María Ignacia García Escobar died in the Hospital del Rey. One of the first women in Opus Dei, María had been introduced to its spirit by José María Somoano. In 1931 he had told her, "We must pray a lot for something that is going to help the salvation of everyone. And I don't mean pray for just a few days. This is a matter of a great good for the whole world. It will require prayer and sacrifice today, tomorrow, and always."[20]

In the spring of 1932, María asked to join Opus Dei. Although she was already sick by then, her petition was welcomed by Escrivá. Shortly thereafter, an intestinal tuberculosis was diagnosed, which required several operations. A long period of suffering ensued. "It was clear to her," Bernal says, "that she was playing a role from her sick bed in the accomplishment of Opus Dei. 'We have to establish it well!' she wrote in her diary. 'We need to do whatever it takes to make sure the foundation is made of granite, so that what happened in the Gospel to the building built on sand does not happen to us. The foundation is the most important thing — everything else comes later.'"[21] Immediately after her death, Escrivá wrote, "Prayer and patience in suffering were the wheels of the glorious chariot of our sister. We have not lost her; rather, we have received her as a gift. And the realization that she has gone home should immediately turn our natural sorrow into supernatural joy, because now we are sure of an even mightier intercessor in heaven."[22]

In September 1931, Escrivá had taken over the chaplaincy at the Santa Isabel Foundation. Formerly called the Patronato Real, the Foundation incorporated both a school taught by nuns of the Assumption of Mary and a convent of Augustinian nuns founded in 1589 by Blessed Alonso de Orozco.[23] In the convent church of Santa Isabel, Escrivá celebrated Mass for all the nuns, heard their confessions, and gave them spiritual direction. In 1934 he was appointed rector of the Foundation; the difference was that the post included a rectory next to the convent. Except for the interruption of the Civil War, he held this post until 1946.

The church-and-convent building has not changed since then. There is a plain yellowish facade, unobtrusively built into the plane of the neighboring buildings. The rooms inside are poor. At the left of the simple altar there is a screen, separating the altar from the choir of cloistered nuns. Hardly any other still-existing spot in Spain is so deeply connected with the infancy of Opus Dei as the Foundation of Santa Isabel. Whether it houses any artistic masterpieces, as is claimed on a postcard depicting "el Niño [The Christ Child] de Mons. Escrivá," I could not determine. I saw nothing of the kind. But that is unimportant. There is a real treasure in that convent — an exquisite wood carving of the Christ Child. A friendly nun showed it to us in a small room behind the chapel. The foot-long figure, probably carved in the seventeenth century, shows an infant boy lying on his back, with his arms and legs gracefully crossed. The face, which is framed by remarkably lifelike hair, is turned aside. Finely carved eyebrows hover over closed eyes, and a slight smile seems to play about the mouth. The more one looks at the face, the more one seems to see the union of heaven and earth. The good sister explained that for many years now, this Christ Child has been reverenced by the faithful at Christmas. And why is it called the Christ Child "of Msgr. Escrivá"? The founder of Opus Dei, she said, was a young priest who loved the Eucharist above all else and was totally dedicated to prayer. "It is believed that he received a very extraordinary gift of grace...." With the permission of the prioress, Fr. Josemaría would often take the famous image to his apartment, and he would always return deeply moved and beaming with happiness.

Over the last two thousand years, millions of Christians have as a matter of course prayed the "Our Father." It is something quite different, however, to suddenly feel in one's flesh, through the humanity of Christ, a father-child relationship with God so real that it perfects and gives meaning to all one's other relationships. Many Christians strive to preserve and deepen this divine filiation through prayer, reception of the sacraments, meditative reading of the Gospel, and other spiritual exercises. The most important work, of course, is done by God's grace. This grace was granted Josemaría according to the needs of his vocation — in vast amounts. But it did not manifest itself in spectacular ways. The Articles of Postulation give us a glimpse into the way he experienced divine filiation. At the beginning of 1931, we read, "during an especially deep period of prayer, he became aware of his divine filiation with a peculiar and most lively clarity. This awareness was to form a foundation of the spirituality of Opus Dei."[24] We know from Escrivá himself that he was in extremely difficult circumstances at that time, but "in spite of that, he was certain of the accomplishment of the impossible — certain of that which today stands before you as a reality...."[25]

At this discouraging time, he recalled, "I felt the working of the Lord in me. In my heart and on my lips, with an irresistible force, he formed the tender cry 'Abba, Father,' as I was traveling in a streetcar. For the street does not prevent us from having a contemplative dialogue with God; for us, the hustle and bustle of the world is precisely the place of prayer."[26]

A chief obstacle to sensing one's divine filiation is a natural blindness to its connection with the cross, a corollary of which is the stubborn, querulous disposition that tempts one to reproach God. Everyone knows how readily God gets accused of harshness, cruelty, and injustice. "How can God, if he is a Father and loves us, permit this and that ..." — and there follows a long list of horrors and sufferings of every sort. For such questions to arise is admittedly understandable. Children are often dumbfounded, furious, and disillusioned, and there are dreadful sufferings whose causes, meaning, and ultimate consequences are no more comprehensible to us than they are to little children. But an untrusting attitude, if unchecked, can lead to the cooling of love and the loss of faith. Theologians and spiritual writers through the ages, starting with St. Paul, have wrestled with the cross as the secret of the paternal love of God. For Escrivá, divine filiation, sanctification of work, apostolate, acceptance and even love of the cross — all of these formed a unity. Each conditioned, presumed, and depended on the other.

We do not know how the Christ Child of the Santa Isabel Convent brought Escrivá mystically close to the childhood of Jesus, how feeling himself an infant in the hands of God taught him to understand the sufferings he bore. But whoever lovingly contemplates the face of the infant Jesus, as so often portrayed in religious art, will come to see a crown of thorns around the tiny head — a crown that is almost suspended and nearly transparent. The fragile wreath has just a few tiny thorns, barely visible; but it will become more solid, and thick with thorns, until it becomes the terrible martyr's crown of the Passion.

In that same summer of 1931, Escrivá discovered the cross as the center of spiritual life for a child of God. While he was saying the Mass for the Feast of the Transfiguration, "heaven sent the Servant of God a further enlightenment; and from this moment on, he announced more emphatically than ever, and with untiring energy, the apostolic need to 'put Christ at the center of every human activity.'" Such sanctified work makes the worker holy and leads the world to holiness. Such sanctified work will be carried out by those who unite themselves with Christ, with the crucified Christ, through interior life, prayer, and penance.[27]

The founder of Opus Dei spoke often about the relationship between divine filiation and suffering, but perhaps most beautifully in The Way of the Cross, which was not published until after his death. "God is my father, even though he sends me suffering. He loves me tenderly, though he wounds me. Jesus suffers to fulfill the most holy will of God.... And I, who also want to fulfill God's will by following in the footsteps of the Master, can I complain if I meet suffering along the way? It is a clear sign of my divine filiation, for he is treating me like his divine Son."[28] Reflecting on the second fall of Christ, Escrivá says, "Seek comfort in divine filiation: God is your most loving father. This is your refuge, a sheltered harbor where you can drop anchor no matter what disturbs the surface of the sea of life."[29] Of Christ's third fall, Escrivá says, "But have you forgotten that God is your father? He is your omnipotent and omniscient father, full of mercy. He could never send you something evil. What is bothering you is really for your own good, though your earthbound eyes cannot see this now."[30]

If divine filiation is the essence of the relationship between God and ourselves, and if Christ's Passion is the heart of that relationship, joy is its emanation. In other words, joy is what other people should perceive. "Our way," said Escrivá, "is one of joy, of loving fidelity to the service of God. Our joy is not the warm glow of a foolish smile, a sort of physical well-being. It has deep roots. But it is compatible with exhaustion, with sorrow (for we have hearts), and with difficulties in our interior life and apostolic work. For though it sometimes does seem that the world is falling apart, nothing is actually falling apart, for God does not lose battles. Joy is an inevitable consequence of divine filiation, of knowing ourselves loved by our father God, who holds us close, helps us, and always forgives us."[31]

It was this joy of Escrivá's that the nuns of Santa Isabel remembered decades later; this joy had drawn people to him and marked everything he touched. This infectious joy has become a hallmark of Opus Dei. Where joy is missing, you may find good and useful activity; but you will not find Opus Dei.

Opus Dei is a family

I do not remember all the streets we walked after leaving the Augustinian convent; and even if I could, their names would mean little to those unacquainted with Madrid. But they are the streets where Escrivá walked his innumerable miles, hurrying from one task to another. The streets of Madrid, like those of so many other Mediterranean cities, are adorned with many pictures of the Madonna, on walls and monuments and windows. On his long walks, Escrivá spotted every image of the Blessed Virgin, no matter how hidden or insignificant. My guides pointed out one of Escrivá's favorites (I would never have noticed it otherwise) — a mosaic at the peak of a house on Calle Atocha. They showed me a relief, in the wall near the royal palace, before which Escrivá sometimes prayed for an hour, kneeling on the sidewalk.[32] Passers-by thought he was crazy.

These streets served Escrivá not only as links between apostolic tasks, but also as places of work. Opus Dei grew up in the open air — like any healthy child. In the plazas, parks, and boulevards, Escrivá met with the young men who had entrusted themselves to his spiritual direction, who felt a vocation growing within them, or who had already offered their unconditional yes to his new work. He often gathered these young men together in small groups, though he also gave them individual time and attention.

On these instructional walks Escrivá would clarify the ancient novelty of Opus Dei to students, workers, and others who saw piety and church as one thing and "life" as quite another, and who thought that any man who felt called to serve God and the Church in a special way must become a monk or a diocesan priest. He freed them from this dilemma by showing them a practical way to follow God closely in the midst of the world, and by explaining the theory and theology behind it.

Then as now, it was not enough to use the terms of old ascetical manuals, or to accept at face value all of the ideas expressed therein. Platitudes have little positive effect, and can do real harm. Escrivá never used expressions like "develop your prayer life," or "consider your divine filiation." Instead, he explained by word and example how to do these things. For example, he would suggest particular mortifications, particular sacrifices of the senses, whims, or moods. We should, he said, deny ourselves with joy, without making a fuss — not out of contempt for the world, but for the love of Christ. We should, in fact, live like Christ himself, who joined in festivities but lived in the most moderate way, in continual self-giving. He told them, for example, to devote a particular time each day to prayer, regardless of how they might feel at that time. But he advised against restricting conversation with God to those set times each day; prayer could and should continue, like the beating of one's heart, in any environment. This life of continuous prayer would take practice, but a variety of means — aspirations, the rosary, visits to the Blessed Sacrament, greetings to images of the Blessed Virgin, and so forth — would make it possible.

This advice was presented to Escrivá's first followers *en passant*, literally. Occasionally, of course, they would stop someplace, depending on weather, money, and location. On my tour of Madrid, I saw the site of the El Sotanillo cafe, a typical Madrid chocolate shop where Escrivá liked to rest and talk.

After 1932, Escrivá's friends usually met him at his family's house. When he moved from Saragossa to Madrid, his mother, sister, and brother also moved to the capital; until February 1934, when he moved into the Santa Isabel rectory, they all shared a ground-floor apartment at 4 Martínez Campos St. This was, in a sense, the first Opus Dei center. Here the family spirit of Opus Dei took root, and its basic structure and pattern became established. For Opus Dei is not an organization, a society, or an order; it is a family.

It may be difficult to understand this fully, for the expression is more than a metaphor. Opus Dei is a real family, a spiritual one, whose bond is a common vocation. Its members have a natural, familial loyalty that is warmhearted and confident. The marriage that began this family was the spiritual union of Josemaría Escrivá and Jesus Christ, a union effected by the sacrament of Holy Orders and deepened by a life of self-sacrifice. Like every natural child, Opus Dei was the fruit of a union and a gift from God. Of course, all the members of Opus Dei, including those yet to come, were "born," or called, by the grace of God, but they were "conceived" through Escrivá's prayer, sacrifice, obedience, and love — through his union with Christ and with God's will for him. "I cannot stop raising my heart to the Lord in thanksgiving," wrote Escrivá in 1945, "for having given me this paternity, which I have accepted, thanks to his grace, with the full consciousness that my only mission on earth has been to make this a reality. This is why I love you with the heart of a father and of a mother."[33] Years later he wrote, "My children, I brought you into the world as a mother — in pain, like a mother."[34]

Escrivá's paternity of Opus Dei makes the members brothers and sisters; they form a family. This is of crucial importance in understanding Opus Dei. Everything else follows from this family spirit. Like any other father, Escrivá loved his children and desired their happiness — the health of their souls and their joyful following of Christ in the midst of the world, which would lead others to follow along and "light up the ways of the earth."[35] Like any other father, he also wanted his children to love one another, to stand up for one another as brothers and sisters. And he wanted them to wear clean clothes and have their buttons sewn on — to live respectably.

A father's responsibility is not, however, a one-way street. Coming from the other direction is the duty of filiation. "You must pray for me a lot," Escrivá often said. "I am praying for you — please pray for me! This is the way I want you to show your appreciation ... not only out of justice, but also out of love; for I need you to be better than me, to help me and support me. Pray that I will be a child before God and remain strong in my work — I am already old, and night overshadows me — so that I can accept the final call to the journey of love, which I foresee....[36] And when something costs you an effort, then offer it up for me, so that I may be good and faithful and cheerful. How much I offer up for my children in the course of each day!"[37]

There is, of course, more to a family than this. There is all that goes into making a home, all the physical and emotional warmth and care. There is order, as family members take responsibility for themselves and for one another. When someone goes astray, it is a great sorrow for the whole family and a reproach to those closest to that person. Escrivá used to say, "The most beautiful apostolate is seeing to it that none of your brothers or sisters is lost."[38] And all the members must contribute in some way to the support of the family. All must be mindful of the honor of the family wherever they work and hope to bring Christ. They must make the family a source of friendship and joy for as many people as possible.

"Those of my children who most like to stay home within their four walls must learn to get outdoors and see the town. It is our first and essential duty to seek souls where they normally are — all around," says Escrivá. Recalling the Gospel story of the miraculous catch of fish, he then adds, "We must pull them into the boat, infected with love, with the spirit of repentance, and with dedication, or at least with a desire for dedication."[39]

Finally, a healthy family wants to grow, to become bigger and better. Escrivá was ready to overlook any weakness or failing in his spiritual children as long as he knew they had not given up the struggle. There was only one attitude he considered a sure sign of a dying vocation — an indifference toward spiritual fecundity. "Any child of mine who does not want to win others is acting badly. Something is not right with that child, for those who truly love their way feel an impulse to bring others to share their happiness; good is diffusive of itself. Unhappy is the child who no longer has this zeal to win other souls."[40]

A large, dispersed family may have special family days, certain feasts, customs, and traditions. I have even heard of people having family newsletters and magazines to help them keep in touch. Yet no normal person would wear a sign saying, for example, "I am a member of the Meyer family," or come up with an introduction like this: "My name is Carl Miller; I belong to the Meyer family, so I would like to repair your washing machine." It is part of the nature of a family for each of its members, according to personal circumstances, to work independently in society.

Opus Dei is a truly lay and secular family. Some of its members are clerics, but this is true of many Catholic families. Occasionally people complain that Opus Dei is not cooperative, because it never sends representatives to this meeting or that congress, it does not appear as a group, pass resolutions, advertise, wear insignia, or wave a flag. But it cannot do these things since, as in any other family, its members each have the right and duty to act according to their own judgment. The only limit to this right is the requirement of adherence to the teachings and laws of the Church.

As early as May 1935, Escrivá wrote in his *Instructions:* "Do not forget that single people, married people, widows, and clerics [in Opus Dei] all continue to be members of their own environments, fully bound to their own natural families with all the duties and rights that arise therefrom."[41] The present prelate of Opus Dei, Bishop Alvaro del Portillo, later added the following commentary: "The members' bonds to their natural families remain the same as they were before membership in the Work, but God's call has sketched out a new divine path on earth for them. To the extent that they raise to a supernatural level their feelings, affections, and all the rights and duties involved in their family life, new horizons of joy and peace open before them. Everything is transformed by the grace of the vocation facilitating their encounter with God. Inasmuch as they try to build bright and cheerful Christian homes, the divine grace of vocation easily becomes contagious, and the families become fruitful centers of sanctity."[42]

There is a connection here between dedication and freedom. Regarding family bonds, Jesus had some clear, unequivocal words to say — words that can at times be quite tough to live by. When he spoke of the sword he had come to bring, he was referring to the difficult but necessary severance of all relationships standing in the way of a full response to his call. His is the sword of definitive love, a sword which cuts all ties holding the heart fast and preventing it from giving itself fully.

In a heart thus freed, secondary attachments can find their proper place, and indeed become deeper, richer, and more fruitful than ever. Christ did not demand that one not love father and mother, son or daughter; only that they not be loved more than God. This does not entail any weakening or denigration of natural ties and affections; on the contrary, it intensifies them by filtering them through the most perfect love of Christ.

Dolores Escrivá, with the help of her daughter Carmen, managed the household in the apartment on Martínez Campos St. She made sure that the young men who followed her son understood "family" not as a mere concept or symbol, but as a tangible reality. With the spiritual guidance of Josemaría, she made that apartment a home.

Seeing her photograph, I was first struck by her natural, unforced dignity. She had a remarkably high, clear, determined brow, which led me to suspect that the "Aragonese hard-headedness" to which Josemaría frequently confessed came principally from her. Around her mouth there lingered a hint of roguishness, but she seemed very self-possessed. We know she endured the hard blows of fate without complaint or bitterness.

By all accounts, she had a strong character. She was busy and self-disciplined, but at the same time affectionate and funny — a happy combination of traits that she had passed on to her son. He had always taken to heart her sturdy advice. For example, she had told him one day when he was little (and embarrassed at having to wear a new suit), "Josemaría, never be ashamed of anything — except of sin." And from that day forward, those words had formed a cornerstone of his entire life.

Later, what had been rooted in the natural family of its founder was to become typical of all centers of Opus Dei, and especially of those fortunate enough to have an "administration." Made up of, or managed by, members of the women's branch, an administration helps to create the family environment of the centers by taking responsibility for meals, cleaning, and care of oratories. Until her death in 1941, Dolores Escrivá directed this work herself and trained other members of the women's branch for these tasks. Afterwards, Carmen Escrivá became the organizer and soul of the administration, an apostolate which naturally became more complex with the global expansion of Opus Dei.

"Unless the grain of wheat falls into the earth and dies, it remains alone; but if it dies, it brings forth rich fruit" (Jn 12:24). The early 1930s gave Opus Dei not only those who became "grains of wheat" by their holy deaths, but also those who through long lives of service fulfilled the words of Christ as he more generally meant them; they died to themselves and brought forth a rich spiritual harvest. I would like to describe two of these early followers of Escrivá's — not to single them out, but to offer them as examples representative of all those trying to walk the path of Opus Dei.

The first of these was Isidoro Zorzano, who lived from 1902 to 1943. Along with Luis Gordon, he was one of the very first members of Opus Dei. (Outside of Opus Dei, his name will become known only when his process of beatification, begun in 1965, is completed.) Born of Spanish parents living in Argentina, Zorzano was able to retain dual citizenship, which proved to be of great importance to Opus Dei during the Spanish Civil War. He grew up in Spain; the family moved there in 1904, intending to return to Argentina when the children's education was complete. Isidoro and Josemaría met in the secondary school in Logroño. But then their paths separated. Zorzano became an engineer and worked for some time at a shipbuilding wharf in Cadiz. Then in 1928 he took a position with the Andalusian Railroads in Malaga. "It was a monotonous job," notes his biographer.[43]

One morning in August 1930, the two friends chanced upon each other in Madrid. Escrivá had for some reason taken a street he ordinarily did not use. The meeting renewed their old friendship, and out of it sprang a vocation to the barely begun Opus Dei. In accordance with the nature of his vocation, Zorzano kept his job, but "now he tried to do his work in a way that would make it an instrument of sanctification and apostolate."[44] He had understood Escrivá well. On the other hand, if Opus Dei was to grow, there would have to be student residences, centers of formation, and circles. All these things would demand helpers who could do some of the hard work; for Escrivá was still virtually alone. When that time came, Zorzano would have to be totally available. "If the Lord calls me," he said, "I must be ready to say yes."[45] But it had not reached that point yet. Zorzano's destiny for the time being was to remain where he was, with the new love for Christ that drives the lover to be holy and to help others to be holy for Christ's sake.

Zorzano was also the first to benefit from long-distance personal and spiritual contact with Escrivá. They corresponded regularly, and Zorzano regularly made short visits to Madrid to deepen his spiritual formation and his understanding of the essence and practice of Opus Dei. But until 1936 his workplace remained "red Malaga," and there he carried out a magnificent youth apostolate reminiscent of St. John Bosco's.[46] He took the poorest street urchins, whom he literally found in the gutter, and found a home for them in the orphanage run by the Jesuit priest Fr. Aricarda. There he served them at table, ate with them, and played soccer with them. He did not take them to church processions or force them to pray, but when he urged them to study, work, or play fair, he would repeat very energetically what Escrivá had said to him: "You won't be worth a thing if you don't change!" The boys did not understand right away. (Neither did Zorzano himself immediately grasp the full meaning of what Escrivá was saying.) Gradually, the boys recognized their duty to do things in an orderly, conscientious way, and they began to feel something growing in their hearts that brought them closer to God. No one understood how Isidoro found the time to do all that he did.[47] (Shortly before the outbreak of the Spanish Civil War, he was transferred to Madrid. We will speak more of him in the next chapter).

Of the seventy thousand members of Opus Dei, none has been a member longer than Juan Jiménez Vargas, who was a nineteen-year-old student when he met Escrivá, in 1932. I met him in 1981 in Pamplona, where he was a professor of physiology, and he mentioned that first meeting. "I had heard of Escrivá from my friends," he said, "but I was not interested — I just dismissed it all as mysticism. A first casual meeting made no particular impression on me, and until August 1932, nothing happened."[48] Jiménez Vargas explains this further in his memoirs for the cause of Escrivá's beatification. Spain was in a state of feverish agitation. Religious, political, and social tensions were mounting as the nation began to split into two hostile camps. In this atmosphere, he says, "the young people understood very little or nothing [of what Escrivá was saying]. All they were interested in was political solutions, and their activism fixed their attention on violent solutions."[49] On August 18, 1932, there was an attempt at a rightist putsch by General Sanjurjo, which collapsed within twenty-four hours. In the arrests that followed, many young rebels, including students with opposing ideological and political views, were incarcerated.[50] Escrivá, sometimes accompanied by Jiménez Vargas, visited the imprisoned. He did not worry about how this might make him look in the eyes of the political authorities, nor did he make any distinction, in his conversations through the visitor's grill, between "red" and "black," leftists and rightists.

Without mentioning Opus Dei, he was always indirectly speaking about it, for everything he said reflected the spirit of Opus Dei. In this hardly propitious situation, he exhorted the students to study and work. He brought them books. He talked them into giving their political sentiments a rest and playing soccer in politically mixed teams, with a sense of humor and fairness, which ended up doing them far more good than their hour-long disputes. He went against customary pastoral practice by not requiring Catholics to belong to one specified political party; he insisted on political freedom for Catholics within the bounds of Church teaching. Above all, however, he remained a priest always and everywhere. And a priest, as he never tired of stressing, "cannot and will not speak of anything but God."

Fifty years later, Jiménez Vargas recalls that what most impressed him was the way Escrivá talked about the sacrament of Penance, which he called the "sacrament of joy," and the very natural and deeply human love with which he spoke about the Mother of God. He never sounded otherworldly, esoteric, or extravagant. Everything he said resonated with the heartiness of a true father, showing great and broad comprehension and also detailed knowledge. He was well informed about the political situation in Spain, but he did not spend much time talking about it. He knew only too well how easily such discussions could become entanglements; but he also knew how, as Jiménez Vargas put it, "to give an apostolic twist to every conversation."

Throughout his life, Escrivá remained in contact with the university world. Though he spoke to the hearts and minds of people in all walks of life, he felt especially at home among students, and students trusted and confided in him. Among the first members of Opus Dei were many students. For the first twenty years, the various vocations came mainly from their ranks. This had nothing to do with elitism; mostly it had to do with the need for growth and development. The grafting of Opus Dei onto society required young, malleable souls who could understand and embody its spirit. These young people would mature and advance in their professions and become multipliers, each one a powerhouse transmitting the contagious love of Christ.

At the end of January 1933, Juan Jiménez Vargas asked to be admitted to Opus Dei. He made the decision after a long talk with Escrivá, who explained the foundations of Opus Dei and showed the young man the greatness and beauty of this new way of sanctity. Escrivá had been making a novena to the Holy Spirit, asking him to give his grace to Jiménez Vargas.[51]

The work of the archangels

The apartment on Martínez Campos St. no longer exists, but the nearby house at 33 Luchana St. still stands. In December 1933, in a

The first home of the DYA Academy was in an apartment in this building on Luchana St. in Madrid.

second-floor apartment of this building, the DYA Academy began its work. It was the first "corporate work" of Opus Dei. This is an arrangement whereby Opus Dei as a whole guarantees the Christian principles of an institution, and Opus Dei members take responsibility for administrative and spiritual direction. Today there are many corporate works, comprising a wide variety of apostolic activities in many countries. Among them are universities, trade schools, student residences, and youth clubs. All of them have an exclusively apostolic goal: to prepare people of every social situation to turn their environment into a *terra firma Christi*, a land of faith to which many settlers will be attracted. The principles behind these corporate works have not changed since the founding of the DYA Academy — they are simply the spirit and aim of Opus Dei.[52] These undertakings, therefore, are not church-related; they are secular activities established in accordance with civil law, and their organizational structure is completely lay. Managing these corporate works is the professional career of those who run them.

The initials "DYA" have a double significance. They stand for "Derecho y Arquitectura" (Law and Architecture), the chief disciplines studied there. They also stand for "Dios y Audacia" (God and Daring); as early as 1928 Escrivá had adopted this expression as a motto. The Academy offered courses in professional disciplines and in Christian doctrine. Aside from the spiritual and apostolic formation of the few members of Opus Dei, Escrivá was also responsible for the religious care and formation of the many other young people who sensed something special in him and sought his counsel.

Needless to say, establishing and supporting the Academy, despite its modest set-up, entailed serious material and financial difficulties. With respect to such difficulties (a rather weak word for what were often dramatic setbacks), little has changed in Opus Dei since that time. Escrivá was and remained poor, and the same is true of Opus Dei. The fact that the houses are always well cared for and tastefully furnished stems not from the riches but from the spirit of poverty of its members. They give Opus Dei as much as they possibly can. What seems so comfortable and attractive is the fruit of the hard work, personal sacrifices, and self-denial of the members of Opus Dei. It depends, too, on the help of many friends and members, and on the generosity of individual donors. Escrivá's family sold all that they owned — it was not much, just a small piece of land — and contributed the proceeds to the first centers. The furniture in the Luchana St. center came from Escrivá's mother. Economic straits were a constant then, and they have been ever since. Whenever Opus Dei begins an activity, it starts with next to nothing. It has no property of its own, and it does not build up capital. In accordance with its lay status, the individual members are responsible for gathering the necessary means through their professional work and the generosity of others. Begging is a familiar part of Christianity, certainly nothing unique to Opus Dei. It is a school of humility, and not just where money is concerned. Msgr. Escrivá begged for the alms of prayer like a child begs for candy. Millions of starving and sick people beg today, as has been the case since the beginning of human civilization, and those who beg either in silence or out loud for a little love cannot be numbered. Anyone who has never met a beggar has never encountered Christ, and anyone who has never begged has never followed Christ.

Every great institution or servant of God has inevitably met with opposition, misunderstanding, and malice. This was true of Christ and his Church, and it was true of Escrivá and Opus Dei. As soon as Opus Dei's first center had a face and a name, it met with opposition and detraction. The opposition grew as Opus Dei grew, though the Work has clearly outdistanced it.

In 1933, however, and until the Civil War, opposition from outside was not worth worrying about. There were more pressing problems, such as finding members. Opus Dei was open to everyone, but in order to spread the Work around the globe, Escrivá needed a core of young, healthy, intelligent men and women who could give their whole lives in the service of Opus Dei. They would have to be the cornerstones, or the "apostles," as Escrivá liked to say. "When Christians," he says, "understand the catholicity of the Church and live it, when they feel within themselves the longing to announce the message of salvation to all creatures, then they also know that they must become all things to all people, in order to save all (1 Cor. 9:22).[53] And as for us, whom God has wanted in his Work, to us he has also given an apostolic mode of working, which leads us to understanding and forbearance and a refined charity towards all souls."[54]

This is an ideal to which many are naturally disposed, but which can be lost over the course of a life. High aspiration has to be gradually impressed on young souls and given an apostolic twist. Both Salvador Bernal and Juan Jiménez Vargas tell us about the day this really came home to Escrivá. While walking through a poor neighborhood, he noticed a picture of the Blessed Virgin, torn out of a catechism, lying in the dirt. When he bent over to pick it up, he suddenly realized, with full clarity, that God wanted the St. Raphael work to be the first stage in the development of the Work. This is an apostolate involving youths who have not yet embarked on professional careers or decided to get married. Later the St. Gabriel work, an apostolate for married people, was added. The backbone of Opus Dei, made up of members living a life of celibacy and complete availability, was entrusted to the special protection of the archangel Michael. The celibate members of Opus Dei are called "numeraries." With full dedication and unlimited availability, they devote themselves to the apostolates of Opus Dei. Ordinarily they live in Opus Dei centers. "Associate" members are also celibate, but they carry out their apostolate in the framework of certain permanent family or professional requirements; they do not live in centers, but on their own or with their families. Most members marry, and these are called "supernumeraries." In the 1930s, there were no supernumeraries. The married people and secular priests who then enjoyed a close personal and spiritual relationship with Escrivá and the fledgling Opus Dei could not be members yet. This would require the authoritative approval of Opus Dei as an institution within the Church. So at that time, Escrivá concentrated on building a strong backbone of numeraries who could work closely with him in his youth apostolate. He encouraged young men and women to follow Christ as lay people, teaching them the importance of seeking complete dedication and sanctity in everyday life. A small, loyal, self-sacrificing band of followers enabled Escrivá to open, in the autumn of 1934, the DYA Academy, which was the first student residence of Opus Dei.

Naturally, the St. Raphael work and the St. Gabriel work are inextricably linked. When adults draw near to Christ, they bring their children with them. Teachers and workers bring their students and younger colleagues. And when young people dedicate themselves to Christ, they draw their parents, teachers, and older friends along. "I have made it clear to you," Escrivá said in 1960, "that you cannot approach your apostolic work as though it were some kind of a laboratory experiment, taking one isolated strand and calling it St. Raphael work.... No, our apostolate is all of a piece, with a single weave. Where there is St. Raphael work, there is also St. Gabriel work along with it, and all sorts of vocations for our family, and as a result we have St. Michael work and the corporate works."[55]

Without departing from this unified approach, Escrivá insisted nonetheless on the vital importance of the youth activities of Opus Dei. How long can any community survive without new blood? True, no one is ever too old for Opus Dei. The grace of God that rejuvenated our biblical ancestors can still summon octogenarians to service in the vineyard. Nevertheless, it is usually the young people who let themselves be sent far afield to labor for the harvest. Although it is wonderful to labor for the Lord for that last hour before sunset, the kingdom of God is in great need of those who can bear the burden and heat from the break of dawn to the end of the day.

Someone asked Escrivá why he put so much emphasis on the St. Raphael work — surely there must be many vocations to Opus Dei from outside the St. Raphael work. Escrivá replied, "Certainly, my child, and there always will be. But the richest harvest comes from there. That is the way, and there is no other."[56]

Once, in the 1970s, he was asked how it had been possible to get this apostolate going at all. He answered, "How does one begin anything? Any way one can! And where? Wherever it takes you. My children, I could not count the times we carried out the work of St. Raphael in the apartments of friends, in hotels, in rented rooms, anyplace... — but it was done! For us, it was as necessary as breathing.... What do you mean, how did I begin? In my mother's apartment, with three fellows ... — that was over forty years ago."[57]

Escrivá himself determined all the details of the spirit and practice of this St. Raphael apostolate. It rests, one might say, on five pillars: catechesis, which secures and deepens the knowledge of doctrine; a life of piety, which means a real personal relationship with Christ in prayer and the sacraments; sanctification of work, whether manual or intellectual; service to the poor and the sick, through works of charity and mercy; and a cheerful, friendly family atmosphere where people work, share, and celebrate. This is the unshakable foundation of the apostolate of Opus Dei. "It is not in our hands," wrote Escrivá in 1934, "to omit, shorten, or change anything that pertains to the spirit and practice of the Work of God."[58]

He also cautioned against losing heart. One must, he said, carry out the class or meditation even if only one person were to show up instead of the eight or nine expected. In 1935, he reminded his followers how he had begun the work of St. Raphael: "As I began to give the blessing with the Blessed Sacrament," he said, "I didn't see just the three young men in front of me, but three thousand, three hundred thousand, three million ... white, black, red, yellow, men of all languages, all lands."[59] All sorts of difficulties — attacks from outsiders, material worries, personal failings, innumerable disappointments — would come. The cross is never far from a work of Christ; it can never be absent. But victory and defeat depend only on the inner life of the soul, on the holiness of the individual and the group.

The seed sprouts

In September 1934, the DYA Academy had moved to a second-floor apartment at 50 Ferraz St. It was here, as we mentioned, that Opus Dei's first student residence was set up. There have been many firsts in these pages: the first St. Raphael circle,[60] the first female vocation, the first center, ... and now there was the first chapel and tabernacle in an Opus Dei center. Escrivá obtained permission from the bishop of Madrid to have an oratory in the student residence, and to keep the Blessed Sacrament reserved there. The prerequisites were extremely strict; this was an important step forward for the Work. It did not entail an ecclesiastical approval of Opus Dei, but it was an expression of trust by the hierarchy toward Josemaría and his spiritual sons. From the beginning, Escrivá had maintained a close relationship with the universal Church, with the hierarchy and the local ordinaries. This was not a tactical maneuver, but a manifestation of his love for the Roman Catholic Church, the family founded by Jesus Christ. He could not imagine a work of genuine Christian renewal that would be separated, or somehow alienated, from the pastoral and doctrinal jurisdiction of the Church.

It was not always easy to explain the heart of Opus Dei to Church authorities, much less to enthuse them. The bishops' outlook was often shaped by the spirit of the times and the general conception of the clerical, religious, and lay states that had developed over the centuries. Perhaps for this reason, some were puzzled by Opus Dei. Of course, many of the Spanish bishops were friends and supporters of Escrivá and his work. With the permission of the pope and the encouragement of many bishops, Escrivá's process of beatification began just six years after his death. The roots of this popularity go back to the earliest days of Opus Dei.

Bonds of friendship, upright and permanent, bound Escrivá to numberless religious and secular priests. Many of these men eventually held positions of authority in the Church. Among the striking collections of written testimonies about Escrivá that were gathered for the beatification process, there are many accounts from friends of the 1930s and 1940s who later became bishops.[61] Two particularly close friends were the vicar general and later bishop of Madrid, Casimiro Morcillo, and the bishop of Vitoria, Xavier Lauzurica Torralba, who wrote the preface to the first edition of *The Way*. These and many other friends who met Escrivá between 1924 and 1934 remained in contact for the rest of their lives. Their statements are wonderful sources of information. For example, Laureano Castán Lacoma, the bishop of Sigüenza-Guadalajara, was a seminarian in 1926 and lived in Fonz. He occasionally served the Masses that Josemaría celebrated there when he made short visits to see his priest-uncle Teodoro. Castán remembers many private discussions with Fr. Josemaría between the years 1931 and 1935. "He spoke to me about the foundation that the Lord had asked him to make. He spoke of it as 'the work of God.' Although he told me he was laboring to bring it into existence, he presented it as an already existing reality. He saw it that clearly, quite obviously through the grace of God, and projected it into the future."[62]

"He told me," Castán continues, "that in time I would come to know the members of Opus Dei — young people with elegance and distinction, but living mortification and a spirit of penance. They would have professional careers, well-paid jobs from which they could live comfortably if they so wished, but they would voluntarily choose to live total poverty. The founder particularly lamented the way some teachers, 'mentors of youth,' clipped the wings of young people, not developing within them the capability of full dedication to apostolate and interior life."[63]

A particularly interesting witness from the 1930s is Pedro Cantero Cuadrado, archbishop of Saragossa, who died in 1978. He met Escrivá in the fall of 1930 at the University of Madrid. "Our lifelong friendship," he writes, "began with our first meeting." This happened quite frequently with Escrivá, which gives one some idea of his extraordinary charisma. Like many other young Spaniards in that turbulent period before the Civil War, Cantero was deeply involved in politics and, as he says, "was dreaming of a professorship."

One can easily imagine him: a gifted young theologian, ambitious and somewhat introverted. His friendship with Escrivá changed him. As by now we would expect, Escrivá encouraged him to work harder, but his influence went deeper than that. "His example," says the bishop, "caused a complete change in my outlook on life." In a letter written in 1931, Escrivá minced no words. "Look, Pedro," he said, "you have become an egoist now! Look at the situation of the Church in Spain now — and at Spain itself. You think of nothing except yourself! We have to think about the Church and consider the situation of Catholicism in our country. We have to consider what we personally can do to serve the Church."[64] Pedro, who had been one of the hospital helpers and a friend of Somoano's, mentions that Escrivá never spoke to him about a vocation to Opus Dei. "He respected everyone's freedom to choose their own path, and to follow their own personal judgment. Even more, he helped people to follow their own chosen paths."[65]

This respect did not contradict his understandable zeal to win new members for Opus Dei. "We are destined by God," Escrivá said in 1935, "to spread extensively in a short period of time."[66] But such expansion takes place only when God calls whom he wants, and they freely respond to his call. Of course, God often uses certain individuals as instruments to attract others to his service. Escrivá always spoke of personal friendship as the chief transmission line for apostolate and new vocations. He insisted, however, that friendship should never be instrumentalized to attain the aims of Opus Dei. If friendship was true and selfless, God could always make it an instrument of his for the good of the friend, whether or not that was readily apparent; and this might or might not involve a vocation to Opus Dei.

Escrivá united a penetrating eye for character and personality with a talent for helping people, through friendship and trust, to realize their divine calling. This explains why he immediately encouraged some people to join Opus Dei, while in other cases he waited years before raising the issue, and often counseled someone to get married or to join a religious order. It also explains why his friendships never suffered as a result of the advice he offered.

That first residence at 50 Ferraz St. has not survived, and the apartment house at 16 Ferraz, into which the Academy moved in 1936, was destroyed in the war. Today there is a beautiful park across the street, where the barracks of the Cuartel de la Montaña once stood. The storming of these barracks by the Republican militia on July 19, 1936, ignited the Red Terror in Madrid. Walking along the street, I tried to imagine those days. Political, ideological, and social confrontations had intensified between 1930 and 1936. By 1936, there was bitter enmity between the traditional Catholics and the socialist-anarchists in Spain. Chasms of hatred ran through regions, towns, social classes, and families. It took great supernatural conviction for Escrivá to continue building Opus Dei in the face of these violent cleavages in Spanish society. Although he was never nervous or anxious, but always optimistic and in good humor, he was completely realistic and had no illusions about the dying peace in his country.

Even though he found helpers and generous benefactors, in the last analysis everything still rested on his shoulders. He bore the burden of taking all the initiative. He begged for money. He worried about buying and furnishing the centers. He gave meditations and talks — several each day — and many hours of instruction. Between 1934 and the outbreak of the Spanish Civil War in 1936, hundreds of students received a deep Christian formation from him — a formation both natural and spiritual. Escrivá refused to get involved in the lengthy theoretical discussions that were common at any gathering, even within Church circles. He always insisted on practicality.[67] He said little about the virtue of humility or the usefulness of the rosary; instead, he spoke of being humble and saying the rosary.

A resident of 50 Ferraz (years later, after his marriage, he joined Opus Dei) recalls forty years later, "Often it was enough to hear him say just two words — 'my son' — to give you a push forward."[68] With a childlike piety, in the face of endless financial difficulties, Escrivá prayed this request to St. Nicholas: "Sancte Nicolae, curam domus age!" ("St. Nicholas, take care of this house!") Notwithstanding all the difficulties and the obvious storm clouds looming over Spain, Escrivá was still planning to spread Opus Dei to Valencia, and even beyond the Spanish border, to Paris.

On March 31, 1935, he was able for the first time to celebrate Mass, give Holy Communion, and reserve the Blessed Sacrament in the chapel of an Opus Dei center. This first chapel was simple but dignified; the tabernacle of gilded wood was borrowed from members of a religious order. Escrivá had hoped to celebrate the first Mass on the Feast of St. Joseph (March 19th), but there were still no candlesticks, wine and water cruets, or a missal stand. He did not know where to turn. Then a big parcel was delivered to the building caretaker by an anonymous friend. It contained all of these items. The origin of these gifts has remained a mystery to this day.[69]

Opus Dei, by the way, owes a great debt of gratitude to Leopoldo Eijo y Garay. As bishop of Madrid, he not only authorized this first oratory, but also promoted and defended Opus Dei in the years just after the Civil War, when the Work faced especially great difficulties and stern opposition. With him begins a long line of episcopal friends and benefactors of Opus Dei throughout the world. Eijo y Garay, formerly the bishop of Vitoria, became the bishop of Madrid-Alcalá in 1923, and held this office until his death in 1963.[70] Like Cardinal Soldevilla, he belonged to that generation of bishops who considered themselves not only fathers and shepherds but also rulers, and he acted accordingly. But he combined his exercise of authority with a certain grass-roots spirit. Bishop Leopoldo summoned diocesan synods, expanded the seminary, and established new parishes in the rapidly growing suburbs of Madrid. He occupied lofty positions in educational and professional organizations, but he was always a man of the Church, a bishop who considered the care of souls his chief responsibility.[71] And it was this concern that led him to understand Opus Dei so quickly and to support it so vigorously.

Escrivá had the chapel placed in the best room of the apartment, and then he took the poorest room for himself. His tiny room received its only light through a small window that opened onto an interior courtyard. It was furnished with a desk, a table and chair, a cot, and a small wardrobe. Escrivá worked, according to all witnesses, an eighteen-hour day; aside from his short meals, he did not have a free minute. And in spite of this, it is almost inexplicable how he managed to fulfill all his duties: being rector of Santa Isabel, visiting the sick, teaching at the DYA Academy, seeking financial assistance, and doing apostolate with his countless friends. This apostolic activity consisted mostly of conversations, often during walks, and letter-writing. In addition, there was the spiritual and human formation of the members of Opus Dei, the developing of a family atmosphere and a specific spirituality. The expansion of Opus Dei and its eventual approval by the Church hierarchy was an arduous process, taken one step at a time; for the bureaucracy of the Catholic Church is certainly not something designed to accommodate the impatient. And as if all that were not enough, during these same years Escrivá wrote a tremendous amount — not only personal letters and internal instructions, but also books. One of these was *Spiritual Considerations*, published in 1934; this book was later expanded and republished in 1939 as *The Way*. In the same year, 1934, after morning Mass in the convent of Santa Isabel, Josemaría penned *Holy Rosary*, an almost poetic work of spiritual literature, at a single sitting.

Besides the extreme self-discipline which prevented him from wasting a single minute and carried him past exhaustion, he also seems to have enjoyed something like a miraculous multiplication of time. He never took shortcuts in his prayer, spiritual reading, or other ascetical exercises, nor in his continuing scholarly studies. Nevertheless, those who knew him agree that he was never uptight, hectic, or nervous. He never seemed distracted in conversation, or haunted by the clock — after 1946 he did not even own a watch. "I don't need one," he said. "I just finish one job and go on to the next."[72]

He never complained of being short of time. In fact, his time seemed to increase the more he used it. In 1956, Escrivá said, "We can never have time to spare — not a second. I'm not exaggerating. There's a lot of work to be done. The world is big, and there are millions of people who have not yet heard the teachings of Christ clearly. I ask each one of you: Do you have time on your hands? You might in turn want to question me: Why should we strain ourselves? Well, it is not I, but St. Paul who answers you. 'The love of Christ presses us.' A lifetime is not long enough to fill the radius of our love."[73]

In light of all this, it is not surprising that during the summer of 1935, while all of Spain seemed to be gripped by the impending catastrophe, Escrivá did not break stride in the least. He spared no effort in moving the center to 16 Ferraz St. In fact, at no time — either before or after the outbreak of the war — did he know one moment of malaise. And that is saying a lot. For at the end of the Spanish Civil War, he stood before the rubble not only of the house at 16 Ferraz, but also of much that had been done to develop Opus Dei. He had to begin again, almost from scratch. And he did not shed a tear.

It could probably have been said of every center of Opus Dei ever founded that the timing and circumstances were wrong, that some obstacle made the situation hopeless. There would always be wars, revolutions, and crises to get in the way. But as far as Escrivá was concerned, his mission and goal remained changeless, determined from eternity. "We can't remain passive while we await the return of the Lord, who will then take possession of his kingdom. The spreading of the kingdom of God is not just the official job of those members of the Church who represent Christ on the basis of the ordination and powers they receive from him. 'Vos autem estis Corpus Christi.' You are indeed the body of the Lord. Without being called missionaries, you are indeed apostles with a mission — an unequivocal command to bring forth fruit with your responsible work until the coming of the Lord."[74]

In May 1935, Escrivá made a pilgrimage from Madrid to the shrine of Our Lady of Sonsoles, near Avila, and a few days later he spoke about it in a meditation. He compared the difficulties of the journey — the heat, the dust, the thirst, the mountains and valleys, and the sudden curves through woods and hills, which revealed the shrine one moment and hid it the next — to the interior life of a soul seeking God.[75] For him they symbolized the deepest struggle, the journey of the soul toward God. But only one thing really mattered: to finally reach the destination, to continue on the road tenaciously and faithfully, undaunted by either an unexpected precipice or a quiet meadow's invitation to rest.

On October 2, 1962, Opus Dei was thirty-four years old. The path of its founder had been incomparably steeper, rockier, and more dangerous than the road to Sonsoles. "You cannot imagine," he told the members who celebrated that day with him in Rome, "what it cost to carry the Work forward. But also — what a wonderful adventure!"[76] And he continued in the present tense, in the speech of the timeless present. "Yes," he said, "it is like cultivating a wilderness. First you have to fell the trees, tear out the thick underbrush, and gather up the stones. Then you plow the earth, deeply. The next thing you do is spread fertilizer and let the plowed earth rest, so that it is thoroughly aired out. Only then do you sow the seed; and afterwards, the plants need a long period of cultivation.... You have to prevent diseases. And there is always the fear that a storm could uproot the tender plants. It is necessary, my children, to hope a lot, to work a lot, and to suffer a lot before the wheat is finally in the barn." After a short pause, he added, "Grains of wheat — that is what we are. We are grains of wheat in the pierced hands of Christ, soaked with his blood."

Chapter Five

WAR IN SPAIN

Background

A glance at the course of Spanish history reveals a marked tendency toward national unification and centralization, on the one hand, and regional autonomy, on the other. These two forces have been in constant and usually balanced tension throughout the history of Spain.[1] The seven-hundred-year struggle against the Moors, which ended in 1492 with the reconquest of Granada, was essentially a religious struggle for the restoration of a unified, Christian Spain. The long struggle made Catholicism more secure in Spain than in other European countries where the faithful had not borne such long and severe pressure. The absolutist monarchy of Philip II, which grew out of this unified Spain, maintained a veneer of homogeneity that lasted until the end of the nineteenth century.

The emigration from Spain following the conquest and conversion of Central and South America sapped the vitality of Spanish society, because it took the most energetic and dynamic individuals to colonize overseas, establish new countries, and finally gain their independence from Spain. In the seventeenth century, under the Hapsburg successors of Philip II, Spain fell into a creeping decay, symbolized by the last Iberian offshoot of the House of Austria — the poor, degenerate Charles II. The War of the Spanish Succession brought the Bourbons to the throne in 1713. Under their rule, there was gradual improvement in the state, and certain internal adjustments were made. Corruption declined, and administration of the country became more efficient. But it was in those years, during the reign of Charles III (1759-1788), that the "two Spains" developed: an orthodox, traditionalist Spain, and an Enlightenment-based liberal

Spain. Both remained Catholic, but the split between the two camps became so wide that by the beginning of this century it had become a chasm. A crescendo of violence and unrest arose that culminated on July 18, 1936, when the chasm filled with the blood of a civil war. At the end of the eighteenth century, so much "Enlightenment spirit" blew over the Pyrenees into Spain that the mindset of the educated class was completely altered; but this led to neither an organically developed liberalism, as in England, nor to a victorious revolution, as in France. The faith of the ruling classes often deteriorated into skepticism, but no alternative ideal took its place. There would be no reconciliation between the Church and the rationalist secular spirit of the times, no compromise between obstinate feudalism and explosive socialism.

The revival of a unified Spain during the war against Napoleon, who was regarded as both a national enemy and an enemy of the Church, did not last. Soon after the French were expelled, the deep rift reasserted itself in innumerable uprisings and coups, called *pronunciamentos*. There was a concerted struggle for the transformation of Spain from a feudal agrarian society with a Catholic, absolutist monarchy to an egalitarian industrial society with a secularist, parliamentarian democracy. This transformation along the lines set by the rest of Western Europe would have required the dissolution of the thousand-year union of church and state, the reduction of aristocratic privileges, and the modification of the Spanish throne according to the British model: that is, by elimination of its power.

But this transformation did not occur.[2] Spain, like Russia, skipped the bourgeois, liberal-capitalist phase of the nineteenth century. As in Russia, this caused a sharp collision between retrogressive conservatism and the ascendant modernist socialism. The thin democratic-liberal class of propertied, educated citizens was insufficient to balance the two extremes. A broad middle class could have been a buffer between a politically dependent peasantry and a Marxist-communist working class, thus fostering the development of a parliamentary rule of law. But such a buffer was lacking when the Second Republic arose after the elections of 1931.[3]

It is generally accepted that Spanish democracy simply did not work, either in the First Republic of 1873-1874 or in the Second Republic of 1931. The contradictions deep within the Spanish national spirit — polarized into "Catholic-conservative" and "socialist-revolutionary" ideas — broke through the thin crust of formal republicanism and pressed toward a bloody revolution.

One year after Alfonso XIII dismissed Miguel Primo de Rivera, the dictator who governed Spain from 1923 to January 1931, the monarchy fell; or rather, it capitulated without a fight, more from imaginary fears than by necessity. As soon as the Republicans won the municipal elections of April 12, 1931, the government threw in the towel and the king fled the country.[4] The Republicans, a confederation established by the Pact of San Sebastian, organized a provisional government. In May there were outbreaks of violence against the Church, burnings and plunderings that began in Madrid and spread south toward Andalusia. Even such liberal intellectuals as Ortega y Gasset, Marañón, and many members of the Socialist Party were appalled — not because of any love for the Church, but on aesthetic and strategic grounds. During the elections for the constitutional convention held in June (from which the Monarchists inexplicably abstained), the Socialists won 117 seats, and the leftist Republicans received 80 seats; together these two factions formed a coalition majority, which was opposed by a heterogeneous grouping of 80 conservative Republicans and 100 antisocialist and anticlerical radicals.

On the ninth of December, the Constitution of the Second Republic was adopted, by a vote of 368 to 88. This constitution, no masterpiece, can be considered liberal-progressive. It was not socialist, but it facilitated the drift towards leftist socialism. It resembled the German Weimar Constitution of 1919 in its provisions for a single-chamber legislature, a powerful president, and state-of-emergency laws.

The Republican regime managed to improve the miserable lot of the peasants — particularly the farmhands on the large estates in southern Spain — and the proletariat in the big cities. Three factors, however, boded ill for the Republic:

(a) the growth of radical anarchism along with a Marxist communism that was determined to establish — by force, if necessary — a socialist society with a dictatorship of the proletariat;
(b) the weakness of the executive branch and the general inefficiency and slowness of administration; and
(c) the growing conflict between church and state; or to be more precise, the persecution of the Catholic Church by the state.

"Spain has ceased to be a Catholic country," declared Manuel Azaña, the president of the Republic from 1936 to 1939. "The political task, therefore, is to organize the state in a way adapted to this new historical phase of the Spanish people."[5] This naive and rather premature assault sparked a movement of resistance that grew dramatically after 1933. "The anticlerical laws," writes one historian, "called forth a Catholic counter-movement. The opposition circles on the right began to organize themselves politically. Out of the Acción Nacional of Angel Herrera, José Maria Gil Robles formed the Acción Popular, and in February 1933 he joined with several right-wing groups to create the Spanish Confederation of Autonomous Rightists (CEDA — Confederación Española de Derechas Autónomas). The motto of this new party was the defense of God and country. Choosing a political system was considered a secondary task, so the possibility of parliamentary cooperation within the Republic was open. The CEDA expressed its support for a social Catholicism."[6]

This party must be distinguished from the Falange. The Falange was a mixture of nationalism, strict Catholicism, feudal ideas of the state, and fascism. The leader of the Falange was the thirty-year-old José Antonio de Rivera, son of the former dictator. Part of their uniform was a blue shirt with a bound bundle of arrows as an insignia, a device borrowed from the coat of arms of the *reyes Católicos*, Isabella of Castile and Ferdinand of Aragon.

The Republican coalition collapsed in September 1933, and from the elections in November the rightists emerged victorious, but they could not form a clear majority. The political situation in these last two years before the Civil War resembles the climate in Germany before the rise of Adolph Hitler. Each of these nations witnessed a growth and radicalization of Right and Left forces, between which moderates were crushed and crippled. Each nation also experienced the physical impotence of a government no one wanted (at least in its present form) — a government incapable of controlling private armies and keeping terrorism at bay.

After a seesaw political battle in 1934-1935, the February elections of 1936 brought a victory for the Left. They received 4.7 million votes, while the Right took 3.9 million. The Center collapsed, with barely 500,000 votes. The triumph of Hitler and the Popular Front of Leopold Blum in Paris stimulated the already fanatical political climate in Spain. At least half a year before the revolt of General Franco and his cohorts, Spain was ripe for war. Franco's junta imagined itself saving nationalist, Catholic Spain from Marxist socialism and from an eventual Soviet dictatorship — the declared goal of Moscow and its allies, but a goal that would surely have been rejected by most Spaniards.

Only with a certain hesitation can one assign blame for the Spanish Civil War. Isolated culprits seldom exist either in private life or in the history of nations. The Falangists' murder of the lieutenant of the Guardia de Asalto, a Republican militia, occurred in a hate-charged atmosphere. But so did the murder of a non-Falangist monarchist deputy, José Calvo Sotelo, by the police of the Republic. The government's share of the blame in Calvo Sotelo's death is uncertain, but it is a fact that in the Communist Party, the murder plan was known among the highest officials.[7] In any case, political violence was claiming a steadily growing number of victims across the board.

It is true that Franco and his allies had planned an uprising for some time, but they were not the only ones looking forward to the destruction of the liberal-democratic Republic. The socialists and communists were as eager for a political system like the Soviet Union's as Franco was for a fascist dictatorship. (I use the term "fascist" loosely, for even the Falange, upon which Franco first based his power, was not fascist in the strict sense.)

Eyewitness accounts of the Spanish Civil War are often unreliable; both the Republican refugees and the Nationalist victors offered partisan views. Nevertheless, a few conclusions seem tenable:

(1) By the early 1930s, hate and fear had split the Spanish people — after nearly one hundred fifty years of a growing antagonism — into two hostile camps. There was no longer any bridge for objective, sympathetic understanding, and the eruption of a political volcano was virtually inevitable. The question of Spain's political future would not be discussed, negotiated, or resolved without the shedding of blood.

(2) The Spanish Civil War had two salient characteristics: terror (in part attributable to the communist international brigades) and large-scale foreign intervention. As history shows, civil wars tend to be particularly ferocious and brutal. And forty years after the fact, there is no way to view the intervention of German and Italian troops for Franco and of Russian and various other international brigades for the Republicans as having been simply a preparation for maneuvers in World War II.

(3) Hitler may have wished to test his troops and weapons, but he also realized the consequences a communist victory would have. It was only natural that the fascist regimes in Berlin and Rome should lean toward the antisocialist, antidemocratic Franco, while Stalin's Russia supported the left-wing Republicans.

(4) The stand of the Western democracies was politically misguided. They were seeking to defend, and quite inadequately at that, something that did not exist: a stable, parliamentary, liberal democracy. That is just what Spain was not. The crisis in Spain was not over democracy à la 1776 or 1789, but — at least after the war began — over the Catholic or communist future of Spain. Inasmuch as the true democracies supported a false democracy in Spain, they served neither themselves nor the cause of freedom, but only Stalin.

(5) The assistance of Hitler and Mussolini in Franco's victory should not alter history's judgment of them or of him. To be sure, it made Franco's position in Europe awkward for decades and gave him bad marks among history teachers, but few in Germany, France, England, or the United States wanted to see the Iberian Peninsula become a Soviet base. As the Spanish historian Rodríguez Casado has stated, "The Civil War was not a battle between 'Republicans' and 'Fascists,' but between Catholics and Communists."[8]

When, after three years, the Civil War ended with the marching of Franco's troops into Madrid, more than half a million dead lay buried in their common homeland. "Even more horrifying than the battlefield losses," writes the historian Konetzke, "was the number of people killed in acts of terrorism and summary executions."[9]

The eye of the storm

One may wonder what Escrivá thought of the Spanish tragedy — a tragedy that sadly lacked a moderate third position between two deadly enemy camps. Of course, he hoped for the preservation of Spain's great Christian tradition — its innate, rich, explicit Catholicism — and the unhindered work of the Church in educating its children. For the country he loved, Escrivá wanted a government and a social system that would make this possible. Obviously he could not support an atheistic Marxist state that persecuted priests and the Church; at least in this regard, Franco seemed clearly the lesser of two evils. And independent of any personal preference for this or that form of government, Escrivá was always a loyal citizen. But he was never what one could call a Franco supporter, and the question of republic or monarchy, later widely discussed in Spain and Italy, left him cold.

For the Christian, the Catholic, and especially the priest, there are some clear criteria in political matters. One cannot consent to anything — Marxism, for example — that goes against the commands of Christ and the teachings of the Church, no matter how humanitarian it may seem. "Today as yesterday," Escrivá wrote, "the reality of communism means the persecution of the Church and continued assaults upon the elementary rights of the person. Some, it is true, make declarations against violence. But deeds do not follow these words; and as anyone can see, the Church is as mistreated by one group as by another."[10]

Escrivá was convinced that any defense against injustice must begin with people individually following Christ in their own daily lives. In this defense, organizations and political instruments can be either helpful or dangerous. The danger is that one will lose one's personal dedication to Christ — perhaps unconsciously — in a collective activism. In the zeal for group involvement, both the ability and the readiness to "look God in the eye" can be lost. "It seems substantially better to me," Escrivá once said, "that there be many highly qualified Catholics who, while not posing as 'official' Catholics, work within the political structure from positions of responsibility to create a true Catholic presence, sustained by an upright love for their co-workers."[11] Ever a realist, Escrivá knew that there would always be political, social, and ideological conflicts; they are an inevitable part of secular society. As lay Christians we cannot stand apart from them; we cannot float above political affairs as neutral observers. We must bring Christ into them, even and especially at moments of crisis. While political views may differ, fidelity to the Church must be a constant. The founder of Opus Dei never renounced these principles. And in the heated and fanatical atmosphere of that summer of 1936, he taught them to his followers.

Just who were these followers? They were merely a dozen young men, most of them students about twenty years old. Among them were Isidoro Zorzano, Juan Jiménez Vargas, and Alvaro del Portillo. Besides Zorzano, there was only one other man of Escrivá's age (thirty-four). This man, José María Albareda, was already a well-known research scientist and university professor.

Albareda was a chemist and pharmacist who had made breakthroughs in agricultural chemistry. Because of his academic prestige and his international experience (he had worked in England, France, and Germany), he was in 1939 named the secretary general of the highest Spanish council for research and science.[12] He later became the first rector of the University of Navarre, in Pamplona. At the age of fifty-seven he was ordained a priest; he died seven years later, in 1966.

His biographical writings, together with the sketches of Jiménez Vargas and Pedro Casciaro, provide a good glimpse of the life and work of Escrivá during the Civil War period.[13] Albareda was a striking and fascinating personality around whom a considerable number of friends and students gathered. To him, as to Zorzano, Escrivá had shown how professional life could be seen as a *materia sanctitatis* granted by God. "You are a scientist, a man of the laboratory; you are a professor. That is your place — the laboratory and the lectern; that is where you encounter Christ."[14]

Albareda's biography by Gutiérrez Ríos describes a meditation given by Escrivá in May 1936, in the chapel of 50 Ferraz St. (In a meditation, the priest expounds upon a passage from the Gospel, or from some spiritual book, and leads his listeners to reflect on its message in silent prayer with Christ until they resolve to incorporate it into the way they think and live. Intellectual analysis is not as important as a simple readiness to accept God's word and live according to it.) Escrivá's published meditations are called "homilies." This is an established form of spiritual literature; strictly speaking, however, the term is inaccurate. Even though a meditation does include preaching and instruction, commentary and explanation, its essence is a real encounter between Christ and the one who listens or meditates; it is a silent dialogue, a supernatural tête-à-tête. Msgr. Escrivá's "homilies" are actually prayers, the prayers of the speaking priest and the listening faithful. Ideally, this meditative prayer is done alone in silence before the tabernacle, but any place will do — at home, on the train, in the doctor's waiting room, or during a stroll. Escrivá often suggested to those who were easily distracted, or who felt temporarily dry, that they should take the Gospel or some spiritual book with them to prayer.

Since the meditation given by a priest in an oratory is an essential norm of piety for Opus Dei, a norm which Escrivá developed in a special way, this early description from Albareda's biography is of great historical interest. "Before Mass, the Father gave a meditation. He sat beside the altar, at a small table with a dark green covering,. A small lamp threw a circle of light on the tabletop. He took a small crucifix from the pocket of his cassock and placed it before him, along with his watch. Next to it was the Gospel and a medium-sized notebook with notes for the meditation.... Two candles were lit, one on either side of the tabernacle. He himself was half in shadow — only the Blessed Sacrament and his words commanded attention. He spoke about the sanctification of ordinary work. He often opened the Gospel to passages he had marked with strips of paper. He read them slowly, almost letter by letter. From there, from the holy Scripture, he elaborated on everything. From time to time, he looked at the tabernacle and spoke to Christ in glowing words — the meditation became prayer."[15]

He never tired of repeating the simple, clear truths that were the message of Opus Dei, its core. This message was stamped indelibly on Albareda. "We have to transform every part of our lives," said Escrivá, "into the service of God: work and leisure, laughter and tears. In the field, in the workshop, in the study room, in the political arena, faithfully persevering in our normal lives, we must make everything an instrument of sanctification and an apostolic example."[16]

In order to sanctify ordinary professional work, while also taking part in social, domestic, and religious life, the thousand little things that make up a day — to sanctify all this, seeing Christ in one's neighbor, one must "love freedom," Escrivá went on to say. (This was in May, just weeks before the Spanish Civil War began, and three years before the start of World War II.) "Avoid," he said, "the abuse of freedom. This abuse is becoming more dangerous in our times. It is manifest throughout the world. It arises from the desire, contrary to the legitimate independence of men and women, to force them all into a single mass, so that they are forced to believe things that are really matters of opinion as though they were spiritual dogmas. And this perverted view is promoted through power and propaganda, in a scandalous way."[17]

Escrivá's words were charged with emotion as he urged his young listeners, "You are very free! Listen to me well: you are very free!"[18] And he explained to them how one should express this freedom: by defending the freedom of others and loving others as oneself, accepting them with their weaknesses and their mistakes (of which everyone has plenty); by helping others, through the grace of God and with human kindness, to overcome their defects, so that eventually all would be worthy of the name "Christian." Freedom, when understood in this way, would mean tolerance regarding those things that God has left to the judgment of each person. "Respect the freedom of others," Escrivá concluded, "and defend your own!"[19]

There is a formidable obstacle, however, to this work of Christian renewal — the perverted intellectuality which has spread itself out like a swamp between the modern soul and truth. Men and women cannot reach Christ or construct a better world without first crossing or draining this swamp. "The intelligence," says Albareda, "must not simply construct fantasies, demonstrate its wit and eloquence, organize dramatic scenes ..., divorced from the common good."[20] His words hold true to this day, not only for Spain but for the whole Western world. "Even if it were not to lead to sorrow and regret," he points out, "this intellectualism ... would be enough to cause weariness with its fierce back-and-forth play of exhibitionism. It is an intellectual one-upmanship that must prove its prowess before the wondering eyes of the public in a bullfight without bulls."[21] In the memory of many Spaniards, the first third of this century seems to have been an "epoch poisoned by the bitter fruit of intellectual dilletantism and hatred."[22] In 1936, the fruit of this superficiality and hatred was often violence in the streets of Madrid — daily brawls, demonstrations, street fighting. Everywhere there were fanatical youths with red kerchiefs and fists raised in the proletarian salute. This was a city of miserable and angry masses. Their dark eyes burning with violent intent, they waited for their hour, a powder keg to which the fuse was already attached.[23]

Witnesses all agree that Escrivá, not only in the years before the Civil War but during it as well, remained free from fanaticism, bitterness, fear, and illusion.[24] He neither sank into discouragement nor harbored false hopes. He never doubted that the war would be long and horrible. Nor did he doubt that Opus Dei would survive it — strengthened, in fact, and still growing.

This combination of realism and supernatural faith was characteristic of Escrivá. "He saw the gravity of the situation perfectly clearly," writes Jiménez Vargas, "but he never lost his sense of humor. He never let himself be infected by the generally spreading unrest, or be crippled in fear of what everyone saw coming. Nothing could make him insecure or keep him back from his apostolic work."[25] Only one thing counted: "The normal life of the Work went forward — ... to do the will of God without a shadow of pessimism, come what may. We took great pains to imitate him in this. The unity of the Work came first. So, for example, each of us took part in the elections in a normal way, with great prudence so as not to take part in any activity that could harm the Work or give grounds for identifying it with any political view, or for uniting it to any political faction."[26]

Escrivá knew how easy it would have been for these young men to fall into a mere political activism, stressing the purely human side of things at the expense of spiritual life and interior union with God, and thus thwarting the development of Opus Dei. According to Jiménez Vargas, they did not always understand his concern, especially when it came to particular, personal cases. For example, Escrivá did not want them to take part in demonstrations and things of that sort. This was not a curbing of their freedom, but simple common sense. In those dangerous days, members of Opus Dei were still so few in number that certain activities, later to be left to individual discretion, had to be ruled out as unsuitable.

A year of living dangerously

The Spanish Civil War began as a revolution — a Red revolution, in fact. The assassination of representative Calvo Sotelo brought the Republican state itself under suspicion of murder. "The indignation over this incident," writes historian Helmut Dahms,[27] "was mixed with concern and the fear of new crimes. Well-known personalities began to leave the country — liberals like Marañón,[28] Ortega y Gasset[29], Unamuno,[30] and Menéndez Pidal."[31] These liberals did not flee from the fascist dictatorship of Franco. They fled from anarchy, from the cruelties of internecine war, from a regime that was becoming criminally degenerate. Several days before Franco's uprising, the revolutionary militias had already occupied positions in front of public buildings in Madrid and Barcelona. Together with armed groups of peasants, the militias desecrated churches and monasteries and also plundered government buildings, where they burned documents and public papers. The socialist and communist organizations CNT (*Confederación Nacional de Trabajo* — National Federation of Labor), FAI (*Federación Anarquista Ibérica* — Iberian Federation of Anarchists), and POUM (*Partido Obrero de Unificación Marxista* — United Marxist Worker's Party) confiscated lands and property on their own initiative.

Immediately following the murder of Calvo Sotelo, thousands of Falangists were arrested. The liberal prime minister, Santiago Casares Quiroga, who bore partial blame for the collapse of state authority, forbade distribution of the important newspapers *Ya* and *La Época*, because they accurately reported the assassination.

Franco's national uprising, although it had been planned in advance, occurred in response to an anticipated socialist coup; the imminence of such a coup could no longer be doubted, since two hundred fifty thousand militia members had already been mobilized. (For decades, Western democracies have been offered historical accounts of these events that are colored by leftist ideology.) On July 17th, the "National Uprising" began in Spanish Morocco. Franco, who was not at first generally recognized as its supreme leader, was in Tenerife. On July 18th, he arrived in Las Palmas, in the Canary Islands. Mallorca then joined the uprising. With every passing hour, other garrisons of soldiers, supported by a large part of the population, joined the revolt against the Madrid regime. Seville was the first large city to fall to the rebels.

The Popular Front in Madrid reacted quickly. A general strike was announced. Militias, including the Guardia de Asalto, erected barricades, arrested people haphazardly, shot officers, and killed many "rich" or "distinguished" persons. Priests became hunted animals. The "two Spains," which had coexisted for so long in a precarious patchwork of national unity, rapidly fell into battle formation.

Until September 1st, the two sides were busy consolidating their forces. The country was divided roughly into an eastern and a western half. The Madrid regime held the entire eastern half, plus a large bulge of territory in the middle of the peninsula, almost reaching Badajoz, and the coast of the Bay of Biscay from Oviedo to the French border. The Nationalists ruled the western half, with a bulge of their own in the northeast area of Teruel. In a period of less than a week, between Monday the 13th and Sunday the 19th of July, the socialist revolution became a civil war.

As in Barcelona and Valencia, the military revolt failed in Madrid. The new center of Opus Dei at 16 Ferraz St., to which Escrivá had moved just a few days before, stood directly across the street from the Montaña Garrison, the focus of the battle in Madrid. Escrivá and his followers could watch the bloody events from their window. In the words of Dahm, "On the afternoon of July 18th, several thousand militiamen surrounded the Montaña Garrison, from which the missing locks for fifty thousand weapons were to be delivered. The sentries denied them entrance, and bloodshed threatened to begin. General Joaquín Fanjul encouraged the troops to revolt, gathered volunteers, and opened fire on the militia. But the attempt to break out of the garrison failed, because many civilians had been pressed against the gates, with the women and children in front.... Towards morning on the 19th, the militia brought out their cannons and armored vehicles. The five-hour bombardment, including aerial bombing, battered the soldiers. Cell members [Red agents] within the garrison were able to take charge and encourage surrender. Still, many others continued to fight. Finally, the Montaña Garrison was stormed by shock troops early on the morning of the 20th. The cell members separated out the 'class enemies' among the soldiers, according to the decree of June 6th.[32] They were herded into the courtyard and executed by firing squad. The disarmed officers were simply thrown to their deaths from the highest floor of the building."[33]

At the express wish of Escrivá, all those members of Opus Dei whose families were still in Madrid left the Ferraz St. center at about ten o'clock in the evening on Sunday the 19th. Among those who left were Alvaro del Portillo, Jiménez Vargas, and José María Hernández de Garnica.

The triumph of the militia in Madrid meant not only Republican control of the capital, but also the continuation of the war and the rapid development of a communist state apparatus. July 20th marked the beginning of a dramatic period in Escrivá's life, 498 days when his life was in constant danger.

While even in Red Spain there were moderate zones (such as Valencia and Alicante, where the most extreme horrors did not occur), terror reigned in Madrid. On the day after the massacre in the Montaña Garrison, Jiménez Vargas, who returned to survey the damage, saw piles of corpses at the city morgue.[34] On the morning of the 20th, Escrivá had left the center. Being recognized as a priest would have meant certain death, so he dressed as a mechanic and made his escape, together with Isidoro and a few remaining companions who had spent the night with them. His priestly tonsure could have betrayed him, but no one noticed, and he was able to find refuge in his mother's house. Once there, he had to remain completely out of sight. He could not even venture onto the street for some fresh air, because everyone in the area knew he was a priest. He might at any time have been arrested and killed by a militia patrol. In fact, a man in the neighborhood was mistaken for Escrivá and hanged. In a sense, this unfortunate man was a martyr for Opus Dei. From the moment he learned of this tragedy until the end of his life, Escrivá prayed and made sacrifices for him.[35]

On July 25th, the house at 16 Ferraz St. was confiscated. But Escrivá was expecting this — he had removed all the documents about Opus Dei and given them for safekeeping to his mother. She kept them throughout the war, some of them in the mattress of her bed.

What was the future of Opus Dei?[36] If the communists and their allies won, Opus Dei could not continue in Spain. "But if God arranged for the Work to begin in Madrid," Jiménez Vargas and del Portillo told each other one day as they were taking a walk, "it is not likely that he would have done so only to have the Work begin again somewhere else. One has to assume that all will go well, and that the Work that has been begun will be continued in a normal way." Immediately, Juan jotted this sober and faith-filled conclusion down in his notebook. Forty years later, he wrote, "We did not doubt for a second that nothing would happen to the Father, but at the same time we realized immediately the need to do everything we could to protect him."

The source of this confidence was, of course, Escrivá himself. More than any lay person can readily imagine, he suffered from not being able to celebrate Mass, receive Communion, and pray in front of the Blessed Sacrament. (All the churches had been closed.) But he was not disheartened or depressed, even though his apostolic work seemed to be destroyed, the little flock was scattered, and everyone had to go under cover wherever and however possible. No hiding place was safe for long. They lived quite literally from one day to the next. Houses were frequently searched, and all the streets were guarded. Every apartment and every room had to be registered; everyone needed a pass that told their occupation and place of work. A knock at the door, a ring of the bell, a footstep on the stairs, the mistrust of a landlord or the vindictiveness of a personal enemy, the gossip of a neighbor or the senility of an aged relative, the innocent noise of children or the bark of a dog — anything might mean arrest, torture, or death.

Meanwhile, Fr. Josemaría continued to show himself a father to each of his children in Opus Dei. He cared in the depths of his soul not only for their physical security, but also for their spiritual progress, the ripening of their interior life with God. "Don't neglect your prayer," he wrote. "And be sure to follow a daily schedule (*plan de vida*).[37] Seek out the Lord regularly,[38] asking him to shorten this difficult time of trial."[39] It was fortunate that Isidoro Zorzano was an Argentinian citizen. Since he could travel with relative freedom, Escrivá was able to maintain contact through him with the other members of Opus Dei, usually by letter. Besides, Zorzano was earning money; this was quite important, since Escrivá was completely without means. Isidoro remained in Madrid throughout the entire war and assisted Escrivá's family, who also remained. After Escrivá fled into the Nationalist Zone, Zorzano *was* Opus Dei in the Republican Zone.

The danger of discovery increased with every day that Escrivá remained in his mother's house, and the consequences could easily have been fatal for all concerned. So on August 9th he left the apartment and hid out in a friend's house. The elderly servant there was deaf, which turned out to be providential. On August 30th, militia soldiers came to search the house, and they had to shout so loudly in the entryway that Escrivá and Jiménez Vargas were alerted and managed to flee by a back stairway.[40] The place of refuge for September was the apartment of an Argentinian family who were friends of Alvaro del Portillo;[41] after receiving warning of imminent danger, Escrivá left this refuge on October 1st. For a few days he hid himself in various places, with different friends, for a few hours at a time. The fact that he did not have a valid pass meant that any street or house inspection — and these inspections were taking place with increasing frequency, especially at night — could have meant the end.

Every day brought new reports of arrests, imprisonments, and shootings, and rumors of massacres. Notwithstanding his trust in God and confidence in his vocation, Escrivá had to do something if he hoped to survive. He could not live indefinitely the way he was living now — like a hunted animal creeping into this hole today, that one tomorrow. A strange, even somewhat macabre, solution presented itself. A former classmate of Escrivá's named Dr. Suils had become a psychiatrist and the director of an insane asylum in the Ciudad Lineal section of Madrid. Though the two of them had not seen each other since their days in Logroño, Dr. Suils now came to the rescue. He accepted Escrivá as a mental patient in his clinic. Escrivá stayed there almost five months. Although — or perhaps because — the asylum was under the control of the Socialist UGT (*Unión General de Trabajadores* — General Worker's Union), it turned out to be relatively safe. Of course, great caution was necessary; Escrivá could not attract attention in any way. When one of the patients began to suspect that he might not be sick at all but only faking, he did his best to act insane. Discovery would probably have meant death not only for him but for Dr. Suils as well.

Because of the bitter cold, the hunger, and the terror, the winter of 1936-1937 was hard for everyone in Madrid, but especially for Escrivá. A rheumatic arthritis kept him bedridden for weeks. Separated from his natural and spiritual families, and virtually a prisoner, he could communicate with the outside world only through Isidoro Zorzano. (Because of his Argentinean citizenship, Zorzano could visit him regularly.) His one major consolation was that he could now, in secret, do something he had not been able to do since the war began — celebrate Mass.

Eventually, it became clear that Escrivá would have to move again. No end of the war was in sight. The Madrid front had stabilized; the Republican regime had established its power; the communist-socialist radicalism had only increased. Organized terror had become a basic part of the system of government. And the relative security of Escrivá's insane status had begun to dwindle.[42] After all, a healthy person can endure life as a patient in a psychiatric institution for only so long. Escrivá would have to leave as soon as possible.

Fortunately, it did not take long for an opportunity to present itself. Since the beginning of the reign of terror in Madrid, some Spaniards with the right connections had found refuge in the foreign embassies of countries like Holland, Portugal, Norway, and Panama. Among these refuges, the "legation" of the Republic of Honduras was surely one of the lowliest. In terms of diplomatic law, it was not really a legation, but only a consulate which took care of the interests of the small Central American country. But apparently it had a bighearted director. The consul had been able to gain for himself full diplomatic status and even respect for the extraterritorial status of his residence, with a guard posted at the entrance. Through at least three intermediaries, it was possible to gain his permission for Escrivá's admittance. In the first days of March 1937, Escrivá moved in.

This move meant some major improvements in his life. He was able once more to say Mass every day in a provisional but dignified and proper manner. He was no longer alone, because Alvaro del Portillo and two friends also took refuge in the consulate; and at the beginning of April, Juan Jiménez Vargas joined them. But though they found themselves in relative security, they were also trapped. There could be no thought of leaving the building without papers — even the shortest walk might have had fatal consequences.

Living conditions in the overcrowded house were totally abnormal and quite depressing. "About thirty people were housed on the same floor," relates Jiménez Vargas. "Married people with children, persons of dubious character with a tendency to gossip, young girls, members of religious orders — they were all crowded together in a stifling atmosphere, which resulted in a pervasive slackness."[43] In this atmosphere, Escrivá and his friends stood out — a source of encouragement to some, an annoyance to others. Point 687 of *The Way* reads, "Jesus, wherever you passed, not a heart remained unmoved; you were either loved or hated. When apostolic men and women follow you, carrying out their duties, is it surprising — if each of them is another Christ — that they should provoke similar responses of aversion and love?"

Escrivá knew (as any prisoner of war will confirm) that in such circumstances, only a well-organized daily schedule can prevent laziness, boredom, and spiritual chaos. Therefore, his first concern was the exact observance of the daily schedule he set for himself and the members of Opus Dei. There were specific times for prayer, spiritual reading, work, and friendly relaxation and conversation. The work was mostly cleaning, making small repairs, studying, writing letters, religious formation, and learning foreign languages. (Even here, Escrivá was looking ahead to the global expansion of Opus Dei.) Naturally, they also spent a lot of time talking with the other refugees. Living in such tight quarters, they had to struggle to get time alone for undisturbed prayer, which sometimes became a source of misunderstanding and criticism.

Isidoro Zorzano continued to be their contact with the outside world. Through him, Escrivá tried to keep in touch with all the members within reach in order to maintain the unity of Opus Dei. Some of those who remained within the Red Zone were quite far from Madrid. He wrote to them on a regular basis — a course of action not chosen without hesitation. He knew the risks involved in such correspondence. All mail passed through the hands of censors, and one of them could easily have become suspicious. The volume of letters or repetition of addresses might have attracted attention. On the other hand, a minimum of communication had to be maintained in this young spiritual family.

A sketch of the small room in the Honduran consulate shared by
Fr. Escrivá and five others during the spring and summer of 1937.

There was no other way. Escrivá trusted, in his deep faith, that all
would turn out well. He felt compelled to write to each of his distant and perhaps endangered children often and at length. Those
of his sons who shared his "Honduran cage" felt the burden of
his responsibility, yet they also tried to slow down this dangerous
correspondence.[44]

Then, for the third time since the start of the war, the question
again arose: What next? The end of the war was still not in sight.
Priestly and other apostolic activity was virtually impossible. The
stay in the legation, which in the long run would have deleterious
consequences, was proving more and more tortuous. In any event,

it would have been impossible to stay in that place for long, because the security there was so tenuous. In April 1937, plans for leaving the Republican Zone were discussed. One option was to take an escape route through the front; this was a possibility because some members of Opus Dei were serving in the Republican Army, either as draftees or, in order to avoid something worse, as volunteers. But the plan proved to be unmanageable and had to be dropped.

Escrivá was now determined to get hold of any kind of a personal document that would provide him some security and enable him to travel in the streets. Finally, on August 31st, he received a pass that identified him as an official (*intendente general*) of the Honduran legation, and he left the consulate the next day. For the first time in thirteen months, he walked the streets with relatively little risk.

He moved into a small attic room on Ayala St., in an area where no one was likely to recognize him. He had become very thin, and in his baggy gray suit, complete with tie, he did not look at all like a priest. And so he set out, with remarkable speed and intensity, to launch a broad priestly apostolate. He spoke with many people as a friend and spiritual director. He celebrated Mass (secretly, in apartments) and distributed Holy Communion. He even gave retreats. One of these lasted three days, and five or six young men participated, including Zorzano and Albareda. Each came alone. They listened to a meditation and then left, each going in a different direction. Strolling the streets, they could reflect on what they had just heard and quietly pray the rosary. For the second meditation, they met in another apartment; for Mass, in a third.[45]

Every day that passed safely in such circumstances was a special gift from God. Escrivá and his companions never doubted for a moment that the Nationalists would win and the persecution of Christians would cease. God had saved his Church from the persecutions of the Roman emperors, from Arab and Turkish invasions, and from the French and Russian revolutions; God would see it through this civil war as well. Still, their faith and the lessons of history did not tell them exactly what to do in this particular situation.

It was not clear whether Escrivá should remain in Madrid or flee to another part of Spain. Did he have an obligation to flee? God demands trust, but not passivity. Faith does not exempt the Christian from responsibility. Escrivá had a childlike, obedient faith, but this faith was linked to a keen sensitivity to the promptings of the Holy Spirit. What was the will of God in the specific circumstances of the autumn of 1937? That was the question. Escrivá might simply have argued to himself: "If the Lord wants me to accomplish Opus Dei, then he can protect me where I am, in Madrid — even in the dungeons of the Red secret police." Such an argument might have come across as childlike, humble, trusting; yet there would have been something presumptuous in it, something cavalier. Imagine a son in trouble saying to his father, "You take care of it, Dad. You brought me into the world, so you can carry me through. After all, that's your job; I'll just sit back and wait." The good son tackles his difficulties himself, choosing for himself a way to overcome them. His father loves him, and so will not inhibit his freedom. In Escrivá's case, the choice was extremely difficult. Did the responsibility for continuing and developing Opus Dei demand that he flee the Red Zone? By leaving himself in daily, hourly danger of arrest and death, was he not tempting God?

On the other hand, his mother, sister, and eighteen-year-old brother were still in the capital. Isidoro, Alvaro, and many others could not leave Madrid, because they were soldiers in the Republican Army or had some other binding duties. Would not flight mean leaving them in the lurch? Would that not show a cowardly lack of loyalty? Escrivá had to choose the path most compatible with the love of God. To stay or to flee? The question tormented him in his prayers, even after he decided to flee.[46] Apparently this was one of the most difficult decisions of his life. In the following months, thoughts of those left behind gave him painful doubts, and more than once he was on the verge of turning back.

Escrivá's spiritual sons saw the decision as an opportunity to put into action their obedience, fidelity, and practical ability. They realized it was their duty to go along with his decision, and they felt the weight of responsibility for saving him falling on their shoulders. Of course, they discussed every detail of the escape with him; but whenever he seemed to be wavering or uncertain, they did not hesitate to use hard, even rough words to put an end to his indecision. This was not lack of respect, but a sign of love. They could do nothing but good by strengthening Escrivá in this difficult decision. It was a matter of life and death; prolonged indecisiveness would have meant total failure and danger for all.

Time was running out; the government was said to be considering the evacuation of Madrid. Only people with certificates attesting to the importance of their work to the war effort would be allowed to stay. The inspection of passes and guarding of the streets were systematically tightened. September was spent planning, going over all the contingencies. In the greatest poverty, the group managed through daily exercise to get themselves into physical condition for a march on foot through the Pyrenees. This was to be the escape route — one that many others had already taken, with varying degrees of success.

The first phase of the escape was a trip to Barcelona. There one could obtain the necessary papers (personal documents and travel permits) and contact one of the guides who organized groups of refugees and led them from the Catalonian capital through the high mountains to Andorra. These guides — tough, daring youths, smugglers of human contraband who knew the mountain paths and valleys like the backs of their hands — demanded substantial payments. Their trade was mortally dangerous, for themselves as well as for the refugees they guided. Often these groups were caught by the border guards and immediately executed.

Because of the proximity of the front lines, no trains ran in and out of Madrid; one could leave the city only by car. To obtain a car, the necessary gas, and the precious travel permit was as difficult as it was dangerous, but it was finally managed. The hour of departure arrived. Escrivá bade farewell to his mother, brother, and sister, and to Zorzano and del Portillo. On October 7th, he left for Valencia with Albareda, Jiménez Vargas, and Tomás Alvira, a student and a friend of Albareda's whom Escrivá had met in September.[47] There they met Pedro Casciaro and Francisco Botella, two architecture students who had joined Opus Dei; both had decided to accompany Escrivá.

Casciaro, a soldier of the Republican Army serving in Valencia at the chief supply headquarters, later recorded a discussion with Botella that shows the attitude these young men had. "From that afternoon on," he says, "we had to be, so to speak, the older brothers in the family of the Work; the Father was going to need us to bring about what God wanted. 'Don't forget this,' I said to Paco [as Botella was called]. 'After today we're no longer a couple of carefree kids; now we have no choice but to be responsible men.'"[48]

Casciaro and Botella were to wait in Valencia until they received further news and instructions from Barcelona. On the night train to Barcelona, Escrivá and the others traveled the two hundred miles in the company of Christ, for Escrivá carried the consecrated hosts with him in a small leather case around his neck — in those days, the only tabernacle of Opus Dei. According to Albareda, Escrivá prayed in uninterrupted silence, with serenity but also with deep concern for those left behind in Madrid and Valencia. Because of the continuously blasphemous and obscene conversation of the other passengers, he decided he should consume the consecrated hosts. The only place he could do this was in the restroom of the car. Afterward, he sometimes spoke of this midnight Communion, which remained deeply engraved in his memory.[49]

From one Spain to another

In Barcelona, nearly six weeks of anxiety were in store for Escrivá and his companions. First of all, anyone heading north had to get a special permit to leave the city. These permits were illegal, forged, and extremely expensive. Everything depended on money. Without money, there was no way to get a pass or join a refugee group. The guides demanded payment in banknotes issued by the Bank of Spain before July 18, 1936. This showed whose victory the guides were expecting — the provisional junta in Burgos had announced by radio that once the war ended, money printed by the Republic after July 18th would not be negotiable.

Just surviving in Barcelona cost the group dearly, even though they spent little and often went hungry. They lived in three separate locations. Escrivá, Jiménez Vargas, Tomás Alvira, and Manuel Sainz de los Terreros, another student from Madrid, formed one group. At first they lived in a hotel, but after a few days they had to seek less expensive shelter. They found it in the home of a colonel's widow.[50]

The second group consisted of Pedro Casciaro, Paco Botella, and Miguel Fisac, a student who had hidden in the attic of a farmhouse in La Mancha ever since the beginning of the war. All three had been brought to Barcelona, at great risk, by Juan Jiménez Vargas, who was becoming the real leader of the enterprise. (These three youths, all deserters from the Republican Army, not only were in constant danger themselves but also posed an especially high risk for the entire group, since they were the ones most likely to be recognized.) They took refuge in a house where hunger displaced decorum. In desperation, the poor, hungry dog of the house ate Paco's leather belt, some socks that had been hung up to dry, and a bar of soap — which caused it to belch foam!

José María Albareda stayed in his mother's house with his two nephews, aged five and seven, whose parents had had to flee to France. These children would stand in line for hours to get a ration of tobacco for some soldier who would then reward them with a piece of bread. The plight of these undernourished children cut Escrivá to the heart. "Play with them a little," he used to tell Pedro. "Do something for them." Once Pedro asked them if he could draw something for them. "Yes," they begged, "draw us a pan with two fried eggs." This the good-hearted Pedro did, as well as he could. When he mentioned the incident to Escrivá, the Father said, "Don't you understand, my son, that it wasn't right to draw a thing like that for those hungry little kids?"[51]

With considerable difficulty, Escrivá and his companions finally made contact with the guides. But then in late October, a large group of refugees who had already reached Andorran soil, but in a valley overlooked by Spanish hills, was spotted by Republican troops and mowed down with machine guns; no one survived. The press reported the incident with great jubilation, and contacts with the guides immediately went underground. Security at the Pyrenees border, and along the paths leading to it, was tightened. One blow had made escape seemingly impossible. Escrivá's group did not lose heart, however, but just waited for another opportunity.

During this long waiting period, Escrivá came across an old classmate from the University of Saragossa who now held an important judicial post in the Republic. Despite the man's office, Escrivá, apparently able to read souls, confided to this judge that he planned to go to France with some youths, and asked him to do everything in his power to save them if they failed to make it. The judge entreated him to call off the attempt. He pointed not only to the October tragedy but also to the recent decree calling for the execution of anyone suspected of having attempted to flee.

The judge, who was obviously quite fond of his former classmate, offered to secure for him a position as a lawyer in Barcelona. Escrivá refused the offer, seeing no way that he as a priest could be a jurist for a regime that murdered people just for being Catholic. Then the judge asked him to come to the courthouse the next morning. When Escrivá arrived, the judge led him to a room adjoining the courtroom. Through the open door, he listened as several people were tried for having attempted to flee; they were all condemned to death. He was deeply moved, but he did not change his mind. Finally, the judge said, fully realizing the danger to himself and his family, that if Escrivá was seized and not shot immediately, he should claim relation to the judge. That would give him some slight chance of avoiding execution. The man was not a Christian — in fact, he was in the enemy camp — but he had a soft spot in his heart for this priest. Often, Escrivá remarked later, he prayed in a very special way for this man.

The days of waiting were a torment. The only blessing was that Escrivá had an opportunity to say Mass; not all of his companions could attend, but they all found ways at least to receive Communion. The first rule of conduct in Barcelona was not to attract attention. They had to call themselves evacuees who had regular jobs in the city. Discovery was always possible, but in the open there were usually chances to avoid or to run from danger, so they spent most of the day outside — usually on their feet, often praying. Without a peseta among them, they had to ignore their constant hunger and just bypass the food stands in the street. Even resting on a park bench was risky. Every policeman they saw made their hearts pound, and every day that passed made the trip more urgent; it was already November, and winter would make the Pyrenees impassable.

Finally the middlemen started showing signs of life again. Exact instructions were issued, dictating what the small band should do. The route was never in question; for all practical purposes, there is only one. Anyone traveling from Barcelona to Andorra today takes the highway and reaches the eastern corner of the tiny country after a hundred-mile trip over the Pas de la Case, at an altitude of six thousand feet. The altitude diminishes along the rest of the thirty-mile border to the west. The city of Andorra itself, at about three thousand feet, lies on the valley's only highway, which connects it with the Spanish city of Seo de Urgel only five miles from the Andorran border. This was the route by which the refugees in those days sought safety in this tiny agricultural republic squeezed between France and Spain.

The first stage of the journey — leaving Barcelona to the northwest — would be done by bus. From then on, it would be nightly marches on foot over little-used and treacherous mountain paths that only the guides knew. There were to be three phases in the dangerous expedition:

(1) the trip from Barcelona to the point of rendezvous with the rest of the refugees (November 19th – 22nd);

(2) a waiting period there until November 27th; and

(3) the actual crossing of the mountains to the border of Andorra (November 27th – December 12th).

On November 19th, Escrivá, Albareda, Jiménez Vargas, Botella, Casciaro, and Fisac left Barcelona.[52] (Alvira and Sainz de los Terreros were to catch up with them a few days later.) Divided into groups of three, in order not to attract attention, they boarded the bus to Seo de Urgel. (Since he was the one who could do so most easily, Albareda had bought the tickets. While he was buying them, his heart almost stopped when a distinguished old man in the long ticket line asked in a polite, innocent, and very loud voice, "Is this the right place to get the bus for Andorra?"[53] Not all six took the bus all the way to the village of Peramola, the place of their first rendezvous; for security reasons, Paco, Pedro, and Miguel got out earlier and took a footpath the rest of the way. The fact that they did not arrive in Peramola exactly on schedule caused Escrivá a few anxious moments. He was also troubled about the fate of Tomás and Manuel.

Ordinarily a refugee group marched at night and stayed hidden during the day. The first rule was not to make decisions on one's own; success demanded unconditional obedience to the guide. The guides were courageous men, accustomed to hardship, who worked partly to resist the Madrid regime and partly to make a fortune from an unusual situation. (Most of them lived in poverty, and it would hardly be realistic to expect them to have risked their necks simply out of the goodness of their hearts.) The guide who brought Escrivá, Albareda, and Jiménez Vargas from the bus stop to Peramola was a forty-five-year-old man named Tonillo. He was the proverbial village handyman: postman, sexton, mayor's assistant, watchmaker — an irreplaceable citizen. He immediately hit it off with Escrivá. The fact that Escrivá did not hide his priesthood impressed him greatly. Many years later, Tonillo recalled his first impression of Escrivá: "He was friendly, decisive, courageous. One could see that he was very sensible. I told him, 'If you make it, you'll go places.'"

The night of November 19th was spent in a barn in Peramola. The second stop, at a farm in the small village of Vilaro, was filled with anxiety because the two students had not yet appeared. They finally arrived the next morning, just in time for Escrivá's Mass.[54] In the evening, they all left the place together. It was very cold, and their clothes and shoes were completely inadequate for winter weather.

After a hike of many hours, they reached the hamlet of Pallerols. Here they found decidedly unconventional quarters — an old bakery oven, with its floor covered with straw for protection against the cold. The six tried to fit in as best they could. "In the dim light of a small candle," wrote Pedro, "I could just make out the downcast expression of the Father. I had never seen him like that before. He was speaking quietly with Juan Jiménez Vargas, but it sounded like a dispute. Suddenly I heard Juan say something that really shocked me: 'We are going to get you there dead or alive!'" Young Pedro could not believe his ears; he had never heard anyone speak to Escrivá in that tone of voice. Escrivá was shaken by a convulsive sob. Juan had not, however, been lacking in respect. He was just convinced that only by speaking harshly could he help Escrivá hold on. Apparently, Escrivá was losing his determination in the danger of the situation. Doubts tortured him. Had he been right to abandon some of his spiritual children? He wanted to turn around — right now, on the spot — and return to Madrid.[55]

While the others fell exhausted into a sound sleep, Escrivá spent the long hours till morning in prayer. He asked God and the Blessed Virgin for a sign — a sign to confirm his decision and restore his determination. When it was light, he got up to walk around while he prayed. On his walk he discovered a destroyed, burnt-out church in the area. After half an hour, he returned completely altered; he was beaming with peace, joy, and calm. In his hand he held a carved wooden rose. This was his sign: a rose in November, a rose from the Mother of God. It was from an image of Mary that had been in the church; the rose had remained, unscathed, under the blackened debris from the fire, just waiting for Escrivá to find it. The date was November 22, 1937. He preserved the rose carefully. Today it is kept in the headquarters of Opus Dei in Rome, and copies of it decorate the altars of Opus Dei centers throughout the world. It is a symbol of God's love.[56]

For five days, the refugees hid in the forest through which the Rialp River runs. They were still in the vicinity of the first station, Peramola. (The guides were waiting until there were enough refugees to make their trip profitable — it was a business, after all.) Thanks to the support of the rural population, it was at least possible to stay close to the villages. Of course, there were the occasional traitors who reported refugees to the authorities. And the guides themselves were not as a rule particularly idealistic. In the case of discovery, some of them would follow the principle of "every man for himself" and head for the hills, leaving the refugees to their fate. These men saw no reason to let themselves be murdered along with everyone else. They made no allowance for exhaustion or illness; anyone who could not keep up was left behind.

Some of the guides, however, were flamboyant romantics attracted by the extreme danger. Most of them were quite young, few over the age of twenty. Some were real heroes — fearless, self-sacrificing, iron-nerved. Luckily, the three guides who helped Escrivá and his companions were of this last type.

In the woods of Rialp, Escrivá's group stayed in an earthen hut that hardly showed itself above the ground. It was immediately nicknamed the House of St. Raphael, in honor of that mighty archangel who is the special protector of travelers.[57] Even here, Escrivá kept some semblance of order, following a daily schedule and routine. In the morning he gave a meditation, and then he celebrated Holy Mass before a cross in a grassy clearing, on an altar made of rocks and tree trunks. (Both crucifix and altar had been erected earlier by other fleeing priests.)

Each person had a special job. Juan and Paco, for example, had to hunt for food. (The menu was mushroom, wheat grains, and roasted squirrel.[58]) No one was idle. The architecture students sketched busily. Albareda brought out his Russian grammar book and learned vocabulary. Talks were given, and prayer and Gospel reading were done together.

Not all of Escrivá's companions were members of Opus Dei, but this made no difference. The norms of piety in Opus Dei — the basic foundations for contemplative piety in the midst of daily life — are suitable for anyone. In this extraordinary situation, the spirituality, the whole way of life of the young Opus Dei proved workable and resilient. Opus Dei proved itself to be not some wild notion for eccentrics, but a practical way for everyday Christians to live their vocations.

Escrivá and his friends were not the only forest dwellers in the area. Other refugees (who would later join them) were waiting in their own hiding places. About three miles away, there also lived several local priests who had been hiding out since the war started. Escrivá paid them a fraternal visit (a rather unlikely convocation of clergy![59]) He encouraged his brothers and tried to provide a pleasant hour for them in their long, difficult trial.

At midday on November 27th, the real climb into the mountains began, the final stage of the escape. Escrivá and his companions joined up with another group of refugees — aside from one student, all twenty-five in this group were simple Catalan farmers.[60] During the night they reached a cave, where they were able to catch a few hours of sleep. Then they proceeded to the rest station, Ribalera, at the foot of Mount Auben (4600 feet), which they reached at dawn. It was Sunday, so Escrivá said Mass. The altar was a stone covered with a white handkerchief; a small glass served as a chalice. Afterwards Escrivá kept some of the hosts in a cigarette case. (Mass would not be possible again until they got to Andorra, and only God knew if Escrivá would live to celebrate it there.) Another group of ten refugees then came to join them. They all remained at Ribalera during most of the day, breaking camp in the afternoon while it was still light.

As darkness fell, a youth named Antonio appeared.[61] He was the guide for the last stretch — the deadly stretch. Only twenty years old, he was as strong as an ox and as rough and wild as the rugged peaks he knew so well. Everyone liked Antonio. He instilled confidence immediately: "Here," he said, "I'm in command, and nobody else." He started giving orders right away. They were to walk in single file; there would be no talking; any instructions were to be whispered from one person to the next.

It was cold and raining, and the climb was steep. Tomás sprained his foot and had to sit down. Antonio said, "Let's go, with or without him." When he saw the passive resistance of the others, he explained that they would have to reach the mountaintop before nightfall in order to descend to the next safe farmhouse by dawn. Besides, anyone who was weak now would never survive the next few days. But when Escrivá took Antonio aside and spoke to him, his severity softened. And after they relieved him of most of his heavy pack, Tomás was able to limp along.

Before daybreak on November 29th, the caravan arrived at the lonely farmhouse. A warm stable sheltered them. They threw themselves on the straw, completely exhausted by the twelve-hour march. Not all of them were able to sleep; every bone ached, and every nerve trembled. The next day, some women at the farmhouse prepared lunch for them. These women also tried to mend their clothes and repair their shoes. Once more, the refugees broke camp at sunset, and faced another mountain. Near a village, the group of forty-five had to cross a road that was occasionally lit by the headlights of passing vehicles. Then there was a climb, even steeper than the one the night before. Loose stones cascaded behind those in front, showering the others. Escrivá's strength began to give out. He lost his breath, and, panting heavily, he fell behind. Antonio became impatient, but he did show a certain sympathy. Paco and Miguel helped Escrivá along.

They spent Tuesday in another barn. As soon as night fell, they marched to the small, twisting Arabell River. They had to wade through it a dozen times, their shoes and socks growing heavier and heavier with its icy waters. At daybreak on December 1st, they saw below them the lights of Seo de Urgel. They were less than six miles from the border. But these were the most dangerous miles. During the bitter cold days, they hid among the rocks, with hardly anything to eat. Then it began to snow, though only lightly.

It was the thirteenth night since they had left Barcelona. Suddenly strangers, over a dozen, arrived. They were carrying rifles, and, on their backs, knapsacks from which wafted the scent of perfume — smugglers! These men joined the group. After a few hours they all entered a valley; and then, without warning, Antonio disappeared with the smugglers. Completely soaked, the refugees lay down on the freezing ground. They shivered miserably. Escrivá seemed to be at the end of his strength. His limbs were so numb he could hardly move; his teeth were chattering uncontrollably. Juan tried to warm him by massaging his legs. The guide was gone for so many hours, they were afraid Escrivá might completely collapse, in which case everything would have been in vain.

But at last Antonio did return, with two men. Now he drove the refugees faster than ever. Again there was a river to cross, and then a road.... Deep darkness returned, and they were told to stop and hide themselves again. Not far away they saw the lights of a house and a brightly blazing fire. The sounds that drifted their way indicated that there was a border patrol in the area. After a half hour of waiting, Antonio gave the order to start moving again. Then dogs started barking furiously. The refugees were startled, but their guide paid no attention to the noise, apparently confident that the coast was now clear. In another two hours the convoy, by crossing a small valley and woods, reached the opposite slope. "Halt!" shouted Antonio. "Well," he announced, "you are now in Andorra! Wait here until it is light, so you don't wander out by mistake." And he disappeared as though swallowed by the woods.

Thursday night, December 2nd — cries of joy, cheers, laughter, jubilation, hugs. Everyone gathered around Escrivá, and suddenly everyone fell silent. He intoned the Salve Regina in a loud voice, and the song of thanksgiving rose from all their grateful hearts into the night sky.

As soon as the sun rose, they walked along the road to Santa Julia, where they bought food and rented some rooms in a small hotel at the hot springs resort of Les Escaldes. For the first time in almost sixteen months, Escrivá celebrated Mass in a church. But then it began to snow so hard that travel became impossible. The eight men had to spend a full week in Les Escaldes.[62] Their funds thus exhausted, there was then no way for them to reach France except by foot.

After Mass at dawn on December 10th, they set out; and after an eleven-hour hike through snow up to three feet deep, they reached the border. Awaiting them there were two taxis ordered by Albareda's brother, who had been notified by telephone of their escape. The taxis took them to St. Gaudens, where they spent the night. On the following day, they made a pilgrimage to Lourdes, where Escrivá said Mass. On the evening of the same day, they arrived in the French-Spanish border town of Hendaye. Thanks to the mediation of the bishop of Vitoria and Pamplona, they had no problem in crossing the border to Irun.

Here Escrivá briefly separated from the others and journeyed to Pamplona to visit his old friend Marcelino Olaechea, who had become bishop of the Navarran capital; Olaechea had invited him to stay at his residence. Escrivá made a retreat to thank God for

A photo taken the day after the successful escape into Andorra.
(Left to right, standing: Tomás Alvira, Manuel Sainz de los Terreros,
Fr. Escrivá, Pedro Casciaro, Francisco Botella; sitting: Juan Jiménez
Vargas, Miguel Fisac, José María Albareda.)

his graces of the preceding months, and to gain strength for the
coming days in Nationalist Spain.

Burgos: the preparation for peace

Burgos lies in northeastern Castile, in what is called "Old
Castile." To art historians and tourists, this city in the Arlanzon
Valley is known chiefly for its cathedral, which is one of the finest
Gothic churches in the world. Its population in the 1930s was
about sixty thousand, and today it is nearly double that. For a
time, it was the coronation site of the kings of Castile. It was in
Burgos that the national hero El Cid was born, and he is buried
here.[63] In 1808 the city was captured by Napoleon, but only four
years later it was recaptured by Wellington. On July 20, 1936, it
was taken by General Mola, one of the military leaders of the
national uprising. Until the end of the war, Burgos remained the

seat of the Nationalist regime. A central junta was established there on July 26, 1936, and on October 1, 1937, Francisco Franco was named the new chief of state.

Josemaría Escrivá settled in this provincial capital, where he hoped to find good conditions for apostolate. At the beginning of February, he returned from Pamplona and moved into the modest rooming house on Santa Clara St. where Albareda, who had obtained a position with a government agency, was already living. Later they moved into the very modest hotel Sabadell.

Naturally, any young man who had escaped from the Red Zone, and especially any deserter from the Republican Army, was sure to be immediately drafted into the Nationalist Army. By the end of the war, practically all of the members and friends of Opus Dei were in the Nationalist armed forces, most of them in the front lines. Since in this fraternal struggle prisoners were almost never taken — and certainly not those who had changed sides — one can imagine how heavily the uncertain fate of each of his sons weighed on Escrivá.

Paco Botella and Pedro Casciaro, both of whom had crossed the Pyrenees with him and were serving in Burgos, were able to visit Escrivá almost every day. They became his faithful helpers. The memoirs of Casciaro, who is now a priest in Mexico, are an important record of this period in Burgos. Casciaro's account shows Escrivá from all sides. It shows his industriousness, his heroic spirit of poverty (sometimes involving the cheerful endurance of severe material deprivation), his patience and wisdom in difficult situations; his constancy in teaching, his warmheartedness, his unpedantic authority; his spirit of sacrifice, his steadfastness, and sense of humor.

We learn from Casciaro that the history of Opus Dei includes not only many holy, courageous, and talented people, but also a clown here and there. Botella and Casciaro himself played their share of practical jokes. In one case, Escrivá had been given a Roman hat by his friend the bishop of Pamplona. It was very old, and he was to use it only until he could buy a new one. But their money was barely sufficient to pay for room and board, and so he kept wearing the hat. It became shabbier and shabbier, until finally it started turning a little green. Paco and Pedro decided Escrivá had to get a new hat. But talking did no good; Escrivá refused. "So," writes Casciaro, "we decided to act.... We were just in the process of sending out a new edition of our newsletter ... to our comrades at the front, wherever they might be. How they would rejoice if, together with the letter, we sent them each a piece of hat as a remembrance of the Father! Then he would have no choice but to get a new one.... I think I made the first cut. Once we had begun, there was nothing to do but to finish the work of destruction. Paco and I did this with gusto. The pieces had to be very small so that the already stamped envelopes would not weigh too much. Then we took them to the post office right away so that the *corpus delicti* would be gone by the time the Father got home. All's well that ends well. We got a sharp reproof, but the Father got a new hat, like it or not."[64]

A similar attempt, this time in connection with an ancient cassock, failed. The two youths took the cassock and tore it from top to bottom, but this time they miscalculated. When they came back to the room, they found Fr. Josemaría sitting there, sewing the cassock back together. He never said a word to them about it. He wore it for quite a while longer; only now, of course, it looked even worse than before.[65]

During the day, while Albareda and the two soldiers were at work, Escrivá worked alone for many hours. In these months, he expanded his book *Spiritual Considerations*, which he had written in 1934, and put it in the final form in which it would appear in 1939, retitled *The Way*.

Most of the points were handwritten, and almost all of them came from his own spiritual experience or his priestly activity with particular individuals. Escrivá had the habit of immediately jotting down thoughts, ideas, reflections, and experiences that seemed worth remembering, on small pieces of paper that he kept in the left pocket of his cassock. He often did this when speaking with individuals or groups, almost as a reflex — it was the matter of a moment, hardly noticeable. In the beginning he typed the notes himself on an old typewriter, making plenty of mistakes. (In many matters, he was not manually dexterous. When he shaved, for example, he would often cut himself; and whenever he had to erase something, he would tear holes in the paper.) Later he became accustomed to speaking into a tape recorder and then correcting the draft.[66]

Also from Burgos came a book that we have already mentioned, *La Abadesa de las Huelgas* [The abbess of Las Huelgas]. Escrivá spent many mornings in the archives of the Cistercian convent, which lay off the beaten track and required a considerable walk to reach. He was studying documents and records that spanned a period of seven hundred years. The nuns there still proudly point out the room, complete with table and chair, where the founder of Opus Dei used to work.[67]

Escrivá devoted many long hours each day to the apostolate of writing letters. This was still the only way to maintain contact with most of the members of Opus Dei and their friends. But he did not consider the letter a mere substitute for more direct contact; he saw it as an intrinsically valuable means of dealing with people. He was a passionate letter-writer. The letters that poured from his pen glow with a warmhearted naturalness and a divinely inspired drive to bear witness to the love of God.

He speaks of this letter-writing apostolate in *The Way*. "I don't always find the right words," he says, "for putting down things that might be useful to the friend I am writing. But when I begin, I tell my guardian angel that all I hope from my letter is that it may do some good. And even though I may write only nonsense, no one can take from me — or from my friend — the time I have spent praying for what I know that friend needs most."[68]

The monthly distribution of the newsletter (the predecessor to the internal magazines of Opus Dei) was expanded, reaching practically every region and battle front of Nationalist Spain: the Madrid, the Teruel, the Northeast, and the Andalusian fronts. Its contents increased along with the number of those receiving it. Now it contained advice, encouragement, spiritual suggestions, messages from Escrivá, and quotes from incoming letters. The Burgos correspondence was not a one-way street; the members of Opus Dei and their friends also wrote frequently, and whatever was of general interest in these letters was passed along to the others. In this way, an efficient communications network was established — an essential precondition for rapid resumption of work after the war.

Opus Dei, now ten years old, was to all appearances badly set back by the war. But appearances can be deceiving. As the great apostolic explosion of the next decade demonstrated, it had been growing from within. "We are continuing our work," wrote Escrivá on March 19, 1938 (the Feast of St. Joseph, which is always a special feast in Opus Dei), "with the same enthusiasm as ever, just as our natural duty and our supernatural vocation demand. Ten years' work! In the eleventh, which will begin soon, Jesus and I are expecting a lot from you! Even now — in the camps, in the trenches, at your posts, in the exhausting duties in the hospitals — how much you can contribute with your prayer, your purity, your successes and your failures, to push the Work forward! We want to live an intense communion of the saints, so that each one will feel, whether in a time of inner struggle or in military battle, the same joy and the same strength I find here: that of not being alone."[69]

But writing was only a part of his activity in Burgos, and not even the biggest part. Escrivá kept a constant eye on the future of Opus Dei. As soon as the guns were stilled, Opus Dei must blossom in Spain and then branch out to the whole world.[70] Everything depended on bringing into the ship more "apostles of apostles," as well as continuing the formation of those already on board. The war had affected them also. The young men had fallen prey to the feelings of emotional turmoil that a long war, especially a civil war, tends to induce. It requires great inner stability, combined with acumen and tact, to deepen one's life of piety and virtue in the midst of war.

Escrivá's visits to his sons at the front strengthened their ascetical and apostolic formation in the spirit of Opus Dei. He showed them how this spirit could be lived by soldiers. When someone began to feel he was losing the strength to follow his vocation, Escrivá would come to him quickly, take him by the hand, and put him on his feet again. Often Escrivá took long, uncomfortable trips to be at a son's side, sometimes right on the front lines. When it came to helping his children, nothing was too difficult for him. Needless to say, this love was repaid. The young men also made sacrifices and spared no effort to visit him. Many of them spent a large part of their short furloughs in Burgos; some traveled for twenty hours just to speak with him for an hour.

In addition to his personal apostolate, Escrivá took on general pastoral and catechetical work for the local bishop. He taught catechism, preached days of recollection, and gave retreats, not only in Burgos but also in Vitoria, Avila, and Salamanca. Escrivá understood well that what was most important for his listeners was not what they considered important but what mattered in the eyes of Christ. Casciaro offers an example in his memoirs.[71] One Sunday, Escrivá preached a day of recollection at a church in Burgos. Many intellectuals came: scientists, professors, and state officials. When he saw this select audience, he told them he felt like a watchmaker in a workshop full of expensive watch parts — gears of platinum, small screws with sapphire tips, and so forth. Individually and collectively, these parts were clearly of superlative quality, but if one tried to make a watch out of them, one might discover that they did not fit together. As a final product, one might end up with a watch that could not be wound up, or one that would stop after a few minutes.[72] "In short," said Escrivá, "if it doesn't work, it is useless to me. Instead of this, I would rather have one of those cheap alarm clocks you can get at any five-and-dime." As in the Gospel story of Jesus' homily in the synagogue (Lk 4:16-30), some of the listeners did not appreciate the comparison used to describe them. But Escrivá went right on. He explained that just as all that platinum, quartz, and sapphire was absolutely useless if the watch did not run well, so it is that the greatest talents, the most select gifts, and the costliest materials acquire value only through love, justice, and service to God and neighbor.

He then reiterated something that he had often said before: that culture, like scientific research, should not be made an end in itself, something hoarded by a smug, self-congratulatory elite. It was wrong to plot phony intellectual coups, or to run a research institute like a closed shop, or to convert a professorship into an instrument of power.[73] "It is not a matter of being 'higher' or 'lower,'" he said as he ended the meditation in Burgos, "but only of serving God and your neighbor; putting God, not yourself, at the top of all your concerns. Only then will your work be holy and make others holy."[74]

During the sixteen months in Nationalist Spain, Escrivá's connections with the Red Zone were kept alive through Isidoro Zorzano. Through a friend living in France, his detailed letters reached Burgos and the answers to them were sent back to Madrid. Escrivá's mother, sister, and brother were alive. Alvaro del Portillo and a few companions had been able to leave their hiding place and were now soldiers in the Republican Army. While a few of their friends (among them Ricardo Fernández Vallespín, who joined Opus Dei in the summer of 1933) had already managed to get from the Red Zone to the Nationalist Zone, others were not able to do this until the fall of 1938. On October 12th, these others succeeded in escaping (on the Guadalajara front, where the lines had stabilized — about thirty miles northeast of Madrid), and they reached Burgos on October 16th. Those who crossed the line served for the last five months of the war on the side that now seemed certain of victory.

Between March and July of 1938, Franco's troops broke through to the Mediterranean and cut the Republican territory in half, separating Catalonia from the rest of the Republic. This was the turning point, the event that sealed the fate of the Red regime. On January 26, 1939, Barcelona fell, and on March 28th the Nationalist forces entered Madrid, without resistance. The war ended officially on March 29th.[75] "La guerra ha terminado" ("The war has ended") was the last communique of the Nationalist high command. The war had lasted two years, eight months, ten days. It had cost over half a million lives. Begun as a revolution, it ended as a liberation, since the overwhelming majority of Spaniards vastly preferred an authoritarian Franco regime to a totalitarian communist one.

Josemaría Escrivá returned to Madrid on March 28th, just as the first columns of troops were entering the city. On Ferraz St., as he stood in front of the ruins of the house that had been No. 16, he saw something lying in the rubble and bent down to pick it up. It was a parchment he had hung on a wall of the study room. On it was this quotation from St. John's Gospel: "Mandatum novum do vobis, ut diligatis invicem; sicut dilexi vos, ut et vos diligatis invicem. In hoc cognoscent omnes quia mei discipuli estis, si dilectionem habueritis ad invicem." ("A new commandment I give to you, that you love one another: that as I have loved you, you also love one another. By this will all know that you are my disciples, if you have love for one another"— Jn 13:34.) Deeply moved, Escrivá took this parchment with him. Six months later it found a home in the new center of Opus Dei on Jenner St.[76]

Chapter Six

THE MIRACULOUS CATCH OF FISH

"We are for the multitudes."

My all-too-brief tracing of Escrivá's footsteps on the Iberian Peninsula led me to 14 Diego de León St., the building that now serves as the headquarters of Opus Dei in Spain. I was not sure what to expect, but what I found was a beehive of activity, geared toward directing a spiritual family that numbers in the thousands. (Spaniards account for a good fifth of Opus Dei's membership.) More than anything, I sensed the almost physical presence of the founder of Opus Dei. This is where he lived after moving from his first stable post-war residence, 6 Jenner St. After he moved to Rome in 1946, this was the house where he stayed on subsequent trips to Madrid. (During his twenty-nine-year residence in Rome, he visited Spain twenty-three times.[1]

Here I "met" Escrivá: in the rooms, with all the furniture, the heirlooms, the distinctive style that bespeaks a living family — especially in the chapel, his small office, and the even smaller bedrooms. I caught glimpses of him in the crypt where his parents are laid to rest. Finally I met him in a nautical souvenir: a ship's compass, helm and bell. Nearby is a photograph of the small steamship they came from, the J. J. Sister. A mail-carrying freighter, the J. J. Sister was the ship on which Escrivá first voyaged to Rome. (Traveling between Barcelona and Genoa, it was in 1946 the only connection between Spain and Italy.) This was his first trip abroad, not counting the eight days in Andorra, thirty hours in France, and occasional visits to Portugal. It was a foundational trip of the first order, a major step for Opus Dei and for the Church. It meant that this "child," now nearly eighteen years old, had come of age and was about to be enlisted in the service of the Church. The Aragonese priest had moved not only from Madrid to Rome, but also from Spain into the world.

That trip, across the sea by ship, had a rich symbolic meaning — something I grasped as I stood staring at the treasured remains of that long-since scrapped freighter. How deeply Escrivá loved those Gospel passages that speak of the sea, boats, fishing nets, and fishermen. How often he would say that the apostolate of Opus Dei must be a "sea without shores ... *duc in altum*, set out into the deep." (One of his favorite directives, this was an echo of Jesus' challenge to Simon Peter: "Go out into the deep and lower your nets for a catch.") And how emphatically he would tell them, "Cast off your laziness and selfishness! Make your life uncomfortable! In the name of Christ, throw yourself into the waves of the world!"[2] But he himself was the first to follow his own advice, as was evident when he undertook that first trip. This was something that could not be postponed. Alvaro del Portillo, who had already been doing preparatory work in Rome, had written to tell Escrivá that he alone could obtain canonical recognition of Opus Dei. So Escrivá set out, despite the fact that since 1944 he had been suffering from diabetes (an even more dangerous disease then than now). His physical condition was, in fact, so bad that his doctor forbade the voyage. But what alternative did he have? He was forced to disobey the doctor. And then, as if that were not enough, the trip turned out to be much worse than anyone had foreseen. A violent storm, unusual for that time of year, pounded the ship for most of its twenty-hour crossing. The J. J. Sister, fifty years old and a mere fifteen hundred tons, pitched "like a floating shipwreck," as sailors like to say.

Alvaro del Portillo was waiting for Escrivá at the dock in Genoa. He now wore a Roman collar and a priest's hat. Two years earlier, on June 25, 1944, the bishop of Madrid, Leopoldo Eijo y Garay, had ordained him and two other numeraries as the first Opus Dei priests. This had been a necessary step, because Escrivá could no longer take care of the multiplying membership of Opus Dei single-handedly. The step had not been an easy one; it had required a third foundational grace. Escrivá received this grace on February 14, 1943, when the Priestly Society of the Holy Cross entered the history of Opus Dei and the Church. This was, poetically speaking, a towrope thrown to Escrivá by God himself, so that the boat of Opus Dei would be tied fast to the rock of St. Peter.

The need for priests in Opus Dei arose from a supernatural phenomenon, a "Spanish miracle" that brought a flood of vocations after the Civil War. In 1939, Opus Dei resumed its apostolic efforts on the same Madrid street where the Civil War had erupted three years earlier. By 1946, when Escrivá went to Rome, there were already Opus Dei centers in Madrid, Barcelona, Bilbao, Santiago de Compostela, Saragossa, Seville, Valencia, and Valladolid. The first retreat house opened its doors at Molinoviejo, near Segovia, in 1945, and in the following year, the first center outside of Spain was established in the Portuguese city of Coimbra.[3]

In the meantime, Escrivá had also resumed his work at the Santa Isabel Foundation. Contagious disease was all too common, but there was at the same time something we might call a contagious cure. Spain was still bleeding from a thousand wounds inflicted by the fratricidal war; poverty was widespread, as was fatigue from front-line and rear-guard battles. Nevertheless, hope was abroad. From the scars came the will and the enthusiasm to heal the country. There stirred in many Spanish hearts a readiness for forgiveness and Christian renewal. Among the young people of Spain, a growing number realized that the future — their own and the nation's — depended not on ideological and social systems, but on personal identification with Christ. Had not God been willing to spare Sodom because of the presence of ten just men? Spain was in desperate need of just men and women, to serve as leaven in society.

When World War II broke out, Opus Dei had just taken root in a country which had undergone a terrible prelude to the global catastrophe, but which was spared direct involvement. While World War II held the world's attention, there occurred offstage a quiet, unspectacular chain reaction of conversions in the hearts of a few hundred people. Who would have imagined that such an unlikely and strictly spiritual revolution would have the potential to cause profound and lasting changes in the world, perhaps to change the course of human history? Yet when a handful of men and women pledge themselves to the imitation of Christ for the rest of their lives, the cumulative impact can outweigh that of all the nuclear warheads in the world.

In the years following the Spanish Civil War, Escrivá gave regular spiritual guidance to hundreds of people — men and women;

singles and couples; professors, students, and blue-collar workers.[4] Many of these people eventually became members of Opus Dei. Escrivá seemed to possess a special gift for perceiving in souls the slightest glimmer of love for God; even if it was just barely smoldering under a pile of ashes, he could usually fan it into a bright flame. Normally the vocation to Opus Dei develops gradually over a period of years. In the early 1940s, however, God seemed to have pressed a fast-forward button; sometimes this interior development took place within a few weeks, if not just days or hours. Though such accelerated cases were relatively rare, the apostolic harvest in Spain during the forties ripened quite quickly and abundantly.

What was Escrivá's role in all this? He preached the message of Opus Dei unstintingly. But he never tried to hurry vocations along except by prayer, mortification, and fidelity to Christ. By talking with those who sought his counsel, he could easily determine the dispositions of their souls. He would thus recognize whether or not they had a vocation to Opus Dei, or to another path within the Church, and if so, whether they should proceed with haste or caution. This insight did not influence his friendship, spiritual advice, or estimation of others in the slightest. After all, it is God who calls. And it never pays to rush the divine call. For his part, Escrivá put all the focus on just not falling behind. His personal message caused many a sleeper to wake up, throw open a window, and peer out to see the Divine Suitor coming from afar. Escrivá saw romance and drama in everyday life. "We are people of the street, in the midst of the world; equals among our peers, among all kinds of people. With arms open to all souls, we are light and salt. We have no need of distinctive clothes or an insignia. Only one thing distinguishes us, and that is an intimate affair of the soul: the vocation the Lord has given us."[5] To catch and spread this divine fever, one could not live isolated in an ivory tower.

Escrivá was always on the move. Did he not need more people? Had not Christ sent his disciples out in twos? The very word "apostle" means "one who is sent." Escrivá traveled regularly to all the larger (and many of the smaller) cities of Spain. He gladly sacrificed the popular idols of contemporary society: weekends, free time, recreation. After his usual eighty-hour week, he traveled

Saturday afternoon and on into the night by train to distant cities. (The trains were not the sleek express trains we know today, but slow, uncomfortable, rickety affairs, with smoky engines; ten- or twelve-hour trips on wooden benches were not unusual.) No well-furnished, accommodating Opus Dei center awaited him at the end of the line. To whoever would come, he preached meditations in a dingy hotel room; much of the time, his penetrating advice was given on park benches, in small cafés, or on the street. Then on Sunday evening it was back to Madrid, where he began work again the following morning.

Opus Dei's apostolate has not changed much since then. No matter how many countries it has reached, or will reach, it always begins in the same way: with trust in God, hard work, a sense of humor, and little else. For Escrivá this meant meager fare (one substantial meal a day), modest living, and cheap travel. Buying tickets for apostolic trips was often a problem. Once, he later recounted, he did not have enough money for the train trip from Cordoba back to Burgos. He emptied his pockets and plunked a few pesetas on the counter, telling the ticket agent, "Give me a ticket for as far as this will take me towards Burgos." The puzzled man complied, and Escrivá managed to make it to Salamanca, about a hundred fifty miles from home.

"The desire to be detached is not enough," Escrivá used to say. "You have to learn to be detached."[6] He was a master of the art of poverty. If he was alone, he ate sparsely and quickly; but if there was a guest, his hospitality knew no bounds, even if it cost him his last peseta and he had to fast afterwards. He walked countless miles through the streets of Madrid; but whenever he invited some tired, lonely colleague to dinner, he would have him picked up and taken home in a taxi. When Opus Dei's headquarters in Rome were under construction, he slept on the floor. His bedroom was extremely spare in its furnishings; for many years he even did without a bedspread. But guests at Villa Tevere are astonished at the elegant, comfortable decor of the reception areas and the rich beauty of the chapels.

No Opus Dei center has ever been ready for use at the time it was bought. Even when Opus Dei has built centers from the ground up, they have always been opened prematurely, out of a feeling that God cannot wait. Where does the money come from? First, from the members' incomes. But since this is never enough, they also have to solicit money. How? By going through the grind of following leads, waiting in reception rooms, sometimes getting thrown out, braving inclement weather to receive perhaps nothing but a pittance and good wishes — in short, by begging. Unpleasant though it is, this duty often yields great apostolic fruit. While some hearts remain hard, others show a readiness to help, out of Christian generosity and solidarity. The payoff — in souls even more than in money — always comes, for God does not let himself be outdone in generosity.

It would constitute a betrayal of the spirit of Opus Dei if members did not seek to inspire others to dedicate themselves fully to God in the midst of the world. For the seed of a divine vocation to sprout, the ground must be cultivated; members must give the personal, spiritual instruction and formation that enables others to take this step. The first prerequisite for inviting others to seek holiness, to follow Christ in their everyday lives, is a lively desire for one's own sanctity. Apostolate springs from intimacy with Christ.

Hard work is also indispensable. At first, Escrivá bore this burden alone. He crisscrossed Spain to spread Opus Dei, laying the foundation for every single center with his pastoral words, his discussions with the local bishops, and his contacts with the civil authorities. Meanwhile, he dedicated himself untiringly to the spiritual growth of the members of the Work, stressing to them how vital it was "to win the battle of formation."[7]

The letters Escrivá wrote to members in those years, the "Instructions" he composed for this battle, reveal something of his soul's ardor. "The Lord is expecting from you and me," he wrote in 1940, "that with a joyful thanksgiving for the vocation he placed in our souls, we become a great army sowing peace and joy along the paths of men and women. Our numbers will be such that no one will be able to count the souls who join in our chorus: 'Sing to the Lord a new song — sing to the Lord, all you lands!'"[8] In a letter he wrote in 1942, he commented on the parable of the wedding feast in which the head of the household commands his servants, "Go out into the highways and hedges and compel the people to come in (compelle intrare), so that my house may be filled!"(Lk 14:23-24). He said, "This compelle intrare is not like a physical shove. Rather, it is the fullness of light and doctrine; it is the combined weight of the many sacrifices that you offer up; it is the smile on your lips because you are God's children. This childhood gives you a quiet happiness which others see and envy. Add to this your warmth and good nature, and you have the essence of the *compelle intrare.*"[9]

A year later he wrote, "My dear daughters and sons, realize fully what the Lord, the Church, and all people expect from Opus Dei, which is now like a grain of wheat buried in a furrow. Realize the true greatness of your vocation, and love it more every day. Say yes to becoming the instrument the Lord needs; make it a yes filled with optimism, joy, and supernatural outlook.... You must be firmly convinced in head and heart that we will attain nothing if we are not holy."[10] And again, the next year, "If we ask anything in the name of Jesus, it will be granted to us by the Father; be certain of that. Prayer has always been the secret — the mighty weapon — of Opus Dei. So often we have had no other recourse — and it will be the same in the future! Prayer is the foundation of our peace and our apostolic effectiveness.... That is why I insist upon it so much with you. You must believe that the Lord will grant what we ask for."[11]

Especially touching is his letter of May 6, 1945. Two days before the end of the war in Europe, he wrote: "We are here for many, my children — for the multitude. There is no soul whom we do not love, whom we don't want to help. It is our mission to become 'all things to all people.'[12] .... My sons and daughters, I am concerned about all creatures; I want to lead them all to God. Souls make me suffer. Often I can't understand at all how my heart and head can endure such pain. But that is our spirit. We have to listen to the woeful cries of the many, many desiccated hearts simultaneously calling out to us, 'Hominem non habeo': 'I have no one who can lead me to the light and warmth of Christ.'... Each of us is another Christ, called to be a co-redeemer.[13] Our life as God's children in his Work cannot possibly be separated from our apostolic zeal."[14]

How often did Escrivá voice this basic drive. It was his raison d'être; it is the very meaning of life in Opus Dei. "Whoever does not thirst for all souls," he explained, "does not have a vocation to Opus Dei. As children of God..., you and I must think of souls when we see people. We must say to ourselves: there is a soul that needs help, a soul that seeks understanding, a soul that craves fellowship, a soul that must be saved."[15] Yet this concern for all souls precludes neither the wisdom nor the duty of concentrating attention on those who can respond most readily. As early as 1934, Escrivá had presented a list of personality types unfit for a vocation to Opus Dei. "The egotistical, the malicious, the gossipy won't do," he said. "Neither will the pessimistic or the lukewarm, the foolish or the lazy, the timid or the frivolous. But those who are sick, God's favorites, will do, and all who have big hearts, even if their mistakes have been even bigger."[16] What about scholars and other intellectuals? "They will be welcome in the Work," said Escrivá, "but we will be satisfied if the majority — all the rest — are simply competent in their profession or work."[17]

Again and again we see his refreshing sense of reality. Great spirits, important personalities, high fliers are fine and good; but what Opus Dei needs, and what God wants to see in it, is a plentiful supply of "men and women who are well-mannered, holy, obedient, and energetic. They will be the ones to carry the Work ahead; this will be the reward for their humility."[18] He had his own idea of the kinds of people God might be especially interested in. "There should be vocations among people who, by their occupation, already have a continuous public around them, and thus a built-in opportunity to become catalysts: artisans, public officials, barbers, pharmacists, salesmen, midwives, mail carriers, waiters, newspaper vendors."[19] Not exactly an elite. Escrivá was looking for people who were ready to serve as Christ's leaven in the bread of humanity, not those who felt compelled to be the raisins and the nuts. For this reason, he looked towards those who were already yeast in the dough of society, those who needed only to add a supernatural dimension to the tasks they were already carrying out.

Youthful enthusiasm for Christ

The women's branch of Opus Dei had suffered greatly during the Civil War. While Escrivá was able to resume the work of the men's branch with a handful of loyal followers bound together by common dangers and tribulations, he practically had to start the women's branch all over again. The reason was simple: the war had made it impossible for Escrivá to maintain contact with the first members of the women's branch. Communication soon broke down; for a while there was even a rumor afloat that Escrivá had died. When the war started in 1936, Opus Dei's spirituality had just begun to germinate in the souls of the female members; it had not developed strong roots. Denied Escrivá's spiritual care, many of the women went their own way. Some of them ended up adopting lifestyles more appropriate for nuns.

Escrivá recognized and tackled the problem early on. Even during the war, while he was in Burgos, he started to plan the "second beginning" of the women's branch by gathering data regarding the female relatives of his sons. By now it must be obvious that Opus Dei did not spread through organized advertising campaigns or public relations networks. Then as now, it spread from friend to friend and within families, so it was only natural that the families of Escrivá's sons should have provided the first vocations to the women's branch.

As before, the women went to confession to Escrivá in the church of Santa Isabel. He gave them classes on spirituality in the apartment on Jenner St. where he lived with his mother, sister, and brother. In 1940 they moved into the house on Diego de León St. Part of this large building was reserved for Escrivá's family. In another part, the women's branch found a better (though still provisional) place to meet, where Escrivá would teach and offer spiritual assistance to the young women. But by 1942 the quarters used by the women's branch had become too crowded, and a center — their first — had to be established.

In 1978 one of the earliest members of the women's branch, Encarnación Ortega, wrote (for the beatification process) her memories of Escrivá. Her reminiscences cover the period from 1942 to 1952. Perceptive and detailed, they describe the critical decade during which Escrivá suffered the most severe persecution, the Priestly Society of the Holy Cross was founded, Opus Dei moved to Rome, the Church first approved Opus Dei, and the Work began to expand throughout the world. The special value of this document is its perspective. This richly factual history is shot through with a vivid portrait of Escrivá's personality as seen through a woman's eyes.

Ortega worked in different centers of the women's branch in Spain, in the regional government, and for years in the women's headquarters in Rome. Today she is again working in her native land. She often met with Escrivá and has first-hand knowledge of more than three decades in the life of Opus Dei and its founder.

When she first met Escrivá — on Palm Sunday of 1941, in Valencia, where he was holding days of recollection for girls who taught catechism[20] — she was fifteen years old. She was taking part, she reports, out of curiosity; her brother had told her about an unusual priest whom he called "the Father," and she wanted to get a look at him herself. "We went into the chapel," she says, "and our Father came in shortly afterwards. His interior recollection, full of naturalness, his genuflection before the Blessed Sacrament, the perfect devotion with which he said the preparatory prayer before the meditation — to make us realize that the Lord was present there, that he saw us and heard us — all this made me forget my desire to 'experience a great preacher.' Instead I felt compelled to listen to God and to open my heart to him."[21]

After the meditation, Encarnita, as she was called, had an opportunity to speak with Escrivá for a short time. In a few words, right in the doorway, he explained Opus Dei to her in passing, just "as a hypothesis." Encarnita had not yet heard of Opus Dei — her brother had only mentioned Escrivá, not Opus Dei. The idea, she says, was "to seek holiness in ordinary work, without leaving one's state in life; to be in the world, without being of the world; to lead a contemplative life without being a nun; to make the street your cell, but without doing anything extraordinary.... [The Father] spoke to me of divine filiation as the dominant personality trait of the one who lived this way, and about its great importance; about concern for apostolate; about human virtues like sincerity, industriousness, and courage."[22]

The young lady was deeply stirred. She felt a call; yet, as so often happens, she resisted it. "I made a resolution never to get into a face-to-face meeting with the Father again. But despite this decision, I couldn't eat or sleep. I saw that God needed valiant women to accomplish his work on earth, and that he had told me this — why, I did not know — through the founder of the Work.... These ideas stayed with me, strong and continuous."[23] In the last meditation of that day of recollection, Escrivá spoke about the Passion of Jesus. Perhaps "spoke" is not the right word; he saw it so clearly and made it so vivid that his listeners became witnesses themselves. Escrivá shook their indifference, took away the anonymity of it all. He said then what he would later repeat in *The Way of the Cross*: "I love Christ on the cross so much that every crucifix seems to me to be a loving reproach from my Lord: 'I am suffering, and you — you are a coward. I love you, and you — you forget me. I am begging, and you — you are saying no.'"[24] In those thirty minutes of meditation on the Passion, the young Ortega found herself making the decision of her life. "I only wanted to tell [Escrivá] one thing: that I was ready for anything."[25] Escrivá did not leave anyone unclear about what awaited those who wanted to serve Christ, the Church, and all humankind in the Work. Life would be hard; the poverty would be extreme. One had to be completely available, ready to go to distant lands — perhaps even to Japan, which would mean having to learn Japanese. "None of that," recalls Encarnación, "made any difference to me. I had come to a decision so firm that, with the help of God's grace, it was sure to overcome all difficulties."[26]

Opus Dei is sometimes accused of leading young and impressionable people to make decisions whose consequences they cannot foresee, decisions they are neither capable of making nor entitled to make without parental approval, decisions which can cause lasting damage and suffering. But when we look at the history of the Christian vocation, the complete dedication to Christ and his Church, one of the first things we notice is that the Holy Spirit does not bother about birth certificates when choosing the souls he wants. The age at which a person grasps and can follow the divine will varies considerably. There are senior citizens to whom the door of wisdom remains closed, and children for whom the light already shines brightly. A few years ago, the well-known theologian Wilhelm Schamoni published a short work entitled *Young and Holy*, in which he presented thirty-two portraits and short biographies of young saints and other youths who lived in a saintly way. Alongside such famous figures as Aloysius Gonzaga, Theresa of the Child Jesus (the "Little Flower"), Dominic Savio, and Maria Goretti, we find many youths that most of us have never heard of. A book like this should find its way into the hands of all Catholic parents, especially those who out of a misguided love are creating difficulties because they cannot understand how a child can authentically be called to a particular path of holiness. In the foreword of this book, we find a beautiful passage that speaks to the concern of such parents: "Children are like an opening bud, youth like a blossoming flower. They are full of promise. Sanctity lets this promise find fulfillment."[27]

It is a great grace when young people are called to follow Christ and they obey this call. The parents should be deeply grateful. After all, it is all too evident how capable young people are of making a decision and following through on it when it comes to embarking on a life of sin; just think for a moment of the worldwide epidemics of substance abuse, sexual promiscuity, and gang wars among teens and even preteens. Surely young people are no less capable of loving God with pure dedication. And whatever amount of impressionability and lack of foresight may be involved in their decisions, these are realities that must be factored in for better or for worse; in one direction or another, young people are going to be influenced. It is, it seems to me, a mistake of the greatest magnitude to treat adolescence as something arbitrary. I cannot understand, for example, why parents will allow a teenager the decision to drop out of religion class, but not the decision to serve God and the Church. The time-tested experience of the Church is, indeed, that a young person can generally recognize the signs of a divine vocation and at least begin to pursue it.[28] Countless biographies of young saints show parents fighting tooth and nail against a child convinced of having such a vocation. In particular (there are many cases in point, including that of St. Thomas Aquinas), a vocation to celibacy "for the sake of the kingdom of heaven" (Mt 19:12) seems capable of arousing outright hysteria and absolute rejection. Young people in such a predicament experience early, in their own homes, the pain of the cross involved in following Christ. But they can be comforted by the words of

Escrivá: "I especially want to tell you," he says, "that age brings with it neither wisdom nor holiness. On the contrary, the Holy Spirit places on the lips of young people these words: 'I have understood more than the ancients, because I have sought to fulfill your commandments' (Ps 119:100). So don't wait till old age to become holy — that would be a great mistake!"[29] And to parents he says, "Have a special reverence and a deep love for the vocation to perfect chastity, which, as you know, is even higher than the married state; and really rejoice when one of your children, thanks to God's grace, embraces this way. It is not a sacrifice. It is an election, transmitted through the goodness of God; a motive for holy pride; a desire to serve all people, gladly, out of love for Jesus Christ."[30]

As with his sons, Escrivá explained the future of Opus Dei to his daughters as though it already existed. He was a realistic visionary, a loud and convincing prophet. As early as 1942, reports Encarnación, he described in detail future areas of activity of the women's branch throughout the world. Rural schools for farm wives, professional schools for women, student residences for girls, activities in the field of fashion, nursing homes, mobile libraries, bookstores — any of these could serve as the basis and instrument for one's most important task: personal apostolate.[31] The women needed supernatural optimism and confidence in Escrivá's daring dreams, because the future was barely conceivable in even its vaguest outlines. In 1941, the women's branch consisted of only six young ladies, three of whom soon left. And though the other three persevered, there were still only a handful by the end of 1942. But when Escrivá died (in 1975), there were more than two hundred study centers, sixty-two residences for girls, and numerous schools and other educational institutions in seventeen countries.

In the summer of 1942, the women's branch — the handful of young ladies just mentioned — acquired its first house, a small unfurnished villa at 19 Jorge Manrique St. The most necessary furnishings were either brought from their own homes, bought in secondhand stores, or received as gifts. The women's spiritual formation, their apostolic work, and their observance of the norms of Opus Dei in its characteristic family atmosphere corresponded exactly to that of the men's branch. Regarding the value of the person and one's divine filiation, Escrivá made no distinction between man and woman.[32] This divinely ordained equality is, in fact, what conditions, sustains, unites, and makes fruitful the divinely willed differences between the sexes. In 1967, Escrivá recalled the misunderstanding and opposition he had encountered a quarter of a century earlier in his efforts to enable women members of Opus Dei to receive academic degrees in theology.[33] By no means was he trying to create women priests, but he did want to improve their training so that they could better serve the Church in catechesis and other teaching roles.

Within the women's branch, a special field of work developed: the "administration." The English word smacks of bureaucratic coldness, but it signifies something entirely different for Opus Dei. The administration is responsible for the pleasant atmosphere of Opus Dei centers, and the physical well-being of the residents and guests; it does, in short, the work of a good mother in a home. Escrivá referred to the administration as the apostolate of apostolates.

At first, Escrivá and his sons did the housework, but when his mother and sister took an apartment in the same building as the center, the two women started taking over more and more of the work. Joyfully, as though it were their God-given prerogative, they took care of the household, even doing laundry and sewing for the young men. Dolores and Carmen Escrivá formed the first administration of Opus Dei. After the death of her mother in 1941, Carmen continued for some time alone, but with the expansion of Opus Dei, some other solution became necessary. Since Opus Dei constituted a spiritual family, the solution was obvious. Just as they naturally would in any other family at that time, the women would manage the household; they would support themselves and their apostolates through this work. This opened up for Escrivá's female followers a broad and important field for sanctification, a professional task of unique importance to the family atmosphere of Opus Dei. The possibilities for apostolate in the field of domestic arts and family management can hardly be overestimated.

In the summer of 1943, when the new student residence of Moncloa opened, the women's branch was for the first time entrusted with formal administration. Encarnación Ortega has vivid memories of this beginning.[34] She and two other young ladies, all three of them still in their teens, were totally inexperienced in running a household, especially one so complicated; the residence consisted of two houses across the street from each other — a serious logistical problem.[35] Maintaining order in the students' sleeping quarters, the living rooms, and the chapel; shopping, preparing menus, cooking, washing, ironing, sewing, keeping accounts, and trying to make do with the money available; and on top of all this, trying to keep up with the norms of Opus Dei (daily Mass, prayer, spiritual reading, the rosary) — all of this was enough to drive anyone to frustration and discouragement. Seeing the flood of chaos rising around them, the young ladies felt they were failing completely. When Escrivá arrived, two days before Christmas, their despair broke loose. "We just can't continue to work this way — it's impossible!" And they poured out all that was troubling them. Escrivá remained silent, just listening to them with heartfelt understanding and sympathy. And then they said that with so much work, they did not even have time to pray. Though they tried to fit it in, their attention was elsewhere.

Suddenly Escrivá's countenance changed, revealing not simple concern but deep sorrow. Could it be that all his teaching had been in vain? Had they forgotten all he had taught them on unity of life in the constant presence of God, on a continuous union of work and contemplation, on the joy that should spring irresistibly from one's sense of divine filiation, no matter how difficult things might get? Had his daughters failed to grasp the essence of Opus Dei? Would the women's branch, still young and not yet tested by fire, crumble again? He broke into tears and wept for several minutes. The young ladies were stunned. In all her years with Escrivá, wrote Encarnación, "it was perhaps this moment that left the greatest impression on me. On no other occasion — not when he was slandered, not when he was persecuted — did I see the Father moved so deeply."

Then he asked for a note pad and wrote on it, "1. Lack of dishes; 2. Construction workers are everywhere; 3. No practical entrance; 4. No tablecloths; 5. No storage room; 6. Lack of personnel; 7. Inexperience; 8. No division of labor." Under this he wrote, "1. With a lot of love of God; 2. With full trust in God and the Father; 3. Don't think about this trouble — until tomorrow, during the day of recollection." He asked his daughters not to discuss this occurrence among themselves right away. He made them promise to make a good meal that day, amuse themselves, and just relax.

The following day, Escrivá told Encarnación why he had wept. It was, he said, "because you had not done your prayer. And for a daughter of God in Opus Dei, this is the most important work; it has to take precedence over everything else."[36]

One cannot speak of the invaluable service offered by the women's branch in their administration apostolate without confronting the reality of what this looks like in the context of the world today. With due allowance for differences of time and place, there is a problem here that transcends not only cultural differences but the whole question of gender bias. This problem is a general, sweeping disdain for service as such, and for domestic service in particular, that today has reached epidemic proportions. Domestic work is denounced as exploitation by those benefiting from it, while willingness to provide such service is considered proof of effective propaganda by the exploiters and of mindless subservience on the part of those exploited. While service as such is perceived as a major obstacle to self-realization, any type of domestic work incurs a special disdain and horror.

In our day the problem is compounded by the confusion between equality and freedom from having to serve. When men have shown an unwillingness to serve — because they have been told that it is not for the dignified and intelligent, that it is virtually subhuman and definitely not manly — that attitude has, until fairly recently, been perceived as being perhaps less than ideal, but not catastrophic. It has been tacitly taken for granted that no matter how many men abdicate their responsibilities to serve, all necessary services will still get done as long as there are women. We are now only beginning to discover how baseless, unjust, and dangerous this assumption is.

Escrivá did not consider any kind of service to be beneath him. Not only did he cheerfully do domestic work himself, he also repeated for nearly fifty years the cry, "*Serviam*... I will serve!" Spoken out of love for God and neighbor, this impulse to serve is the heart of the struggle for sanctity and the strong foundation of an indestructible joie de vivre.

On hundreds of occasions, Escrivá denounced the distinction between "higher" and "lower" classes of work. The true measure of a work's value, he said, is the amount of love with which it is done. And from this point of view, it is precisely housework, whether done for one's family or for an employer, that particularly shines. Here a practical love comes into play that seems to come naturally to many women, even if it is not a gift universally and exclusively belonging to women. The thousand little things that go into making a home pleasant for others can all be acts of love. "Let us not forget," Escrivá told a woman reporter in 1968, "that though people have tried to represent this work as demeaning, it is not so at all. The woman who does such work today must be a professional too. Any meaningful activity within society is, in the best sense of the word, a service; the activity of a domestic servant is just as valuable a service as that of a teacher or judge. For me, the work of a domestic servant who is a member of Opus Dei is just as meaningful as the work of a member with a title of nobility."[37]

From the beginning, he encouraged the women's branch to found schools of domestic science. There, young women could learn to do housework in a highly skilled fashion, taking advantage of the most recent advances in technology. They could also learn how especially dear to God this work is when done with love. Throughout the world, many women find their vocation to Opus Dei in this special task of service.

Escrivá had enormous love for his daughters in the administration. He showed it with many signs of affection and in the special concern he showed for them. He was always ready to pitch in and get his hands dirty to help them out. One day, when he happened to notice one of his daughters hesitating before a messy job, he took the bucket out of her hand and began to do it himself. "My daughter," he said, "I am not doing this without a reason, but because I am your father and mother — since you had no foundress — and because I have to teach you. I would like you to leave everything spotless; you should be able to see your reflection."[38] Under a dripping faucet he saw a small puddle that the young woman had not noticed. He took a wash rag and wiped it up. "That's the way to do it, my daughter: with a silent prayer to Our Lord or to Our Lady — perhaps for your sisters, for your Father, for whatever — but always with a love of God."[39]

This love expresses itself not in sporadic fireworks, but in the minutiae of daily life — minutiae that come together in a splendid mosaic. Neglect of the tiniest matters could upset Escrivá, because he saw such neglect as a direct offense against the very essence of Opus Dei. There was, for example, the time he visited the women's center on Lagasca St. Upon entering a room with four large cupboards, he noticed that one of them did not close properly. "Such a thing must not be!" he exclaimed. "Where is the presence of God here?" The next cupboard was in disarray. Anger began to arise in him. Then he happened to glance at the table, where the groceries were still lying about. "You must have a sense of responsibility, in everything!" he shouted. Then he recollected himself. "Lord, forgive me," he prayed, and then he turned toward the young lady beside him. "My daughter, you too forgive me," he said. "No, Father, you are right," she stammered; to which he responded, "Yes, what I said is correct, but I should not have said it in that tone of voice."[40]

Priestly soul and lay mentality

It has often been said, and quite truthfully, that Escrivá not only founded but *was* Opus Dei. For more than a decade, he was its sole representative. Only after the Civil War was he able to delegate the religious education and spiritual formation of new members to some of the older numeraries — such as Isidoro Zorzano (who died in 1943), Alvaro del Portillo, Ricardo Vallespín, and Pedro Casciaro — and others who were able to spread Opus Dei and to shoulder the tasks of leadership. The number of members sharing in their founder's grace of foundation increased, but there was one insurmountable barrier: what Escrivá called the "sacramental wall." The growth of Opus Dei made it impossible for Escrivá to hear all the members' confessions, so they had to confess to any priest available. Because frequent confession is an important part of the spiritual formation of Opus Dei, this presented a serious problem. The essence of Opus Dei, the quest for holiness in ordinary life, includes fighting against venial sin, personal frailty, and omissions. The most important weapon in this battle is the sacramental presence of Christ in the Eucharist and in confession. As long as Escrivá was the only priest in

Opus Dei, however, this dimension of the ascetical struggle lay mostly in the hands of the priests whose assistance he had to solicit.

Of course, any Catholic can validly receive the sacrament of Reconciliation from any Catholic priest.[41] The advice, encouragement, and instruction of a faithful Catholic priest will always be profitable and should be heeded. For members of Opus Dei, however, confession is also a chance to go deeper into the lay and secular spirituality of Opus Dei. One cannot expect a priest who knows little or nothing about Opus Dei to be able to provide a thorough, in-depth formation in it. Misunderstandings may arise, for example, regarding venial sins, the thousand small failings of every day that, insofar as they concern the conscientious fulfillment of one's daily duties, are a touchstone to one's fidelity to the vocation. A priest unfamiliar with Opus Dei might too readily assume that his penitent was afflicted with scrupulosity. For sixteen years, Escrivá himself was in this unfortunate position. According to his own testimony, he confessed at least once a week (occasionally two or three times), and he liked to add, "I am definitely not scrupulous, but I know what my soul needs."[42] He loved his confessors. José María García Lahiguera (later the archbishop of Valencia), to whom Escrivá confessed from 1940 to 1944, wrote in 1976, "He was not a complicated, but rather a simple, upright, straightforward soul. Every confessor knows that those who confess briefly are the most thoughtful. He talked to me, I talked to him — period."[43] After more than thirty years, the bishop still recalled a trait of Escrivá's that he had particularly appreciated: "He never presented himself as the poor victim."[44]

It was obvious that Opus Dei would need priests from its own family in order to continue its progress in the world. These priests, coming from among the laymen in Opus Dei, would combine with their sacramental priesthood the "priestly soul/lay mentality"[45] that is characteristic of all members of Opus Dei. This solution, of course, presented a difficult pastoral problem with serious practical, theological, and canonical ramifications. How could laymen in Opus Dei become priests without compromising the integrity of the vocation to Opus Dei? But this much was certain: The divine reason for the founding of Opus Dei was to rejuvenate Christianity, to renew it in the spirit and after the example of the early Christians, by forming a specific spiritual family that would, like the early Christians, understand the world and everyday life as the raw material for the sanctity and sanctification desired by God.

Through the grace of baptism, every Christian — single or married, lay person or priest — possesses a priestly soul. Opus Dei rediscovered this universal priesthood of all believers, which differs in character from the sacramental priesthood, but likewise arises from Christ's life in the soul. (Here Escrivá's teaching anticipated one of the central doctrines of Vatican II.) At the same time, all members of Opus Dei must have a lay outlook: they must seek sanctity and do apostolate through their professional work and their responsibilities as citizens of the world. To strive for holiness does not require any change of status. In short, in Opus Dei the layman struggles for sanctity as a layman, the secular priest as a secular priest.[46] The numeraries called to the priesthood (relatively few of the total number) need not experience an identity crisis, because their vocation to Opus Dei remains unchanged. As Escrivá made clear, ordination does not change the essence of the vocation. The "lay mentality" of the priest includes performing his professional work, his priestly duties, as perfectly as possible. Because they have led professional lives before being ordained, this lay outlook comes naturally to Opus Dei priests, and it immunizes them against the dangers of clericalism. They are not at all likely to interfere in matters incompatible with their priestly status, matters that should be the sole responsibility of lay people.

Escrivá himself possessed this lay outlook that he so vigorously advocated. As a priest who talked only about God, he always respected freedom of conscience and refused to "commandeer" souls or to interfere in matters outside his competence. He rejected clerical privileges. He wanted, he said, to live "in the cassock, but never off the cassock."[47] He abhorred the idea of laymen becoming pseudo-clerics, but he abhorred just as much the idea of priests becoming politicians, economists, and secular scientists. In his mind, a lay person hovering about the sacristy personified a harmful clericalism, while a cleric dedicated to worldly activities embodied an equally pernicious secularism. "I am anticlerical," he said in 1972, "because I love priests."[48]

His message that the world must be sanctified by ordinary Christians challenged the accepted notion that sanctity necessitates a new status of professional dedication to perfection and a retreat from the world ("world" understood as the realm whose prince is the "adversary"). While Escrivá certainly held holy orders in the highest esteem, he knew it is not a *sine qua non* for following Christ perfectly. He held in high regard the period in Church history when the religious orders, from the bastion of *contemptus mundi*, penetrated society in a most pronounced and blessed way, through their prayer, sacrifices, hospitals, schools, and missions — services they are still rendering and will continue to render in the future. On the other hand, he was not oblivious to the changes in society calling for new approaches to evangelization and sanctification. In today's world, the apostolate of religious orders can sometimes reach its limit quickly, because of increased specialization and the incompatibility of such professional specialization with the religious state. And even in Catholic countries, the secularization of all fields limits the orders' presence and efficacy.[49]

It is no accident that in this age of secularization and materialism, Divine Providence has entrusted the task of evangelization to souls who cannot be excluded by prohibitions, or decrees, because they are just everyday, mainstream citizens. "My children," wrote Escrivá, "we can honestly say that the anxiety and responsibility for the whole Church lies with us. When we support the official responsibility of the pope and the bishops, which is a legal responsibility of divine right, we serve the whole Church, not with a legal but with a divine and ascetical responsibility, because of love; then we serve the Church with a professional service, because we are citizens who carry the Christian witness of example and teaching into the farthest corners of society."[50]

What today sounds simple and obvious seemed radical and daring in the 1940s. How there could be a unity of priestly soul and lay mentality within the sacramental priesthood was not immediately clear. For almost a decade, the three young men first ordained in Opus Dei had followed their vocation as laymen in the world. The call to the priesthood might well have seemed contradictory to their original vocation. What today is readily apparent to everyone,

Escrivá had to explain to his sons step by step. And on June 25, 1944, when these three became priests, Escrivá himself had mixed feelings. "I love the lay character of our work so much," he said, "that it hurts me to destine these sons of mine to become clerics. On the other hand, the need for priests within Opus Dei was so obvious that it must have been pleasing to God when they approached the altar."[51]

Besides the problem of training laymen to become priests, another difficulty had presented itself: Opus Dei had not yet been approved by the universal Church, but merely by the bishop of Madrid. (To assist Opus Dei against slanderous attacks, he had, on March 19, 1941, recognized it as a pious association within his diocese). Although Escrivá did not yet see how this Gordian knot could be untied, he nevertheless had full confidence that God's grace would open the right doors. With this certainty, he had the three above-mentioned young men begin preparation for the priesthood. They were José Hernández de Garnica, José Luis Múzquiz, and Alvaro del Portillo. All three of them were in their late twenties; all three were engineers who had joined Opus Dei before the Civil War.

With the bishop's energetic help, Escrivá assembled a college of distinguished theologians, mostly Dominicans. It came close to qualifying as a private university. The curriculum had to conform, of course, to the general requirements for clerics in Spain. The young men were spared nothing: they had to take the Grand Latinum and philosophy exams in the Madrid seminary, as well as theology exams before tribunals of three professors each in the Diego de León center. Not only did Escrivá follow their studies with paternal encouragement, but he also impressed on them, in their daily dealings, the image of a priest that he himself embodied. "The dominant passion of the priests of Opus Dei," he wrote in 1945, "must be preaching and the hearing of confessions. That is their service and their specific task — the reason for their priesthood."[52] Twenty-five years later, when the Church was troubled by controversy and confusion after the Second Vatican Council, he said, "A priest who stands to the left? One who leans to the right? One who is somewhere in the middle? No, there are no priests of either the middle, the left, or the right; there are only priests of God. Only as a priest of God can a priest serve all souls; and only thus can he defend personal freedom in secular matters, and in all that the Lord entrusts to people's free will."[53]

The foundation of the Priestly Society of the Holy Cross, like that of the women's branch, occurred during Mass on February 14th. "After I had searched for years, without success, for a legal solution," recalled Escrivá, "the Lord gave it to me in clear detail. When I finished celebrating Mass, I was able to speak of the Priestly Society of the Holy Cross."[54] Encarnación Ortega reports that after Mass, Escrivá went into the library of the house and asked for some paper; in a few minutes he reappeared, obviously excited. "Here, look!" he said, and showed them a sheet of paper on which he had sketched a circle with a well-proportioned cross fit into it. "This will be the seal of the Work. Not a coat of arms; no, Opus Dei has no coat of arms, but a seal that shows the world and, planted in the midst of it, the cross." Together with the rose of Rialp, this symbol — a perfect graphic definition of Opus Dei — is seen in many centers and on many altars of Opus Dei.

Through the energetic support of Bishop Leopoldo, the new branch on the trunk of Opus Dei received the approval of the Roman Curia on October 11, 1943. This was the first legal recognition by the Holy See of Opus Dei on the diocesan level. Now the way was free for the ordination of numeraries to the priesthood. (By the time of Escrivá's death, there were about a thousand priests in Opus Dei.) The full name of Opus Dei then became the Societas Sacerdotalis Sanctae Crucis et Opus Dei. This was to remain its formal title until it became a personal prelature in 1982.

On June 25, 1944, the bishop of Madrid ordained the three men in his own chapel. It was a great moment in the history of Opus Dei, but Escrivá was not there. He wished to avoid anything, particularly on this day of triumph, that might make him the center of attention, admiration, and praise. According to the testimony for his beatification, "he stuck to his normal daily schedule." This astonished Bishop Leopoldo, who asked later where Escrivá had really been. He was told, "During the ordination, he celebrated Mass and prayed for the three new priests. José María Albareda assisted him. They were alone in the chapel of the Lagasca center, praying and giving thanks."[55] The next day, Escrivá was the first person to confess to Don Alvaro del Portillo, who from then on was his regular confessor.

The secularity of a secular priest consists in his seeing and fulfilling his priestly service within the context, the very texture, of everyday life — including its demand for professional competence. This principle was the key that opened the doors of Opus Dei to secular priests. During the years just after the Civil War, many Spanish bishops asked Escrivá to give days of recollection and spiritual exercises for their diocesan priests, and he soon became one of the most sought-after priests in Spain. His deep love for his fellow priests impelled him not only to accept the bishops' invitations with joy, but also to refuse no sacrifice in this service. (It was for a priests' retreat that he had to leave the side of his sick mother, who died in his absence.[56]) He constantly pondered the possibility of incorporating diocesan priests into Opus Dei. Toward the end of the forties, he even considered leaving Opus Dei to found a separate institution that would be dedicated to the sanctification of diocesan priests.[57] However, he was spared this sacrifice, because that need found an answer in the Priestly Society of the Holy Cross: in consequence of the final approval of Opus Dei as an institution under papal law, it became possible for diocesan clerics to join Opus Dei. A particularly urgent wish of Escrivá's was thus fulfilled. And the fruits were not long in coming. "The real miracle of the fifties in our country," the counsellor of Opus Dei in Spain told me, "was the explosive increase in vocations of associate and supernumerary priests to the Work."[58]

Misunderstandings

I am a historian, and though I am far from knowing history, I believe I possess a certain eye for basic patterns resulting from the nature of the human race and the conditions of earthly life: relatively stable values that have formed the basis for human behavior throughout history. One of these constants is that every endeavor encounters opposition. Ideas and movements invite contradiction, especially from opportunists, tacticians, and pragmatists — people who base their actions and attitudes primarily on fashion and opinion, as dictated by the media. Human nature being what it is, one cannot afford to feel superior to people who are thus carried away by every gust of popular opinion. Tolerance has its limits, however, when justice, decency, virtue, the family, and society hang in the balance, when what is at stake is nothing less than the salvation of souls. Those who think passively and regurgitate shallow theories, instead of personally seeking truth and justice, easily become pawns in the game of history. In contrast, there is no telling how far a person might get who honestly struggles for knowledge and judgment; the grace of the Holy Spirit is a great help, flooding the intellect with supernatural light.

I mention these things by way of introduction to a short discussion of opposition to Opus Dei. Most of the nonsense that excited Spain forty years ago would be boring to read about now. In the long run, however, I would say that there is one main thread running through whatever opposition Opus Dei has encountered through the years, and that is this: people have a problem with simplicity. Let's face it, it is a very difficult and uncomfortable challenge to human nature to take a simple, direct, uncompromising approach to Christianity that involves conversion of one's entire being. It is easy to be critical of people who shy away from this kind of commitment and settle instead for learning to speak and think in highly sophisticated, avant-garde theologisms, but who of us can honestly claim immunity from this temptation? It is far from easy to live up to the standards of *Humanae Vitae* or the many social justice encyclicals. It takes a great deal of grace and fortitude to take a resolutely forthright approach rather than retreat through the back door of circuitous reasoning. I believe this is what people really mean when they tell me they find the meditations of Opus Dei "primitive," or its theology "unoriginal"; just going ahead and *doing* the truth can be a very disconcerting thing.

From the autobiography of St. Teresa of Avila, we know that she suffered much from the suspicion, misunderstanding, and unfriendly judgments of people who were themselves good, pious, and desirous of holiness.[59] A similar thing happened to Escrivá. Spain is Catholic bedrock. The richness and depth of its native piety and creative Catholic vigor are unsurpassed throughout the world. Its life, land, and history are so tightly packed with monasteries, convents, clerics, orders, processions, saints' feasts, and folk piety that the idea of encouraging lay people to make a serious attempt at intimacy with Christ during the workday seemed at first to be downright redundant. As a Spaniard, you were by definition Catholic; that was not a matter for further reflection, especially among liberal intellectuals. I am reminded here of what an Italian friend said to me: "Though I don't actually believe in God, it's still obvious that I'm a Catholic."

An enthusiastic call to fulfill one's Christian vocation in the world would often get a response like this: "But what do you want from me? I am already a Catholic." Nowhere has this response ever been as common as it was in Escrivá's Spain. Often the reply was not even articulated; hearts and minds were simply impervious to his message. "What is he really after?" people would ask themselves. "This 'sanctification of work' reeks of Protestantism! And don't we already have hordes of priests and nuns whose vocation it is to accept Christ unconditionally? Good heavens, the Catholic faith is the state religion; it saturates our education and culture. What more can Escrivá want?" If Opus Dei had fought *en masse* for Catholic culture, press, or education, shoulder to shoulder with other Catholic organizations, it would at least have been understood. When Escrivá rejected such collaboration (even in a friendly way, with great respect for others' projects), he alienated many people. Opus Dei in Spain was really caught between a rock and a hard place. On the one hand, secularists wished to radically curtail the influence of the Church. On the other hand, the more militant Catholics were shocked by Escrivá and distrusted him.[60] They did not understand the essence of the apostolate of Opus Dei — it never works as a group for causes, nor does it issue directives for professional, civic, or social life. Each member cooperates with such causes and institutions according to his or her own judgment. By the very nature of the Work, members cannot form "Opus Dei groups," or participate collectively in political, social, or ecclesiastical life.

Some early opposition to Escrivá, and to his followers' way of being Christian, came from members of religious orders and members of Catholic organizations committed to a traditional institutionalism. At no time, however, was this group a majority or even a large number. Some people were simply unable to understand the essence of Escrivá's message. Teachings now generally accepted as fruits of Vatican II — the responsibility of the laity in the Church, the universal call to sanctity, the personal freedom and responsibility of individual Christians with regard to secular issues, daily life as the normal arena for full dedication to Christ — sounded at the time like heresy.

When Joseph Cardinal Frings, then archbishop of Cologne, visited Spain and Portugal in the summer of 1952, he met in Madrid with Bishop Leopoldo Eijo y Garay. "The bishop of Madrid," reports the cardinal in his memoirs, "told me in detail about the founding of Opus Dei. One day a Jesuit had come to him and said, 'Excellency, do you know, a new heresy has started: Opus Dei.'" Bishop Leopoldo, however, had replied that he had already investigated the matter and given it his approval, and that he had in fact always supported Opus Dei. The cardinal also describes his visit to an Opus Dei residence and mentions similar houses in Cologne, especially the women's residence. "The latter," he recalls, "was set up by Carmen Mouriz, who lived in Germany for a long time and moved to Rome only last year. From her I learned that in the beginning some people had reproached the founder of Opus Dei, Msgr. Escrivá, for teaching that the laity, on the basis of baptism and confirmation, are obliged to give witness for Christ in the world. Msgr. Escrivá, who is still living today [1973], has pointed out with joy and satisfaction that the Second Vatican Council espoused and openly proclaimed these ideas of his."[61]

During the forties, a small but very active group of Spaniards waged a campaign against Opus Dei and Escrivá. Hard to believe but true, this opposition stemmed in large part from jealousy — a jealousy of the strong apostolic appeal this young spiritual family was exerting throughout Spain. From jealousy to envy is a small step, but a grave one, since it is a crossover from mere weakness to the vice of malice. So, for instance, in the families of those in contact with Opus Dei, mistrust and suspicion were deliberately sown, often with deliberately slanderous intent. The subject of the slander, varying from case to case, was not and is not the main point; slander is slander. At that time, Escrivá's book *The Way* was publicly burned as a danger to souls, and warnings were issued about "renewers" who were supposedly attempting to destroy religious orders and replace them with a new status within the Church. It was even suggested that Opus Dei was a dangerous kind of freemasonry.

Slanders do have a life of their own, usually acquired by attachment to the intellectual trend of the day. Fortunately, however, slander often backfires, though some lies always manage to stick. In spite of all adversity, Opus Dei grew rapidly in Spain during the forties and fifties. And although some Spanish sacristies fostered genuine hatred, Opus Dei was blessed with a veritable torrent of vocations.

The enemies of Opus Dei were a minority, but they were not without influence. After 1937, all the bishops and Catholic organizations in Spain supported the Franco regime; personal political sentiment aside, this support did seem necessary to the survival of Spanish Catholicism. In this situation, it was inevitable that the insinuations of certain Falangist spokesmen against the Work should have aroused hostility towards Opus Dei within the party as a whole. It seemed suspicious to some Falangists that Escrivá proclaimed the universality of Opus Dei, that he energetically championed personal freedom, and that he absolutely refused to link dedication to Christ with a particular political stand. They could not understand Escrivá's loving Jews as much as any other race — and perhaps a little bit more — just because Jesus, Mary, Joseph, and the apostles were Jews; or why he did not place Opus Dei at the service of the "new Spain."[62] They suspected him of internationalism, anti-Spainism, and freemasonry. Such misunderstandings became dangerous when national passions ran high and Franco demanded a "strong state."

It was many years before the passions stirred by the Civil War abated. In the final analysis, Franco — in spite of his personal faults and those inherent in his political system — did further the process of recovery. Favored by the vigorous maturity of the postwar generation, Spain finally entered modern times. However, the ecstasy of the 1939 victory brought with it an urge to forge in Spain a party unity on civic and religious matters.[63] To such an attitude there could have been no more direct a contradiction than Escrivá's notion of personal liberty. In 1970 he declared, "If Opus Dei had ever played politics — even for a minute — I would have left the Work at that very moment of error. For, on the one hand, our means and aims are always and exclusively of a supernatural character. On the other hand, every single member, man or woman, possesses in secular matters an absolute personal freedom — respected by all — as well as the personal responsibility that follows as a logical consequence. Therefore it is impossible that Opus Dei would ever be associated with undertakings which are not of an explicitly spiritual and apostolic nature."[64]

Although Escrivá constantly reiterated and guarded this principle, "Franco-philia" has proven itself the most tenacious charge against Opus Dei. The truth is far different. During the first decade of Franco's regime, Opus Dei and Escrivá were attacked with a perseverance bordering on fanaticism, not by the enemies but by the supporters of the new Spanish state. Escrivá was even reported to the "Tribunal for the Fight against Freemasonry." In this case, as in others, the accusation was thrown out for lack of evidence. Sometimes it was a closer call; there was, for example, a time (in the early forties, in Barcelona) when Escrivá was in danger of being arrested.[65] The most damaging thing, however, was the continuous dissemination of warnings that youths were being drawn away from normal, orthodox Catholicism. Escrivá suffered all of this patiently; he prayed for those who attacked him and the Work, and warned members of Opus Dei against anger, bitterness, noisy confrontation, and discouragement.

The testimony of José López Ortiz, titular bishop of Grado, which he composed for Escrivá's beatification process, pinpoints the origin of this opposition to Opus Dei. "About 1941," he writes, "we began to recognize certain patterns. The main attacks were coming from the direction of several clergymen who with envious eyes noticed that an apostolate was spreading that was not their own; these men allowed jealousy to master them. Further opposition came from university professors who distorted the apostolate that Opus Dei was performing among intellectuals. To this opposition was added, as early as 1942, the Falange, which wanted to politicize the Work."[66] López Ortiz records one particularly grotesque and absurd attempt at character assassination. Some members of Opus Dei, to give their cultural and apostolic activities some basis in civil law, had founded a society called "Socoin," — an acronym for "Sociedad de Colaboración Intelectual." Now a certain professor of public law came forward to report that he had found the secret meaning of the abbreviation in a Hebrew dictionary. In this rabbinical dictionary, the word "Socoim" was given as the name of a sect of murderers, or something of that sort. Starting from there and ignoring such trifles as the difference between "n" and "m," the professor spread the word that Opus Dei was "a Jewish sect of freemasons," or at least "a Jewish sect connected with freemasonry."[67] In spite of their obvious absurdity, such tales had unpleasant consequences.

A good number of the young people educated by Escrivá eventually reached prominent professional positions; some held professorial chairs at universities. These professors soon began to meet with suspicion and mistrust from certain Catholic factions that were jealously guarding their position as the "official Catholic presence" within the universities. These groups projected typical behind-the-scenes rules of conduct — favoritism and infighting — on the behavior of members of Opus Dei. They could not believe that the professional advancement of Opus Dei members was not the fruit of political maneuvers, but a logical result of the spirituality of Opus Dei, which emphasizes personal sanctification through well-done professional work.

Antonio Fontán, who was a president of the senate in the young monarchy of King Juan Carlos, has commented on this rather dim view of academic professional advancement. It would have been strange, he says, if there had not been any members of Opus Dei on the faculties of Spanish universities; it was not at all remarkable that there were some. But the reports in the press that Opus Dei members exercised "collectively a virtual dictatorship over the Spanish university" and held in their hands "the key to the occupation of professorial chairs" were bald-faced lies.[68] Granted, a basic misunderstanding was involved that had grown out of ignorance. There had been a careless mixing of gossip and factual information — and, of course, occasional resentment over professional failure. The truth, however, is this: nobody has become a university professor in Spain by belonging to Opus Dei, but many professors are members of Opus Dei. And that is the most natural thing in the world.

Fr. Escrivá visiting the mother of Francisco and Jacinta at Fatima in 1945. With him (left to right) are Fr. Alvaro del Portillo, Bishop José López Ortiz, and a Fr. Galamba.

Fontán goes on to explain the persistence of myths about Opus Dei's secret, dangerous power in universities. He says, "The appearance of Opus Dei in the life of Spain came as a surprise to many people. Opus Dei had existed since 1928 and was never a secret, but its apostolic activity and the personal initiatives of its members reached the general consciousness of the public only some years later, when they gained stature in educational and professional work.[69] Ordinarily, the fact that someone belongs to Opus Dei is known only to family and friends. This was hard for poorly informed people to understand."[70] In those days, people could not imagine Opus Dei as being something truly different from the existing establishments in the Church, as having norms and customs unlike those of religious orders and congregations. Because they were unaware of its uniqueness, they assumed that what was going on must be sinister intrigues and the machinations of a secret society.

Laureano Castán Lacoma, bishop of Sigüenza-Guadalajara, claims that many people did not understand something that had become clear to him in conversations with Escrivá: namely, that the

most praiseworthy of Christian actions is secondary in importance
to, and nothing without, the personal conversion of a soul to God
and that soul's resolve to give itself totally to him while still in the
world. In short, useful Christian activities can bear full fruit only in
the context of radically personal conversion.[71] Many activists have
unconsciously built up a social project as an escape from, or a substitute for, total surrender to God. Escrivá's attitude was bound to
hit a sensitive nerve or two.

According to the bishop, the wariness many Catholics have
toward the idea of seeking sanctity in the world involves two false
assumptions: (1) good Catholics are not obliged to such holiness,
because sanctity is a matter for religious orders; and (2) the universal call to holiness might hurt the Church by emptying seminaries
and novitiates. (This last attitude was at that time fairly common
among members of religious orders.)[72] Such thoughts are admittedly understandable, but they are based on an error regarding the
nature and variety of vocations. It is not true that someone who
marries might just as well have embraced celibacy, or that whoever
comes to Opus Dei could, under other circumstances, have become
a monk. The grace of vocation does not come from a divine piñata,
where each person grabs something at will and then decides to keep
it, trade it in, throw it away, or whatever. Christ calls each person by
name to a specific vocation. Whomever he calls to Opus Dei, a religious order, the secular priesthood, marriage, or any other vocation,
he has called once and for all. It is absurd to suppose that suppress-
ing Opus Dei would stimulate vocations to religious orders. The
same logic would suggest that as more marriages break apart, more
people will flock to the religious orders.

Many did not realize that Escrivá had no problem loving and
admiring what he did not choose for himself. His heart and mind
were quite capable of selfless objectivity. Augustinians, Carmelites,
Jesuits, modern congregations — he loved them all. For years, the
Jesuit Father Valentín Ruiz was his confessor, and in his capacity as
their spiritual director, Escrivá advised many souls to seek their
vocation in religious orders.[73] Yet he steadfastly maintained that he
himself, according to God's will, could not have been a member of
an order, and that Opus Dei was not a religious order.

He was without prejudice regarding secular organizations, provided they were not enemies of the Church. Here his relationship with Angel Herrera is particularly revealing. Born in 1886, in Santander, Herrera studied law and became an important journalist. More to the point, he also became a leader of a Catholic Action political movement. (In 1940 he became a priest. Seven years later, he became bishop of Malaga, and in 1965 he was made a cardinal. He died in 1968.) As president of the National Catholic Association of Defenders of the Faith, he hoped to find an ally in Opus Dei. He was impressed by the young members he had met, and he wanted them to join his movement. In two or three long discussions with Escrivá, Herrera argued that they should work together for the good of the Church. Since his organization and Opus Dei shared the same ideals, they should join together, and then the members of Opus Dei would also be Defenders of the Faith. Evidently it was not easy to convince Herrera that Opus Dei did not operate in closed ranks; that because they were left completely free in all political matters, there was no possibility of Escrivá's "marshaling" members of the Work; that the alliance of Opus Dei with a political movement was out of the question.[74] Herrera, a politician through and through, could not understand Escrivá's political abstinence. It seemed otherworldly, and Opus Dei's personal approach to apostolate seemed ineffective.

It is impossible to completely understand Escrivá and Opus Dei without first appreciating his extraordinary regard for the personal freedom of each individual. In this connection, López Ortiz has quoted two statements of Escrivá that bear repeating. The first one is this: "The innate human freedom to decide upon one's own actions, including political ones, is fundamental to the Work. For the sake of deeper spirituality, much is demanded of those who come to the Work, but whatever does not concern this spirituality remains untouched. Complete freedom reigns, so that they can serve God wherever they want. If they want to carry out some political project, I will not interfere. If one has this political opinion and another has that, I merely warn them that these differences must never go against charity; that with all our differences of political opinion, charity must be preserved. And I also see to it that nobody tries to make a personal opinion a norm for the rest of the

Work, because that is not what it is; rather, it is just the concern of that one person. Complete freedom within the guidelines that the Church proclaims for all Catholics!"[75] And the second statement is this: "As far as politics is concerned, I can neither impose nor recommend anything to those who are in contact with the Work. In their relationship with God and in their spirituality, yes, but not in regard to political preferences: to each his own. There is an element of freedom in temporal matters that is sacred to me."[76]

Exercising this freedom, some members of Opus Dei did in fact help the Defenders of the Faith, and others served as ministers in Franco's government. These ministers are frequently cited as evidence of the fascism of Opus Dei. Not only is this a gross slander against Opus Dei, it also reflects a naive image of Franco as a fascist bogeyman. Franco's government is best understood as having been a last, rather anachronistic, attempt to create an authoritarian, clerical-minded technocracy. Far from ideal? Without a doubt. But let's face it, the moral rectitude of Western democracies is hardly of such a caliber that we can afford to throw stones.

In 1957, Franco restructured his cabinet with a view toward restoring the economy of Spain and guiding the nation toward a modern fiscal system. With such purposes in mind, he appointed a number of talented young bankers and economists.[77] Four of them were members of Opus Dei. Alberto Ullastres Calvo, a professor of world economic history at the University of Madrid, became Minister of Trade; Laureano López Rodo, a thirty-seven-year-old scientist, became Technological Secretary of the State Department; Mariano Navarro Rubio, the managing director of People's Bank, took over the Treasury Department; and in 1962, Gregorio López Bravo Castro became Minister of Industry. Sociologists call this the technocratic era in Franco's regime, because of the shift of emphasis from ideological to practical concerns. But if this was indeed a technocratic era, members of Opus Dei were by no means its only technocrats. There was, for example, the young lawyer from the University of Madrid, Manuel Fraga Iribarne, who transformed the Ministry of Information and Tourism into something incomparably more important than the name suggests. Since I am not writing a history of Spain under Franco, I cannot describe the many accomplishments of these young men. Suffice it to say that within a short period of time, they helped make Spain a modern state with an efficient and productive economy. The members of Opus Dei who were involved acted within their rights as free citizens of the state. Dedication to Christ, fidelity to the Church, and the particular spirituality of Opus Dei did not preclude service to their country. There was historical precedent for such action, and there was nothing criminal about it. The contention that Christians can work only for Anglo-American and Jacobean democracies is an absurdly arrogant parochialism.[78]

But there was never any question of a political bandwagon. In fact, some members of Opus Dei were alienated from Franco and worked for political change: Professor Rafael Calvo Serer, for example, who was arrested several times. And Escrivá never boasted of his followers in the cabinet. When (in 1957) a cardinal felt obliged to congratulate him on the honor of the appointment of one of these new young ministers, Escrivá responded somewhat brusquely, "It does not concern me. He could be a chimney sweep, for all I care. The only thing of interest to me is whether he sanctifies himself in his work."[79] Actually, all told, very few members of Opus Dei have been active in politics. But whether or not they engage in politics, as well as what opinions they hold, is entirely up to them. It is a matter of individual conscience and discretion; it does not involve the other members of this spiritual family.

At the beginning of this chapter, I mentioned Escrivá's emigration to Rome. He had come to the conclusion that Opus Dei belonged in Rome, near the Chair of Peter. That was to be his home and office, not only because Opus Dei needed papal approval and some provisional legal status within the Church, but also because, although born and raised in Spain, it belonged to the world, to the universal Church, and therefore to Rome. Escrivá saw the mission of Christ in the world as being indissolubly linked to the Chair of Peter. Furthermore, the time had come to leave Spain. His presence there provided too convenient a focus for hostility against the Work; as Scripture says, "I will strike the shepherd, and the sheep will be scattered" (Mt 26:31). He left his country because it could not afford him the freedom he needed to bring Opus Dei to the rest of the world. It was a painful decision, because Escrivá loved his country, but he had to obey the demands of his vocation. He was not an emigré in the traditional sense of the word — he visited his homeland almost every year. But he was an apostle to the world in the great tradition of Paul, Ignatius of Loyola, and Francis Xavier; like them he encircled the world with the message of Christ. And he was also like Augustine, Thomas Aquinas, and Francis de Sales, in that his apostolic impact was made through a broad spiritual influence that took many forms.

Chapter Seven

ROMAN AND MARIAN

The approved revolution

Eight weeks after Escrivá's death, Cardinal Frings, who had been archbishop of Cologne from 1942 to 1967, wrote a letter to Pope Paul VI. He described the founder of Opus Dei as a pioneer of lay spirituality who had clearly perceived the necessities and dangers of the times, and predicted that the Work would be of decisive importance for the future of the Church.[1] The pope did not by now need any persuasion; for him the question had been settled several years earlier.[2] He was already firmly convinced of Escrivá's extraordinary position in Church history. As a substitute in the Secretariat of State, he had helped the Spanish priest, then completely unknown in Rome, to negotiate the frequently tortuous paths of the Curia. He had helped to obtain for Escrivá a private audience with Pope Pius XII on December 8 (Feast of the Immaculate Conception), 1946. He had also given him advice and assistance during the establishment of the central house of Opus Dei in Rome, and had promoted his designation as a papal domestic prelate, which took place on April 22, 1947.[3]

Just the bare sequence of dates gives pause for reflection and allows one to sense something of the unbelievable intensity that must have been characteristic of Opus Dei's founder. His first stay in Rome lasted only nine and a half weeks, from June 23 to August 31, 1946. He spent the autumn in Spain and returned to Rome on November 8, 1946 — this time to stay permanently for the twenty-nine years that would make up the second half of his life. Considering how rare it is for an institution as well-rehearsed over the centuries as the Roman Curia to act with anything approaching impulsiveness, one can only marvel at the relative speed with which things proceeded in this case. It took only four weeks for Opus Dei to be granted its first papal audience, three months to obtain the *Decretum Laudis* (on February 24, 1947), five months for Escrivá to receive his designation as a domestic prelate, and three years for Opus Dei to be given full approval (in the summer of 1950).

Until November 28, 1982, when the Work became a personal prelature, the special approval of the Work was based on a general foundation that had had to be created for it. The apostolic constitution *Provida Mater*,[4] dated February 2 (Feast of the Presentation), 1947, preceded the *Decretum Laudis* by only three weeks. One of Escrivá's many gifts was a sense of how to combine the boldest and farthest-reaching dreams with brass-tack reality. He had always known when to drive ahead and when to wait, in just the way each situation and separate problem might require. He recognized, as soon as it came out, that *Provida Mater* provided an adequate basis for the legal anchoring of Opus Dei in the Church, and that it was the most that could then be achieved in view of the novelty of, and the pastoral problems created by, the explicit commitment of lay people to perfect holiness. It was a great, courageous step into the future. Nevertheless, he realized that whatever practical applications and benefits might flow from this constitution — the above-mentioned *Decretum Laudis*, for example, and the full approval of Opus Dei on June 16 (Feast of the Sacred Heart of Jesus), 1950 — it could not really do justice to the original charism and living reality of the Work.

Provida Mater is basically a kind of legal framework. Its purpose is to establish and fix in very general terms the canon-law prerequisites for a new Church entity to be known as the "secular institute." The document consists of a historical and legal introduction embracing thirteen points, and then ten articles explicating the "particular law for secular institutes." The structure adapted by any individual secular institute must fit into this framework.

Anyone who reads the constitution impartially today will surely conclude that in spite of all its good intentions — to keep pace with the times, to support and strengthen a striving for perfection by lay Christians in the world, and so forth — the fundamental view seems to be that what is at issue is just a modern variation of the classical ideal of the religious order. One gets the impression of an attempt to apply by adaptation the statutes of a religious order to the secular affairs of lay people. What we have here seems to be a sort of parallel model for people in the world who are striving for "higher" things. In complete conformity to the traditional understanding of religious life, the "evangelical counsels" (the vows of poverty, chastity, and obedience) are emphasized.[5] In fact, every secular institute is subjected to the Congregation for Religious.[6]

Despite all its limitations, however, *Provida Mater* is what enabled the Work to become, within three weeks, an institute under papal jurisdiction, and to expand throughout the entire world with the blessing of the Church hierarchy. As early as 1948, the founder of Opus Dei sent some of his spiritual sons to North and South America to establish contact with the local bishops and to prepare the way for apostolic work. Opus Dei was now able to take its first steps across the Atlantic: in 1949, to Mexico and the United States; in early 1950, to Chile and Argentina. In Europe, it was now represented in five countries in addition to Spain: Portugal, Italy, and England since 1945; France and Ireland since 1947. Everything always proceeded just as it had in the early days in Spain. Three or four young men, among them a priest, would arrive with a few suitcases, funds for one month at most, a couple of addresses, an inexhaustible supply of good humor; love for the Holy Father in Rome, for the Church, for everyone; patience, inventiveness, and a willingness to do hard work. They always took up professional work immediately (or, if they were students, their studies); often they were forced to earn their living with great difficulty. Usually members of the women's branch followed them after one or two years.

That the unity of vocation in Opus Dei was recognized in theory and applied in practice as its governing principle — equally valid for men and women, laity and clergy, celibates and couples — was certainly due to Escrivá's powers of persuasion, supported by the prayer of his whole spiritual family. But it also owed much to the benevolence and foresight of the Curia. Shortly after the *Decretum Laudis* was promulgated (in 1947), it became possible for married men and women to be received into the Work, in accordance with the guidelines established by the Holy See. This was just eighteen and a half years after the foundation. In the early years after the foundational dates of October 2, 1928, and February 14, 1930, Escrivá had understandably concentrated on winning and forming a nucleus of numerary vocations. Beginning in the mid-thirties, however, his apostolic endeavors were also directed toward the religious formation of those Christians who would one day belong to Opus Dei as married members, and who would even — of this he was completely sure — come to constitute its majority.

As it ever was, human society is now and ever will be based on the family, as prescribed by natural law and revelation. For all Christians, therefore, the opening of Opus Dei to married people had tremendous significance. It could now be said to be anchored biologically in humanity. To be sure, it is and always will be a spiritual family; but because this spiritual family is essentially linked to the natural family — and even in part consists of natural families — it has, in my judgment, a unique character. It makes it clear that following Christ in the world, which constitutes the essence of Escrivá's message, need in no way exclude that source of all future apostles: marriage and the family. (Even celibate apostles — priests, religious, numeraries of Opus Dei, and others — must, after all, first be born!) Beyond this obvious connection, however, the admission of married people, and of singles called to or at least desirous of marriage, has had enormously beneficial consequences. For one thing, the number of members has multiplied through a veritable flood of supernumerary vocations.[7] By the time the Second Vatican Council declared apostolic responsibility of the laity and total commitment of married people to Jesus Christ to be the will of God, there were thousands of families all over the world already following this mandate in Opus Dei.

"Your son," I recently heard one father ask another, "also belongs to Opus Dei?" The response was a nod, so he went on to ask, "As what?" "He's a numerary." "You don't say! Already a full member!" It was not easy to clear up the misunderstanding. The technical terms "numerary" and "supernumerary," descended from the Latin into bureaucratic and official usage, are probably largely responsible for the erroneous opinion that there are "full" and "affiliate" members. In reality, the two groups follow identical vocations, just in different circumstances. This is all the significance there is to these terms; they were chosen more or less by chance, as a natural outgrowth of the early development of Opus Dei.

We have already discussed the fully secular character of the numerary vocation and its role within the institution of Opus Dei. It is not hard to understand the tendency to discriminate in one way or another against people with this vocation; after all, otherwise ordinary citizens living celibacy (and the other evangelical counsels) in the midst of the world for the sake of Christ and the Church are not something common in Church history. Some would even claim that this way of life is not compatible with the spirit of the twentieth century. Nevertheless, people renouncing marriage for Christ's sake have been a phenomenon in the Church from the very beginning, although their lifestyle (after the first few centuries) has as a rule been quite different from that of the numerary in Opus Dei. Judge this as one may, this is a phenomenon comparatively easy to understand — at least it has a history. What has been more difficult for many to understand is the new message of Escrivá, and then of the Council, that marriage and the family are, and furthermore *must be*, the matter and place for sanctification; that married people are called and qualified to live all the Christian virtues — love, hope, faith, humility, chastity, justice, poverty, courage, obedience, honesty, patience, and every other Christian virtue — on a par with those who voluntarily commit themselves to celibacy. Those who understand this receive a new and great happiness. "What happy eyes I have often looked into," wrote Escrivá in 1959, "when men and women who all their lives had thought total surrender [to God] was incompatible with a true and pure [human] love, have heard me say that marriage is a divine way on earth."[8] Marriage is not only a biological, social, and legal institution for assuring the continuation of the human race, it is also the means willed by God to increase and extend the People of God; for every newborn child is called to membership in the Body of Christ. "The Lord," Escrivá repeated again and again, "wishes to crown Christian families with many children. Receive these children with joy and gratitude, for they are a gift and a blessing of God — and a proof of his trust."[9]

The letter *Dei Amore*, which Escrivá addressed to the members of Opus Dei nearly thirty-five years ago, is dedicated in a special way to the theme of supernumeraries. Because it has lost none of its urgency, especially in its bulls-eye assessment of the human situation, I should like to go into it in some detail here.

In the beginning, Escrivá talks of the three great "manchas" (stains) which pollute the world. First there is "esa mancha roja" (that red stain, Marxist atheism), "which is spreading with great speed over the earth, demolishing everything, striving to destroy even the tiniest trace of supernatural outlook."[10] The second stain is the great wave of unleashed sensuality, wholesale carnality, that is causing people to act like beasts. Finally, there is the "stain of another color," the growing denial that God and Church have objective reality and importance, the increasing tendency to relegate them to a corner of private life under the guardianship of an arbitrarily subjective "conscience" — in other words, the ousting of faith and its manifestations from public life. These three stains portend lasting and pernicious dangers. Should not, asks Escrivá, the almost unbelievable progress of civilization in so many countries, the technical developments, the rise in material standards of living, have led to a religious renewal, gratitude towards God, and praise of the grace by which he makes possible and grants such blessings to humankind? "However," he points out, "such is not the case. Men and women, in spite of their progress, have not become more humane. They cannot be so, because human life without its divine dimension is just animal life, no matter what material benefits one may enjoy."[11] We achieve a distance from the animal kingdom only by opening ourselves to the divine. In a certain sense, religion is "the greatest rebellion of the person who does not want to be an animal."[12]

In 1959, on the threshold of a tumultuous decade in which dogmatic truths of faith would be called into question and explained (sometimes even within the Church) as socio-historically determined products of the subjective human mind, Escrivá speaks with prophetic clarity: "In the field of religion,[13] my daughters and sons, there is no progress, no possibility of any special new advance. The peak of progress has already been reached: Christ is the Alpha and the Omega, the beginning and the end. Therefore, one can invent nothing new in the spiritual life. It remains only to struggle to identify oneself with Christ, to be 'another Christ' — *ipse Christus*, Christ himself — to fall in love with, and to live with, him who is the same yesterday, today, and for all eternity.... Do you understand why I am always repeating, over and over again, that I have no other prescription for you but this: personal sanctity? There is nothing else, my children, nothing else."[14]

After these fundamental statements, Escrivá examines the particular possibilities and tasks of supernumeraries. In this connection, he recalls two figures of the Gospel: Nicodemus and Joseph of Arimathea. The former was a knowledgeable scholar, a prominent member of society, several times a member of the Jewish high council, the Sanhedrin; the latter was a rich, distinguished member of the highest authority in Jerusalem. "They acted," notes Escrivá, "discreetly and quietly. In public life they followed their consciences with determination; active and courageous, they faced the world in the hour of peril. I have always thought to myself, and have often told you, that these two men, if they were alive today, would understand the vocation of supernumeraries in Opus Dei very well. Just as it was among those first disciples of Christ, the entire human society of today is present among our supernumeraries, and it will always be thus. Intellectuals and practitioners, specialists and artisans, entrepreneurs and working men and women; people from the worlds of diplomacy, trade, agriculture, finance, and literature; journalists, actors, performers, and athletes; the young and the old, the healthy and the sick — we are always going to be a 'disorganized organization'[15] of the apostolate, because all human professions that are by nature decent and honorable can become apostolic, divine professions."[16]

What does all this mean? It means, first of all, not to be satisfied with finishing one's daily work with the least effort possible; not to view time at work as an interruption of leisure; not to dash right after work into the nearest bar, or jump into slippers and the easy chair in front of the television; not to shut oneself off in a cubbyhole. It means being an apostle and making Christianity credible through work well done, cordial cooperation, and loyalty to one's fellow workers. It means ongoing education; it means participation in professional, political, and social activities. It means being present in the normal, everyday world where souls swim about like fish in the sea — a simple, natural presence, without ostentation and without any play for applause or honors.[17]

Admittedly, Escrivá was probably assuming a political context providing for, or at least permitting, the free participation of citizens when he wrote that Christians quietly working in the above manner and organizing themselves in accordance with the law could influence national law, "especially in those matters that are crucial to the life of nations, such as the laws governing marriage and education, questions of public morality or private property."[18] Obviously, Msgr. Escrivá was a rock-solid Christian "conservative"; but at the same time, and with a profound logic, he was arguably the greatest Catholic "revolutionary" of the last two hundred years. One must understand these terms correctly. To profess firm conservatism means to maintain that the revelation necessary for redemption and salvation is closed and complete, that its content has been validly formulated by the Holy Spirit, once and for all, in a conceptual and verbal manner that can be transmitted and accepted throughout the world, by every age and generation. It means opposing the basic error of our time: the idea that the deposit of faith is only a cultural and historical collection of definitions, and thus is permanently adaptable and in need of adaptation. It therefore also means insisting that the state, as an institution of divine will and law, cannot simply be neutral but must be guided by moral law, by the traditions of its people, and by the general and individual needs of its inhabitants. Proper to this role are such matters as fighting racial discrimination, spouse abuse, and corporate greed. But the role of the state must also encompass the defense of the unborn, the protection of young people — and hence the fundamental protection and encouragement of marriage — and care for a certain public order of morality, among other things.

All of these concerns involve "conserving" somebody's life, dignity, health. Anyone who is not "conservative" in this sense is not liberal or up-to-date either, but rather antiquated — just one more person who has relapsed into eighteenth-century philosophical positions and still older heresies already proved false both in theory and practice. What I call "revolutionary," then, is something entirely different and infinitely more exciting: it is to penetrate society with the fundamental and total imitation of Christ.

Though *Dei Amore* is addressed to all the members of his spiritual family, Escrivá has a special word to say to the few who were active in politics at the time [1959].[19] He seizes this opportunity to outline the rights and duties they have as Christians in political life. Every Christian, of course, has a right to be professionally active in politics and in the life of the state. (To deny this, one would logically have to ban Christians from every form of civic activity.) In fact, to avoid a call to political activity, assuming one is suitably equipped for it, could constitute a sin of omission. What Escrivá says directly to his politically active followers holds true generally. "In fulfilling your mission," he says, "act with honesty of intention without losing the supernatural perspective, but don't mix the human with the divine. Do things just as they should ordinarily be done — without forgetting that the order within [material] creation has its own principles and laws that one can't disregard as if one were an angel. The worst praise I could give to one of my children would be to say, 'He is like an angel.' No, we are not angels, we are human beings."[20] He concludes his letter with this charge: "Fulfill your mission with courage, without fear of committing yourselves. Stand up for your mission. People are too often afraid to exercise their freedom. They prefer pat solutions for everything. It's paradoxical, but people very often hunger for rules at the price of forsaking their freedom, from fear of otherwise having to take risks."[21]

The spiritual family of Opus Dei finally reached its full extendedness in 1950, when Escrivá received permission from the Holy See not only to accept diocesan priests into the Work, but also to welcome non-Catholics and even non-Christians into the ever-growing number of "cooperators," that is, active friends and sympathizers. What the circle of friends and acquaintances is for the natural family, the circle of cooperators represents for the super-natural family of Opus Dei. It is a sphere of sympathy and personal friendship that takes concrete shape to the extent that each cooper-ator pitches in and thus has a claim to the Work's means of spiri-tual education — such as participation in retreats, seminars, and evenings of recollection. The founder had foreseen such a collabo-ration already in May 1935, when he said (in an Instruction he put into final form in the autumn of 1950), "Cooperators, without being members of our family, form a distinct community, inseparable from the Work."[22] Individual cooperation can range from the prayer of a person confined to a wheelchair to major economic undertakings or cultural initiatives. There are practically no limits to the possibilities for cooperation. Voluntary financial contribu-tions are, of course, a great help. What is most important, however, is a closeness to the spirituality of the Work, the readiness to fur-ther educate oneself in religion, and (for Catholics) an eagerness to propagate the spirit of a lay and secular Christianity in absolute loyalty to the Church and the pope. Naturally, many vocations to the Work come from the ranks of the cooperators. The youthful vigor of Opus Dei in a given geographical region can, in fact, be determined according to the number and activity of cooperators.

Love for Peter

Point 520 of *The Way* reads: "Catholic, apostolic, Roman! I'm pleased that you're very Roman, and that you wish to make a pilgrimage to Rome, *videre Petrum* [to see Peter]." In a multitude of similar remarks, Escrivá made it clear that not only did he view the papacy as histori-cally important, and as essential to the unity of the Church and its effectiveness in the world (non-Catholics and even non-Christians also recognize this), but he truly loved the pope as the visible head instituted by the Founder of the Church, Jesus Christ. He saw the pope as the one who represents Christ in the course of human his-tory. The personal character of the successor to Peter is not what makes this love all-important, but the fact that he is in essence Peter. When Jesus chose a visible leader for the Church, he did not have in mind a purely temporal, worldly institution, nor was he thinking in terms of just the first three or four decades of its existence. Rather, he wanted there to be on a permanent basis a supreme shepherd for the people of God — someone who would act not only as ruler of his episcopal co-shepherds, but as father and brother to all Christians, and even non-Christians; someone who would personify the love, truth, unity, and authority of Christ.

The key to ecumenism and to the success of its every effort seems to me to be acceptance of this concept of the Petrine office. It may appear that other points of controversy — the doctrine of justification, for example, or some of the teachings on the sacraments (especially regarding the Eucharist), the emphasis placed on Scripture or tradition, dissent regarding the priesthood, and so forth — are more profound and more difficult to resolve. We may even grant this. In fact, however, the issue of papal primacy has the closest and most inseparable relationship possible, both theologically and practically, with all the above problems. Before Christians can seek unity again concerning those things that cannot be seen, they must unite again around the person everyone can see: the successor of Peter, the pope. This must be the beginning and not the conclusion of an honestly meant ecumenism. It is a fact of human nature that it takes humility and obedience to be able to recognize the truth, remain in the truth, and/or return to the truth. A close look at Church history also teaches that heresy follows schism far more often than the other way around.

In this sense, to be truly Roman means to be truly ecumenical, and vice versa. This is a truth often forgotten today. Msgr. Escrivá once mentioned to journalists that during an audience with Pope John XXIII, he had said to him, "All men and women, Catholics and non-Catholics, have found in our Work a place where they feel comfortable; I haven't first learned ecumenism from Your Holiness."[23] This remark, which on the surface might sound proud, touched on something so important for Escrivá that he repeated it twice (in an interview with a Spanish newspaper and then with a French paper). But in addition to what he was obviously saying, this was also an attempt to correct some confused notions of ecumenism that had spread everywhere after the end of the Council.

Being a man of clear criteria and clear definitions, Escrivá distinguished between a common activity of people of good will — that is, of those who are ready to serve the common good on the basis of their individual belief in Christ — and a unity in faith. He knew beyond doubt that the latter can never be restored by a negotiation or compromise in which each side gives and takes a little, but only through a conversion on all sides that is a gift of the Holy Spirit. Among other things, this means that those who are not already there need to come home to the common Father's house. The love we owe to others can never come at the expense of the truth.

Escrivá always distinguished between the error and the erring person; while he opposed the former, he loved and respected all people and defended their freedom, including their freedom to err. But he never permitted the impression to be given that Opus Dei is "nonsectarian," to use the expression so popular today. Quite to the contrary, Opus Dei was and is Catholic through and through — but that is precisely what makes it open to all, though in various, graduated ways. "Naturally," he said, "the members are Catholic; and, what is more, they are Catholics who make the effort to live their faith consistently. Since the beginning of the Work, and not just since the Council, we have endeavored to live with an open Catholic spirit: to defend legitimate freedom of conscience, to meet all people, whether Catholic or not, with love, and to work together with all men and women in solving the many questions that trouble the world."[24]

In the fifth volume of the meditations written for the spiritual formation of the members of Opus Dei, there are eight readings on the theme "The Unity of Christians,"[25] one for each day of the Octave of Christian Unity. These readings explain the foundations of Christian unity and the basic premises for recovering it. In Jesus Christ we find ourselves united with all creatures. To live this unity well, we must personally join ourselves with Christ and move those about us to identify themselves with him in the same way.[26] This living unity is not a mishmash of religious feelings, it is not a new stage in social and historical development, nor is it a spontaneous convergence. Rather, it is the living Church: a community of divine foundation, a community bearing the criterion of the universality that is characteristic of Catholicism.[27] Within the Catholic Church, there is certainly place for men and women of every kind, with many differences in viewpoint, though a clear distinction must always be made between what can and cannot be modified. There is, however, room for only one entire truth of faith. This truth is not doomed to unending flux, a permanent state of becoming (Hegel's *status nascendi*); rather, it is present wholly and definitively, as a *depositum fidei perfectum*. An honest ecumenism must combine firmness regarding the deposit of faith with an accommodating kindness toward those who are still on the way toward its fullness.[28] Inner unity in belief and faithfulness to the deposit of faith within the Catholic Church exert the strongest magnetic pull for the return of separated Christians.[29] The certain guardian of this inner unity, and the focus for restoration of unity among all Christians, is the pope.[30] "After the Most Holy Trinity and our Mother, the Virgin Mary," Escrivá once said to a journalist, "there follows, for me, the pope in the hierarchy of love."[31] Escrivá never set foot in St. Peter's Square without reciting the Creed and praying especially for the pope. He requested all members of Opus Dei to adopt this habit. The first place for any of his spiritual children to visit in the Eternal City, he said, should be St. Peter's, as a sign of loyalty to the Roman Church. He himself had personal contact and lively correspondence with three popes: Pius XII, John XXIII, and Paul VI.[32] Twice he experienced a conclave in Rome. In the Articles of Postulation we read that "as soon as he saw the white smoke rise, he knelt — and all those about him knelt with him — and without yet knowing who had been elected, he recited this prayer: 'Oremus pro Beatissimo Papa nostro.'"[33]

During the first decade after the Council, when the Church was afflicted with steadily spreading inner erosion — heresy, rebellious theologians, the general collapse of discipline, the defection of priests, and capricious experimentation in the liturgy — Escrivá confessed, "I'm suffering — why hide it? And I suffer especially when I think of the pope's pain."[34] According to the Articles of Postulation, he offered his life to the Lord every day for the Church and the pope. He prayed that God might take his life as a sacrifice of reparation for the Church, begging God to bless her with a new blossoming of holiness and sound doctrine, a pentecostal new beginning. "When you have grown old," he said to his spiritual children, "and I have long since given an accounting before God, tell your brothers and sisters how much their father loved the pope, with his whole soul and with all his strength."[35] Escrivá offered the same love and reverence to all the members of the hierarchy. He felt that bishops, simply because they are the successors of the apostles, have a right to people's love and respect, as well as obedience. The founder of Opus Dei enjoined its members to pray for the pope and their own bishops every day, and to remain loyal to them in thought, word, and deed.

Popes and bishops rewarded the love and devotion of Josemaría Escrivá with affection, admiration, and support, although not all of them recognized the full dimensions of the phenomenon of Opus Dei and the greatness of its founder. In terms of visible success, curial approval, and hierarchical support, however, Escrivá was one of fortune's favorites.

We know that Pope Paul VI used *The Way* in his personal meditations.[36] Pope John XXIII once said to his secretary (later to become prelate of Loreto) that "the Work is destined to open up undreamt-of horizons of the universal apostolate in the Church."[37] Both Opus Dei and its founder were accepted by Popes John Paul I and John Paul II as significant historical phenomena and as the beginning of a new apostolate in the world. All these popes were — as the Polish pope still is — at the helm of the ship of Peter in the stormy years of the Vatican II era. The situation of Pius XII was different. Though he had to lead the Church through the catastrophe of World War II, the Church at that time seemed to be strong and healthy internally — and so it probably was, at least for the most part. Between 1946 and 1958, the prestige of the Church and the papacy (as well as Pius XII's personal authority) reached a peak that had not been thought possible since the Reformation.[38] This pope nevertheless recognized — at a time when no inner danger seemed to menace the Roman Church, and external persecutions such as those in Communist countries only heightened her *splendor martyrum* — that what was needed was a new and intense apostolic activity in the midst of the world. Further, he saw the "Work of God" of that Spanish priest as a divinely willed instrument for this task.

His perception of its importance at this early point is certainly of great significance.

With four other members of the Work, Encarnación Ortega had traveled to Rome in December 1946, to take up the administration of the central house. At the request of the general secretary, Alvaro del Portillo, who was well respected in the Vatican, she and Escrivá's sister Carmen were granted what Escrivá had expressly wished for them: a private audience with Pope Pius XII. Her description of the event is as touching as it is interesting; it communicates both the charm of Pope Pius and the childlike innocence of the visitors.[39] "Don Alvaro accompanied us, to conduct us into the Vatican and to wait with us," recalls Encarnación. "We passed various sentries — the Swiss Guards, the Palace, and the Noble Guards — and proceeded through several rooms. In the antechamber of the audience salon there was a deathly stillness." Don Alvaro then began to explain Opus Dei to the gentlemen of the Guard waiting there. At last the ladies were called inside. Encarnación is now remembering so vividly, she moves into present tense. "We enter," she says. "After we have knelt and kissed the hand of Pius XII, we explain that Carmen is the sister of our founder and that I am a member of Opus Dei, one of those who have come to Italy to begin our work. We tell him how much we love the Vicar of Christ, and that we learned this from our founder, and we request that the Holy Father might pray most especially to God the Father for the work of the women's branch of Opus Dei in the Eternal City and for Msgr. Escrivá. He replies that he has already been doing this every day since the visit of Don Alvaro del Portillo in 1943." At the time of that visit, Pope Pius then told them, Don Alvaro was not yet a priest and he showed up in the uniform of the engineers. "'At that visit,' says Pope Pius, 'he requested that I pray for the founder of Opus Dei. Since then, I have been doing this every day, and I keep on my night table the copy of The Way which he presented to me.'"

"The pope then mentioned," continues Encarnación, "that he had received a visit from another member of the Work, José María Albareda. He had been impressed by his spiritual and scholarly bearing." The response of the two women is noteworthy. "We told him that in the Work the members sanctify themselves in their work: the researcher in his research, the teacher in her instruction and care for her pupils, the housewife in the loving fulfillment of her family duties; and that if work is a means of encountering God, it is only logical to expend on it the greatest possible care." That comes across as a real lesson; its frankness astonishes me, especially when I think back on my own meeting with Pius XII in 1953. Ortega remembers that they also told the Holy Father details about their apostolic work and the growth of the women's branch. "I know that we also mixed in some anecdotes," she says. Surely the pope could sense their completely authentic innocence and see in it the childhood in God that is a part of the spirit of Opus Dei.

The close relationship of the president general of Opus Dei to the Holy See remained unchanged until Josemaría Escrivá's death and has continued under his successor. In 1957, Msgr. Escrivá was appointed a member of the Pontifical Academy for Theology and also an advisor to the Congregation for Seminaries and Universities.[40] Four years earlier, the prefect of this congregation, Cardinal Pizzardo, had expressed in a document his admiration for the structure, direction, and work of formation of the Collegium Romanum Sanctae Crucis, the educational center in Rome of the men's branch of Opus Dei, founded in 1948.[41] In the same year (1953), the corresponding center for the women's branch was opened — the Collegium Romanum Sanctae Mariae.[42] In 1952, the first level of the future University of Navarre (in Pamplona) had begun its work. Moreover, there were already many schools run by Opus Dei in several countries. And in 1957, a priest belonging to the Work was entrusted with the care of the Prelatura Nullius Yauyos in the Peruvian Andes, an extensive territory divided by peaks over fifteen thousand feet high, populated by impoverished Indians.[43]

In 1961, John XXIII appointed Escrivá a consultor to the Pontifical Commission for the Authentic Interpretation of the Code of Canon Law. As the Articles of Postulation discreetly remarks, there was never a lack of "difficult assignments from the Holy See" for the founder.[44] But Escrivá never rushed a decision or judgment. As he used to say, "One must hear every bell ring and, if possible, also get to know the bell-ringer."[45] Escrivá never shirked the duty of clarifying the situation. He once quoted a cardinal as having passed on to him a principle widely held in the Curia: "One often has to lie low to keep from getting killed." Escrivá went on to say that he had always made a special point of expressing himself clearly when dealing with the offices of the Holy See. He never let himself be stopped by the consideration that some unpleasantness might befall him if he spoke up for the truth that he bore in his heart.[46] The wisdom of this approach — at least over the long run — was confirmed by the steadily growing and deepening understanding of the Church authorities toward him.

Aspects of humility

Every pope is, of course, to some extent both "Roman" and "Marian." Pius XII, however, was so to a very special degree. A Roman by birth, he stands at the conclusion of a historic phase of the papacy which might be called absolutist, princely, imperial, stamped by a ruler's dignity and authority. Though he displayed great holiness and was noted for his kindness, he did in fact retain an aura of majesty and pronounced distance. Nevertheless, he was loved and revered as no pope of modern times before him, and not only by Catholic Christians. The world viewed him with awe. A film about his life, called *Pastor Angelicus*, was shown all over the world; for months it played in sold-out theaters. Never before had anything like this occurred.

Despite the advent of automobile, telephone, radio, and television, the Roman baroque as the curial style of administration reached one last peak with the pontificate of Pius XII. (In fact, it ended with him.) And his pontificate was Marian in a quite explicit and official way. On November 1 (Feast of All Saints), 1950, he proclaimed the dogma of the Assumption of Mary into heaven. He declared 1954 a Marian year, in commemoration of the one hundredth anniversary of the dogma of Mary's Immaculate Conception. Attached by a deep personal faith to Our Lady of Lourdes and of Fatima, he tried to inculcate in all of Christendom her message of love. The founder of Opus Dei therefore found during this time a most favorable situation in the spiritual climate of the universal Church for the growth and spreading of the Work.

It was in that Marian year of 1954 that Opus Dei's internal magazine *Crónica* began publication. Escrivá introduced the first issue with the following preamble: "Our Opus Dei was born and grew up under the protection of Our Lady. This is why the everyday life of the children of God in this Work of God is filled with so many Marian customs. You can imagine how great is my joy that the Holy Father has consecrated this year, 1954, to the Blessed Virgin. We will correspond to the pope's wishes by practicing devotion to Mary, the Mother of God, with even greater love — if this is possible. Moreover, we take on ourselves in a special way this year the duty of propagating the rosary and the making of three pilgrimages, in the usual way, to shrines of Mary: in February, May, and October."[47]

In many centers of Opus Dei one finds the inscription "Omnes cum Petro ad Jesum per Mariam" — "All with Peter to Jesus through Mary." This is another version of that quintessentially Catholic couplet "Roman and Marian." One flock under one shepherd; a single way, firm and secure; a common goal — that is what these seven words express. We have already spoken about "cum Petro"; the entire book talks of "ad Jesum"; there remains only the "per Mariam" to discuss.

Escrivá did not create or propagate a new Mariology. He never created any new theology — though the spiritual message of Opus Dei does carry with it an enormous enrichment, full of youthful dynamism, for theology. Rather, he simply proclaimed the doctrine of the Roman Catholic Church, as handed down without interruption and as universally binding. He exhorted the members of the Work to adhere to this doctrine with faith and humility — that is, without doing egocentric cartwheels to come up with spurious interpretations. In this regard, there was never anything original or sensational about either him or Opus Dei. All there has ever been is something simple, something perhaps unnerving only because of its simplicity: keeping the faith. Maintenance of this loyalty acquired an unusual and peculiar character only during and after Vatican II, when Catholic doctrine began to be challenged and then shaken to its foundations by certain theologians, with the consequence that traditional piety began to waver. Now, thirty years later, we are still

Msgr. Escrivá visiting a shrine with his sister Carmen and some
members of the Work in the early 1950s.

not finished suffering from the fallout. Think of how few Catholics
today, including those who go to Mass every Sunday, know what
the Catholic faith is and what beliefs cannot be done without. This is
all due to three main problems: (1) lack of knowledge, (2) the error
of thinking that there are no unchangeable truths of faith, but only
subjective statements and opinions which arise out of the stream of
history and sink back into it again, and (3) the supposed incompatibility of faith with science. These three factors mutually produce,
influence, and intensify one another.

To know the faith, to live it with heart and mind, to radiate it
and transform it into an action of love — these are things that ought
to concern every Christian. In the case of Catholics, this presupposes
(among other things) a closeness to Mary, the Mother of God. To foster this closeness, the founder of Opus Dei did not need to dig up or
invent anything. The Church has developed and proclaimed a comprehensive set of teachings concerning Mary. More than sixty generations of Christians have revered the Virgin Mother of God with a
steadily growing treasury of devotions. Nevertheless, Escrivá, whose

utterances concerning Mary can hardly be counted, let alone individually listed, because they were as the breath and pulse of his spiritual existence, found an individual, personal, and unmistakably true note when he spoke about Mary, and to Mary. Not only did he conclude almost every one of his meditations with a loving reference to the Mother of God, not only did he engage in a never-interrupted dialogue of the heart with Mary, but he also gave devotion to Mary a new spiritual and lyrical beauty perhaps unparalleled in twentieth-century Marian literature. He gave Marian piety a new pride,[48] leading it in a unique way out of the ghetto of routine or superficial piety so rightly deplored by contemporary Christians. He thus contributed substantially to overcoming the prejudice that devotion to Mary is just a religious crutch, something needed only by simple souls unable to comprehend religious truths intellectually. To dispel this misconception, he put the following caveat at the beginning of *Holy Rosary* (1943): "These lines aren't written only for old women. They are written for grown men, for very manly men who at times, no doubt, have raised their hearts to God. At the start of that way, whose end is the complete madness of a life for Jesus, stands a trusting love for Mary. Do you want to love the Virgin? Then get to know her! How? Pray well the rosary of Our Lady."[49]

I am sure the reader will by now be convinced of the great importance of Opus Dei for the life and future of the Church and all humanity. It is indeed a work of God: a saving measure of the Divine Physician, to heal and aid in recovery the Mystical Body of Christ, which, so weakened by the decline in faith, at times limps through the world as though on crutches. To take part in this healing process requires standing up against the spirit of the times. It requires that one grow strong in the virtues most contrary to this spirit, most hated by it: humility, the readiness to serve others, obedience, the overcoming of self, chastity — the principles in the life of the "earthly Trinity," as Escrivá liked to call the Holy Family of Nazareth. Nothing will succeed without the renewal of these virtues: not the reform of industrial society, not the much-needed development of the Third World, not the preservation of peace and the consequent preservation of our biological existence on this planet. Nothing good will come about in the absence of these virtues. One cannot, therefore, come to Opus Dei and hope to persevere in it — or, for that matter, be any kind of active follower of Christ — without cherishing these virtues and being ready to strive toward them seriously in a personal daily struggle. Consciousness of being a child of God and perseverance in this state are certainly, as gifts of grace accepted in freedom, the foundation of all sanctity. Humility, however, is the indispensable cement for this edifice.[50] "I am worth nothing, I have nothing, I can do nothing. Nothing!" This brief exclamation was Escrivá's motto throughout his life.[51] From him it was absolutely believable, because it was absolutely sincere. This transparent sincerity stands in pure contrast to that most revolting impostor, false humility. Let's face it: regardless of the general unfairness of it, the perennial caricature of the clergyman who while feigning humility is actually power-hungry, sly, and lustful is hardly a great advertisement for religion! Feigned humility is not, of course, the only kind of false humility there is. Cowardice can pass for discretion, and what appears to be holy deference can be simply an inferiority complex. But all types of false humility have one thing in common: just as workaholism gives diligence a bad name, so false humility in any form makes true humility seem suspect.

Escrivá's humility was of a kind far removed from hypocrisy, cowardice, or an inferiority complex. "In spite of our personal shortcomings," he wrote in 1931, in his second letter to the members of Opus Dei, "we are bearers of the divine and have inestimable value, for we are tools of God. Because we want to be good instruments, the Lord will give us everything that we lack; and the smaller and poorer we consider ourselves to be with true humility, the more he will give us."[52] An almost infallible characteristic of true and healthy humility is its unobtrusiveness and silence. All the virtues are interrelated; they form a network, animating and complementing one another. Nevertheless, some virtues (courage or justice, for example) can at times be almost isolated. They can dominate a personality or an action. True humility, however, is always an attendant virtue; it never appears alone. Humility is the virtue that preserves all the other virtues from corruption. It does not shrink from achievement, office, responsibility, or defense of one's rights; rather, like a child, it renders these gifts back to the Parent from whom they came.

In the company of Christ, the Christian can and should accept humiliation "joyously, as reparation, as purification, and as an act of love for the Lord."[53] So said Escrivá, who never defended himself from unjust accusations or made a scene, yet never indulged in self-pity.[54] Whenever Escrivá made a mistake or thought he had wronged someone in any way, he asked the person for forgiveness immediately, even if there were others present.[55] "I too receive corrections," he said, "and I receive them with a lowered head. Whenever I find myself thinking they are baseless, I just have to correct myself and see that it is I who have erred."[56]

Humility goes hand in hand with the spirit of childhood. Together they make it possible to show awe and admiration without any envy or introspection. One day in February 1947, Escrivá heard a broadcast on Vatican Radio that spoke of his importance to the Church. Although the broadcaster was making extremely flattering statements about him, he seemed not to notice. "He was, on the contrary, lost in thought," says a witness. "I would almost venture to say he was praying without absorbing what was being said about him."[57] Another time, watching television, he was lost in wonder at an old professor who was proudly displaying a whole mountain of published works, the fruit of many years of labor. The next day, Escrivá said he felt ashamed before the Lord when he saw that after so many years of vocation he had nothing completed to offer; he felt he had accomplished nothing and was only a beginner in the spiritual life.[58]

The paths of humility and secularity join at an intersection that is full of potholes and blind spots. It seems to me that this was the only area in the life of Escrivá where he stepped cautiously, often following the advice of his children rather than his own instinct. For someone with considerable power and responsibility, it is not always easy to decide which course of action represents true humility. Humility and fidelity to his vocation led Escrivá to decline the tempting offers that would have launched him on a brilliant career in the Church. In 1928 he declined an offer to become Chaplain of the Royal Household, an honorary position that was then the dream of many clergymen.[59] And in the thirties he turned down an invitation to be canon at the cathedral of

Cuenca;[60] it was also in the thirties that he turned down Angel Herrera's offer to make him spiritual director of the Catholic Action headquarters in Spain.[61] To Herrera he said, "No, no. Thank you very much, but I cannot accept this position. God is calling me to a different way, and I must follow. Moreover, I cannot accept this because, as you yourself say, the best priests in Spain will be meeting in that house. It seems obvious, then, that I am not fit to direct it."[62] The words, their childlike humility (they may come across as ironic, but that is not the way he said them), remind me of St. Thomas More's manner of speaking.

The path of humility is often more ambiguous and obscure than these examples suggest. Full of uncertainties, it can become as hard to stay on as a tightrope. But for Escrivá's children there is a constant point of reference: Christ's thirty years of hidden life in Nazareth. Keeping that focus in mind, Opus Dei does not try to attract attention. The rationale is perhaps best expressed in this anecdote related by Alvaro del Portillo. During a visit with Escrivá to Montecatini, Italy, a high-ranking official of the Curia approached them to ask how many centers they had, and other questions of that kind — organizational, statistical questions. Escrivá answered by talking about the effectiveness of prayer, penance, and work performed in silent humility. "How," asked Escrivá, "can one make statistics of these sorts of things, which are the only things that count?" The prelate's astonished expression prompted him to explain. "There are some," he said, "who do the work of three and make the noise of three hundred. We have to do the opposite: do the work of three hundred with the noise of three — with humility. There are those who do not understand our way of working. They can't understand why we do not seek either personal praise or honor for our organization."[63] In light of the heartfelt convictions he spelled out here, it is certainly not hard to understand why Escrivá did not like spotlights, microphones, and interviews, why he ignored articles about himself and never appeared at a press conference or on television.

Escrivá was not, however, against mass communication as such. And though the "house of Nazareth" that Opus Dei tries to keep has not changed its spirit of prayer, warmth, and simplicity, its furnishings have kept in step with the times. Radio, television, newspapers, and other means of mass communication are an inescapable part of life — certainly of secular life. Everyone is affected by them; there is no way to escape their influence entirely. But one can participate in forming and guiding them. On this point, Escrivá never had a doubt. He was adamant in his conviction that he and his children would have to be apostles in an industrial and technological age. He would have to fulfill God's mission in the twentieth century, and do this all over the world. Men and women must be made aware that Christ walks through the world of assembly lines, printing presses, supersonic transport, atomic reactors, and microprocessors, just as he once walked the dusty streets of Palestine.

Escrivá always supported the apostolate of the mass media, which involves so many professions. He tirelessly urged those active in the media to do justice to their apostolic responsibilities, not only through personal commitment and professionalism, but also through the creation of new means to convey the message of Christ. This was the impetus behind the school of journalism at the University of Navarre. Through the initiative of Opus Dei members and their professional colleagues, many publishing houses, newspapers, and magazines were founded. Escrivá wanted to cover the world with printed matter (understood in the best apostolic sense) that would spread the teachings of Christ and his Church. However, neither Opus Dei as an institution nor its prelate in his official capacity appears in public for the sake of these personal initiatives; it was only after great hesitation that Escrivá agreed to have his catechetical journeys after 1972 filmed, and only in the hope of drawing attention to Christ, the Church, and the Gospel.[64]

While he did not look for honors, neither did he refuse those bestowed on him. Such a refusal would have been a type of pride in disguise. It would also have contradicted the secular nature of Opus Dei. Life in the world, after all, does include whatever recognition and rewards one's efforts may merit. In 1947 (just after the first curial approval of Opus Dei), Don Alvaro del Portillo, in the name of the General Council of Opus Dei, petitioned the Holy See for Escrivá's appointment as a domestic prelate. Escrivá knew nothing of these efforts. When the appointment came (on April 22nd), Don Alvaro had to persuade the reluctant Escrivá to accept.[65] But he was always accessible to rational and spiritually motivated arguments, even when they clashed with his personal sentiments. There are photographs and portraits of Escrivá in the full crimson dress of a prelate, with pectoral cross and buckled shoes — clothes that he called "otro cilicio" (another kind of penitential garb).[66] And whenever an honorary doctorate, the keys to a city, or any other honor was granted him, he invariably remained as calm and grateful as when slander or humiliation struck him. There was, for example, the time he received a major decoration of the state, and a military officer who was also a member of Opus Dei congratulated him in Rome. "My son," Escrivá replied with a smile, "for you soldiers a decoration like this is significant, but not for me. Only one cross interests me — and in the long run, you too — the Holy Cross."[67]

"I do not direct the Work alone."

Josemaría Escrivá, who became the president general of Opus Dei when it was approved as a secular institute, resided in Rome from 1946 on. But the governing board of Opus Dei, the General Council, did not. It remained in Madrid, with the permission of the Holy See, for another full decade. Only when a fully detailed and methodical history of Opus Dei is written will it be possible to analyze the effects of this unusual separation, this split-location leadership. But whatever difficulties it caused were apparently overcome, for it was during this decade that Opus Dei expanded worldwide.

In August 1956, a General Congress of Opus Dei in Einsiedeln, Switzerland, resolved that the General Council should move to Rome, because of the spreading of the Work and the consequently more complex duties of direction. (Escrivá himself initiated the motion.) There are, as we have mentioned, two branches of Opus Dei — one for men and one for women — which are united in the same vocation, the same apostolic work, and the same prelate. (Canonically speaking, he is a prelate, but inside the organization he is the father of one family.) Next to the prelate stands the "spiritual director" of both branches. The General Council is organized as follows: the vicar general, the prelate's right-hand man; the procurator general, who is responsible for relations with Church authorities; the priest-secretary for the women's branch;[68] the three directors of the works of St. Michael, St. Gabriel, and St. Raphael (for numeraries, associates, supernumeraries, and the youth apostolate); the prefect of studies, who is responsible for the education of the male members of the Work; and the general administrator, who is in charge of finances. These officials work at Opus Dei's headquarters in Rome and form the permanent "cabinet." They are not, however, the entire General Council. The General Council also includes delegates from the individual regions of Opus Dei throughout the world. Various advisory groups participate in the government when needed. The structure of the women's branch corresponds to this schema, though the names of the offices are different. The representatives of both branches elect the prelate for life tenure. (After Escrivá's death they elected Alvaro del Portillo, on September 15, 1975.)

The governing bodies in the individual regions correspond to the structure of the Roman headquarters. Each region has a regional vicar or counsellor, a priest who represents the prelate in that land. He is appointed by the General Council for a fixed term.

This structure may seem complicated, but it rests on two simple principles: decentralization and collegiality. The principle of decentralization, which Escrivá often referred to as "disorganized organization," represents, in his words, "the primacy of the spirit over the organization." What does this mean in practical terms? "Members don't live in a straitjacket of directives, plans, and conferences. Everyone is free, joined with the others through a common spirituality and a common drive to be saints and apostles."[69]

Insofar as is possible, each member acts independently. In fact, not only every center, but every Opus Dei enterprise (such as a student residence, an agricultural school, or a school of economics) functions independently. While all the units are faithful to the spirit of Opus Dei, they each act on their own initiative and responsibility. They are also financially independent of one another. Through the income of the members, state assistance in the case of educational institutions, rent paid by residents, the generosity of friends, and special trust funds, the centers support themselves. But because this money is never abundant, the demands of financial independence are a constant burden for any director in Opus Dei. Whatever qualifications they may have in other areas, directors must also be beggars for Jesus' sake.[70]

Escrivá explained his idea of collegiality in this way: "The duties of direction in Opus Dei are always performed by a group, never by an individual. We despise tyranny because it violates the dignity of the individual. I do not direct the Work alone; decisions are made in the General Council, which has its headquarters in Rome but currently has members from fourteen countries.[71] The General Council limits itself to establishing the guidelines for the apostolate of the Work worldwide and leaves to the directors in the different countries a free hand for their own initiatives."[72]

Opus Dei directors occupy a unique place in the Church. They are responsible not only for the legal and organizational dimension of apostolic enterprise, the maintenance of installations, and the operation of their respective centers in the context of Opus Dei as a whole, but also for the spiritual direction of other members of Opus Dei, for the furthering of their spiritual education and formation as lay persons. The continuing growth of Opus Dei eventually made it impossible for Escrivá to personally communicate the spirit of Opus Dei to each new member. He entrusted this duty of care and direction, of personal attention, to capable sons and daughters.

In the past, the Christian who sought total commitment to Christ always depended on the help of a spiritual director. Normally, the spiritual director was a confessor, although spiritual direction by lay persons has existed from the first Christian centuries. It is not only kings, queens, monks, and nuns who have sought counsel from confessors and struggled for perfection with their help; many simple men and women, yearning to love God and the Church more profoundly, have also walked the road of spiritual maturation through the sacrament of Reconciliation and spiritual direction.

Escrivá was convinced that in order to live Christianity in all its fullness, the ordinary person needs continual spiritual direction from his or her own peers.[73] In my opinion, this is a great breakthrough in Catholic spirituality and pastoral theology. Escrivá's perception and the practical form it takes in Opus Dei constitute a veritable revolution in the pastoral work of the Church.

All the means available must be used to make Christ everything to his followers so that, following the example of St. Paul, they can be "all things to all people" and can do all things "in him who strengthens them." In addition to prayer, sacraments, meditation on Scripture, other spiritual reading, and doctrinal formation, a Christian needs the help of another Christian. In Opus Dei, no one lacks this help; no one is without a director. The directors of Opus Dei by delegation share in the grace of direction of the prelate. In a real sense, the directors serve as conductors or transmitters of this grace.

Escrivá succeeded in combining the principles of paternity and fraternity in this system of direction; collegiality is combined with brotherly (or sisterly) pastoral care. We read in a letter of 1957, "Realize clearly that direction in the Work depends on trust. All in Opus Dei enjoy a relationship to their directors that is characterized by fraternal, childlike openness, without fear or suspicion, for they know it would be a great evil for their souls and for the effectiveness of the apostolate if they assumed, because of false respect or to avoid correction, an attitude of timidity towards those entrusted with the duty of direction. If trust disappears, disquiet and disorder arise, and serenity and calm vanish. For this reason I have always tried to form your brothers and sisters in this intimate atmosphere, and also the St. Raphael boys, with whom I took great care."[74] In the same letter, Escrivá made the oft-quoted and touching assertion, "You — every one of you — I trust more than a hundred notaries who would unanimously assure me of the contrary."[75]

Strength through adversity

Villa Tevere in Rome is the heart and head of Opus Dei. It is the final resting place of the founder, the seat of his successor, and the headquarters of both the men's and women's branches. It is a whirlwind of activity. The prelate has visitors from around the world. Pilgrims visit the tomb of Josemaría Escrivá [now beneath the altar of the Prelatic Church of Our Lady of Peace], the number of visitors growing every year. Cardinals of the Curia, bishops, scientists, the young and the old, members of Opus Dei, non-Christians — no one who knocks is ever turned away. Often Villa Tevere overflows with people. During Holy Week, thousands of students from around the world gather in Rome to celebrate Easter and to fortify themselves in the spirit of Opus Dei for the ethical and spiritual renewal of Christianity and the world. Though Villa Tevere is not a place of solitude, it is not noisy and hectic either; a busy silence prevails. It is a place to seek holiness in the midst of the workaday world. Every wing of the building has a tabernacle, and on every staircase the Mother of God, represented in a statue, relief, or painting, watches over and greets the guests.

The three-story building, erected in the 1920s, was originally the Hungarian embassy to the Vatican. Urged by Cardinals Montini and Tardini to establish his own house in Rome, Escrivá found this building in 1947, but its acquisition involved monumental financial difficulties.[76] (The countless occasions when Escrivá's prayers brought miraculous solutions to financial crises would make a lengthy chapter. Suffice it to say, his prayers somehow attracted contributors and connected with the commercial minds of creditors and salesmen, and astonishing turns of fortune were recorded.) Providentially, the owner of the property on Viale Bruno Buozzi, sensing that something extraordinary was afoot, developed such an admiration for Escrivá and del Portillo that he agreed to a low purchase price and easy terms of payment. He did, however, require payment in Swiss francs. "We don't mind," said the Father. "We don't have any Swiss francs, but we don't have any lire either, and they are all the same to Our Lord."[77]

In July 1947, Escrivá and some of his sons moved into the doorkeeper's lodgings in the building, which he christened "Villa Tevere." Here they lived in extreme poverty, hunger, and cold, sleeping on the floor. These conditions lasted until 1949, because the old tenants, Hungarian diplomats stranded by the Communist takeover of Hungary, could not leave. Nevertheless, on June 29, 1948, the Roman College of the Holy Cross began classes there. The first students entered these primitive surroundings to further their spiritual and intellectual formation. (Since that time, thousands of members of Opus Dei, most of them young men already having acquired college degrees and some career experience, have studied philosophy and theology at the Roman College. Many of them are now serving the Church and Opus Dei as priests. The college's provisional quarters at Villa Tevere remained in use until 1974, when students began attending classes at Cavabianca, the new facility on the Via Flaminia. Under construction since 1971, Cavabianca was not completely finished when classes began. Escrivá did not live to see its completion, but he did get to witness the start of classes at the place he jokingly called one of his "ultimas locuras," or "last follies.")

The construction of Villa Tevere lasted over a decade. The facade of the Hungarian embassy remained mostly intact, but the interior was completely rebuilt. Funds and material assistance were virtually nonexistent. The postulation for Escrivá's beatification refers to the establishment of Opus Dei's headquarters in Rome as part of a "divine logic." Transforming that logic into an effective instrument of apostolate in the form of Villa Tevere was a great adventure. Escrivá was constantly concerned about the progress of construction, from the architectural planning down to the smallest detail. Hardly a day passed when he did not take several walks through the construction site. "He thought of everything; he coordinated, directed, and checked everything."[78] Naturally, he supervised the construction of the chapels with special care.

Poverty was a faithful companion in those years. Del Portillo was in charge of finances, and every Saturday he had to perform a minor miracle: paying the workers their weekly wage. The project was never far from bankruptcy; del Portillo showed heroic dedication in the face of seemingly insurmountable obstacles. Recalling all the sacrifices it had taken to complete the construction of the building, Msgr. Escrivá said, after blessing and setting the last stone (on January 9, 1960), "These walls appear to be made of stone, but they are made of love."[79]

The part of the Villa Tevere complex reserved for the women's branch was called the Villa Sacchetti. It was there that the Collegium Romanum Sanctae Mariae, founded in 1953, was lodged. But the number of students increased so rapidly that by 1959 the space had become inadequate. So in July of that year, shortly before the com-

Msgr. Escrivá on the construction site during work on Villa Tevere.

pletion of Villa Tevere, Escrivá had to embark on a new construction project mandated by that same divine logic. The Holy See had donated some property, near the papal summer residence in Castelgandolfo, to the women's branch. Its reconstruction into the Villa delle Rose began that year — once again, a task of several years' duration.[80] By the time it was finally completed, in 1963, the preparations for the construction at Cavabianca had already begun. Thus it can be said with little or no exaggeration that Escrivá lived among Roman construction sites for nearly thirty years.

While he was confirming Opus Dei's universal character by establishing its headquarters in Rome, Escrivá also directly or indirectly reinforced its Marian character through three consecrations of Opus Dei, in 1951 and 1952. Roman and Marian: so Opus Dei had been born, and so it grew. With the buildings and the consecrations, these characteristics were publicly proclaimed to the Church and to the world. As the Gospel says, "A city set upon a hill cannot be hidden" (Mt 5:14).

Unfortunately, official approval of Opus Dei did not alleviate all misunderstandings and animosities. In the early fifties, influential parties in the Church tried to cut off the women's branch from the rest of Opus Dei, possibly as a first step toward dissolving Opus Dei entirely. Apparently they came dangerously close to achieving their goal. Earlier attacks on Opus Dei in Spain had been focused on the alarming of parents and other family members; these tactics were now used in Italy. "Alarming" is perhaps too mild a word; people were actually trying to convince mothers, fathers, favorite aunts and uncles, and grandparents that their relatives in Opus Dei were suffering harm to body and soul and were very possibly on the road to perdition. One can easily imagine the sorrow, pain, and damage such misinformation caused. The only possible defense was trust in God. Therefore, on May 14, 1951, in the chapel of the Holy Family in Villa Tevere, Escrivá consecrated the families of his spiritual children to the Holy Family of Nazareth.

The flood waters, however, continued to rise. In retrospect, it is clear that the continuation of Opus Dei hung by a thread sustained only by the grace of God. A decade later, Escrivá, in a voice full of gratitude, spoke of the great peril he had been in, and how God had rescued him. "They refused to speak to me," he recalled. "They gave me no opportunity to explain anything or clarify the situation. It was a very bitter experience for me. Despite our having received the approval, the slanders did not cease. Since I did not know to whom to turn on earth, I turned, as always, to heaven."[81]

In July 1951, after returning from a trip to Florence,[82] Escrivá received a message from a cardinal warning of imminent danger.[83] So on August 14th he traveled to the town of Loreto, where, according to tradition, the house of the Holy Family (now covered by a splendid Renaissance church) is miraculously preserved.[84] The following day, the Feast of the Assumption, he celebrated Mass here and placed Opus Dei once more under the protection of the Mother of God.

Finally, there followed the consecration of Opus Dei to the Sacred Heart of Jesus, performed October 26 (Feast of Christ the

King), 1952, in the chapel of the Sacred Heart in Villa Tevere.[85] These three consecrations — to the Holy Family, to the Blessed Mother, and to the Sacred Heart of Jesus — are renewed annually in every center of Opus Dei. And with their help, eventually the dangers passed. Someday, when the time comes for the archives to be opened, we will know in greater detail the dangers faced and how they were overcome. In the meantime we do know this much: Opus Dei emerged strengthened from its time of persecution — strengthened enough to start going to work all over the world. The where-and-when list is impressive in and of itself: Mexico and the United States in 1949, Venezuela and Colombia in 1951; Germany, 1952; Peru and Guatemala, 1953; Ecuador, 1954; Switzerland and Uruguay, 1956; Brazil, Austria, and Canada, 1957; El Salvador, Kenya, and Japan, 1958; Costa Rica, 1959; the Netherlands, 1960; Paraguay, 1962; Australia, 1963; the Philippines, 1964; Belgium and Nigeria, 1965; Puerto Rico, 1969. And the list is still growing.

An Opus Dei member sent from Rome to Ireland in 1952 has left us an account of how the Work began in new lands, and of how Escrivá sent his children into the world. "When we begin our work in a country," Escrivá told her, "we cannot isolate ourselves in it, but must form roots in it. Otherwise nothing will succeed; for it is not our business to represent national interests, but rather to serve Jesus Christ and the Holy Church."[86] This meant adapting to local customs regarding eating, drinking, and dress, instead of asserting one's foreign background. Escrivá dictated to her a list of twenty-nine notes on everything from details on the maintenance of centers to apostolic dos and don'ts.[87] This is one of them: "We must not forget, while employing all the natural means at our disposal, to exhaust the supernatural means as well: conversations, confession with our priests [always respecting the complete freedom to confess to any authorized priest], and the study of doctrine." When he finished his dictation, he took the pad from her hand and wrote, "In Dublin, in Rome, in Madrid, just as in the middle of Africa, souls! That's what matters!" And then he added, "Eat! (One must eat! That is part of humility, for if you don't eat, you'll collapse and won't be able to serve Our Lord.[88]) And sleep, at least seven hours — better eight, but never more than eight unless a physician directs otherwise." Before giving the pad back, he drew a duck with an open beak. "That's you. Ducks, swim!" he said. "If I request anything from you, my daughters, never say it's impossible — I know that already. Since I began the Work, the Lord has requested many impossibilities from me. Even so, things worked out! That is why I want you to be like ducks who dive into the water without hesitation or fear. If God asks for something, one must do it, one must swim — forward, and with courage. Now do you understand why I love these creatures so much?"

Chapter Eight

Day-to-Day Life

In the minds of most people, day-to-day life has two main divisions: workdays and weekends.[1] In fact, the workday is more or less defined by way of contrast. Workdays are the price one pays for time off — weekends, holidays, vacations. A workday is something gray, monotonous, exhausting. The less work one can do (without losing money), the better; the less effort one has to put into it, the better. A jaded, half-dead, really depressing outlook, yet one with which many of us are all too familiar. What has ruined the reputation of the workday is not so much the work itself as it is the boredom associated with relentless uniformity, regularity, and repetitiveness. But for most people, most days in their lives are going to be workdays of this type, and so this daily toil is worth a closer look. For as many people have already discovered the hard way, a quasi-metaphysical hostility towards workdays will end up ruining not only that large percentage of one's total time on earth, but also one's capacity for enjoying time off. One is either satisfied in the workday and able to find the meaning of existence in it, or one is satisfied in nothing and with nothing, and unable to find meaning in anything. In this context, the message of Escrivá and the founding of Opus Dei have much to offer. The consecration of the workday as a gift from God — a gift which Christ offers to the Father, and which the individual Christian offers "through him, with him, and in him" — has significance beyond what anyone can dream of; it can, in fact, transform political and social life on earth.

Since classical times, one of the most effective slanders against Christianity has been its depiction as an idealistic theory for social conduct that is well meant, but out of place in the "real

world." In fact, nothing could play better into Satan's hands than
enervated Christians who consider a world run according to the
precepts of the Gospel an impossible dream. Having thus capitulated, they have no choice then but to turn tail and run for shelter
under the amorphous recommendation that everyone should be
good according to individual taste. In contrast, Escrivá has once
again reminded us that world crises are caused by one thing
alone: the absence of saints in daily life.[2]

One day in Rome

While visiting an Opus Dei center in a large German city, I was
struck by the elegant furnishing of the spacious living room, and was
reminded of critical remarks I had often heard. Opus Dei reportedly
had luxurious houses; the furniture was too expensive; apostolic
poverty was ignored. Even though I hold such criticisms to be, for
the most part, social hypocrisy (since they usually come from people
who vacation five times a year and have a second house, a vacation
home, and a small fleet of cars), I raised this subject with my hosts.
They were not surprised; they had heard it all before. In response,
the director said that he would like to show me the entire center.
And sure enough, the perspective changed once I saw the whole picture. Besides the carefully furnished chapel (the most beautiful room
of the residence) and the above-mentioned living room, there was a
smaller dining room, simple but comfortable, and a sober, utilitarian
study. Then the young man led me through a small, dark passage to
a pair of tiny rooms overlooking the back yard. Each room had a
bed, a table, a chair, and a narrow wardrobe like a locker. That was
all. "These," he said, smiling, "are our private rooms."

The spirit of poverty, as the founder of Opus Dei taught and
lived it for his whole life, does not consist of saving at the expense
of others, but just the opposite. The best things available go to the
chapel, the dwelling of Our Lord in the Blessed Sacrament. The second best goes to visitors, guests, and friends, so they feel at home.
Whatever resources are left (usually next to nothing) go for the
members' personal needs. Here, too, priorities and proprieties are
observed. As an ordinary person in the midst of society, a member

of Opus Dei will not dress in rags, but decently, in suitable attire. A cab driver will dress more simply, while a mayor will have to dress up for work or social occasions. Regardless of social position and occupation, however, all members of Opus Dei are to share a personal unpretentiousness, a Christian openness to the rich and the poor, and an inner detachment from all possessions.[3]

This spirit of poverty is evident at Villa Tevere. A large, complex building and a pleasant and dignified dwelling, it is the very image of Opus Dei. True, if today a catastrophe were to destroy the central office, a provisional office would surely be rebuilt in the ruins or in a shed, and the prelate and his sons once again would sleep on the floor. But to have built the center of the Work in the first place as a shed, in an ostentatious display of poverty, would not have been detachment, but hypocrisy.

Josemaría Escrivá observed the principles of truth and propriety always and everywhere — when he was with only his closest associates, when he stood in view of the world and was subject to public opinion, and when he was alone with God. Villa Tevere is the testimony in stone that as father, priest, and friend, Escrivá always remained the same person, in surroundings that were functionally appropriate and consonant with the expectations of others. The chapel of the president general, in which he offered the holy sacrifice of the Mass daily as the founder of Opus Dei, is, fittingly, of extraordinary beauty, a real jewel. His bedroom, in contrast, is a small, dark, and scantily furnished room without any comforts. The reception area and dining rooms, where cardinals, bishops, scientists, and other dignitaries were his guests, are furnished not luxuriously, but in a solid and comfortable fashion. His work room, however, where he spent the greater part of his Roman years, is a different story. Located on a very high floor, it has especially small windows — I found it to be the hottest and stuffiest room of the entire labyrinthine structure.

There is an unusual aspect of this office, though, an aspect that reveals the real "heart of the work," as the present prelate explained to me. It was, as a matter of fact, not the office of the president general at all. That office was located next to Escrivá's bedroom, yet he almost never used it. Instead, he came to the office of the secretary general (del Portillo) to work together with him. They usually sat across from each other at a massive rectangular table of dark brown wood. (Nothing of this has changed, except that Don Alvaro now sits at the other side of the table and has relinquished his former seat to Don Javier Echevarria, the current secretary general. Escrivá's armchair is no longer used, but it stays next to that of his successor as a reminder, a stimulus, and, now and then, a consolation.) Mountains of letters arrived at this desk from over six dozen countries. There were personal letters, ranging from the simple greeting or thank-you note of a Mexican farm worker to the moody, soul-searching epistle of a poet or the *Zeitgeist* analysis of a scholar. Then there was the mass of reports, requests, suggestions, and notices from various regions — the actual internal administrative correspondence. And the out-box was just as full as the in-box. The personal answers from Escrivá numbered in the thousands; and these were never routine replies or form letters smacking of bureaucracy. He lived by the advice he used to give his fellow workers: "Behind every piece of paper you must see a soul!"[4]

Escrivá's day began exactly when his alarm clock rang — at about six o'clock — whether he had slept a long time, only a little, or not at all. For long periods of his life he frequently remained awake all night in prayer. Praying was to him like breathing: indeed, his every breath and heartbeat was a prayer. He was constantly engaged in a spiritual dialogue with God, which he said did not terminate even in sleep. He was convinced that one could pray while sleeping. Later, as the weight of years made itself felt, he was told that he must absolutely preserve his rest at night, or else he would be exhausted in the morning, his energy depleted. In his last years, when insomnia increased, he never arose before the set time, even when he lay awake. One of many acts of obedience, this was done at the express direction of one of his sons, a doctor.[5]

After dressing, he went to the chapel to spend half an hour in contemplative prayer, which also served as preparation for Mass. No one who ever attended one of his Masses remained untouched by it. The witnesses are legion. For many people, participation in a Eucharistic sacrifice celebrated by Josemaría Escrivá became the starting point of a new phase of their life, of an interior conversion and renewal, sometimes even of a vocation to Opus Dei.

There followed an extremely frugal breakfast: a cup of coffee with milk, and a little bread. The same held true for the other meals of the day. If he was alone, Escrivá often fasted totally, not even taking a drink of water. Just as he practiced the art of poverty, he also practiced the art of mortification, bringing home a serious point with his joking reminder to "mortify yourself, not others."[6]

The whole idea of mortification calls for some discussion. The word "mortify" does not, after all, commonly appear in the vocabulary of our times. Highly esteemed as it was by no less a figure than St. Paul,[7] this word is actually repellent to many people.

Well, it is not an especially pleasant word. In fact, to mortify oneself — to overcome oneself through sacrifice — is not a very pleasant thing. Yet it is something very necessary and desirable. For if we truly believe that Jesus Christ has enlisted us once and for all to follow him, we must realize that this means imitating him and identifying ourselves with him. Furthermore, if we believe that Christ has made us capable of this, surely we will want to answer the grace of such an insight of faith with a readiness to cooperate. This cooperation, however, ultimately involves concentrating so intently on the goal of following Christ that one pays less and less attention, and finally none at all, to the clamoring of one's ego. That is the core of St. Paul's teachings and the core of Christianity. This exchange of goals, wherein Christ takes the place of the ego and thus presents the possibility of eternal happiness with God, generally does not take place dramatically or instantaneously. It demands a lifelong struggle of hard labor with oneself — a work of mortification. Mortification is a constant attitude of inner detachment and exterior independence from the thousand demands of selfishness, with all its tricks and enticements to comfortable compromises. By no means does it consist only of those greater or lesser self-conquests that concern the material, physical, libidinous realms of our existence. On the contrary, it embraces every small act or attitude, taking priority away from the self and giving it to the "thou" of God and of others. Escrivá describes mortification in very concrete terms: "The appropriate word you left unsaid; the joke you didn't tell; the cheerful smile for those who bother you; that silence when you're unjustly accused; your kind conversation with people you find boring and tactless; the daily effort to overlook one irritating detail or another in those who live with you ... this, with perseverance, is indeed solid interior mortification."[8]

Genuine mortification is discreet and tactful, a form of conversation with God — not a Spartan or Prussian drill. Here, too, Msgr. Escrivá invented nothing. The disciplining of the ego and its incessant bodily, sensual, and spiritual demands for pleasure helps one to draw closer to Christ and to become more transparent and useful for his activity within one's soul. For this reason, mortification has been a key element of all Christian asceticism from the first days of the Church. What the founder of Opus Dei did was simply to rediscover this asceticism as something necessary for a more profound interior life, and to awaken awareness of its vital importance in the lives of people "in the world," the everyday churchgoers. Calling mortification the "prayer of the senses," he said it must be "as uninterrupted as the beating of our hearts; only then can we have dominion over our own selves and succeed in living the charity of Jesus Christ with the people around us."[9]

One aspect of the family atmosphere of the Work — an aspect which Escrivá taught from the beginning and with great insistence — is doing small acts of kindness and courtesy. These small acts must be done in an unforced, natural manner, and they must be accepted in the same way; otherwise, no human warmth is created. Mortification does not mean refusing good gifts, but rather, not indulging oneself constantly and immoderately, and especially not in front of others.

So much for our digression into the meaning and importance of mortification. Now let us continue with our description of a day in the everyday life of Msgr. Escrivá. After breakfast he read his breviary and then went to work at his desk; at noon he interrupted his work for a few minutes to recite the Angelus. Noontime was usually reserved for private visitors who wished to meet with him. Among them were often members of the Work who were traveling through Rome, or temporarily staying there. These receptions took place mostly between 12:30 and 1:15 p.m. in a small, elegant, almost boudoir-like room; the founder was usually accompanied by the secretary general (Fr. del Portillo) and an assistant from either the men's or women's

branch, depending on the situation. Everyone sat in comfortable closeness (there were sofas and armchairs around the table), and Escrivá's
often humorous cordiality banished all constraint or stiffness in conversation. The talk was always a dialogue; Escrivá never "held court,"
but asked questions and let himself be questioned.

After lunch, Escrivá visited the chapel to offer Christ his love
and adoration. In this way, he put the visible confession of the real
presence of Our Lord in the tabernacle in the middle of every day.
(He never took a siesta; never, except perhaps during an illness,
did he take any rest at all during the day.) On a normal workday,
he would then have an informal get-together for thirty or forty
minutes with his closest colleagues or with his sons who happened
to be at Villa Tevere (usually students of the Collegium Romanum
Sanctae Crucis). For many, these frequent, familiar gatherings with
Escrivá were the most decisive and lasting spiritual and formative
experience of their years of study in Rome. Here they encountered
his whole, rich, fascinating personality. He possessed enough
charisma not only to attract people, but also to inspire them — no
matter how burned-out or "sleepy-hearted" they might be — with
his love for God, for Christ, for their fellow men and women. "Hijo
mio" or "hija mia" ("my son," "my daughter") — two such simple
words could sink indelibly into a person's memory, often giving
direction to someone's entire life.

The long afternoon-into-evening hours, from about three to eight
o'clock, brimmed with activity. There were visits to be made — to
sick people, to Church authorities, or with his daughters in Castelgandolfo — and visitors from all over the world had to be received.
Then there was the daily administrative work: internal discussions,
meetings, and so forth. Escrivá himself drafted the documents that
established the directives for the spirituality and apostolate of Opus
Dei in the world. He also prepared spiritual meditations to give to his
sons and daughters, later working them into the final literary form in
which they would appear as books.

After supper, he dedicated another half hour to conversation
with his sons and then retired, usually around ten o'clock. He closed
the day in deepest silence, reviewing it in the light of his examination of conscience. Before going to bed, he lay prostrate on the floor

and prayed the great penitential psalm: "Miserere mei, Deus, secundum magnum misericordiam tuam." ("Have mercy on me, O Lord, according to your great mercy.")[10]

Journeying like Paul

Travel was a part of Escrivá's everyday life. Sometimes he lived for weeks and months at a time as a virtual prisoner of his work, practically locked up in Villa Tevere.[11] Just as often, however, he subjected himself to exhausting travels. The twenty-nine years in Italy saw a truly Pauline apostolate of travel from the Opus Dei center at Rome. The reasons for this lie in the universal mission of Opus Dei itself and in its global expansion. Escrivá made several European journeys from the late forties into the early sixties to explore the possibilities for opening branches of Opus Dei in different countries, and to strengthen the members in fledgling centers. (Members in these new centers usually faced grave material problems, and since success often came very slowly, they needed the encouraging presence of their founder and father.) He also had to make frequent trips to Spain, since the General Council was still there, and since Opus Dei had so many members there.

With the exception of Spain and Portugal, France and Switzerland dominate the list of countries visited by Escrivá. He went to France about twenty times, to Switzerland about fifteen. In contrast, he visited Austria only three times. He went to West Germany eight times, making seven visits between 1955 and 1960, none thereafter. Every trip had its own unique circumstances. I do not know the rationale governing his travel plans and accounting for their very uneven pattern — perhaps later research will yield insights into this. But this much is certain: Escrivá never traveled capriciously. Most of his travels were determined by the administrative necessities of the moment and a purposeful planning for the future. He liked to link these travels with pilgrimages — to Lourdes, to Fatima, to Einsiedeln — or with recreational getaways from the overwhelming heat of the Roman summer. From 1958 to 1962, for example, he spent his summers in England.

Escrivá traveled mostly by automobile, with one of his sons at the wheel. Whoever was assigned this task had to understand quite a lot about automobiles, for the used cars (it was many years before they could afford new ones) had their quirks, and it took a considerable amount of skilled maintenance to keep them running for any length of time. In addition to the driver, two other close associates usually accompanied the Father — del Portillo was almost always one of them. While on the road, they did their daily prayer — sometimes individually, in silence, and sometimes together, using a text recited aloud. They also said the rosary, read from the Gospels, or did some other spiritual reading. But conversation and jokes were never lacking. (Neither were songs. Escrivá liked to improvise on the lyrics, and he was fond of telling people afterwards that they had "paved the roads of Europe with Ave Marias and songs."[12]) One of his favorite themes of discussion was the special aspects of the apostolate in different countries. Escrivá possessed an uncanny flair for discerning not only the personalities of individuals, but also the personalities of the different nations in which Opus Dei was active. He could diagnose their strengths and weaknesses with a high degree of accuracy. He viewed, for example, the self-control of the British and the diligence of the Germans as splendid foundations for an understanding and implementing of the lay spirituality of Opus Dei, yet their dark sides did not elude him. He knew very well how easily a natural disposition for religious conversion can be blocked when self-discipline becomes a fortification of the heart against God and neighbor, or when industriousness becomes a soulless rat-race or an obsession with organizing just for the sake of organizing.

As I was working on my biography of St. Thomas More,[13] an evocative photograph stood before me on my desk: Josemaría Escrivá and Alvaro del Portillo in St. Dunstan's Church in Canterbury, where the head of the Lord Chancellor is buried. (Thomas More was canonized in 1935 by Pope Pius XI.) Escrivá loved this martyr a great deal, not only because he followed the law of God as transmitted by his conscience and mounted the scaffold for the unity of the Catholic Church, but also because he did this as a layman, a loyal citizen of the world, a father, husband, and politician who had sanctified himself in both his life and his death. Escrivá named him as intercessor of Opus Dei for all matters dealing with the civil authorities.[14] He used to say of the great Englishman, "If he had lived in our time, he would have been a supernumerary of Opus Dei."[15]

Catholics in England have been fully free to practice their religion only since 1829,[16] and many of them are descendants of immigrants or of families converted during the years of the Oxford movement of the nineteenth century.[17] The number of English members of the Work was small, and their apostolic work still resembled a closed bud, when Escrivá visited Eton and the university towns of Oxford and Cambridge. Of the two colleges, so splendid and rich in tradition, he said, "God must be brought into these places!"[18] He urged that the specific apostolate with students begin as soon as possible, starting with Oxford, and that the youth work of St. Raphael be intensified. His listeners mentioned to him the reticence of the English in personal matters. He was told of the interior resistance Britons tend to have toward any talk, no matter how friendly, which touches on the private sphere of the individual — especially concerning religion. "You must," he countered, "intervene in the lives of others in just the same way as Jesus Christ has intervened in mine: without asking permission!" He was saying, in other words, that the real obstacle for the apostolate is not so much the reserve of the person addressed as it is the false tact of the speaker afraid to mention spiritual subjects; the root of the problem is inhibitions that often are nothing but laziness or cowardice in disguise.

On August 15, 1958, Escrivá renewed, as he did every year, the consecration of Opus Dei to the Virgin Mary. This time the renewal took place in the Church of Our Lady of Willesden (whose ancient image was brought to the papal Mass held in Wembley Stadium on May 29, 1982). In Westminster Abbey, the citadel of the national, Anglican conscience, tourists were amazed to see a priest praying the rosary before an image of the Mother of God. Msgr. Escrivá returned four times to visit England, even though — or rather, because — he found not only joy and confidence there, but also sadness and disappointment. Years later, in a meditation, he admitted this to his children. They should not, he said, consider him some kind of miracle man, somebody immune from temptation. They should see him for what he was: a regular flesh-and-blood person, well acquainted with weariness and the temptation to capitulate. He felt the impact of all the indifference to God he met with every day; it hurt him to the core, because he loved God so much. "As I viewed the entire panorama one more time," he said, "I lost my composure somewhat and felt incompetent and powerless. *Josemaría, you can't do anything here.* Without God, I could not even pull a blade of grass from the ground. My whole, miserable weakness was so apparent that I almost grew sad — and that is bad. Why should a son of God be sad? He can be weary, like a faithful donkey pulling a cart. But sad? Never! Sadness is evil. Suddenly, in the middle of the street, where people from all corners of the world were crossing paths, I felt within me, in the depth of my heart, the motion of God's power. I felt him reassuring me, 'You can do nothing, but I can do everything; you are weakness, but I am strength. I shall be with you, and that will have an effect. We shall lead souls to happiness, to unity, to the way of salvation. Here, too, we shall sow peace and happiness in abundance.'"[19]

In 1958, right after his trip to England, Escrivá visited Germany for the sixth time. After stopping in Holland for three days, he arrived on September 21st in Cologne, where the headquarters of this new region of Opus Dei was located. On the same day, he also traveled to Bonn, because the first German student center had just opened there; and on the next day, he made a pilgrimage to Maria Laach. (This was the third in a series of five two-day visits he made to Germany.[20]) The visit was intended to build the confidence of the tiny flock and to embolden them to take courageous steps into the future. Indeed, it was in the sixties that Opus Dei expanded most rapidly in Germany. The same was true of Austria and Switzerland. When the successor of the founder returned to Germany eighteen years later (in 1978), there were centers of Opus Dei — some flourishing, some just beginning — in Cologne, Bonn, Aachen, Berlin, Essen, Munich, and Münster. Since then, Düsseldorf, Jülich, and Trier have been added. From these centers, the apostolic work of Opus Dei reaches the entire territory of the Federal Republic of Germany. Until the first centers could be established in Stockholm, the German outreach even included some of the Scandinavian countries. The scope of this apostolate is admittedly modest in view of the fact that Germany has some seventy-five million inhabitants, of whom about forty percent are Catholic; it is also quite modest in comparison to the outreach of Opus Dei in Spain, Portugal, or Latin America. In light of its point of departure, however, it is a major accomplishment.

When I met the prelate of Opus Dei in January 1981, in Cologne, I asked him what his predecessor had thought of Germans.[21] He told me that Josemaría's father, José Escrivá, had been an enthusiastic admirer of Germany. Josemaría, therefore, had had a favorable impression of Germany from the earliest years of his childhood. Holding in high esteem the natural virtues of the Germans, he regretted the fact that so often these virtues were separated from religion and supernatural guidance, and thus could bear no fruit. Discipline, order, diligence, drive might all be present; but what good are they in the absence of receptiveness to grace? Del Portillo tells us that Escrivá was familiar with German philosophy and intellectual history, and that he was especially familiar with those ideas — the "Krausism" of the thirties, for example — which had found a home in Spanish intellectual circles.[22]

Escrivá held one thing paramount with regard to Germany: he placed great hope in a rich apostolic harvest in Germany and, through the German culture, in Central Europe, Scandinavia, and Eastern Europe. Though he could offer no timetable, he stood firm in his conviction that faithfulness to one's vocation and the readiness to act in accordance with it necessarily bears fruit that sooner or later will be harvested. He was also convinced that the Germans, the Austrians, and the Swiss had a particular Christian, apostolic vocation.

The first journey to Central Europe lasted thirteen days, from November 22 to December 4, 1949.[23] En route from Milan, Escrivá wrote a short but characteristic letter to his followers in Portugal: "May Jesus protect you, my beloved children! About to visit Austria and Germany for the first time, I am moved by the memory of my first trip to the blessed land of Portugal. Pray hard for my undertaking, so that the Lord will look not on our wretchedness but on our faith, so that soon we may finally begin our work in Central Europe. A warm embrace for all and the blessing of your father,

Mariano."[24] Escrivá and his two companions spent two days at Innsbruck. One of his fellow travelers reports that he liked the colorful peasant houses of Tyrol (many have fresco paintings on their exteriors), and that he liked even better the obvious piety of the people. He said that the Work must begin soon in Austria and Germany, because there would be many vocations in these two countries. From there they went (by way of Garmisch) to Munich, arriving there on Thursday, December 1st. The sight of Munich in 1949 did not portend a bright prognosis for Germany. Everywhere lay traces of the terrible war that had ended five years earlier. "The city," Escrivá recalled later, "was half destroyed. In the hotel where we stayed, we had to keep close to the wall when using the stairs, because there was no banister."[25] The phrase of the day was "poor but respectable." When dessert was ordered for Msgr. Escrivá, the waiter produced, on a large silver platter, one apple.

Escrivá said Mass on the day of his arrival, probably in the Cathedral of Our Lady.[26] Michael Cardinal Faulhaber received him afterwards — they conversed in Latin. The cardinal showed great interest in Opus Dei and spoke of the vast pastoral problems caused by the influx of millions of Catholic refugees from the east.[27] Escrivá thus obtained firsthand insight into one of the most grievous consequences of the German collapse of 1945, one which would have a decisive influence on the history of the newborn Federal Republic. He returned to Rome by way of Venice, having traveled over twenty-one hundred miles on wintry roads. Escrivá had spoken with an important German prelate, and the first German furrow had been plowed for the apostolic fields of the future.

The first members of the Work arrived in the summer of 1952.[28] They were three young Spaniards: a priest and two students (both of whom are now professors at German universities). They knew little German, and they had no money, housing, or connections. A few years later two women came, also with next to nothing. And from this handful of young people came everything that Opus Dei can claim in Germany today — centers, student residences, and youth clubs for both branches, as well as an intense personal apostolate extending over the entire nation. In memory's eye these first years may appear wonderfully exciting and rich in instructive and funny anecdotes, but the fact remains that they were very difficult years; these were hard times. The young people did their best to earn money as translators, but they went hungry for days and often did not know where they would eat or sleep next. As one of these pioneers tells us, "We felt depressed, because our search for housing in the first months remained unsuccessful. The Father, in Rome, must have sensed our courage waning, because from time to time a letter would arrive from him to cheer us up. We had to look harder, he wrote; 'your steps through the streets of Bonn will resound like a peal of bells in heaven.'"

On May 1, 1953, the young men finally found a dwelling in Bonn — in an old-fashioned villa lying like a monument to the nineteenth century in the midst of the regional government's buildings. Soon this house became the student center "Althaus." But two years were to pass before Opus Dei received its first German vocations. Josemaría Escrivá visited Althaus many times.[29] The first visit was on May 1, 1955 — he had intended to travel directly to Austria from Switzerland, but his desire to see these sons of his again and to restore their courage won out and cost him a six-hundred-mile detour. Escrivá certainly understood the restrictions of poverty, but he urged them to make every conceivable effort to improve the furnishings of their center, especially in the oratory. Here, as so often elsewhere, he reminded his children that when Opus Dei started, he had been much poorer and the situation had been more difficult. He told them all about the Roman College at Villa Tevere and announced the imminent beginning of the Work in Switzerland and Austria. They should pray often, he told the young men, that the women's branch could come to Germany as soon as possible.[30]

A talk that Msgr. Escrivá gave to his sons in Bonn during that visit was preserved on a tape recorder. The following is an excerpt:

> I am very happy to be in Germany, and I have the greatest expectations that the Lord will soon grant a multitude of vocations. You shall see; the hour of the harvest has come. My child, doesn't it make you happy to see the trust that the Lord puts in us? It's clear that the fruitfulness of the Work depends on how faithful we are. What a great responsibility we have! And how much we feel like sons of God

when he shows us this much trust! What joy the thought of the harvest gives us, the harvest that is ripening on German soil! The Work is a field cultivated for the harvest, even though twenty-seven years is very little for an institution, and even less for a family that the Lord wished to found so that it might last as long as there are men and women on this earth — a family serving the Church, spreading the kingdom of Christ for the salvation of souls, and making people happy by bringing them to God.

When del Portillo was asked what impressed him the most in Germany, he answered with a touch of humor, "Nothing yet, really, since we traveled on the Autobahn from Switzerland, and that's like taking an airplane — until Bonn, we saw nothing. Here, however, I like just what the Father already mentioned: the joy that is exactly the same as in all the other centers. Moreover, I have great faith in the good qualities of the German people and especially in the many vocations they will receive in the service of God and the Church."

After an unlucky trip up the Rhine Valley on May 3rd (during which the old car broke down, and sightseeing was confined to garages instead of landscapes), Escrivá and his companions reached Mainz that night. The next day he celebrated Mass in the cathedral and returned in the afternoon to Althaus. In a short get-together, one of these early members recalls, "he admonished us again to love Germany very much, but nevertheless — without diminishing this love — to be always ready to move to another country should this be necessary for the cause of Christ."

Escrivá revisited Cologne and Bonn in December of that same year.[31] This time, however, he traveled further — through Munich and Innsbruck to Vienna, where he arrived on May 7th.[32] Austria was at that time still divided into four zones of occupation: American, British, French, and Russian. The jointly administered city of Vienna was similarly divided. A sense of déjà vu touched Escrivá as the car crossed the famous Enns Bridge, which separates the Soviet from the American zone. "It was adorned," he said, "with a large crucifix, before which stood a Russian sentry. This made a deep impression on me, for I had lived under communist rule for a year and a half during the Civil War in Spain, and had seen so many churches burned down...." Nevertheless, he found that the Russians were just men and women like everyone else. One day, Escrivá walked by a hotel in Vienna that had been transformed into a Soviet military barracks, and there was a group of soldiers standing outside; he later commented that they had seemed like good kids to him, especially the younger ones with the friendly smiles.

The Spaniards slept in a modest hotel next to the Franz Josef railroad station in the American sector. During the day, the three of them — Escrivá, Alvaro, and Georgio (the driver) — remained constantly on their feet. "To get to know a city," Escrivá said, "one must walk about the town in every direction. We saw that Vienna was still a city of wonderful riches, possessed of an imperial splendor, although it had suffered much in the course of time." Later he remarked, "This is the only city I've seen with a monument to the Most Holy Trinity!"[33] On the base of the famous column, which is crowned with a statue of Mary, Escrivá and del Portillo discovered an inscription: "Deo Patri Creatori — Deo Filii Redemptori — Deo Spiritui Sanctificatori." ("To God the Father, Creator; To God the Son, Redeemer; To God the Spirit, Sanctifier.") Escrivá had these words carved into the altar at Villa Tevere where he celebrated Mass.

Several months later, Escrivá returned to Vienna, coming once again from the Rhineland. The Allied and Soviet occupation of Austria was over. He celebrated Mass on December 4th in St. Stephen's Cathedral; then, kneeling before the miraculous image called "Maria Pötsch," he placed the Work in Austria under the protection of the Mother of God.[34] He prayed "Sancta Maria, Stella Orientis, filios tuos adiuva!" ("Holy Mary, Star of the East, help your children!"), meaning, "Please help your children to succeed in Austria and, in the future, to move from Austria to other lands." And so we see that the motto of "the Ruler of the World" Charles V — "Plus ultra!" — is far from obsolete. In the world of politics, "Ever onward!" may be a rash thing to say; but in apostolic work, it is something that must be said.

And thus it was that the one-time political slogan "Austria is the gateway to the east" became for Escrivá a promise. He had an optimism that was supernatural in origin, yet thoroughly in touch with everyday reality; it was anything but quixotic. This realism was very much in evidence, for example, during a visit he made the last time he was in Cologne, to one of the women's centers. In the course

of conversation, one of the young ladies had enthusiastically proposed that Opus Dei go to Russia. What Escrivá said in reply did not
seem to address what she had said, but that was because he wanted
to bring her back to earth gently. One must act, he said, with both
natural and supernatural prudence; then, and only then, things
would eventually work out. He spoke about his first visit to Vienna,
when it was occupied by the Russians, and then he added, "My
daughters, I pray for the unity of your country! I also pray for Berlin.
That is a duty of justice. You must work throughout Germany —
what an unlimited field of opportunity awaits you!"[35]

In the course of time, not only the geographical range but also
the agenda for Escrivá's travels broadened. Making penitential pilgrimages and teaching the faith were emphasized more and more.[36]
Escrivá seized every opportunity to offer the Mother of God reparation for himself and all the members of Opus Dei, for their own sins
and the sins of their fellow Christians. (This characteristic love is
one of the cornerstones of the Christian religion.) Between 1967 and
1969, he undertook frequent pilgrimages to the sites of Marian
apparitions and other miracles in Italy, Switzerland, France, and
Spain. On April 1, 1970, in the face of all the tribulations the Church
was suffering from so much internal confusion and the infidelity of
some Catholics, he began a penitential pilgrimage. This brought
him to a number of sites of Marian devotion on the Iberian peninsula: Saragossa (Our Lady of the Pillar), Torreciudad, and Fatima.

In May, Escrivá made his first transatlantic journey.[37] This, too,
was a pilgrimage of penance, and so he began and ended his month
in Mexico by visiting the shrine of Our Lady of Guadalupe.[38] But
there was something different about this trip. Escrivá was now "going public," addressing thousands of people at once. In Rome and
Pamplona he had already spoken to large gatherings and had managed to give these meetings a personal flavor, entering into an intimate dialogue with the crowd. Now, at the end of his life, he was
to carry this large-scale format of catechesis throughout the world.

Naturally, he went first to Spain, Portugal, and Latin America,
where Opus Dei was most developed. In October and November of
1972, Escrivá made a catechetical journey covering the entire Iberian
Peninsula.[39] Over 150,000 people saw him in person. For each one

there, it was a personal encounter — he never addressed "crowds" as such, but always individuals, even when they came in huge numbers. But there was more to his journey than these very public gatherings. To emphasize the necessity of the contemplative life and his love for it, he also visited the convents of contemplative nuns in every Spanish and Portuguese city he entered, encouraging them to remain faithful to their particular vocation and their founders' rules. He knew of only one People of God, whose members had to pray for and support one another. Jealousies between the various families within the Church were incomprehensible to him.

As if Escrivá knew his allotted time on earth was running out, his desire to reach more souls grew greater than ever. Like a runner on the last lap, he picked up the pace and wrung out the last drops of adrenalin, though he was already exhausted. On May 22, 1974, at the age of seventy-two, he embarked on his longest and most fatiguing journey ever.[40] This journey, which lasted until August 31st, took him to Brazil, Argentina, Chile, Peru, Ecuador, and Venezuela. He visited numerous centers of Opus Dei in these countries and met tens of thousands of people. As priest, apostle, and father, he spent himself spiritually, mentally, and physically. The hot weather, drastic altitude changes, and long plane flights were a heavy burden as well; for weeks, he fought bronchitis, fever, and altitude sickness. His health barely held out at all through the last leg of the trip through Venezuela. Finally, after spending a few weeks in Spain, he returned to Rome on September 30th, totally exhausted. Yet six months later his apostolic restlessness drove him across the Atlantic again. On February 4, 1975, he arrived in Caracas and continued where he had left off in Venezuela. From Venezuela he flew to Guatemala. There he suddenly became so ill that he was forced to return to Rome on February 23rd. Perhaps he sensed that his last — or rather, penultimate — journey was over.

In the early seventies, Escrivá finally allowed his apostolic travels to be recorded on film. These color films serve as an excellent introduction to Escrivá and Opus Dei. (There are more than a hundred of them, and they are shown fairly often at the various centers.) Preserving the unique dialogue between Escrivá and people of every age, race, and social status, these films convey the seminal energy of this work of Christian renewal. They cover a broad range of topics, but three main points seem to surface, especially during the South American trip: an affirmation of God's gift of life and the Catholic family; an insistence on fidelity to the doctrine of the Catholic Church, and on its eternal validity; and a call for Catholics to return to the sacrament of Reconciliation. He wanted to make sure everyone realized that without penance, there is no reconciliation with God; without reconciliation with God, there is no spiritual growth; and without life, truth, and mercy, there can be no personal friendship with Christ and no renewal of either the Church or the world.

At a meeting in Barcelona in 1972, a mother of ten children complained of the lack of understanding — and even open hostility — she was encountering, simply for having so many children. Escrivá answered, "All men and women know the teaching of the Church; all know it.[41] But then egoism, brutality, and passions arise, and powerful propaganda joins in. In this way, people lose their sense of sin and commit horrendous crimes, even the killing of children." On a visit to Buenos Aires in 1974, he said, "In the Church of God, the priests have taught the same things for two thousand years. So if you hear things that appear completely new, they are not from God. We men and women — I especially like this metaphor — have not created religion with votes or plebiscites. Get an old St. Pius X catechism[42] and read it in peace, to protect the faith of your children."[43]

Genuine faith demands deeds. To accomplish works of love, faith must shape hearts that have not gone to sleep or turned to stone under the rubble of perversion or worldly attachments. The heaps of refuse that arise from our weaknesses and lack of love must be periodically hauled away. This is what the sacrament of Reconciliation does through the whole process of confession of sin, contrition for it, resolution to avoid it in the future, and forgiveness of it. This spiritual restoration is not something subjective or probable, but something objective and guaranteed by Christ himself.

On a visit to Tabancura College in Santiago, Chile, Escrivá spoke eloquently of the immeasurable value of this sacrament. "For many years," he said, "I have told a story — it may seem trivial, but it means a lot to me. I was in Portugal, speaking to people, as I am now. Some of my children gave me a present of a big soup tureen — a bowl for a large family. This tureen had been used every day for many years. It had been broken, repaired with iron clasps, and used again. I looked at them and said, 'Well done; you've taught me an important lesson' — for just as you are doing now, they used to teach me lessons, and I encouraged them to. I said, 'Yes, indeed, I am like this bowl: broken to pieces and fastened with iron clasps, but still in service; usable again thanks to the holy sacrament of Penance, which I receive every week to ask forgiveness from the Lord for my sins and to renew repentance for everything in my life that has injured him.'" Escrivá told his audience at Tabancura, "Confess, confess, confess, confess! Because Christ poured his mercy out upon his creatures. So much is lost when we do not go to him to purify ourselves, to cleanse ourselves, to inflame ourselves again. Lots of exercise, sports — that's good, that's fine! But what about that other sport, the sport of the soul? What about that other water that cleanses, purifies, and strengthens us? Why don't we go receive this grace from God, in the sacrament of Penance and in Holy Communion? Go and receive! But don't receive Communion if you are unsure that your soul is pure. First there must be penance — personal penance, individual penance, like in the past. Any other way is impossible — unless, of course, an earthquake were to catch us off-guard. If that were to happen now, I'd say, 'My children, I absolve you — but you're under obligation to confess if we survive!' And I would only be telling you what the Church has always said, for the Church cannot change. She teaches just what she taught two thousand years ago; and two thousand years from now, she will still be teaching what she is teaching today."*

Opus Dei and the Council

The ninth chapter of the Articles of Postulation for Escrivá's beatification is entitled "Attorno al Concilio 1958-1970," which can be loosely translated as "In Connection with the Council." It describes the conciliar era: the time of preparation from 1958 until 1962, the Council itself, and the first five years of its implementation.

---

*RHF, 20771, p. 214. [Ed.]

An ecumenical council is a worldwide gathering, summoned by the pope,[44] of those men who, according to canon law, exercise authority in the Church: cardinals, ruling and residing patriarchs, primates, archbishops, bishops, abbots, prelates nullius,[45] the heads of the exempt clerical religious orders, and, upon special invitation, the titular bishops and heads of other religious orders. These are the "council fathers." The advisers (called *periti*), theologians, and representatives of non-Catholic religions can assist, observe, and accompany the council, but they are not council fathers. Although they may exert considerable influence, they make no decisions and bear no responsibility for decisions, apart from their responsibility before God of giving good counsel.

In the context of a Church council, "ecumenical" does not mean "interdenominational"; it means "universal" with regard to participation by the Catholic hierarchy. An ecumenical council is an assembly of the bishops with the pope presiding. A lack of clarity on such a basic point can cause great confusion. In union with the pope, an ecumenical council does exercise supreme doctrinal and pastoral authority over the Church. But it cannot exercise this authority without the pope, whereas the pope can exercise supreme authority by himself. This issue, clouded for centuries by the opposing tides of papal and conciliar movements, was resolved in the Council of Florence (1431-1442) and finally defined by the Council of Trent (1545-1563). Vatican I elaborated on this resolution with the doctrine of papal infallibility. Vatican II reaffirmed this doctrine, but also emphasized the principle of collegiality, the principle of brotherly love in the relationship between the pope and all other bishops.

The three most recent councils — Trent, Vatican I, and Vatican II — mark three profound crises in the Church, hurricanes in which the ship of Peter was threatened by stormy seas. Since the Church exists in the world, and Christians — always children of their times — are subject to formidable social and personal pressures, such crises have both spiritual and secular dimensions. These councils were convened in different stages of the particular crisis at hand, but each of them was an attempt to give the Church new strength by taking the measures necessary to fulfill Christ's saving mission in a changing world.

The Council of Trent was really a response to the crisis of Protestantism — not a mere crisis, I would say, but a catastrophe, the terrible consequences of which are probably yet to be fully appreciated. The Council of Trent defined what is Catholic faith, and what is not.

Vatican I is understood superficially if, as is often the case, it is viewed simply as the council that declared the pope infallible. It was the first part of the Church's long-delayed answer to what has often been called "modernism." Since this is a tired term, I prefer to say that Vatican I marked the beginning of the Church's adjustment to the new situation in the world that arose from the Enlightenment and the democratic revolutions of the eighteenth and nineteenth centuries.

The doctrine of infallibility declares that the pope is free from error when, speaking ex cathedra (as the successor of St. Peter), he formulates and solemnly defines a statement of faith or morals to be held by the universal Church. All Catholic Christians are thereby obligated to accept this teaching. Papal infallibility, however, is only a part of the whole answer to the modern world. In his apostolic letter *Aeterni Patris* (June 29, 1868),[46] Pius IX clearly stated his reason for summoning a council: it was to discuss the Church's defense against the errors listed in the "Syllabus of Errors" (December 8, 1864).[47] These errors, direct offspring of the age of "enlightenment" and revolution, never did disappear; they have, indeed, become a permanent challenge to the Church. In eighty sentences the "Syllabus" listed them. Essentially they are errors of subjectivism — an intellectual attitude that, enhanced by popular strains of relativism, seems to have won a total victory in the one hundred twenty years since Vatican I. Little by little, these errors have infiltrated the minds of millions of Christians of all denominations. This has been, of its very nature, a mental victory.

The Second Vatican Council had to address this situation. The pope and the other shepherds of the Church gathered to discuss and determine how the Catholic faith should be lived, and the mission of Christ carried out, in a world dominated by relativistic subjectivism. For we are now living in a world that denies the existence, or at least the perceptibility, of a single truth; a world that pays homage to the historical relativism supposedly operative in every dimension of human existence and behavior; a world in rebellion against any subjection or obedience to an absolute norm — which, for Catholics, is the salvific will of God operating through the Church. The Council fathers sought to ensure that Peter's ship remained seaworthy. Council fathers, however, are not test-tube creations, and they do not wear surgical masks; they breathe normally and inhale the same germs everyone else does. The council hall is not a sterilized operating room. Council fathers of Vatican II, the second half of the Church's answer to modernism, faced a new challenge. In a world permeated by the errors of modernism, the doctors themselves were more susceptible to the disease they sought to cure than their nineteenth-century predecessors had been.

The style of the Second Vatican Council was also new. It took place in the public eye, facing continuous direct and indirect publicity. The penumbra of *periti* supplying information and materials sometimes overwhelmed the less sophisticated bishops with the weight of their scholarly status. A bishop needed to have a strong personality to remember that his authority came not from specialized knowledge, but from the teaching mission of the apostles, the apostolic succession, his episcopal consecration. Vatican II cannot be fully understood unless one takes into account the varying influences of the accompanying horde of assistants (pious and not so pious, perceptive and obtuse), reporters, and interpreters of every kind.

The Council was, of course, permeated by the action of the Holy Spirit. Individual Council fathers might offer ill-advised opinions, but the decisions of the Council were guaranteed by the Holy Spirit. On the other hand, while the Council documents were necessarily safeguarded by the Holy Spirit, their interpretation was not. The novelty of this pastoral council was that it produced "open" documents, rather than statements. In taking this risk, the Council fathers demonstrated true Christian optimism and faith in Divine Providence, relying on the action of the Holy Spirit in the souls of believers. Unfortunately, when dogmatic formulas chiseled with Roman precision were replaced with voluminous reflections on the faith and beautiful essays on the Catholic's life with Christ, unscrupulous manipulators also set to work — and with considerable success.

Three years after the conclusion of the Second Vatican Council, Karol Wojtyla, then archbishop of Krakow, published an essay titled "An Introduction to Vatican II: An Attempt at Clarification."[48] In this essay he wrote, "The Council looks at the Church in the mirror of revelation and, at the same time, situates and reaffirms the Church in the experience of the world today. And thanks to the Council, the Church also sees itself from the viewpoint of modern men and women's needs and problems. In this manner, the Church blooms by recognizing its mysterious supernatural essence. This opening up, or rather, this openness of the Church, signifies its new enclosure — not within itself, but in the setting in which, as Paul VI writes in his encyclical, 'the hand of God has placed us.'"[49] Pope John Paul II might today reread these words of his with sorrow. Not that there is no longer room for Christian optimism; that is far from the case. But the potential expansion of the devil's field of action in conjunction with the openness of the Council must have been something beyond the Council fathers' imagination; for the devil, the third determinative force in world history (after Divine Providence and free will) is hardly mentioned in the Council documents. The statement of the archbishop of Krakow makes the post-conciliar dilemma clear. The rich openness of the Council documents is nourishment for Catholics who are already well-intentioned, pious, and faithful; but when misinterpreted, they offer a foothold for those inside and outside the Church who are fighting for an alternate type of Catholicism.

Trent and Vatican I sought dogmatic and legal consolidation after historical events that seemed catastrophic. Fortifications were erected out of the granite blocks of definitions and laws. Vatican II, on the other hand, relied on friendly persuasion and the will to convince. The approach was to be "dialogue," something the Church should initiate by "taking root" in the world. Unlike the other two councils, which had tried to create a suit of armor out of faithful obedience and ecclesiastical discipline, Vatican II recommended that Catholics leave the fortress, discard the armor, and enter the marketplace. There, in a stall next to all the others, they should compete with confidence, relying on the merit of their own wares. This recommendation carried along with it a call to exercise personal freedom and other social virtues: friendship, common sense, and a spirit of fairmindedness.

It is undeniably a Christian duty to go to the marketplace and trade with one's talents. The fortress of sound doctrine, however, cannot be neglected, nor the armor of fidelity scrapped. The enthusiastic merchant must bear in mind that the Lord of both the market and the fortress prohibits the burial of talents and commands that they be multiplied through hard work and prudent investment,[50] not by a debasing of the currency.

Notwithstanding his first-rate intelligence and ability to diagnose current affairs, Escrivá remained free of that arrogance that accepts no institutional limitations and that likes nothing better than to advise God himself. He recognized authority and did not deem it necessary to summon every ecclesiastical statement before the court of his own opinion so that he could then proclaim his verdict.

In Pope John's call for an ecumenical council, Escrivá saw the will of God. He did not second-guess or even question whether such a council was opportune. When the pope promulgated a document of the Council, often the result of protracted debate and controversy, Escrivá accepted it without further discussion as an instrument that would serve the Church and all humanity. This was true with regard to the entire Council. Escrivá understood the risks taken by the Council, and he suffered with the Church when new freedoms were abused, but he never doubted that after this trial by fire, the Church would enjoy a newly kindled, zealous love for Christ.

Escrivá did not participate in the Council directly. He held no office in the gigantic apparatus of preparations, assistance, and advice. John XXIII had wished to appoint him a consultor, but this would have entailed an enormous additional workload and time expenditure, and Escrivá was already pressed beyond endurance. The pope therefore appointed del Portillo to this position. Three of the Council fathers were also members of Opus Dei,[51] and so that Escrivá could indirectly share in the Council process, these three and consultor Don Alvaro were relieved of their obligation of silence with respect to him. Del Portillo was concerned with the preparation of the Council from the start, especially regarding the role of the laity in the Church.[52] He eventually became the secretary of the Council commission "De disciplina cleri et populi Christiani" and a *peritus* on several other committees. In this way, Opus Dei had the privilege of participating in the Council. Of course, the two friends Alvaro and Josemaría discussed all the Council issues. In the four years of the Council, not a day passed without a conversation between these two men who represented the body and soul of Opus Dei. But Don Alvaro was not Escrivá's only contact with the Council. Many bishops, consultors, theologians, and canon lawyers sought Msgr. Escrivá's advice during the four sessions.[53]

We know no details of Escrivá's conversations with his secretary general and these visitors. A discreet silence will probably be observed here for a while, since some of those involved are still living. But some of Escrivá's comments are recorded in the Articles of Postulation, and these comments give us an idea of his views on certain Council issues. There is, for example, his reply to a bishop who, while discoursing on the emancipation of the laity, had said it was their task to fill the world with Christian life and transform the structures of the temporal order. "Yes, your Excellency," responded Escrivá, "but only if they have a contemplative soul! Otherwise, they will not transform anything at all; rather they will be the ones transformed. The result will then be the opposite of what you intend: instead of Christianizing the world, Christians will become worldly."[54] And there is this remark, which he made in a similar conversation: "[Lay apostolate is] all well and good, but first the laity must be in order on the inside: men and women with a deep interior life, souls of prayer and sacrifice! If they are not, then instead of putting society and the family in order, they will just add their own disorder to what is already there."[55] Words that were all too prophetic; for indeed, the post-conciliar turmoil within the Church was caused by the fact that the new emancipation of Catholics was not accompanied by a renewal of devotion. Rather, it went hand in hand with a neglect of religious devotions and a rejection of the hierarchy as such — as guardians of the faith, in all its mystery and integrity. Sadly, such neglect and rejection is often confused with Christian maturity.

Though the history of the Council that is at our disposal is far from complete,[56] one can perceive in it forces that fostered conflict between the pope and the other Council participants over status, rights, and authority within the Church. To some extent, the pontificate of Paul VI was characterized by a battle over papal authority.[57] Escrivá never relaxed in his support of this authority — every pope since Pius XII has known he could rely on Opus Dei in every situation. On February 14, 1964, Escrivá wrote a letter in which he exhorted the theologians and canon lawyers within Opus Dei to "defend the authority of the Roman pontiff, which is derived from God himself, from every possible attack."[58] And twenty months later he wrote, "Remain very close to the pope, follow his teachings, take them to your prayer, defend them with your word and with your pen!"[59] These were not theoretical recommendations. His words stood out in high relief against a darkening background of crisis within the Church. For the years after the Council brought with them a crisis on every front: a crisis of faith for many priests and theologians, a crisis concerning tradition, a crisis regarding Church discipline and hierarchical authority.

In the day-to-day life of Opus Dei, Escrivá ordered strict observance of the decisions of the Council, eschewing any arbitrary license or capriciousness in matters of doctrine and liturgy. In this connection, we should bear in mind that liturgical improvisation, neglect of the sacrament of Reconciliation, and sexual laissez-faireism directly contradict the explicit intentions of the Council.

Moreover, a "new theology" viewing all dogmas as historically determined products of the "spirit of the age," as products which must be continually reformulated in accordance with the unfolding consciousness of each succeeding generation, finds no support in the documents of Vatican II. To deny the physical reality of the Virgin Birth or the Resurrection, to declare them mythical symbols or concepts unique to the magical thought of a prerational and prescientific state of consciousness, is not a fruit of the theological research initiated by Vatican II; it is heresy, and a rather hackneyed heresy at that. Furthermore, the facile claim that Thomistic theology has been

superseded is simply not true.[60] Its central concepts — "nature,"
"essence," "form," "substance," "person," and so forth — do require
commentary, especially in the light of scientific advances. This does
not, however, diminish the value of Aquinas' metaphysics. I asked
Don Alvaro about this, and he pointed out that although St.
Thomas would have written differently in our age, his writings would
undoubtedly have had the same content, for he had discovered and
formulated imperishable truths. In this context it should be noted
that Vatican II, alone of all Church councils, explicitly enjoined theologians and priests to uphold the teachings of Thomas Aquinas. In
a striking way it thus corroborated and reinforced a tradition of
more than six-hundred-years standing; for ever since his canonization in 1323, Rome has recommended Aquinas as an indispensable
guide for the authentic interpretation of the truths of faith.[61]

Pope Pius X made this recommendation with special emphasis
in his motu proprio *Doctor Angelis*. Escrivá quotes this document
extensively in his last major letter (dated February 14, 1974). The
pope says, for example, that it is important to "keep holy and intact
the philosophical foundations that St. Thomas laid, for by proceed-
ing from them we are able to comprehend the created world in a
manner corresponding to faith, to refute the errors of every epoch,
and to determine with certainty what belongs to God alone and
cannot be ascribed to another source. With complete clarity, there
appears before our eyes the analogy of being and the distinction
between God and his works."[62] Furthermore, "the most important
points in the philosophy of St. Thomas must be taken not as just a
set of opinions for discussion, but as foundations upon which rests
all knowledge of the natural and divine realms. If these foundations
are rejected or perverted, it necessarily follows that those who
study theology will no longer even understand the sense of the
words with which the magisterium of the Church proclaims the
truths revealed by God. Therefore, we would like to warn all those
who dedicate themselves to the study of philosophy and of theology that if you leave the paths of St. Thomas, especially in the area
of metaphysics, great damage will result."[63]

These statements quoted by Escrivá are entirely in accord with
the Council. And he was in complete harmony with its intentions

when he wrote this: "I ask my daughters and sons, particularly on this, the seven-hundredth anniversary of the death of the Angelic Doctor, that they conscientiously follow the pertinent recommendations of the Church in their study and teaching."[64]

Although Escrivá suffered deeply on account of the dark shadows shrouding the face of the Church, the Bride of Christ, he certainly did not see the post-conciliar era as an impenetrable night. Quite the contrary. As a matter of fact, Vatican II represented an overwhelming breakthrough for Opus Dei. What the young Aragonese priest had rediscovered through the grace of God three decades before, the Council now raised as a guiding light for the future of the Church. This chapter of Church history saw a certain fulfillment of Christ's words to his disciples: "Nothing is hidden that will not be revealed; nothing is concealed that will not be disclosed. What I tell you in darkness, speak in the light, and what I have whispered in your ear, proclaim from the rooftops" (Mt 10:26-27). From the rooftops of the Council, the Church proclaimed and confirmed the highlights of Escrivá's message:

(1) Unity of life — a congruence between the universal vocation of all Christians to holiness and their everyday lives.

(2) Professional work as both a fulfillment of this vocation and a basis for apostolate.

(3) The freedom of Christians seeking holiness in their work to participate in the ordering of secular things, according to the laws proper to such matters (the only boundaries for this freedom being those implicit in Christ's command of love, which the Church preserves, interprets, and clarifies).

(4) The holy sacrifice of the Mass as the center and root of all interior life — the workday being oriented toward it, and all the strength and blessings of everyday life pouring forth from it.

An accurate perception of Escrivá's relation to the Council was long in coming. But in the end, after many years of misunderstanding, the founder of Opus Dei finally had the satisfaction of seeing such Council fathers as Cardinal Frings (of Cologne), Franz Cardinal König (of Vienna), and Cardinal Lercaro (of Bologna) acknowledge him as a true predecessor of Vatican II, especially with regard to discerning the proper direction of the Church for the future.[65]

Throughout the encyclicals and addresses of Pope John Paul II, there runs an unbroken thread of exhorting and encouraging Christians to embody the spirit of the Council. The desire to renew the body of the Church through this spirit is the driving force of his pontificate. But this constant concern, this ongoing exhortation, implies that the spirit of the Council has not yet really taken hold. To remedy this situation, the pontiff who had as archbishop of Krakow participated so decisively in Vatican II offered a summary of its spirit in his first encyclical, *Redemptor Hominis*.[66]

In this encyclical, the Magna Carta of his pontificate, the pope writes, "At various points in its documents, Vatican II expressed the fundamental concern of the Church that 'life in this world may increasingly correspond to the surpassing dignity of the human being'[67] in all aspects, and 'may be formed in an ever more human manner.'[68] This is the concern of Christ himself, the Good Shepherd...." In the name of this pastoral concern, we read in the Council's Pastoral Constitution on the Church in the Modern World, "The Church, which in no way may be confused with the political community in regard to her tasks and responsibilities, or be bound to any political system, is both a symbol and a guardian of the transcendence of the human person."[69] The same section goes on to say of the Church: "Her solicitude takes the whole person into account, and is sympathetic in a unique way. She concerns herself with people in their individual, irreplaceable reality, which contains the indestructible image and likeness of God.[70] Noting this dignity of the person, the Council adds, 'Human beings are the only creatures on earth that are willed by God for their own sakes.'[71] Inasmuch as we are willed by God, called by him for all eternity to grace and salvation, every one of us is truly human; this is who we are in the light of the mystery of salvation through Jesus Christ, a mystery involving each person who lives on this planet, from the very moment of conception."[72]

If the more than five billion people on earth are to experience the mystery of salvation, each individual Christian (for Christians today form a great diaspora, like seeds scattered on a field) must endeavor to embody Christ, so that whoever meets a Christian meets Christ himself. In short, every one of us must seek holiness. Vatican II directed this demand, to an unprecedented degree, toward the whole Christian people. The Council requires holiness from everyone. This is the "spirit of the Council" that the pope never tires of invoking.

It was not by chance, then, that Opus Dei appeared at the beginning of this century. Though only subsequently recognized as such, it came as the first flash of what was to be a new enlightenment for Christians in the secular world, the new way that the Second Vatican Council would call the path to the future. By the time of the Council, Opus Dei was already mature and well-established, ready to set the pace for the called-for renewal. For there is no contradiction between the supposedly conservative spirit of Opus Dei and the supposedly progressive spirit of the Council. The only contradiction — at times an abyss — lies between the orthodox interpretation of the Council documents by the magisterium and their arbitrary, unorthodox manipulation by unauthorized persons. This conflict overshadowed the entire pontificate of Paul VI. At times the struggle seemed life-threatening; it rocked the inner stability of the Church and drove many souls into confusion. Until his dying breath, Pope Paul explained and defended the Council as a continuation of the unbroken tradition of Christ's Church; and for this he was insulted and ridiculed. A wave of insubordination and flagrant disobedience stormed against him, of such constancy and severity that in his last years, he endured the solitude and powerlessness of Christ in Gethsemane. In this respect, Pope Paul VI died a martyr. It is only in the light of this situation that we can truly understand Escrivá's words before the General Council of Opus Dei in 1970: "I suffer much, my children. We are facing a terrible danger that in the Church's practice, the sacraments — all of them, even baptism — will be emptied of content, and people's consciences will grow cold to the commands of divine law."[73]

Work and holiness

Joaquín Mestre Palacios, a canon at the cathedral of Valencia, recounts how one day he requested from his good friend Josemaría Escrivá, whom he had known since 1933, a photograph of himself.[74] "Sure," Escrivá replied. "Of course — with pleasure. I'll give it to you right away." He went into the next room and returned with a small cast-iron donkey. "Here, take it," he said. "Now you have a portrait of me." Don Joaquín just stared at him, quite bewildered, until Escrivá explained, "Yes, yes, my friend, that's what I am — a little donkey. May God grant that I always remain a donkey of the Lord, his instrument for carrying burdens and for bringing peace."

As already mentioned, Escrivá loved ducks. He loved the brave way these beautiful, colorful birds plunge into water — taking to it as soon as they are born, swimming off in a straight line toward their goal. He wanted the women of Opus Dei to be like this, and he often gave them little ducks made of wood, glass, metal, or clay, as encouraging mementoes. Well, he also loved donkeys. This was partly because they are so drab, poorly fed, and roughly treated, but he loved them most for the way they work — patient, unnoticed, and indispensable, they work until they drop dead. This is how he envisioned the men of Opus Dei. What are we to think of such a vision? In this century, work is all too often a miserable, destructive business, the absence or excess of which can bring disastrous consequences. Precisely at this moment in the evolution of society, along comes a Spanish priest who proclaims a new theology of work and declares the daily grind[75] to be an indispensable means of salvation, the means by which ordinary Christians sanctify themselves and the world around them. Is this some sort of perversity, just plain craziness, or a legitimate challenge?

The threefold saying "Sanctify yourself, sanctify your work, and sanctify others through your work" is probably the most common summary of the message of Opus Dei. (It usually comes in response to a question, like "What is Opus Dei?" "What's it up to?") Unfortunately, this simple synopsis is not always immediately understood. The problem is not just spiritual superficiality or ignorance; there are stumbling blocks in some fundamental characteristics of life in our age of worldwide, technologically advanced civilization.[76]

We cannot understand Opus Dei without grasping the thread that intertwines work and sanctity. I have spoken often in this book about holiness. But to understand holiness in conjunction with work — the essence of Opus Dei — we must first discuss the nature of work.[77]

"God took the man," says Genesis 2:15, "and set him in the Garden of Eden, to cultivate and watch over it." Men and women need to work to feed and clothe themselves, to make shelter, and to survive in any way. Work is an absolute, inescapable duty. First of all, it is our obligation as creatures. But it is more. The Creator made us to work not only to secure our physical existence, but also to cultivate the earth. God himself is our employer. Work as such is neither a consequence of sin nor a punishment for it; it is the privilege God has granted to us of participating in his loving care for the world. True, this participation has been changed by the fall of Adam and Eve; it has suffered an alteration. "Accursed be the ground because of you!" says Yahweh. "Painfully will you get your food from it as long as you live. ... By the sweat of your face shall you earn your food, until you return to the ground, as you were taken from it; for dust you are, and to dust you shall return" (Gn 3:17-19). The circumstances and means of work have thus changed from the serene, idyllic gardening that preceded the fall, just as we differ from our first parents in their original innocence. Nevertheless, work remains oriented toward God and is destined to play a part in our salvation.

Ever since sin made that initial and ineradicable inroad on the dynamics of human life, work has entailed exhaustion, sweat, and tribulation. This is not, however, why it has come to be considered a punishment and something to be disdained. What accounts for the widespread denigration of work is the way in which it has been integrated into the life of society, a way that distorts its essence. For long periods of history, work — especially manual labor — was connected with personal and social bondage: slavery, serfdom, child labor, penal servitude, and so forth. The brutal work in mines, quarries, and galleys was, in fact, real punishment.

Though our own century has set horrible new records for forced labor, political and social advances have brought substantial and far-reaching improvements. But new problems have arisen. There is, for example, the inbuilt drive of technology-oriented industries and factories to put severe restrictions on personal freedom at work, or even to eliminate it entirely. The relationship between work and justice is of vital importance, from both material and socio-psychological perspectives. There is often a gross disproportion between the work performed and the wage received. Exorbitant salaries coexist with pitifully insufficient wages. The hunger and misery of the worker (who sometimes suffers forced unemployment due to layoffs) exists side by side with the over-indulgence and luxurious living of nonworkers, possessors of inherited wealth, and those who live off the work of others.

This unjust situation has deep psychological and social roots. For centuries manual work was considered a degrading way to make a living; only wretches had to live off the work of their hands. Knights, noblemen, and clergy did not "work." It might, in fact, be hard work to manage a manor, factory, bank, or business; to command troops, fight battles, sail the seas; to rule a state, a diocese, a monastery. But neither these privileged classes nor society as a whole thought of these activities as work. The concept thus suffered a drastic diminution of content, until at last "work" came to represent simply a necessary evil for those who did not have other resources and who were not born for higher things. It seemed obvious that princes, scientists, artists, writers, and actors did not really work; work was something ignoble and restrictive, whereas these privileged people were ruling, research-ing, and creating. From this perspective it is easy to see why Adam Smith and Karl Marx were hailed as saviors — they raised "work" to the dignity of commercial assets and political power.

All genuine work has a purpose, but this purpose is not always apparent. A farmer plows the land, sows the seed, fights weeds and pests, harvests the crop, and turns up the earth for replanting. The harvest, in turn, must feed the farmer and others, so it is threshed, milled, shipped, and sold. In short, the farmer's land has been used for a purpose. Yet farmers do not harvest their crops and raise cattle just to feed themselves and others. They work to give substance to their vocation as farmers — complying, most explicitly if they are Christian, with the divine mandate to take care of the earth and one's neighbors for the sake of love. This holds true of all vocations and occupations. When the link between work and the meaning of existence is clear, this is easily perceived and accepted.

Difficulties arise when there seems to be a gap between work and the meaning of existence. Galley slaves, for example, certainly know they are rowing to propel the ship; but to recognize that this rowing can give meaning to their existence, they will have to delve into the Christian significance of suffering and expiation. In other words, they will have to understand their situation as an opportunity for identification with Christ. Otherwise, they will hate their work.

A similar difficulty arises when the fruit of one's labor (not the wage, but the product made) is completely removed from one's ken. Think of the typical assembly line — the endlessly repeated operations of the production process that erode the worker's sense of self, reducing one to a cog in a gigantic machine. The carpenter can say, "I built this table," and feel real pleasure and satisfaction. But an office worker in the shipping department of a large warehouse, or someone who has to stare at a control panel all day on the lookout for a malfunction signal, goes home with little feeling of accomplishment or success. Such lost-in-the-system workers will consciously or unconsciously become unhappy, and soon they will find themselves measuring their lives by vacations, "sick days," and approaching retirement. The emphasis of their existence will thus have been transferred from work to leisure. Meanwhile, the function of leisure has also become a pressing problem.

In the preaching of Escrivá, work has a preeminent significance. This is natural, since work is the standard route to fulfillment of the Christian vocation: sanctity. Christians become, quite literally, fellow workers of Christ's, which means that their cooperative work with Christ is also a "way of the cross" and an apostolate. This coredemptive nature of everyday work is what God revealed to Escrivá as the heart of Opus Dei. "In a mighty inspiration, which God granted him on August 7, 1931," states the beatification proposal, "the Servant of God saw confirmed with even greater clarity that the Lord had wanted to found Opus Dei so that there would be men and women in all walks of life who, united with Christ on the cross, would sanctify the duties of every moment."[78]

Concerning that same day, Escrivá wrote: "Today this diocese celebrates the Feast of the Transfiguration of Our Lord Jesus Christ. While I recommended my intentions to God in the Mass, I reflected on the inner transformation that God had wrought in me during those years of residence in Madrid. This transformation occurred in spite of myself — I can truly say, without my cooperation. I believe that I renewed my intention of totally dedicating my life to the fulfillment of the divine will: the work of God (an intention I renew at this moment too, with my entire soul). The moment of the Consecration arrived. In the very act of elevating the sacred Host, without losing the necessary concentration, without being distracted (I mentally completed the sacrifice of merciful love), I felt the following passage of Scripture echoing in me with unprecedented strength and clarity: 'When I am lifted up from the earth, I shall draw all things to myself.' As usual, I felt afraid of the supernatural;[79] but then came the reassurance, 'Do not be afraid; it is I.' And I understood that it will be the men and women of God who will raise the cross and the teachings of Christ to the summit of every human activity. And I saw the Lord triumph, drawing everything to himself."

Work, understood both as activity and as product, is a fundamental part of human existence.[80] In producing works of our own making, we resemble our Creator, and we should do so consciously and cooperatively. "In this way, work becomes supernatural, because its end is God and because it is done, with God in mind, as an act of obedience," said Escrivá.[81] On innumerable occasions, in print and in person, he insisted that honest work is a service to God. He elaborated on the criteria for honest work — industriousness, sound professional training, attention to detail, care for the quality of the work accomplished — and considered it inseparable from good personal behavior. A letter written in 1948 is especially interesting in this regard. Escrivá wrote, "For you, work can never be a game, something to be taken lightly, a hobby for dilettantes. What do I care when people tell me that one of you is, for example, a bad teacher, but a good son of mine? If you are not a good teacher, of what use is that to me? Because, in fact, you are not a good son of mine if you have not used the means necessary to improve in your professional work. A man without zeal for professional excellence is of no use to me."[82] Professional zeal and enthusiasm are two sides of the same coin. "In the Work," continued Escrivá, "we cannot have loafers. If people were to come to Opus Dei and not work, if they did not fight any inclination to idleness, in a few days they would feel quite out of place. Our vocation demands that we apply to ourselves that phrase from the Gospel: 'To those who have, more shall be given' (Lk 19:26). To the one who already has work, more work will be given; whoever can do the work of ten must do the work of fifteen."[83]

At times, Escrivá's demands sound harsh. But looking back from this forty-five-year distance, we need to keep in mind that some of them were written to shock a society that scorned the wear and tear of daily work, that taxed it and tried to minimize it. It is in this light that we should read a passage like this: "I don't understand how a son of mine could be twiddling his thumbs, killing time. What a pity to kill time, which is a divine treasure! If a son or daughter of mine has time on their hands, they are not doing their duty. I always have to leave things for the next day.... We have to go to sleep loaded with things to do, like little donkeys of God."[84]

Needless to say, this attitude encounters plenty of resistance and misunderstanding — especially when it is separated from joy and love, from the joy unleashed by the love that thrives in work done close to God and neighbor, close to the fruit of one's toil. With the strength of deep conviction, Escrivá lived and preached a unity of life based on the unity between work and contemplation. Work and contemplation should interpenetrate and nourish each other until, as he so beautifully put it, "there comes a moment when we can no longer tell where prayer leaves off and work begins, because our work is also prayer and contemplation, a true mystical life of union with God — a moment when, without doing anything strange, we become like God."[85]

Yet this statement of the ideal, much as it can animate and enthuse the soul, does not tell the whole story. By his teaching and example, the founder of Opus Dei also gave profound and practical answers to the urgent, often complex problems that work can cause in personal and social life. "In the spirituality of Opus Dei," he said on one occasion, "work is fundamental. The whole Work hangs, like a door on a hinge, on the exercise of some task in the midst of the world, to such an extent that if anyone denigrates honest, human work — important or humble — claiming that it can be neither sanctified nor sanctifying, we can say with certainty that God has not called that person to Opus Dei."[86] Unequivocal words, quite implacable, etched in the cornerstone of Opus Dei. With them, Escrivá returned to the reflections he had expressed identically in 1932.[87] And sixteen years later he wrote this: "There is no incompatibility between Christian morality (or Christian perfection) and any licit profession, whether intellectual or manual, whether considered prestigious or menial."[88]

Precisely because they are so categorical, these claims of Escrivá's require explanation, for it is impossible to believe that they are as simple as they seem at first glance. They refer to the nucleus of Opus Dei and touch upon an essential characteristic of the vocation to Opus Dei. We need to examine the concept of work, the notion of honest work, and the idea of sanctification, not in abstract terms, but in the context of everyday life near the close of the twentieth century.

When Escrivá first began to speak about the sanctifying potential of work, when he set out to revive this way for lay people to follow Christ, he used the concept of work that was current at the time. In 1928, work was a simple reality, in no need of qualification or analysis. It was a human activity — intellectual, manual, or a little of both, but not necessarily producing visible results — by which one supported oneself and others, either directly with the fruit of the work or through the money the fruit might earn. But a moment's reflection proves this concept inadequate to the reality. Artists, for example, do real work, even if (as happened to Rembrandt in his old age) no one will buy their paintings. Did Msgr. Escrivá fail to take this into account?

Escrivá was a child of his times; like anyone else, he expressed himself in terms of what he saw around him. There was no way he could have imagined all that would happen in the field of labor over the years. Nevertheless, as founder of Opus Dei he knew — for God gave him light to see — that it would always be possible and necessary to work and to sanctify one's work, regardless of circumstances.

In the Spain of Escrivá's day, people were sometimes without work. But generally speaking, this situation had two possible causes: idleness or unemployment. Though they are both work-related, these are two entirely different problems. Unemployment, a socioeconomic matter involving work as a commercial transaction, may be involuntary. Idleness, however, is another story. The material and moral misery stemming from exclusion from the great circulatory system of work does inevitably involve social degradation. But there is no excuse for idleness, because it is always possible to work outside of the economic process of remuneration. Even the unemployed can and should, for their own good, do something. Surely Escrivá would never have accepted the notion that people who have lost their jobs have no choice but to dedicate themselves to idleness. It may happen that one loses one's job; but one never loses the duty to work. This duty continues before God, for each and every individual.

In this light, any question of early retirement, or of a work week set at thirty, forty, or twenty hours, becomes academic. It may be possible to regulate how many hours and years one will work for a particular employer, but it is not possible to regulate how long one will work for Jesus Christ, one's neighbor, or oneself. Escrivá knew, and he proved it with his own deeds, that this field of opportunity is immense, and totally independent of the job market, so that no Christian can ever be in forced worklessness.

He himself was a tireless worker — and this is a dominant characteristic of his personality and life. Moreover, he worked with great intensity and concentration. Living and preaching the virtue of hard work, he also gave content to it — he was an imaginative patron and creator. He always knew how to awaken the well-disposed but dormant human virtues of the people he met, and how to elevate these virtues to the supernatural level of sanctification. Escrivá not only mobilized the good dispositions people had toward work, but he also set goals and opened doors for them that were as diverse as roads through life can be; the only common denominator they had was the task of sanctification entrusted to all of them by Jesus Christ.

One of the characteristics of human and Christian solidarity is a refusal to stockpile wealth, a resolve instead to make it productive. Among other things, this means not being an egoist or elitist with regard to one's work, but seeing it as a good thing to be communicated and shared. Escrivá practiced this work of mercy generously. His professional outlook and profound grasp of different situations gave him an astonishing ability to spark initiatives around the world. The enterprise might be a textile factory, a language school, an agricultural cooperative, a university in Italy, Spain, Japan, or Mexico, but never did he just suggest or inspire the initiative in some vague way. In each instance he pushed people ahead and involved himself in all the logistical details — all this without limiting the personal freedom and responsibility of those charged with developing these initiatives. And he personally motivated not only the members of Opus Dei, but also the many helpers: the retired workers, the men and women who already held challenging positions elsewhere, and so forth.

Escrivá recommended that the members of Opus Dei remain in their places. His intent was not to squelch healthy ambition or to discourage the quest for professional excellence, but rather to curb a spiritual disease: the restless anxiety, fueled by vainglorious desires, that has reached such epidemic proportions in our times. What is it that is motivating so many nurses to suddenly decide to become teachers, clerks to want to become dentists, and priests to envy engineers? This trend can be attributed not only to the great expansion of personal freedom, but also to the economic and technical progress of the last decades, which has brought with it a growing subjective — and sometimes objective — need to learn new skills, to begin again with a new career. In our technological civilization, fewer and fewer people are maintaining a single profession throughout life. It is this situation that Escrivá addressed when he put people on guard against self-centered anxiety and instability in professional life, against developing a complex he jokingly called "mystical wishful thinking" — wanting to be, do, or have something other than what one actually was, did, or had: "If only I had done this or that...." By no means, however, did he disapprove of the dynamics of prudent professional changes; to him this was just one more natural part of daily work that had to be sanctified. "When you came to the Work," he wrote in 1948, "you were told that you were not being moved from your place in life, from your professional occupation. You know well that this doesn't mean you can't change jobs; it simply means that you can't abandon the world because of your divine vocation, but rather must remain in it with all that it entails."[89]

The professional job is the normal place for the living out of a vocation, but it is not the determining factor. One's profession must serve and be part of one's total dedication to Christ. On occasion, this can mean having to abandon, change, or restart one's career. Members of Opus Dei have the right and the duty to orient their work in accordance with the needs of their spiritual family and social position. They do not lead two parallel lives, but only one life: the apostolic life of an ordinary Christian, with one body, one mind, one heart with which to love God and others, and work for them. "My sons and daughters," says the founder of Opus Dei, "it is the same with you [as with all other Christians]: each of you is just one more soul — an equal among your colleagues at work — and your life is bound by the same laws that govern their lives. And it is this life, with all the vicissitudes that the diverse circumstances in which you find yourselves can bring, that you must sanctify."[90]

As he lived and preached the need for constancy with flexibility in working at one's professional position, he also lived and preached the joy and suffering that belong inseparably to this work, accompanying it throughout life. By joy in work, I mean happiness in the task at hand, as well as in work in general. I have already mentioned that joy of this sort, a joy in one's handiwork, in the what and the how of one's labor, is threatened not only by the extreme dividing and stretching of labor through vast labyrinths of assembly lines and bureaucracies, but also by the constant reduction of the volume of personal work. The technological revolution, which I see as typified by the advent of the computer, has consequences not yet fully understood. Just think of the growing number of factories in which one can walk for hours through cavernous rooms without seeing any employees, except the dozen or so who operate the control room. In the industrial world, work — in absolute, quantitative terms — is decreasing. In all sectors of society (in the home as much as in the factory), there are ever fewer people working, in the traditional sense of the word. It is surely not conceivable that someday eighty percent of humanity will dedicate itself to loitering, or to just standing with arms akimbo (a torment in itself), but the fact nevertheless remains: traditional work is steadily diminishing. It is therefore necessary to deepen and expand our concept of work, to rethink and reestablish it.

People who approach their work with false, grandiose expectations run the risk of misdirecting their lives, as do those with inferiority complexes. Such distorted attitudes can take various forms. Some want to do only those things they find pleasing or easy. Others see work as a necessary evil: the price one pays for survival, prosperity, pleasure, luxury. Still others work themselves to death in order to satisfy a thirst for power, prestige, sensual delight, or personal ambition. There are even those who, perverting an ambition that might have been healthy and life-giving, dedicate all their strength to erecting a sort of monument to themselves. All these motivations are forms of selfishness, of an egocentricity that is neither balanced nor integrated. For the human race to advance along the road to truly human work and a mature happiness, a goal that lies between brute competence and effete indolence, some integration and sublimation will be needed.

What will it take to effect this integration and sublimation? Precisely what Escriva called the sanctifying of ordinary work. One must see work as a way to follow Christ, and thus do it happily— love it. But this is far from easy. Following Christ always involves carrying the cross, and therefore work always includes a cross. Countless times, Escrivá reiterated the fact that most things we have to do are things that go against the grain. Rarely are we naturally inclined to endure the burden, the exhaustion, the dullness of daily work. So whatever transformation the working world may undergo, this much is certain: Christians must forever rebel against nontranscendental work—work separated from the following of Christ.

With compelling clarity, Escriva proclaimed that a day without the cross is a day without Christ, and consequently a day without joy. "The roots of joy take the shape of a cross," he liked to say. The Christian must approach the inevitable pain and fatigue of daily work in the same way Christ accepted and embraced the cross. This is a key element in the vocation to Opus Dei. As early as 1934, Escrivá explained its importance. At the forefront of all human activities, he wrote, there must be men and women who put the cross of Christ into their life and into their work, who raise the cross on high as a means of reparation and salvation, as a visible symbol of both the redemption of the human race and the love that God the Father, God the Son, and God the Holy Spirit—the Most Holy Trinity—have had and always shall have for us. "Beloved, Jesus is urging us! He wishes to be lifted up once more — not on the cross, but in the glory of all human activities, in order to draw all things to himself."[91] And twelve years later, shortly before moving to Rome, Escrivá reminded his followers of God's desire: "Especially from us, he expects this service and cooperation which will contribute to the growth on earth of the fruit of the redemption: the only true human freedom."[92]

I spoke earlier of an epigrammatic "trinity" — "Sanctify your work, sanctify yourself in your work, and sanctify others through your work" — and I called it the shortest and most popular definition of Opus Dei's spirit. This triad was, by God's grace, made clearly perceptible to Msgr. Escrivá so that he could remind the world of it. It signifies a unity that I call "trinitarian" with some real justification, because within it there is nothing more or less, nothing before or after — the three processes of sanctification are simultaneous and of equal worth. This threefold unity, which was the main thing Escrivá had to teach and demonstrate, is the essence of Opus Dei.

To "sanctify your work" means to work just as Christ did when he was on earth, and as he still works in every moment of history through the members of his Mystical Body. It does not matter whether one digs a ditch or does highly specialized research toward a cure for cancer. What matters is that one's work have a single prerequisite, sign, and consequence: living in Christ, sanctifying oneself with the help of God, for love of God. But this sanctification is not an isolated event, something just between God and the individual. It is the platform, the starting point, of an apostolate. Every apostolate is a communication of the life, love, and teaching of Christ to others; it is a guided path to him. This marvelous transmission occurs through a network of sanctified daily work, a network woven together by millions of sisters and brothers who are sanctifying themselves in their work.

To understand this trinitarian formula of holiness and work is to understand Opus Dei, as Escrivá made beautifully clear in a letter of 1940. This is how he explained it: "United to Christ through prayer and mortification in our daily work, in the thousand human circumstances of our modest lives as ordinary Christians, we will accomplish the marvel of laying everything at the feet of the Lord, raised up on the cross, where he allowed himself to be nailed — so much love did he have for the world and for us. By working among our peers and loving God in the fulfillment of our daily duties (the same tasks incumbent upon us before he sought us out), we fulfill the mission of placing Christ at the pinnacle and center of all human enterprises. Since none of them is excluded from our work, every respectable activity thus becomes a testimony to Christ's redemptive love."[93]

It is, indeed, quite possible that the absolute quantity of work in the world may decrease as a consequence of ever-advancing technology. But this is a possibility only for instrumental work — not for creative work or the works of mercy. It is conceivable (even probable) that someday there will be no jobs for typists, train conductors, or road workers, because their work will have been assumed by machines. But many new jobs will arise to take their places. Those fields that cannot be mechanized will become broader and busier: art, science, charities, nursing, housework, gardening, education, and many more. Whatever the future may hold, journalists will still have to compose their articles, mothers will care for their babies, and gardeners will be trimming their roses. Computers and software packages will not change diapers, comfort the sorrowful, wipe runny noses, or visit the lonely. In short, work will never disappear, nor will its essence as a means of salvation. Only its form will change. Opus Dei cannot, therefore, be affected by any structural change in the world of labor. Its mission and the possibility of fulfilling it will always remain. It is "a sea without shores," as Escrivá liked to say. The day will keep its twenty-four hours, the week its seven days. To use this time well — to let Christ mold the world, with or without microprocessors and shortened work weeks — remains the calling of all Christians, particularly those in Opus Dei. That means working around the clock (for even sleep can be a work of dreaming prayer), until our dying breath.

For work to have sanctifying potential, Escrivá laid down just one stipulation: the job itself must be respectable and honest. A seemingly simple and obvious requirement, but it hinges on something that can be quite problematic: an ability to distinguish moral from immoral within contemporary reality. To tell good from evil in professional and social conduct (including indirect participation in immoral activity) is a tricky problem in a society growing ever more complex. The Church, allowing for honest but mistaken consciences, takes this into account. Nonetheless, it should never be forgotten that the Church is guided by the Holy Spirit when she interprets Christ's teaching and sets criteria for Christian ethics. Anyone who accepts the Church's authority and studies the moral teaching of the Church can usually learn what must, can, or must not be done in a given situation. Truly Christian behavior does demand a basic knowledge of faith and morals and a constant formation of conscience.

Because knowledge of Christian doctrine has all but withered away in the neo-pagan environments of Europe and America, men and women are needed to replant this knowledge in the workday apostolate. This is part of what is needed for the radical sanctification of the workday. And so, said Escrivá, "the children of God in Opus Dei have three dominant passions: to transmit the teachings of the faith; to guide, by one means or another, those souls who have approached the warmth of our apostolate; and to love the unity of the Work....[94] A sanctity without joy is not the sanctity of Opus Dei; a sanctity without doctrine is not the sanctity of Opus Dei."[95]

Escrivá considered ignorance, especially religious ignorance, to be one of the most powerful allies of the devil. (Today's religious ignorance is often something pernicious indeed: a pseudoscientific superficiality masquerading as erudition.) And he envisioned Opus Dei as a powerful antidote. Its characteristic way of teaching Christianity — through sanctified and sanctifying work — would make it a worldwide catechesis. Escrivá made every effort to teach all Christians that only work well done can be a service for Christ, that the quality of one's work is an expression and natural consequence of one's love for God and others, that sloppy work should not be offered to God or to anyone else. "It is difficult," he said, "to sanctify work if one does not include in it the human drive for perfection. Without this it will be difficult, if not impossible, to achieve the necessary professional prestige by which one leads others to sanctify their work and conform their lives to the demands of the Christian faith."[96]

What constitutes well-done work is, of course, not always easy to say. It is one thing to determine if a cobbler has made good shoes or a baker a first-rate cake, but how does one evaluate the work of an artist, or that of a teacher? In many cases, quality is hard to define; opinions will differ, and the judgment of God may differ significantly from that of colleagues, critics, and audiences. Occasionally a whole profession may become contaminated with a concept of quality so corrupted that immoral practices are recategorized as professional necessities. Thus lawyers, entrepreneurs, or tax advisers may come to think of certain blatantly immoral practices as being without moral stain. When this is the case, then only those with calloused consciences can aspire to the highest positions and the greatest prestige.

Escrivá understood the problem. What was needed was a fusion of work quality and worker ethics. Consider, for instance, the wife and mother who is a homemaker. She may cook wonderfully and keep an immaculate house, but her work will not be apostolate if she is doing it just to outshine the neighbors. People may praise her, but her work will remain unsanctified. There is no substitute for what Escrivá called "professional culture": the fusion of skill with virtue. He saw every profession as having a distinct culture, with its own set of requisites. The culture of a journalist, for example, demands clear, prompt reporting, diligent research, and a passion for the truth (all of which means sacrifice — possibly delayed promotion or even unemployment). Unique as they are, however, all professional cultures have one thing in common: an inestimable importance. "The culture of, say, a homemaker need not be identical to that of a university professor," explained Escrivá. "In the same way, the culture of an office worker will differ from that of the farmer. But the professional culture of a barber is as important to me as that of a scientist, and that of a maid is as important as that of a scholar. What matters is having the culture for one's own task, the culture appropriate to one's own professional vocation."[97]

To sanctify work, to sanctify oneself in work, and to sanctify others through work: the triangular trademark of Opus Dei is burned like a brand into every vocation. It is a call to work as Christ worked. Admittedly, we will never fully live up to this ideal. The way is too cluttered by obstacles embedded in fallen human nature: frailty, limitations, sin. Nevertheless, with the simplicity of a child, the working Christian must ask, "How would Christ act in my place? How would he want me to act?"

We have already seen some criteria for comprehending Christ's challenging answers. For example, every service done for God and neighbor qualifies as work, whether or not it is done for pay. Poets work even if their poetry remains forever unpublished. Somebody unemployed who takes a disabled person out in a wheelchair is working. Even searching one's conscience and struggling to awaken contrition in one's heart is in some sense actual work. Any kind of self-improvement can be hard work. From this perspective, therefore, there is no such thing as a layoff or a vacation; there is only work in all its different modes, some of which go by the name of "leisure."

It can happen that the moral and religious implications of a given work are incorrectly perceived; an erroneous conscience can lead one to choose (sometimes with self-sacrificing idealism) the wrong road. When we set out to sanctify work, it is crucial first to clarify any moral doubts we may have about that work. If this is not possible, it is essential at least to work with a good intention. And let us not deceive ourselves. Even in the professional circumstances of the world today, it is still possible to distinguish right from wrong. It is always possible to ask and answer the question, "How would Christ conduct himself here?"

It is also possible, regardless of the circumstances, to work with joy. Granted, many kinds of work are not naturally enjoyable. Reluctance and aversion are often inescapable, a fallout of the clash between our limitations and the demands of work. Who loves working in a coal mine? Who could spend day after day monitoring hundreds of control lights without ever feeling restless and dissatisfied? And yet real joy is possible in the most inauspicious of circumstances — the profound joy that comes exclusively from cooperative intimacy with Christ on the cross. For to work is to share the privilege of Simon the Cyrenean, the privilege of helping Christ carry the cross.

This is what Escrivá had in mind when he wrote, "Because of the great human and social value of work, but mainly because of its instrumental function in the economy of salvation,[98] it is our duty to acquire the best possible professional training!"[99] It was also in light of this privilege that he made the following recommendation: "Work in the awareness that God is looking at you! Our work must be holy and worthy of him — not only perfect in every detail, but done with moral purity, a good intention, justice, and loyalty."[100] This is something that is always possible, regardless of the circumstances. Escrivá's meditation on Simon of Cyrene makes this quite clear. "It is not too late," he says, "nor is everything lost. Even though a thousand foreboding voices keep saying it is, even though you are besieged by mocking and skeptical onlookers..., you have come at a good time to take up the cross. The Redemption is taking place — now! — and Jesus needs many Simons of Cyrene."[101]

The man who wrote these lines backed up every word with the authenticity of his life. He saw himself as a donkey — a small, wretched, mangy donkey. In his spiritual notes from 1931 and 1932, he was already referring to himself as "un burrito sarnoso" (a mangy donkey); sometimes he even signed his writings with the initials "b.s."[102] The adjective "mangy" suggests neither false modesty nor self-pity, but rather an honest and cheerful humility — and work. Day after day, for fifty years, work. And so it was that when he consecrated the altar of the new shrine of the Virgin Mary at Torreciudad, and a bas relief of a donkey caught his eye, he kissed it and said softly, "Hello, brother."[103]

Chapter Nine

PORTRAIT OF A MAN AND A PRIEST

The portrait

A single, definitive portrait of a person does not exist. There are, instead, the separate images: of childhood, of adolescence, of old age. Pictures capture events and phases in life: the infant in the cradle, the man or woman in the casket, and everything in between. We see John graduating from high school, Margaret as a bride. Though physical changes can completely transform a person's appearance (there is little resemblance, for instance, between the portraits of Rembrandt young and old), one can still leaf through a photo album and recognize oneself as a child at First Communion, a soldier off to war, the proud new parent. It is not possible to merge these pictures into a single image, but it is possible to detect, in their sequence and range, a unique individual with the same identity from birth on into eternity.

Msgr. Escrivá's portraits show little change over the course of seven decades. Apart from effects of the natural aging process, there is no significant difference between the youth of seventeen and the seventy-year-old man. To his very last day, his face retained a youthful, boyish expression. This was partly due to his soft features — the rounded chin, the full cheeks — and the simple parting of his short, slowly graying hair. Mostly, however, it was his smile. In all the pictures, the same smile plays about his mouth and eyes: a smile full of warmth, amusement, and unaffected concern, yet without any shadow of anxiety. His was a face without any trace of bitterness or ennui; it was transparently guileless, candid, cheerfully interested. It was not a scarred battlefield where elation and sorrow, God and the devil had waged war; it was not a dramatic stage. (That is why his portraits are not as fascinating as Beethoven's or Einstein's.) His face spoke of being a child of

God; it radiated serenity, confidence, joy. And what else would we expect of the founder of Opus Dei? Features dominated by distraction, agony, or ecstasy would have testified against the spirit of Opus Dei, and therefore against his own credibility.

All existing photographs of Escrivá (thousands published and many more not) have one thing in common: they exhibit his constant naturalness. Escrivá never stood on ceremony, stalked about, or made premeditated gestures; he gave himself no important airs. He was always just himself. To become, like St. Paul, "all things to all people," we cannot be self-focused; we must be able to discern the needs and the capacity for understanding of each person we meet. This is a gift that Escrivá possessed in full measure. With a sort of spiritual X-ray vision, he would read souls by the light of Christ's love, never hurting or pushing, but always soothing and captivating.

He was self-confident, but not self-centered; he certainly never played the little dictator. This is obvious in the films, and verified by all who knew him. All his confidence was in God, not himself. Josemaría felt himself secure in God's presence, more and more through the years, until finally this awareness overflowed and enveloped him. This is what enabled him to see the world supernaturally, to see things and people, great and small, all in the light of God's presence. This is why, except when he was loudly praised and celebrated, he never felt embarrassed. One cannot imagine him blushing, stammering, or posing in front of the mighty. An incident from the early forties illustrates this point admirably. At the request of the bishop of Madrid, Escrivá was giving a retreat to Franco and his wife, and he considered it appropriate within this context to remind the generalissimo of the fact of death. Franco's response was that he did think about death once in a while, and he had made the appropriate preparations. Apparently he viewed death as just one more political problem. Don Leopoldo, upon hearing of this meeting, told Escrivá, "Now you'll never be a bishop in Spain!" Whereupon Escrivá replied, "Being a priest is enough for me." He saw in Franco, as in anyone else, primarily a soul, and would never have concerned himself with nonspiritual considerations during a retreat.[1]

As one might guess from his physical appearance, Escrivá's personality developed with unbroken coherence and continuity.

There are no fractures or sudden transformations in his life story — no exciting material for psychologists, private detectives, or novelists. (They look for complicated characters, preferably tragic ones, and saints tend to be disappointing from that perspective.) It was holiness that Escrivá was struggling for — nothing but holiness, nothing but the love of God in action. Because he adored God with the passion of a lover, he could not help but passionately love the world and everyone he

Msgr. Escrivá answering a question on one of his catechetical trips.

met. His burning desire was to inspire as many people as possible with God's love by showing them that it was within reach.

Granted, loving God in this life will never again be the simple thing it was before original sin; our weakened nature makes it inescapably difficult. But it is never impossible. For this reason, true Christianity does not countenance tragedy. Tragedy involves self-centered entanglement, subjective guilt that appears objectively determined and consequently inevitable, and ultimate failure. Christian tragedy, therefore, is a contradiction in terms.[2] Christ's death was not tragic but triumphant; in the strength of his perfect sacrificial love, Christ pulled out the root of tragedy, the pride of life. And so, declared Escrivá, "we never fail!"[3] How often he would insist that God never loses a battle. Even when he had to reckon with the possibility of not surviving the Spanish Civil War, he did not see this as a potential tragedy, but simply asked each of his sons, "Will you continue the Work when I am gone?"[4] And their steadfast affirmation was enough to satisfy him.

Once in 1935, and once again during a time of great persecution in 1941, he had sudden doubts concerning his vocation, wondering if he had not merely sought to assert himself by founding Opus Dei. He prayed, "If the Work was not born to serve the Church, O Lord, please destroy it."[5] And even if such had been the case, he would never have thought of himself as any kind of tragic hero, but simply as a converted sinner. (By his own admission, he returned to the Father many times a day like the prodigal son.[6])

Whenever a beatification or canonization[7] is celebrated in the Catholic Church, the most perfect union possible between Christ and one of his redeemed is certified by Church authority, according to the regulations fixed by Pope Urban VIII's decree of 1634. But since only God knows a soul completely — the degree of its holiness, the depth of its love — it stands to reason that there are in heaven many more saints than appear on the calendar of feasts. Canonization simply guarantees the holiness of a particular Christian whose life has been thoroughly investigated. From time to time in the life of the Church, a soul attains the height of sanctity and the fact becomes clear to the Church and others. These sisters and brothers are presented to us by Christ, through the Church, as shining examples of virtue and grounds for hope.

Being a Christian is possible

The pedagogy of God's love — sometimes bluntly, sometimes sweetly — makes this truth as clear as daylight: It is possible for every one of us to be truly Christian.

Holiness, whether canonized or not, becomes perceptible through one kind of evidence: a life lived for the love of God. Proof of holiness is a life of virtue, a life informed by the theological virtues of faith, hope, and love, and by the cardinal virtues of prudence, justice, fortitude, and temperance. For canonization, a person must have lived all of these virtues, at least one in a "heroic" manner. In other words, there must be proof that the person engaged in a constant, self-sacrificing struggle for perfection, not as a means of self-fulfillment (this is possible only in heaven), but as an expression of love.

Any one virtue does, of course, necessarily imply the many other virtues; none of them stands alone. But one virtue or another, depending on a person's circumstances and talents, is going to stand out. This salient virtue, the one practiced to the most heroic degree, will often be the one that compensates for the saint's natural defects. We especially admire (I suppose the Lord does too) the courage of St. Thomas More because he was timid by nature, the gentleness of St. Francis de Sales because he was prone to anger, and the purity of St. Aloysius Gonzaga because he was surrounded by corruption.

What does it mean when we read that "the founder of Opus Dei died in the reputation of holiness?" Reputation is a sort of mathematical average of public opinion. It is the predominant image conveyed. It is essentially the creation of the contemporaries of the person in question, who supplies the material. Reputation often corresponds to the truth, but errors are possible, and since a good reputation is more vulnerable than a bad one is repairable, the former is as precious as the latter is accursed. This is why slander is one of the most heinous crimes possible. A reputation of holiness, however, is something more than just a good reputation; it is the widespread, stable conviction of someone's extraordinary dedication to Christ.

Although not everyone who met Escrivá appreciated him, understood him, or even considered him a holy priest, his special reputation arose early, during the thirties. The opinion was based not only on the man himself, but also on the fruit of his works: the lives of the members of Opus Dei bore eloquent witness to the holiness of their spiritual father. Pope Pius XII once told an Australian bishop that he considered Escrivá "a true saint, a man sent by God for his time."[8] To Pope Paul VI, he seemed "a man who had been given more graces than others, but who had also given himself up to them with extraordinary devotion."[9] One of the earliest testimonies comes from Bishop Leopoldo Eijo y Garay. It is especially illuminating because it confronts one of the standard misconceptions about Opus Dei and its founder: the accusation of secretiveness. In 1942, the bishop of Madrid sent a letter to the abbot of the monastery of Montserrat, and this is what he had to say of Escrivá: "It is absurd to suppose that Josemaría Escrivá could have founded any kind of secret society. Such a charge could not be made by anyone who knows him. If there is any man as candid and sincere as a child, that man is Don Josemaría. And besides (though he must not hear this), he is a good man, a true saint. Moreover, he is a patriot. Above everything else, however, he is holy. We are so used to venerating saints on the altars, we tend to forget they were people like us, people who walked on this earth just as we do. But Don Josemaría is a saint, and one day we will see him lifted up to the honor of the altars."[10]

In 1930, not long after Bishop Leopoldo first met Escrivá, Marcelino Olaechea also became acquainted with him.[11] At that time, Olaechea was provincial of the Salesians; later he became prefect of the Salesian college in Madrid. Escrivá at once recognized him as an eminent personality in the Church. From the beginning, that priest, who was as pious as he was sophisticated, devoted himself to the religious welfare and education of young workers and members of the lower middle class throughout Spain. In 1935, he became bishop of Pamplona. It was he who sheltered the refugee Escrivá during the Spanish Civil War, making it possible for him to enter Nationalist Spain in December 1937 and offering him a home for the winter. Olaechea played an enduringly important role in the Spanish episcopate and in Escrivá's life. When he became the archbishop of Valencia and Escrivá moved to Rome, they did not see each other often, but their relationship remained close and was crucial in the founding of the University of Navarre. Olaechea told his secretary, "I hold Josemaría as someone truly chosen, a real saint. I will probably die before him, and so will not get to be a witness for his canonization. Therefore I want you to act as my witness and to voice my urgent appeal [for his beatification]." He compared Escrivá to two saints — John Bosco and Vincent de Paul — who were concerned with the formation of youth, as he and Escrivá were, and whom he particularly admired.

Three-quarters of the beatification testimony is devoted to demonstration of the heroic virtues establishing Escrivá's reputation of holiness. As is true with regard to the entire life and work of any candidate for beatification or canonization, such testimony is subject to the judgment of the Church, whose final decision must not be unduly anticipated. Escrivá has been beatified; he may or may not be canonized; and even if he is, that day may or may not come anytime soon.[12] But in any case, it is only natural to take an interest in a person who was one of the great Christians of our century.

The word "heroic" belongs to a vocabulary that is not highly esteemed nowadays. (There are many such words in this book.)

Heroes are supposed to be extinct. But what does "heroism" really mean? Many are ready to laugh it off as madness or triumphalism. For Escrivá, though, it meant an unflagging battle against one's own baseness, inclination to sin, and indolence. The weapons for the fight must be prayer, sacrifice, devotion, and, above all, joyful love, which is the true spirit of heroism. Escrivá used to say, "It is our destiny on earth to fight out of love until our hearts stop. *Deo gratias!*"[13] At Villa Tevere and many Opus Dei centers, you can see this inscription on a plaque or painting: "Vale la pena" ("It is worthwhile"). The "it" referred to is this battle, which is the secret of happiness. But many Christians are no longer convinced of this truth. Deeply insecure, they have lost the sense of their vocation as Christians. The "children of this world," wiser indeed in dealing with their own than are the "children of the light" (Lk 16:8), have made Christians feel quaint and ashamed. In October 1963, Escrivá saw a poster on a wall in Rome that said, "Renew your membership card, and bring along a friend."[14] Did not that slogan, geared as it was toward some political party, tell Christians what they need and how badly they need it? Did it not mean — did it not shout — "Renew your faith, and bring along someone who also wants to serve Christ and the Church"?[15]

There was not a single day of Escrivá's life when he did not feel in his heart a louder call for more faith and an intensified apostolate. And he proclaimed it with corresponding urgency. Opus Dei must, he insisted, be "one big catechesis; the task of transmitting dogma must be a dominant passion for all the members."[16] Faith is certainly a gift from God, but receiving it is just the beginning. We can never afford to underestimate the destructive capability of its enemies, one of the deadliest of which is religious ignorance. What, indeed, is causing the Church more suffering today than the increasing, the spreading, and even the inheriting of ignorance? One generation without a clear, precise familiarity with the doctrinal treasures of the Church can have disastrous consequences. The spiritual edifice starts cracking — sinking here, crumbling there — and millions of souls are set adrift, confused by error. The guideposts are knocked down, or wrongly named, and people get lost in the mist of subjectivism. Thousands of times Escrivá prayed, "Adauge nobis fidem, spem, et caritatem" ("Increase our faith, hope, and love"). Until the very end, he fed his soul and work by reading the Gospel and studying the writings of the Church fathers and doctors, such as Thomas Aquinas and Teresa of Avila, and the works of other sound theologians.[17] He never asked himself why he kept at it. He surely knew the doctrines, and had plenty of things to do, but nothing could replace these norms. The daily routine of a child of God requires exercise, perseverance, and order. This is what experience teaches and love commands.

Faith, hope, and love cannot be compartmentalized in any Christian life. This organic trinity of virtues enveloped Escrivá's life and rendered his every action transparently sincere — one of the keys to his charisma. One day, for example, when he was a young priest in Madrid, he heard of a man who was dangerously ill and without money. This man did not want to die in the street, so he took the only other choice he had: he went to his sister's place, which was a brothel. After gaining permission from his bishop, Don Josemaría went there, along with an older friend. He said to the sister, "I know the way things go here, but I want to let this sick man die strengthened by the holy sacraments. Therefore, I will return tomorrow to administer them to him, but only on one condition: at least for tomorrow, the Lord must not be offended in this house." The poor girl did have some faith left, so she promised to see to it that the condition was fulfilled. The next day, the dying man gratefully made his confession and received the last sacraments. Josemaría stayed with him to the end.[18]

Escrivá would often say that he had only one heart with which to love, and that that heart beat no differently for Christ than it did for those for whom Christ died. And sure enough, if one of his children was injured in an accident, he would cry just like any natural father. But he was really hurt more deeply and more acutely by the sufferings of Christ than by those of anyone else, including himself. When Escrivá visited Peru in 1974, for example, he was shown pictures of a landslide that had taken place three years earlier. This landslide had buried parts of a village, including the local church, with its tabernacle. The thought of Jesus Christ present in those consecrated hosts and, absolutely unprotected, locked up in that box many feet below the ground until one day he would be consumed by the soil of his own creation — that thought was so deeply painful to Escrivá that he stayed up all night, praying to Our Lord in the Blessed Sacrament.[19]

His piety, like that of Francis de Sales or Philip Neri, had an unbelievable range, from the sublime to the tongue-in-cheek. Case in point: 1944 was a year of grave financial problems, so Escrivá told his sons, "Ask the Lord for money, because we are in great trouble. But ask him for millions! He owns everything anyway. To ask for five million or fifty million requires just the same effort, so while you're at it...."[20]

He could laugh at himself honestly and easily. He was well aware that even remorse and penance do not have to be gloomy, that a real smile can cover real pain. And he was never too dignified to tell a joke on himself. He liked to tell the story of one particular time when, confronted with some adversity, he had become quite upset. "I was furious," he recalled, "and then I became furious because I had become furious." In this double rage, he stalked the streets of Madrid until he happened to come upon an instant-photo booth. God invited him to a lesson in humility and joy — he had his picture taken. And then, he said, "I just had to laugh at my angry face.... For a month, I kept the picture in my wallet, and every time I saw that scowling face, I humbled myself before God and laughed at myself, saying, 'What a fool you are!'"[21]

The "touchstone of love"

Escrivá used to say that pain is the "touchstone of love." The truth of this should be self-evident to Christians. It is an alarming fact, however, that this mystery of the Christian religion, the very secret of redemption, is often forgotten, misunderstood, and even explicitly rejected. This is the key to the spiritual malaise afflicting so many Catholics, especially in the affluent Western world. A friend once told me that he considered "the whole theology of the cross" anachronistic and out of step with the worldwide effort to remove suffering and pain from the lives of individuals and societies. He conceded that the traditional Christian view of human suffering is "psychologically astute," inasmuch as it helps people endure all sorts of misery. As so often happens, ignorance had let slip a great truth. For unless suffering is understood in the light of divine love, it is simply another phenomenon to be subjected to academic, psychological research — just as formerly, among the Stoics and the idealists, it was analyzed in terms of philosophy and ethics. Unfortunately, mastering pain through philosophy, ethics, or psychology is skating on thin ice. Just think of the increase in suicides among the terminally ill.

It is impossible to live any virtue heroically without suffering, because suffering is the price one pays to make ordinary virtue heroic. The measure of heroism is not, however, the objective quantity of pain involved, but rather the subjective intensity of one's devotion to the crucified Christ. That is why Escrivá wanted to see his discovery of the sanctifying "greatness of little things" applied by Christians to their suffering.[22] Extreme suffering is rare. Most suffering is on a modest scale. But it is difficult — and without God's grace impossible — to bear the thousand pinpricks of every day, the splinters of Christ's cross, in good humor, seeing them as tokens of God's friendship. Escrivá could never complain of a lack of such tokens, and neither can the rest of us. Whoever loves Christ's Passion will be presented with some of its thorns. "Pain is a tenderness God the Father shows to his spoiled children," Escrivá said.[23] If such is the case, he was spoiled indeed. One could not catalogue all the sources of pain: the loss of friends through death, the slanders against Opus Dei, the lost vocations, the endangered souls, the sins against Christ and his Church. All these were "business as usual." Illness, too, was a constant companion. For ten years (1944 to 1954), Escrivá suffered a bad case of diabetes — an interminable round of exhaustion, impaired vision, special diets, and injections. After a severe hypoglycemic shock, he inexplicably found himself cured of the diabetes, but good health was never restored. For the rest of his life he suffered intense headaches and agonizing fatigue. In 1966, a kidney ailment and high blood pressure set in. His eyes never having been particularly strong, his sight now deteriorated rapidly. Without extremely strong glasses, he was almost blind, though nobody except del Portillo and a few of his other close associates knew it. On March 19 (Feast of St. Joseph, the patron saint of workers), 1975, Escrivá prayed, "Lord, I really can't go on any longer, but I have to be a bulwark for my children. I can hardly see anything three meters away, and still I have to look into the future[24] to show my children the way. Help me, Christ, Jesus of my soul, that I may see with your eyes."[25]

His prayer at the age of seventy-three echoed the "ut videam" which the young man had prayed at the very inception of Opus Dei. The original request had been granted. The young Spanish priest had been shown his mission: to found and to be Opus Dei. For this mission Christ had lent Escrivá his own eyes; starting on October 2, 1928, Josemaría's ability to see the world through Christ's eyes had grown steadily. And how does Christ look at this world? He sees with eyes of infinite mercy, understanding, and love, but also of infinite justice, penetration, and fire. He looks at the adulteress and forgives her; but he sees the fig tree without fruit and curses it. He knows the schemes of the Pharisees, but he does not deny them the temple tax. His vision is the vision of total love: a love that encompasses mercy and justice, forgiveness and punishment, obedience and command.

An incident from the early thirties shows Escrivá's sharing of this vision. When the religious persecution in Spain forced them to leave their convent, the Augustinian nuns of Santa Isabel in Madrid intended to store abroad, for safety, the precious works of art from the cloister and chapel. These objects, however, did not belong to the order, but were public property. Considering the state of affairs in Spain and the position of the Church, it was certainly tempting to disregard this fact, but Escrivá, as rector of Santa Isabel, explicitly forbade the nuns to do so. He gave his reasons as a priest and as a prudent lawyer. First of all, the civil authority of the state had to be respected on principle. The objects, since they did not belong to the Augustinian sisters but to the Spanish state, were legally at the state's disposal. The nuns had to ask permission; there was no circumstance that would justify bypassing the rightful owner. Besides, removing the art would have supplied ammunition for propaganda against the Church, giving the state a pretext for more persecution. But the most important reminder he gave them was this: It is morally inexcusable to prevent possible misfortune tomorrow by breaking the law today.[26]

Escrivá did not believe in preventive sin or situation ethics.[27] Nor did he support any gratuitous provocation of public authorities, or the legitimacy of an all-or-nothing attitude in matters of secondary importance. In this he could be compared to St. Thomas

More. In fact, he felt a special affinity with this saint who had had such a keen sense of balance. Nearly forty years after the Santa Isabel episode, on June 22 (More's feast day), 1972, Escrivá confided to some Opus Dei members: "This morning, during the Mass of St. Thomas More, I saw the point clearly. Until the very end of his life, he was a model of loyalty to the king, yet he never yielded an inch in matters where a Christian could not give in. Even before God wanted to start Opus Dei, I saw clearly the two fields of action: the duties and rights of the citizen, and those of the Christian. And I have defended them both."[28] He was constantly defending their integrity and distinction, and calling for their mutual respect.

Normally, the rights and duties of a citizen and those of a Christian need not clash. Their compatibility is, in fact, a sign and guarantee of a healthy political system. For it is only where Christians are free to live and act as Christians that non-Christians can count on respect for their rights and protection of their dignity as citizens. Unfortunately, such a situation is rare in today's world. Even in liberal democracies, citizens who do not want to be Christian in name only, keep their faith a secret, or enter a monastery, but who want to live an active, apostolic Christianity in secular society — such citizens are destined to live in confrontation with the state. This is not because the modern state is neutral in religious matters and refuses to enforce religious observance as it once did.[29] No. Today's Christian lives in confrontation with the state because its laws tolerate or actively promote violations of human rights and the moral law.

Catholics and other Christians have entered into a battle with civil authorities over the so-called *res mixtae* — matters where church and state spheres of jurisdiction overlap. In questions concerning the family and education, both the church and the state have legitimate rights and responsibilities. Sorting them out is an extremely complicated process. Nevertheless, there are certain rights that cannot legitimately be denied to Christians. For a long time now, Christians have ceased defending on a purely confessional basis their positions concerning social issues. But when basic human rights are involved, further concession is impossible. It is not only un-Christian, it is inhumane for the state to deny legal protection to the family, or to tolerate the destruction of its structure, which is based on marriage, parenthood, and responsibility for children. In laws facilitating divorce and abortion, stifling Christian education, and creating artificial conflicts between parents and children, the Christian confronts not neutrality but injustice.

The preservation and revitalization of the Christian family, the family that lives rooted in Christ, was a central concern in Escrivá's life and preaching. One of the inalienable rights of this family is a certain say-so with regard to education. The foundation of a substantial number of healthy Christian families depends on the existence and effectiveness of Christian centers of education and culture. The worldwide apostolate of education is one of the most important tasks of the Church, and of Opus Dei in particular. From the very beginning, Escrivá kept in mind this need for education and cultural formation.

In 1962, Opus Dei began the construction of a cultural center for workers in Rome's Tiburtino quarter, a predominantly communist area. The building was finished in 1965, and dedicated by Pope Paul VI. I remember well the visit I made there in 1976. Amid the rows of apartment houses in that proletarian neighborhood, there stood a home for two hundred young men — some of them among the poorest of the poor — who were being trained to become skilled workers. Here I saw in action a unique re-Christianization of the workplace. The first thing that struck me was how cheerful they looked as they came home from work. The center includes a high school and training workshops for technical designers, locksmiths, electricians, and so forth. If possible, the boys live with their parents; if not, they live in the dormitory. Built for an occupancy of three, each of the rooms is bright, roomy, and simple. I saw only clean, orderly rooms, each of which had a crucifix and a picture of the Virgin Mary. There were plenty of common rooms, showers, and sports facilities; not surprisingly, all of them were in good condition. On the bulletin board, I read something that gave me a glimpse into the workings of this community: "Giovanni: northern garden; Paolo: southern garden; Francesco: electrical repairs; Luigi: plumbing; Roberto: painting the window frames in the basement; Emilio: in charge of fixing the mail box."

There is a parish church attached to this center, and Opus Dei priests have been entrusted with its care. But every building of the complex has its own chapel. Work, classes, leisure, and religious life constitute (as they should) a unity. Of course, nobody has to live this way; no one checks who does and does not go to Mass. But in many souls a fire, an eagerness to live this unity of life, is kindled. The day I visited, I ate lunch with the residents, and I was surrounded by exuberant cheerfulness. Every one of the young people I met seemed completely natural — unassuming and unaffected, neither subservient nor impudent. The director told me that when they first arrived in 1962, some people spat at them, threatened them, and even smashed their windows with stones. But today, Centro ELIS (Educazione – Lavoro – Istruzione – Sport) is the heart of Tiburtino. "I believe in the Communist Party and in Opus Dei," an old worker told me. And with this remark, we have yet another interesting brush stroke added to the portrait of Msgr. Escrivá.

Another focal point of Opus Dei's contribution to education is the University of Navarre. This university so dear to Escrivá's heart has achieved international renown as a center of academic research and Christian higher education. Marcelino Olaechea tells us how the university came to be.[30] He had been a member and then president of the Spanish Bishops' Commission for Seminaries and Education. By the time the Civil War ended, he had become bishop of Pamplona, and as such he wanted very much to found a pontifical university in Spain, preferably in Navarre, along the lines of the Sacro Cuore University in Milan. But that would require the consent of Franco, as well as that of Pope Pius XII. Franco told Olaechea that instead of founding a pontifical university, it would be better to make all the universities in Spain subject to the Spanish bishops, who could then select professors and oversee the religious education of the nation's youth. The bishop replied that while such a system would be appropriate, a pontifical university would be much more feasible. Besides, no one knew what the future might bring. The supreme power in Spain might some day rest in less reliable hands, and the Church could lose its influence on the educational system. (These words proved prescient indeed.) For quite a while, the generalissimo did not condescend to make a decision, and the memorandum simply languished in a desk drawer. Pope Pius XII was also hesitant. He pointed to the difficulties of the Milan university. He also had doubts about the Pamplona location, fearing for the future of the Navarre region, which borders on the

Basque country.[31] Finally, after long and tough negotiations, Archbishop Olaechea obtained the consent of Franco and of the regional government of Navarre. When the pope then asked him, "And who shall manage the university?" he responded, "Your Holiness, don't we have Don Josemaría and his sons? Won't they joyfully follow the pope's wishes?"

Escrivá was, of course, well acquainted with his friend's efforts. But though he entirely supported Olaechea's educational ambitions, he had slightly different ideas for a university that would be founded and run by members of Opus Dei. Because of the secular nature of Opus Dei, because its members are ordinary Catholic citizens, any apostolic project begun by them would have to be in essence a civil, not religious, institution.

So when the University of Navarre opened its doors in 1952, with a law school linked to the state university of Saragossa, it did so as a civil, not a pontifical, institute. (It was located in Camera de Comptos Reales, a small but beautiful building from the late Middle Ages, in the old city of Pamplona.) The Holy See did, eight years later, establish it as a Catholic university, but this was only because there was no other way that the Spanish government would recognize it as a private university, which Escrivá saw as vital.

In an agreement with the Holy See (signed on April 5, 1962), the Spanish government finally recognized the University of Navarre as a private university.[32] This agreement had far-reaching consequences; it was, in fact, what broke the state monopoly on education.[33] It should be noted that the conditions prescribed by the state for civil recognition of a church university were extremely rigorous. Among other things, the state required that a large percentage of the faculty consist of state-tenured professors, or *catedráticos*. This was fine with Escrivá, for he wanted the university to be among the best in the world. And its forty-year history shows that his dream came true. Particularly because of its high standards and its open-minded dovetailing of research with academic theory, the University of Navarre today enjoys great prestige among private and state universities all over the world. It now features not only all the classical university disciplines, but degree programs in communications, architecture, and engineering as well; there is also a business school in Barcelona. The student body numbers between seven and eight thousand. There are about seven hundred professors on the staff, including a hundred *catedráticos*. Only a minority of the faculty members belong to Opus Dei.

What, then, is so special about the University of Navarre? What is it that makes it an institutional expression of Escrivá's whole life — one among many, to be sure, but a signally important and characteristic one? It constitutes a remarkable portrait of Escrivá in the way it embodies his mission of rediscovering and sometimes creating, in and through Opus Dei, a unity of life — in this case, in the fields of science and education. The organic unity of science and faith, academic and personal growth, career and spiritual responsibility, education and religion, was taught and lived by Escrivá for half a century and is the spirit of the constitution of the University of Navarre. In 1951, one year before the university opened, Escrivá wrote of the critical importance of restoring that unity. "Today," he noted, "heresy and impiety originate more in errors advocated by the secular sciences than in directly theological controversies. Not that the secular sciences do not allow for supernatural truth; the light of reason also comes from God and cannot contradict the light of revelation. But people are moved by the same passions as ever, and some are now trying to find a foundation for atheism and heresy, especially in what are known as the experimental sciences."[34] (Thirty years later, in the Cologne cathedral, Pope John Paul II expressed essentially the same thoughts in a speech addressed to a group of scientists and students.[35])

When I talked about this with Francisco Ponz, a biologist and physiologist, and rector of the University from 1966 to 1979, he explained it this way: "Msgr. Escrivá cared for the education and formation of the whole personality of every human being. 'I am not interested in the cage, but in the birds,' he used to say."[36] Escrivá knew full well that no change in structure can sanctify this world and launch people on their way to heaven. On the contrary, only renewed individuals can change the structures and make them more suitable for the divine adventure. According to Ponz, Escrivá believed that professors of both the natural sciences and the humanities were in particular need of a Christian education combining doctrine, prayer, sacraments, and asceticism. Otherwise they would become vain and unhappy, with disastrous consequences for academia.

On the campus of the University of Navarre, Christ is present in many ways and places. Each complex of buildings has its own chapel. In none of these chapels is the Blessed Sacrament ever left alone; there are always visitors. Young and old, professor, student, gardener, they enter — just for a moment, but that moment is clearly pivotal. They say some short prayer, and then are on their way. Christ is also very much present in all those souls trying to study, do research, or teach according to the spirit of Opus Dei — in all those souls performing one indivisibly secular and divine service.

Escrivá wanted the University of Navarre to be living proof that not only is Christianity compatible with the highest academic standards, it actively fosters them. He wanted his school to be a model for the return of theology to the world of letters, which is ennobled when placed in a divine context. As a Spaniard, he knew and loved his country, anxiously watched its development, and wanted the University of Navarre to act as a spiritual leaven in this society so perennially susceptible to explosive reaction and regional separatism.[37]

Fulfillment of this wish came, in large part, thanks to an active participation in the maintenance of the university by people from all over Spain. In the late fifties, the Society of Friends of the University of Navarre was founded; this organization, which now has thousands of members, raises one third of the funds needed to run the university. The task of procuring money puts thousands of people in contact with one another; the need to be generous brings many people closer to God; and thus the association has become a veritable injection of the Gospel into the bloodstream of Spanish society.[38] This was the first time in Spanish history that the whole country pooled its resources to support one educational center — and in a remote region at that.[39]

Msgr. Escrivá attended the 1964, 1967, and 1972 general assemblies of the association in Pamplona.[40] In November 1964, he told the thousands who gathered in Pamplona's cathedral: "Our love ... belongs to the pope; our love belongs to all souls, whether Catholic or not, whether Christian or not. We are not 'against' anything; we are an affirmation, an affirmation of love. We want freedom for all. My sole mission is a spiritual and priestly one. I am talking about the soul, my children, my brothers and sisters — about the soul only. Freedom which the soul and conscience can decently and honestly exercise — this is what we want to gain with this additional instrument, the University of Navarre, which you support with your prayers, your sacrifices, your love, and your financial assistance.... Help us, Friends of the University of Navarre, because in order to spread the word [sanctification of the world in Christ], we need the right language and means of expression, if we want to be heard. The University is in your hands, which are blessed hands,[41] because they present the Lord with a sublime means for the opening [of hearts], a wonderful soil for his seed."[42]

Afterwards, when Escrivá met with the press, the correspondent of the French newspaper *Le Figaro* asked him what he considered his principal victory. Escrivá said, "Victory? I've never had one. I've never been victorious, because I've never fought with anybody. I hope that my only victory will be at the moment of death."[43] Then the agency director of France Press wanted to know if Escrivá could explain the enormous expansion of Opus Dei throughout the world. "Can you explain it?" responded Escrivá. "I can't. There is no explanation in human terms. The Work is God's own, and only he could satisfy your curiosity." After the Grand Chancellor thanked the journalists for coming, Escrivá bade them farewell. "I don't want to know what you will write," he said. "May God reward you if it is the truth! If not, I'll pray for you, so you will gain something anyway. But I trust your honesty."[44]

Such words characterize Escrivá as a priest. He habitually radiated cordiality and dignity, displaying an almost inexhaustible depth of nuance. He definitely had pedagogical flair, with the finely attuned sense of humor that normally goes with it. In fact, pedagogical flair was a basic component of his personality. We could use the word "charisma," but "flair" better conveys this ability to transmit grace through one's very nature. By way of personal attractiveness, he ignited people with a glorious desire to serve. As a renowned expert on canonizations explained, "If you take someone's picture dozens and dozens of times, these photos, made with or without their knowledge, in the most varied moments, situations, and circumstances, represent a first-rate source for the history of that person."[45] For this reason, I believe there will come a day when beatification cases will rest not only on oral and written evidence, but on visual material as well. Just by looking at the photographs of Escrivá, anyone can see that his charisma, his special efficacy, was not merely something verbal. It was something that can still be read in his smiles, glances, expressions, and reactions, and especially in those of his companions; the reverence and love he inspired is recorded in innumerable photographs. It would be easy enough to take a cynical view of this phenomenon, but one fact remains. Though this love and reverence may well have originated in natural affability and simple human affection, they nearly always led people to a genuine love for Christ, the Church, and all souls. One cannot deny the sincerity of their love, nor the sanctifying influence of Escrivá, who was able to direct these feelings toward God.

Holiness is not, of course, rooted in education. Pedagogy is nothing without the action of grace. Nevertheless, education is a valuable stepping stone. People often complain about the stale dryness of pedagogical advice. Well, allow me one counsel, which though old, is not yet stale: Make sure that the natural dispositions of each person in your care are open to perception of the grace of vocation; develop and mold talents so that each individual will be able and willing to correspond to the grace of vocation with an ever-increasing intensity. Developing talents and natural aptitudes is not excessively difficult. What is really difficult is the work of sanctification, the daily practice of what we know in theory. What made Escrivá such a superb teacher was that in him the discrepancies between duty, desire, and ability (discrepancies due to original sin) were so small as to be unnoticeable, and so whatever he taught had the seal of truth and credibility. What is more, he came across as being a friend of Jesus Christ's, someone eager to introduce Jesus to his other friends. He was richly gifted by his divine Friend; he also shared his cross. (We have already spoken about that.) At first a few, and then more and more people took what Escrivá offered them — sometimes hesitantly, like a careful shopper; sometimes impetuously, like a starving child.

Escrivá's pedagogy was grounded in his obvious, unaffected respect for the unique freedom of each individual in the context of Christ's eternal work of redemption. This fundamental attitude permeated all his interaction with people. Whatever this interaction may have involved, there was one thing that had no part in it: humiliation. Escrivá never humiliated anyone, and no one ever humiliated him. He was a master of the true art of education: guiding the pupil over the peaks and valleys of intellectual superiority and inferiority complexes (often aggravated by inept teachers) to a genuine self-knowledge. While he never humiliated people, he did not refrain from correcting them; he made a person confident enough of his love and affection to accept tough advice, a reproof, or even severe censure, if need be.

Opus Dei is by nature multifaceted, but one of its main roles is to serve as a pedagogical province, an academy of Christian life. To serve Christ and the Church, those called by God to Opus Dei must buttress their yes to his call with education and training. Any serious endeavor requires rigorous training. To become a physician, for example, one must study medicine and work in a hospital. And if medical supervisors failed to correct interns, or if colleagues never called each other's attention to errors and oversights, the entire staff would end up acting blindly and unscrupulously. And yet how much more is at stake in that most important and universal profession of all: holiness. Escrivá was keenly aware that all effective education is based not only on guidance and encouragement, but also on correction. "As a constant means of mortification," he said, "I intend to let not a single day go by without reprimanding where I have to reprimand."[46] He followed this principle, and occasionally his spiritual daughters shed some tears because of it. "We must reserve our tears for the times we offend God," he explained to them. "If you cry when you are given a reproof, you will be taking from me or whoever is in charge the confidence to say what must be said."[47]

Correction could, indeed, be quite painful for Escrivá to have to give. Encarnación Ortega describes one such occasion in her memoirs.[48] In the autumn of 1952, she says, Escrivá began talking of the need to divide the headquarters of the women's branch in Italy from the central headquarters at Villa Sacchetti, as had already been done with the men's branch. But when the women began doing the necessary work, they set about it in a slow, rather fussy manner. Noticing that things were falling behind, Escrivá invited the women over and told them they should leave Villa Sacchetti at once, if they wanted to see the region develop at the pace God expected. And he did mean at once. He looked at the head of the Italian region and told her, "If I were you, I wouldn't even sleep here tonight." So it was; a few hours later they were all gone. That night, Escrivá later admitted, "my heart was all in pieces, but it had to be. If it had not happened this way, nothing would have happened for a long time, and our work would have come to a standstill."

Escrivá made sure that he himself was not exempted from reprimands. He established, as a permanent arrangement for himself and his successors, the assignment of two numeraries to the duty of correcting the head of Opus Dei — simply and clearly, with love and respect, but without any reservations — on all matters concerning his duty of guiding Opus Dei and practicing its precepts himself. He was well aware that for a loving heart, it would be much harder to give than to accept correction. To accept correction is, of course, never an easy thing, for human beings have an innate tendency to be proud; as Escrivá liked to say, one's pride does not die until twenty-four hours after one's death. No exception to the rule, he admitted that it was a challenge for him to sincerely accept a correction — especially when it was clearly well founded. When he was all by himself later on, and feeling the rise of inner resistance, he would say in a loud voice, "The others are right! Absolutely right! Always!"[49]

It is certainly not by chance that the word *lucha* ("struggle") was a constant in Josemaría's daily vocabulary throughout his life. He said it thousands of times, nearly as often as "believe," "love," "child of God," "apostolate," or "perseverance." The reason is plain to see. If you want to walk in Our Lord's footsteps, making him ring in your words, shine in your eyes, and accompany your every step, whether in joy or in pain, you have to struggle. If you want to love him and all people, if you want to be holy, you have to struggle. We know our opposition pretty well. Usually it does not come in the form of a villainous aberration or a full-blown hatred of God. It is far more likely to take the form of what we could call mini-vices: the petty failings that plague our weakened nature like an itch, the insidious weeds that overgrow the path of holiness with their gnarled roots and brambles. It is the little unkindnesses and faults of everyday life that are the chief obstacle to our sanctity, to our following of Christ. Unless we keep struggling against them, these little foxes will eventually destroy the vine of our Christian vocation.

It is true that Escrivá was not the first to discover the greatness of little things (this was revealed by Jesus of Nazareth), but he reemphasized their importance. William Wordsworth could have been speaking for him when he wrote about "that best portion of a good man's life,/ His little, nameless, unremembered acts/ Of kindness and of love." Escrivá virtually created a theology of little things. Proclaiming their sanctifying value and power, he pointed out how little crosses, patiently borne, keep the cross of Christ alive in the world as a living work of redemption. But he also showed how petty acts of baseness and meanness, constantly repeated, keep hell alive in human history. To trivialize or ignore these evils, he said, instead of fighting against them, is to open the door and invite the devil in for dinner — and it is no secret how such feasts end. Such are the insights that God granted Escrivá in 1928, and that he passed on. This is why he hated venial sin so much — it creates tepidity by numbing people to the influence of the Holy Spirit. "You are lukewarm," he warned, "if you are centered on yourself and your convenience, if you don't detest venial sin."[50]

Living the virtues heroically means detesting venial sin and tirelessly fighting the worms that gnaw at the roots of holiness. But we are not talking about a grouchy, humorless rage that cannot forgive itself any slips or signs of weakness — that would be just another self-centered drive, a mania for self-glorification. So how goes the well-fought battle for sanctity in little things? Well, small victories and defeats come and go; the tide of the battle is always shifting. There is never a truce, never a cease-fire, because "the devil never takes a vacation," as Escrivá used to say, and because our nature is continually subject to the same temptations. On the other hand, a firm desire to be a fruitful branch on Christ's vine — a desire strengthened by the grace of vocation, the virtues of faith, hope, and love, and a fighting spirit to achieve all for Christ — is not a Sisyphean exercise in futility.[51] We have been redeemed by Christ;[52] everything we do or leave undone, everything we suffer or refuse to suffer, has a lasting effect. Anyone who loves Christ and is serious about following him will not waste time, because Christ does not waste time. The Christian moves on, following him uphill, heading towards Golgotha. Of course, none of us knows how far our particular road to holiness stretches, but we need not worry about that. We are not going to count the milestones (a most unholy thing to attempt), but we will know if we are falling behind or moving on. There is no absolute certainty of reaching the journey's end, eternal life with God (since our ongoing free will is involved), but there is hope, the virtue that guarantees God's loyalty. For the holiest human being, there is still a precipice to encounter before joining God, who dwells in unapproachable light. But even in this life, Jesus Christ, perfect Man as well as God, is utterly approachable. Otherwise, the whole of Christianity — including the Church, Opus Dei, and this book — would be absurd.

It should, therefore, come as no surprise that Josemaría Escrivá sincerely considered himself a sinner. He was always wholeheartedly and urgently begging God's forgiveness, deeply convinced of needing his mercy very badly. Yet on all occasions he kept his sense of humor and lived in the confidence that Jesus Christ is a forgiving God. On March 28, 1975, his golden jubilee as a priest, he told the members of the women's branch in Rome, "Drawing the line at fifty years and adding them up, I have to laugh at my insignificance.[53] But along with that laughter, I ask from the bottom of my heart for God's pardon, and I also forgive everything, though I've never felt offended by anyone."[54]

These last words touch on an area where Escrivá may, indeed, have been sorely tempted. He was, after all, a headstrong Aragonese and a true Spaniard, with all the sense and prizing of personal honor that this implies. We must keep in mind that for a Spaniard, honor is not only the supreme social attribute, it is also part of his or her very essence as a person. *Honra* is a central topic in Spanish literature; its preservation, loss, violation, and restoration provide the theme for innumerable poems, narratives, and dramas. Even a slight scratch on the ever-sensitive skin of the soul can lead to bloody tragedies. As he said himself (in Buenos Aires, 1974), Escrivá was often cut to the quick, especially in the forties, when he was treated "like a filthy rag."[55] One night, he recalled, he entered the chapel of the Diego de León center, fell on his knees, and prayed, "Lord, if you don't want my honor, why should I want it?" That prayer, which told of inner liberation from one of the most important, precious commodities of the Spanish soul, may well signify Escrivá's hardest victory: parting with a final fragment of self-love hidden deep in a corner of his heart.[56] But this abandoning of his honor to God, difficult as it must have been, was well worth the cost. For the feeling of injured honor dropped from his soul like a useless, antiquated plume, and thirty years later, he could honestly say he had never felt offended.

Escrivá never allowed personal values to dominate his soul — even values as sacrosanct as Spanish honor or Aragonese pride — because that would have meant depriving Christ of his exclusive rule. Nor did he permit any inclinations or talents, such as his penchant for architecture or his flair for writing, to claim a special place in his soul. He certainly used his gifts, but he did not grant them any rights in themselves. Here, too, he had to fight persistently. Perhaps that fight was even more painful, because it was aimed not at defects, but at gifts — against their use for his own gratification.

The writer

I believe writing was Escrivá's secret love. From time to time he would improvise little songs and write verses, but then immediately throw them away. I am convinced that he could have written novels of great power, profundity, and beauty. He saw with the eyes of a poet. Consider his description of the young peasant boy in Perdiguera who could imagine wealth only as having wine soup every day.[57] Or his vivid memory of the simple worker who started every day by going to the church, opening the door, calling out to Christ in the tabernacle, "It's Juan, the milkman!" and then rattling off with his cart.[58] Or his poignant image of a certain beggar, the darkness of whose poverty was penetrated by only one light: the faint luster of a tin spoon, his one possession.[59] Yes, Josemaría had the eyes of an artist, and he might easily have become a great artist had he not chosen instead to spend his life seeing with the eyes of the Good Shepherd. His language was full of poetry; this is more obvious in the original Spanish, but still evident in the translations. Each of his meditations unfolds the drama of redemption and catches the listener up in the action. His *Way of the Cross* and *Holy Rosary* are full of elements from mystery plays, poetical sequences more seen than read.

Pope John Paul II greets Bishop Alvaro del Portillo, prelate of Opus Dei, following the beatification of Msgr. Escrivá before a gathering of some two hundred thousand people in St. Peter's Square.

In 1931, at the age of twenty-nine, Escrivá wrote, "Although I feel devoid of virtue and learning — and I really mean this, without any exaggeration — I would love to write some books so full of ardor that they would sweep through the world like a reveille, inflaming people with light and warmth; yes, books that would transform poor hearts into glowing fires, so I could present them as rubies for Jesus' royal crown."[60] This is the voice of a poet — not a self-absorbed or angst-driven one, but one whose patron and kin is the Lord himself.

The young man's wish was granted. His books swept the world. His first book, *The Way*, had from the start a tremendous impact that has continued unabated. An authentic self-portrait of the young Escrivá, this is a portrait in which all Christians can recognize themselves. Without hesitation, I would call it the most untimely book of this century, compared with which Nietzsche's *Untimely Contemplations*[61] seems dated and shallow. *The Way* has become one of the most widely read and necessary books of the century. If Hugo von Hofmannsthal had known of *The Way*, his *Jedermann* might have been written completely differently or not at all.[62] It is for this contemporary Everyman that the 999 gates to the imitation of Christ that comprise *The Way* are opened. It is Everyman who walks — half pushed, half pulled — along the 999 paving stones that mark the path of an ordinary Christian life. And the Everyman who follows this road will live more happily, die better, and arrive less disheveled at his final destination than Hofmannsthal's character. "I will not tell you anything new," Escrivá announces in the preface, underlining the point so as not to disappoint the intellectual or the pious who are keen on spiritual novelties because they think they already know the old truths. "I will only stir your memory," he says, "so that some thought will arise and strike you, so you will better your life and set out along ways of prayer and of love. And in the end you will be a soul with clear judgment."

The trick to reading this book well is to not get mad at the author's demands, but simply accept them and keep reading. One is likely at times to feel shocked, frightened, or deceived, for some of the points are tough, apparently banal, or incomprehensible at first glance. A friend of mine wanted to throw the book away just because of point 592: "Don't forget that you are just a trash can. So if by any chance the divine gardener should lay his hands on you and scrub you and clean you, and fill you with magnificent flowers, neither the scent nor the colors that beautify your ugliness should make you proud. Be humble: don't you know that you are a trash can?" Well, my friend was quite right. This is offensive — insufferably offensive. But that is because these radical, even brutal words aim straight at the heart and storm our generation's holy of holies: the illusion of wholesale emancipation. In the face of that lamentable cry *God is dead*, here is someone with the only true answer: If that is the case, then you, like it or not, are nothing but a dirty, empty trash can. Without God you are nothing.

One of the secrets of *The Way* is that its 999 points seem at first glance to be simple maxims, but after some reflection they prove to be rules for a life full of wisdom. Reading them for the first time, one thinks, "Okay, this phrase and that one are quite accurate; this other one is less apt, and that one does not apply to me at all; here is one that is only partly true." But both the simple and the sophisticated, if they give themselves a chance, will find themselves more and more engaged until finally they are hooked, having come to realize that every point is an unfathomable well. *The Way* rivals the great works of literature in its ability to suit each mental capacity. Generally speaking, the only ones to whom it says absolutely nothing are those who have little to say for themselves.

Escrivá apparently had more to say than he had the opportunity to put in writing. Point 120 of *The Way* has this intriguing sentence: "I promise you a book, God willing, that could be called *Celibacy, Matrimony, and Purity.*" Some thirty years later, talking with students, he promised a book on university issues; and when asked a few months later how it was going, he responded, "I hope the book will be published, and that it will be of some use to professors and students. Maybe it will take some time, but the book will certainly be published."[63] Since Escrivá never spoke rashly, and both promises remain unfulfilled, two possibilities exist: the manuscripts have yet to emerge from his estate, or — more probably — he had to sacrifice his projects, close to his heart as they both were, for some compelling reason.[64]

A man of many talents, Escrivá could have become an architect. If he had not been called to found Opus Dei, Spain would probably have had one more fine architect, perhaps a great one. His constant participation in the construction of the many buildings, his personal supervision of each project, has already been noted. His talent for sketching imaginative, beautiful, and eminently functional plans has been mentioned. He had a flair for architectural design, but he also knew how to choose the right location for a faucet or a light switch. Construction workers had an immense respect for him, because he would instantly spot bad masonry or a carelessly plastered ledge. Torreciudad,[65] the Marian shrine near Barbastro in the Pyrenees, owes its rediscovery, reconstruction, and revival to Escrivá's initiative. The splendid idea of building a church with "wide open arms" was his, though he in no way impinged on the freedom of Heliodoro Dols, the chief architect.

His last trip took him to his native country, to the places of his youth: Barbastro, and Torreciudad. He arrived there on May 23, 1975, at noon. In the new church's tower, finished almost the day before, the bells were ringing. Outside, Escrivá prayed, "Regina Coeli, laetare, alleluia" ("Queen of Heaven, rejoice, alleluia"). Then he withdrew to the adjacent old shrine of Our Lady of Torreciudad, a small chapel which had, in its own quiet way, proclaimed the faith for more than twenty generations. To that place, where he now prayed the Salve Regina ("Hail, holy Queen ..."), his parents had taken him seventy-one years earlier, to thank the Blessed Virgin Mary for saving the life of their little boy, and to commend that life to her protection. That protection, he realized, had never ceased. He had so much to remember, so much to bring to this prayer. In that moment of deep emotion, he perhaps remembered his parents, his sister Carmen, Isidoro Zorzano, and José María Hernández Garnica. Perhaps he felt a particular closeness to the stranger who had been hanged in his place, or to his spiritual daughter Montserrat Grases, who had died in 1959, at the age of eighteen, and whose beatification process had been opened in 1962.[66] Calling to mind all his beloved friends, and especially his sons and daughters in Opus Dei — those already gone, those still living, and those to come after his time — having them all in mind, he entrusted them all to the one who had always protected him, addressing her as "Mater misericordiae" ("Mother of mercy"). This was not just a token of the habitual gratitude he had displayed on countless occasions. This title was a synopsis of the great hymn he had preached for more than fifty years by word and example: "Praise the Lord, all you nations. Sing his glory, all you peoples. For he has proven to us his loving kindness — the Lord is true to his word forever" (Ps 117). "Mater misericordiae" — this was homage to the woman by whom divine mercy had become flesh and entered the world, there to dwell until the end of time.

A few hours later, Escrivá entered the new sanctuary of Our Lady of the Angels of Torreciudad. Standing in the cavernous nave, which was bathed in amber light, and gazing at the majestic altarpiece, he felt an ineffable joy and exclaimed, "Only the crazy people of Opus Dei can do such a thing! And we are happy to be so crazy.... You have done very well. You have put so much love into it.... But you must complete it fully.... How easy it will be to pray well here!"[67]

To pray, yes, and also to go to confession. For Torreciudad is not just another tourist attraction, a pious stopover. It is a place of pilgrimage, a place where many people renew their communication with God. Its architect had planned twenty confessionals. But Escrivá had said, "Forty!" He must have been able to see into the future, for they have not gone unused. He was the first to receive absolution there — from Don Alvaro del Portillo, his son, friend, helper, alter ego, and soon-to-be successor.

On May 26th, he returned to Rome, to his daily work routine. He had only thirty-one days to live. It has frequently been said that Escrivá had a gift of natural foresight concerning the fate of persons and things. Whether or not he had a premonition of his own death, no one can say; but that would have made little difference to him. His will was so fused to God's will that he could repeat without presumption the words of Jesus, "My food is to do the will of him who sent me, and to finish his work" (Jn 4:34). He had done what God wanted him to do, always and everywhere. Never had he plugged his ears or feigned ignorance in order to get out of doing God's will. Instead, he had always responded promptly, even when he really did not understand what God was after. So what was now left for him to do? Opus Dei had already borne out the parable of the mustard seed; the tiny seed had, indeed, grown into a mighty tree "in whose branches the birds of the air perch" (Mt 13:31-32). And this tree, what was it but just a healthy new sprout on the stem of the perennially budding Church?

Did Escrivá fear for the Church? No. He trusted fully in Jesus' guarantee that "the gates of hell will not prevail against it" (Mt 16:18); he had every confidence in the one who had prayed for Peter "that your faith may not fail," the one who had told Peter to "return and strengthen your brothers"(Lk 22:32). But Escrivá did suffer for the Church. He loved her and felt the pangs of what she was suffering from the disobedience, hostility, and coldness of her children. On the morning of June 26th, after celebrating a votive Mass in honor of the Mother of God, he said, "For years now, I have offered Mass every day for the Church and the pope. Over and over you have heard me say that I have offered my life to God for the pope, whoever he may be."[68]

That morning, he went to Castelgandolfo, with Alvaro del Portillo and two others, to visit the women who were taking classes at Villa delle Rose. There, too, his words were dedicated to the Church and the Holy Father — his last words as father of this family, a legacy of supreme importance. He asked his daughters always to be conscious of the presence of God and faithful in fulfilling their duties, practicing the spirit of Opus Dei. They should endeavor at all times to live close to God, Mary, St. Joseph, and their guardian angels, "to help our holy Church, our mother, who needs our help so badly, because at present she is having a really bad time in the world."[69] And for the second time that day, he made this plea: "We must love very much the Church and the pope, whoever he may be. Pray to the Lord that our service to the Church and the Holy Father may be effective."[70]

Feeling indisposed, he stopped talking, and after a short rest at Villa delle Rose, he returned to Rome. Shortly after twelve o'clock, he collapsed in Don Alvaro's study. His heart stopped beating, but he was still breathing, and Don Alvaro was able to give him the last sacraments. Whenever he had spoken of his own death, Escrivá had always asked Alvaro not to let him go "without that treasure." Every attempt was made to save his life, but to no avail.[71] When his breathing finally stopped, not only a great life — a life which had opened a new chapter in Church history — but also Opus Dei's age of foundation had ended. The first stretch of the journey was over.

The last stone of Villa Tevere, which Escrivá had consecrated and inserted on January 9, 1960, had been engraved with a verse he had chosen from the Book of Ecclesiastes:

MELIOR EST FINIS QUAM PRINCIPIUM.
(Finishing is better than beginning.)[72]

Just five simple words. But although he himself did not realize it, these five words summed up the whole life of Josemaría Escrivá.

Epilogue

Opus Dei as a Personal Prelature

The wonderful figure of St. Thomas More has always appealed to me in a very special way, so much so that I eventually wrote a book about him. What is most appealing to me is the fact that he was both a lawyer and a saint. This fact catches one's attention as something rather surprising, for it seems almost a contradiction. It is not necessarily an easy thing to find any connection between holiness and law. One would hesitate, for example, to look upon the following of Christ, the struggle for holiness, as the defense and exercise of a legal right.

There is also a certain reluctance to define the People of God as a juridical society. The very juxtaposition of the two concepts at first sight repels us, sparking repugnance as if they were totally clashing entities. Such qualms result perhaps from our tendency to reduce love (whether divine or human) to something purely sentimental, to set it up as an antithesis to law. To look at this another way, if we do not attribute to love of God and neighbor the power necessary to create a right order of things, and if we do not understand that holiness and sanctification are the greatest — indeed, the only — obligatory mission of service in our lives, then justice becomes the only reliable substitute, and law the only relevant instrument with which to practice it. Thus love is reduced to mere sentiment, mercy becomes indifference to wrongdoing, and law just partially satisfies conflicting demands by creating a certain balance between them.

The reality, however, is quite different from all this. Human life basically consists of an ongoing effort to create and maintain proper balance between the essential aspects of the one Love: justice, mercy, wisdom, freedom, power. In God, these aspects are united in a mysterious, incomprehensible way. But in us, weakened as we are by original sin, these aspects exist disjointedly and often in contradiction to one another. To understand this, one must begin with the realization that law and justice do not exist primarily for the ordering of relationships among people. They are, first and foremost, real and tangible aspects of the relationship between God and ourselves. Even the plan of redemption, the work of salvation itself, has a legal character. This does not contradict the fundamental principle of the Catholic faith that God is Love, for love does not address itself to passive beings, but rather to beings who are themselves capable of loving. The very essence of love is revealed in God's having created us and endowed us with the power to respond freely. Part of this endowment is our natural capacity to come to a knowledge of his existence; another part is our natural need and desire to worship him. God chose to carry out the work of our redemption in such a way that his perfect love would become apparent and could be personally experienced by us as both perfect mercy and perfect justice.

The distinction so often made between the "hierarchical Church" or "Church of law," on the one hand, and the "popular Church" or "Church of love," on the other, is as detrimental as it is unfounded; for it belies, or at least obscures, the very reality of the People of God, which was established by Jesus Christ and remains alive only in him. Lengthy acquaintance with a comfortable but simplistic image of original sin can trivialize, and in a sense aestheticize away, the real horror of the conduct of our first parents. The fact is that even though Adam and Eve enjoyed an intellectual union with God, a close and loving relationship with their Creator, Preserver, and Friend, they opted instead for the path of treason. In paying heed to the promise of the serpent ("You shall be like gods") and in acting upon it, they committed the greatest crime in the history of the human race: they slapped God in the face.

A moment's reflection will give us some insight into the catastrophic consequences of what they did. The enormity of an offense is, after all, measured not by the status of the person giving offense, but rather by that of the one offended. If the very idea of striking one's father or mother, employer, or parish priest is enough to cause shock and revulsion, then just think how great should be one's shock and revulsion at the idea of treating God this way — deliberately, freely, in cold blood. Such a voluntary abuse of the love of God formed the essence of the first sin, and forms the essence of all sin. At the same time, such an abuse of love was and continues to be a grave transgression of the law. And this offense against the majesty of God would still be a transgression of the law even if there were not this personal bond of love between Creator and creature.

Our adoration, praise, and thanksgiving, whether expressed in word or in deed, cannot increase the glory of God, but they are necessary to our happiness, to the meaningfulness of our lives, and to our salvation. Likewise, our evil deeds, betrayals, transgressions cannot injure God or reduce his eternal beatitude, but they can weaken and pervert us and make us miserable both on earth and (if we do not repent) throughout all eternity. Due to the gravity of their offense, the rebellion of our first parents against God had devastating consequences. Their nature, their very existential status, was weakened and wounded; so would be the nature and status of every one of their descendants. Neither Adam and Eve themselves nor any of their sinful descendants were in a position, on their own, to heal this wound and restore the *status quo ante*. Only the love of God, the One who had been offended, could accomplish this. The divine plan of salvation perfectly demonstrates the union of love and justice in God, making it clear that justice is an obligation that proceeds from love. Since the offense of our first parents was an abuse of divine love, it could be atoned for only by a supreme act of divine love. It was, in fact, expiated by nothing less than the sacrifice of God's only Son.

Thus provided with all the necessary means, we can now live as beloved children before God, and not as enemies or offenders. Furthermore, since God's infinite love and infinite mercy remain forever inseparable, it was fitting that the act of love by which he redeemed us should have been the very act of law that effected reparation. And really it was for our own good that God did not bring about our redemption by means of an arbitrary decree, did not decide to just overlook the fault and waive the reparation requirement. Love cannot bear not to be able to atone for an injury or offense. Thus we see how it was, in the deepest sense of the term, truly for the best that God chose to save us the way he did: through the incarnation, suffering, and death of his Son.

The fact that the legal character of the work of salvation has its origin in the very bosom of the Holy Trinity, that the apparent opposition between love and law has been overcome in Jesus Christ, helps us to understand more profoundly why the Church, the new People of God, has from the moment of its foundation been a community of both love and law. To be sure, the Church did not at first have any formulated statutes or codes, but it did have certain legal characteristics and a defined structure. From the very outset it possessed hierarchical organization, a clearly defined division of responsibilities, and an internal order. These characteristics were already in place during Jesus' earthly life; they were introduced by him. The blueprint is clearly discernible in the New Testament. Jesus is the supreme head of the Church that he founded. He has authority over it, which he exercises: he chooses and calls to himself certain individuals; he imposes demands and gives instructions. He gives Simon, son of John, a new name and makes him his vicar on earth, giving him, and by implication his successors, the power to represent him on earth for all time. Even in that first community that Jesus assembles around himself, a differentiation is made between the apostles and the other disciples. And the circle of the Twelve has its own internal structure: Peter, James, and John are given a special position in the group, while Judas is given the responsibility of administering community funds. When Jesus gives the apostles the power to bind and to loose, he establishes the procedure they should follow in dealing with unrepentant sinners, including, if necessary, excommunication (see Mt 18:15-18). Later we see the primitive Church in Jerusalem, and it has a hierarchical structure. All the faithful have a supreme head in Peter; there is the clearly defined college of apostles, and there is another group to help them in their apostolic work; a clear distinction is drawn between liturgical services and works of charity. All of this implies a body of norms of a legal nature.

It had to be this way. For the new People of God, the Church, is by no means a loose collection of individuals existing independently of one another. On the contrary, it is the Mystical Body of its Founder and Lord — his Body existing within the human race, within its history. At the same time, it is also a *societas terrena*, and as such, a legal body with legal norms, developments, and improvements characterizing its internal structure and its relations with the outside world, especially with the state. And because every member of the Church is necessarily the child of a given era, the Church must play both active and passive roles in human history, sharing in its highs and lows, discoveries and errors, triumphs and disasters. Yet because of the permanent presence of the Church's sovereign Head — in the sacraments (especially the Eucharist), in Scripture, in all its many members living in the state of grace — and because of the constant guidance and protection of the Holy Spirit, the Church's participation and unavoidable involvement in history have not resulted in its decline and self-destruction, but have served instead to open new paths for Christ on earth, thus fulfilling the salvific will of God.

The long history of the Church shows proof after proof of the ongoing fulfillment of Christ's promise that it will not decline or perish. While all merely human enterprises — cultures, empires, civilizations, states, and all other entities — reach their natural end in time, the Church, being immortal in its essence, continues to stride ahead through the entire gamut of historical time and on into eternity. It is ever the same "one, holy, catholic, and apostolic Church" that Christ won by his death on the cross and that the Holy Spirit confirmed on Pentecost. The pilgrim Church, the visible Church on earth, continuously increases the membership of the Church in purgation and the Church in glory, and at the same time continuously receives strength and support from them. In other words, the visible Church shares in all the temporal, historically conditioned elements of progress, the paths, developments, and transformations of human history, with the one striking exception that it alone is exempt from collapse and death.

Not that the Church has ever had an easy time of it. In every chapter of its history, it has undergone some form of trial by fire. In the early centuries, for example, flourishing Christian provinces succumbed to the Moslem onslaught, and the Huns, Germans, Tartars, Mongols, and Turks all cut wide paths of destruction through Christendom. And besides such external, physical peril, the Church has suffered deep internal wounds as well. There has been no end of heresies, schisms, and apostasy. At times the Church has appeared to be on the verge of collapse — when, for example, it was under threat of destruction, from without and from within, by such formidable forces as Arianism, Protestantism, Modernism, and Marxism.

But that is not the whole story. The Church has, in fact, been as constantly endangered by its necessary participation in the world as by these controversies and bloody conflicts. This holds true at every level of its organization. Bishops and priests, religious orders and congregations, and pastoral works — they all take part in, and thus are affected by, the vicissitudes of history. Even the briefest glance at Church history confirms this. Beginning with Constantine's establishment of Christianity as the official religion of the Roman Empire, the historical path of the Church leads from Byzantine caesaropapism to the patronal churches of the Franks and the church-state dualism of the Middle Ages. From there it passes through the worldliness of the Renaissance, the confusion of the Reformation, and the church-state alliance of the Counter-Reformation. Finally, it makes its way through the upheavals of the age of Enlightenment and revolution and finds itself in the midst of all the various schools of thought to which this age gave birth — liberalism, socialism, nihilism — schools which for the past two hundred years, with ever increasing force, have continued to attack the Church.

Throughout these twenty centuries of participation within history, the Church has suffered innumerable wounds — wounds caused by the sins, errors, and confusion of its members, as well as wounds inflicted by its enemies. Nonetheless, the Church has not collapsed. Structures and milieus have come and gone. Medieval ardor, feudalism, scholasticism, the Holy Roman Empire, the European monarchies, the Papal States are no more. But the Church has continued to grow. In fact, it has often grown most remarkably at the very time that one of these other institutions was fading away. It has spread through the entire world, fulfilling and continuing to fulfill its apostolic mission on all seven continents. It has remained faithful to its mission, the salvation and sanctification of all people, and it will continue to do so. It has remained loyal to its Founder and Lord, and it will continue to do so. It has preserved the deposit of the faith from harm; and this will not, cannot ever change. It has accomplished all of this despite the many horrible evils brought about by the mistakes, delusions, and bad example of its members. For besides God's constant safeguarding of its magisterium, the Church has also been blessed with a constant supply of saints. Even in the darkest of times, when the voice of sound doctrine seemed almost inaudible and the face of Christ seemed covered by the thickest of veils, there were saints on earth, shining like bright stars with the crystal clarity of his love.

Many contemporary historians have adopted an attitude that is thoroughly unjust, profoundly antihistorical, and, unfortunately, quite contagious: they have made it fashionable to view the past with the eyes of a righteous judge. Treating the past as though it were on trial, these intrepid judges condemn our predecessors for their appalling lack of political, economic, human, and psychological sense. According to them, sixty generations lived in complete darkness. Then, at long last, the dawn began to break, thanks to the likes of Voltaire and Rousseau, and the sun finally rose with the advent of Marx and Freud. Sadly, many Christians today have adopted this point of view, and they apply it to the Church as if that were the most natural thing in the world to do. As a result, the Church appears to them to be a body dedicated to the abuse of power and the suppression of freedom, the ultimate treason against the "cause of the man Jesus." As a further result, they are able to persuade ordinary, faithful Christians to adopt such extra-ecclesial principles as tolerance, freedom of opinion, democracy, and egalitarianism, and apply them to the Church in order to bring about the changes they desire.

At the heart of this opinion lies a false vision of history. The idea that one's own generation stands at the highest level of historical progress is, to say the least, foolish and naive. It engenders an arrogant and myopic view of history, a view by which one relates the entire past to the present "highest level of historical progress" and then grades it according to the extent to which it has furthered or hindered the progress attained. I would like to point out again that throughout its history, the Church as a whole (and it must be viewed as a whole) has always shaped its theology and spirituality, its pastoral work, its movements, and its legal norms and structures so that it can fulfill its constant mission within the constantly changing relationships of time and place, regardless of how the People of God are divided into different empires, nations, races, or cultures; regardless of how they take their part in the course of history. The Church, as a *civitas terrena*, can be attacked, wounded, or severely shaken, but it can never be destroyed, for it is at the same time the *civitas caelestis et aeterna*. Constantly strengthened by the power of the Holy Spirit, it receives again and again the means necessary to open new paths of spiritual renewal and salvation.

One of these paths is Opus Dei, the subject of this book. Granted, I may have gone far afield here, but I have done so in order to explain why, two years after writing this book, I found it necessary to add an epilogue detailing the definitive juridical situation of the Work — its status as a personal prelature — and answering the basic questions that naturally arise in this connection.[1] The full import of its legal standing can be understood only within the context of the essential unity of the Church as a community of love and law.

II

I was once asked, "What was Opus Dei before it was recognized as a pious union by the bishop in Madrid on March 19, 1941?" I answered that in the eyes of God, and for those faithful Christians following the way of the founder, it was what it had been since its founding on October 2, 1928, and what it will continue to be for all time: the spiritual family of those who, according to their divine vocation, want to be and do the work of God by following the teaching and example of Msgr. Escrivá. From a canonical point of view, however, Opus Dei did not yet exist, since it lacked an approved legal form. The spiritual children of the founder simply exercised a right held by all people, all citizens, all Christians: the right to undertake in common something good and noble (in this case, the following of Christ) in an unofficial and private manner. Nonetheless, the legitimacy of this new undertaking was being called into question more and more as it was growing and attracting greater public interest, demonstrating once again that public recognition and understanding of general rights is to a large extent based on the scope of the rights in question. As we have seen, Josemaría Escrivá and his spiritual family had to suffer accusations of at least borderline heresy on account of his teaching that one can achieve sanctity without leaving the world. To promote and to act on this teaching did conflict with the ecclesiastical discipline and structure in force at that time, particularly in Spain. And because of the close connection between church and state in Franco's Spain, such accusations might have carried implications involving civil and even criminal law. Even in the early years, then, the question of Opus Dei's status within the Church was of paramount importance.

When the bishop of Madrid issued his decree recognizing Opus Dei as a pious union, he took the first step in a process that would take over forty years — a process that would eventually lead to the full, proper, and definitive incorporation of the Work into the legal structure of the Church. The chief importance of that decree centered around the fact that this was the first time an ecclesiastical authority attested publicly and officially to the orthodoxy, loyalty to the Church, and piety of the young organization. However, while Opus Dei needed to be completely integrated into the legal, hierarchical system of the Church in order to fulfill its mission and carry out an effective apostolate throughout the entire world, the appropriate legal framework for this incorporation did not yet exist.[2] The one it was given — that of a pious union — was inadequate; it did not at all correspond with the spirit of Opus Dei. This presented a potential threat to the living out of that spirit, as God had made it known to the founder, and adversely affected the health of the Work itself. There was as yet no legal framework suitable for an organization of ordinary lay people dedicated completely to Christ and the Church in the midst of the world, dedicated to living a life both active and contemplative. Indeed, the very creation of such a framework was not even perceived as something immediately necessary. So Escrivá sought to gain from the Holy See at least a temporary solution which would allow Opus Dei to carry out its apostolate and expand unhindered without having its spirit endangered. He saw this, however, as being simply the least inadequate of the alternatives then available, for even this solution prevented the true spirit of Opus Dei from being seen clearly on certain key points.

The creation of the juridical form of the secular institute was the first result of this effort to incorporate Opus Dei into the legal structure of the Church. For thirty-five years (1947-1982), the longest period in its history thus far, the Work existed in a canonical form (that of a secular institute) which the founder had to accept as a purely temporary solution. At the time, there was simply no alternative. This was the only secular framework that allowed for the universal and central direction of the Work, as well as for the incardination of its own priests. Earlier I spoke of the apostolic constitution *Provida Mater*, promulgated on February 2, 1947, which created secular institutes. I would like to add here a few further observations on the subject. At the basis of this document was the preconciliar notion of the Church in which the laity was defined solely *per exclusionem* and *ex negativo* — that is, not by specific characteristics, but as not having any. The laity consisted of "the faithful" who lacked specific tasks, responsibilities, and characteristics within the Church. They were "the rest." But within this remainder (which, of course, encompassed the great majority of Catholics), there were those who felt called by God to a life of complete dedication, those who were striving to live sanctity in the one way possible to them: as ordinary lay Christians in the midst of the world. Understandably, these people wished to come together in order to better achieve their goal, but this would take some help. So after carefully examining the statutes and practices of such groups, Holy Mother Church took them under her protection and established them as secular institutes, thus making it possible for their members to live, explicitly and formally, a life of complete dedication to Christ outside of a religious order or congregation — that is, outside of a traditional "state of perfection," but assimilated nonetheless into such a state. That is why the members of a secular institute are obliged to live the evangelical counsels (poverty, chastity, and obedience), and that is why the secular institutes are subject to the Congregation for Religious. They exist as a type of variant order, adapted to the spirit of the times (in this case, secularism) and joined to the traditional orders by a sort of interior affinity, a kind of blood relationship.

One must keep all this in mind to understand Don Alvaro's comment that it "cost the founder many tears" to be saddled with compromises regarding the canonical status of the Work while he was striving to preserve intact the nature of its foundation as willed by God.[3] For in order to be approved by the Vatican as a secular institute, Opus Dei had to adapt its *ius particulare* (internal statutes and by-laws) to conform with the general law promulgated for secular institutes. Concessions had to be made for compliance with the regulations established by the Congregation for Religious. One of these concessions was the requirement that every member of Opus Dei make a private vow to follow the three evangelical counsels.

The barque of Opus Dei was thus anchored to the rock of Peter, but not in the proper port. The Work was included among a group of ecclesiastical communities that despite their many differences had one thing in common: their members had a status over and above that of the ordinary lay person. The special status of a secular institute superseded, so to speak, the simple lay status and allowed its members to live a life similar, from a canonical point of view, to that of those living in one of the states of perfection — those living a "consecrated life" — even though, as lay people, they continued to live in the world. They became, in a sense, "extraordinary laity." But this status contradicted the very nature and mission of the Work. Nonetheless, it was difficult then, and it is still difficult today, to show this essential contradiction and to clarify the situation in a manner that is readily understandable to all.

One can understand the true significance of those "many tears" only in the light of a detailed study of the history of Opus Dei from 1928 to 1982, with a focus on its relationship with the Curia, and especially with the Congregation for Religious, upon which it then depended. As long as the universal call to sanctity — and, consequently, the role of the laity in the Church and the genuine lay vocation to Christianize the world — was not clearly understood, or even perceived, the survival of Opus Dei's unique spirit remained in danger. Any modification of its organic structure would have jeopardized its spirit. The fact that this never happened is for me clear proof that the Church and the world needed the Work, and needed it in the exact form in which God had made it known to Escrivá when he revealed it to him and entrusted him with the task of making it a reality. For if any change had been made in its spirit, Opus Dei would have become superfluous.

During this period, Msgr. Escrivá had to live at the same time the highest degree of holy prudence and the highest degree of holy fortitude. He had to remain completely loyal to the Congregation for Religious and at the same time work tirelessly to get his views across. He was deeply grateful to the pope and the Curia for their recognition of the Work as a secular institute, but at the same time he had to keep trying harder to make sure this situation was viewed, both by his own spiritual children and by the approving authority itself, as a purely temporary one. In letters and documents he not only had to explain again and again why Opus Dei was not by its nature a secular institute, but he also had to define the exact legal structure that it should possess in the Church. He had to show how the "suit," as he liked to call it, could be tailored to properly fit the body, and how the reality of Opus Dei — a spiritual, ascetical, and apostolic reality that already existed — should be described in canon law.

From the start, Escrivá had a clear idea of how this could be accomplished, and as time went on, his idea of the proper juridical structure of Opus Dei under canon law became even more clearly defined. As early as 1940 (that is, before Opus Dei was approved as a secular institute), he saw distinctly the outline of the juridical structure that in 1982 would finally become a reality. Pedro Casciaro recalls an incident that bears this out.[4] In 1936, he went to Madrid to visit Escrivá, who was at that time serving as rector of Santa Isabel. Pointing to two gravestones that had been set into the floor at the front of the sanctuary, Escrivá said to him, "There lies the future juridical solution for the Work." The young man did not at all understand what he meant, but he read the epitaphs inscribed on the stones. They were dedicated, respectively, to "Antonio de Sentmanat, Patriarch of the Indies, Chaplain of King Charles IV of Spain, Vicar General of the Royal Armies on Land and at Sea (1743-1806)" and to "Jacobo Cardona y Tur, Patriarch of the West Indies, Titular Bishop of Zion, Chaplain of the Royal House, Vicar General of the Army (1838-1923)." The founder was thus indicating to one of his children (for the first time, as far as we know) the precise direction in which the structure of Opus Dei in canon law was to be sought and found. It would have to be a hierarchical, and thus secular, structure of the Church, of a personal rather than territorial nature.[5]

In order to create a legal structure of this type, a structure that would correctly and justly correspond to the spiritual nature of the Work, it was necessary first to promote a renewed, more correct, and more profound understanding of the role of the laity in the Church.[6] This was achieved by the Second Vatican Council, and clearly formulated in its documents *Lumen Gentium, Sacrosanctum Concilium, Apostolicam Actuositatem,* and *Presbyterorum Ordinis.* It would be good to recall here the essence of these conciliar teachings on the subject.

The Church, the People of God, is composed of all the Christian faithful incorporated into it by the sacrament of Baptism, and especially all those called to full participation in its life by the sacrament of Confirmation. Regardless of their different states, ministries, or functions, all of the faithful share fully in the mission of the Church, the mission entrusted to it by Christ, in three ways. First, all of the faithful are obliged to seek personal sanctity — that is, to personally follow Jesus Christ. Second, all are obliged to strengthen their brothers and sisters in the faith and to strive to bring others closer to God, to Christ, to the Church by their example of living a Christian life, each in accordance with their state in life and situation in the world, and by their words. Third, all are obliged to strive to bring about the *consecratio mundi,* as described in *Apostolicam Actuositatem*: "It is the work of the entire Church to fashion people who are able to establish the proper scale of values in the temporal order and direct it towards God through Christ."[7]

This threefold mission common to all the Christian faithful is fulfilled in different ways, according to the different states, offices, and functions in the Church; clergy, religious, and laity carry out the same mission in distinct ways. In other words, joined to the radical equality of all the faithful, there exists a functional diversity. But this means every group within the Church, including the laity, has specific characteristics and specific missions. No one, therefore, can be a faithful Christian in a general, unspecified manner. Each one has, "according to one's mission as cleric, religious, or lay person, a specific way in which to exercise one's rights and duties." This also means that in addition to the general legal status of a faithful Christian, every member of the Church has a specific legal status as cleric, religious, or lay person, and that this too is further differentiated according to the organic diversity that exists within each of these states.

Finally, every lay person has a vocation that is uniquely his or hers. According to *Lumen Gentium*, the laity "live in the world, that is, they are engaged in each and every work and business of the earth and in the ordinary circumstances of family and social life which, as it were, constitute their very existence. There they are called by God that, being led by the spirit of the Gospel, they may contribute to the sanctification of the world, as from within like leaven, by fulfilling their own particular duties. Thus, especially by the witness of their life, resplendent in faith, hope, and charity, they must manifest Christ to others. It pertains to them in a special way so to illuminate and order all temporal things with which they are so closely associated that these may be affected and grow according to Christ and may be to the glory of the Creator and Redeemer."[8]

Reading this text (one small representative of the language and aim of the conciliar documents dealing with this subject), one gets the impression that these could have been the words of Escrivá himself. Thus one begins to appreciate how truly he was a spiritual forerunner of Vatican II. Twenty years before the Council was convoked (and there are many even earlier quotes to the same effect), he wrote, "The lay state also has a certain characteristic that is proper to it, which constitutes the special ministry of the laity within the Mystical Body of Christ. They are to assume their personal responsibilities in the professional and social spheres in order to inform all earthly realities with a Christian spirit, 'so that God may be glorified in all things through Jesus Christ (1 Pt 4:11).'"9 The profound and intimate connection between the spirit of Opus Dei and that of the Council should be evident to anyone who has even a passing knowledge of them both. To reject the spiritual thrust and goals of Opus Dei is really to reject the spiritual thrust and goals of Vatican II. It is important to read and understand the conciliar texts. They are not, after all, just theological literature; they are an integral part of the solemn magisterium of the Church, promulgated under the auspices of the Holy Spirit.

The laity make up, by far, the largest part of the People of God. Therefore, one of the greatest milestones in the history of the Church was the rediscovery of the real and specific vocation of the laity to sanctify the world. Its rediscovery by Vatican II gave new impetus to the responsible fulfillment of this vocation and ensured its complete protection from a legal point of view. Granted, not all of the faithful, and certainly not all of the laity, understand the revitalization of the laity that was so desired by the Council, especially with respect to the inherently spiritual nature of this revitalization and the proper means for making it a reality. This, however, is a separate topic, and one that need not be pursued here. In any case, the fact remains that the spiritual and legal course set by Vatican II and confirmed by the new Code of Canon Law did pave the way for already existing organizations to be incorporated into the universal Church in an appropriate legal form. And since no other preexisting ecclesiastical institution was as concerned as Opus Dei with the renewal in Christ of the laity, it was fitting, in terms of justice and historical logic, that the first fruits of the new legal situation within the Church should have fallen to the Work. So it was, then, that Opus Dei was finally given its proper legal form, the one best suited to its nature, to its purpose, and to the living reality of the organization: the form of a personal prelature.

III

In the introduction to this book, I provided a brief explanation of this new legal structure created by Vatican II, and of its first application: the establishing of Opus Dei as a personal prelature. Nonetheless, it would be impossible to write a complete biography of Msgr. Escrivá without exploring the issue of this legal structure as the definitive legal solution for the Work. Though he did not live to see it become a reality, the founder spent over forty years seeking this solution, years filled with countless hours of prayer and work; he prepared this solution down to the last detail.

"I have always thought," Escrivá wrote in 1961, "that the law should represent a legal response to a phenomenon of life — not a mere premise, but a deduction made from reality."[10] Here he was referring, first of all, to the internal organizational law of the Work, which had existed since 1947, the year the Holy See gave its approval to the Work. But he was also referring to the canonical situation of Opus Dei within the Catholic Church. Opus Dei's *ius particulare* and its position in canon law should together represent "a legal response to a phenomenon of life," the juridical expression of an already extant reality — in this case, that of the group of faithful Christians united around Escrivá. At the time he was writing these words, nearly a decade and a half had passed since the *ius particulare* of the Work had been approved. This much, at least, was secure and finalized (except, of course, for the concessions that had had to be made so that the Work could qualify as a secular institute). The definitive juridical solution, however, had yet to be found. In other words, while the internal law of the Work corresponded to the living reality, its juridical status within the Church did not.

The preamble to the apostolic constitution *Ut Sit* (promulgated on November 28, 1982), which established Opus Dei as a personal prelature, explains this sovereign act of the Holy See. It was based on a confluence of factors: the nature and development of the Work, the specific wishes of its founder, and the enrichment of canon law brought about by Vatican II. The document states, "Since Opus Dei has grown, with the help of divine grace, to the extent that it has spread and works in a large number of dioceses throughout the world as an apostolic entity made up of priests and laity, both men and women, which is at the same time organic and undivided — that is to say, as an institution endowed with a unity of spirit, of aims, of government, and of formation — it has become necessary to give it a juridical configuration which is suited to its special characteristics."[11] This expresses in a modicum of words the essence of the spirit of Opus Dei.

It was in the interests of safeguarding this spirit that in 1962 the founder requested, "with humility and confidence," that the Holy See grant Opus Dei its the proper juridical configuration. "What we are seeking," he wrote, "is not a total revision of our present law. Rather, we are seeking the ecclesiastical confirmation of this law, but within a different general legal framework."[12] Once again, as he had done so often in the past, Escrivá went straight to the heart of the matter. The members of Opus Dei are not lay people who want to walk the way of sanctification on the basis of privileges they have received or special additions that have been made to their lay status. Nor do they want to assume obligations derived from the clerical or monastic sphere. The vocation of Opus Dei members is the same as that lived by all other faithful Christians who are fully conscious of their calling to be Christians in the midst of the world; that is, to do what, according to the will of Christ, should be considered normal. This normality will be misconstrued as elitism only by those who possess a mistaken notion of democracy. For authentic normality consists in complete dedication to Christ and the Church, which means following the example of Christ, living the counsels contained in the Gospel, and striving to live the virtues to the fullest degree, according to the conditions of one's state in life. This includes (for the married as well as the unmarried) a personal struggle to live the virtue of chastity; a sincere humility based on trust in God; poverty, even on the part of those with substantial economic resources; a life of intense work linked with a faithful fulfillment of one's familial, social, and professional obligations; and obedience in matters concerning one's spiritual life and apostolate.

So who are these Catholics who have dedicated themselves, by means of a special vocation, to living this normality together as a spiritual family gathered around their founder and father? They are a microcosm, as it were, of all Christians who live in the world. They are men and women; young and old; healthy and sick; single, married, and widowed; priests called from among their number in order to serve primarily, but not exclusively, the spiritual family itself; and, joined to them, in an organization of their own, secular priests who seek the spirit of this new normality as a help towards their own sanctification. At the same time, all members of Opus Dei continue to be faithful subjects of the dioceses in which they live.

Having ascertained the nature of Opus Dei (it is a spiritual family made up of lay Christians striving to live their vocation as ordinary faithful in the midst of the world), one naturally wonders how canon law is structured to deal with such an organization; for these ordinary lay Christians are, by definition, members of their respective dioceses, and thus each of them is subject to the authority of the local bishop. As we have already seen, the proper juridical solution to this problem was long in coming. This was for good reason. Certain gradually developed insights into this problem, such as can be found in the writings of the founder of Opus Dei and in the documents of Vatican II, were needed before the proper and competent decisions of Church authority could be made. Certain profound global changes — changes posing no small amount of danger to Christians in general and to Catholics in particular — necessitated the general mobilization, as it were, of ordinary lay Christians. Under the guidance of the Holy Spirit, this mobilization took the form of the spiritual renewal of the laity. Msgr. Escrivá provided perhaps the strongest impetus to this spiritual renewal. Opus Dei represented the first wave of this renewal; it served as a prototype and a most impressive model. Once one understands all of this, then it becomes clear why Opus Dei could not have taken on the legal structure of a religious order or the status of a local church (i.e., a diocese) — either one of these options would have removed its members from normal lay life. So what alternative remained?

The apostolic constitution *Ut Sit*, which established Opus Dei as a personal prelature, continues: "From the time when the Second Vatican Council introduced the figure of the personal prelatures into the legislation of the Church, by means of the decree *Presbyterorum Ordinis*, no. 10 [which was put into effect by the motu proprio *Ecclesia Sanctae*, I, no. 4], to carry out specific pastoral activities, it was clearly seen that this juridical figure was properly suited to Opus Dei." This was "clearly seen" not only by the pope and the Curia, but also by the various competent bodies that with full authority formally, substantially, and personally determined this new juridical form and applied it in this concrete instance; by the vast majority of the bishops who were consulted in this matter; and also by the party that was most immediately concerned, and which was obviously the most apt recipient of this juridical form: Opus Dei. Its founder saw clearly that the form of the personal prelature corresponded perfectly with the nature of the Work. He had sought this form for decades. He had formed the contents (Opus Dei) for a container which for years had existed only in his mind, but which he had tirelessly endeavored to bring into the life of the Church as something very real. It is not surprising, given the pastoral situation of the Church at the time, that the commissions preparing the outlines for the documents of Vatican II foresaw, as early as 1961, the form of the personal prelature. Escrivá himself was, by and large, the one most responsible for the creation of personal prelatures. Assuredly, some future historian will be able to show this in much greater detail than is possible here.

Even though the form of the personal prelature was in the Curia's files by 1966 and in principle could have been applied to Opus Dei then, seventeen more years were to pass before this step would finally be taken. "I must tell you," Msgr. Escrivá wrote to his sons and daughters in the fall of 1966, "that at this very moment, the legal route for us is already opened. But for now we prefer not to put on this suit. It is better for us to wait and continue to pray as if nothing had happened. When the right time comes, we will don the suit, both the slacks and the jacket."[13]

The matter continued to proceed at a snail's pace. Though this was largely because of the great care being taken, Escrivá felt that something needed to be done to expedite things. In response to his request, and in accordance with the norms established by Vatican II, Pope Paul VI encouraged him to convoke a special general congress of Opus Dei at which the issue of its canonical restructuring could be discussed. This congress convened in the summer of 1969 and concluded in 1970. But Escrivá died before the solution decided upon by the congress — the transformation of Opus Dei into a personal prelature — could be officially presented and processed.

A mere six months before he died, Escrivá stressed once again the vital importance of seeking a new and definitive juridical form for Opus Dei. "You should be willing to risk," he wrote to his children, "not just one life but a hundred lives, if you had them, for the Work to be granted its definitive juridical form. In that way, even if I were to die tomorrow, you would be assured of never parting from the spirit of your founder. As I have stated in writing hundreds of times, we can never let ourselves be assimilated with the religious in any manner."[14] It takes no special historical acumen to deduce from this, and from other similar utterances, that there must have been many attempts to rob Opus Dei of its lay, secular character and thus destroy its foundational charism. Only with this background in mind can one understand the struggle of Josemaría Escrivá, and of his successor, Alvaro del Portillo, to find the appropriate legal path for the Work, and their unrestrained joy once this path was found. It was a matter of life or death for Opus Dei.

IV

As one might suppose, the juridical structure Escrivá desired for this spiritual and physical organism that is Opus Dei corresponds almost exactly with the figure of the personal prelature instituted by means of the above-mentioned motu proprio of Pope Paul VI and the new Code of Canon Law (1983). But it should be noted that even though it has until now been applied only to Opus Dei, this juridical form was not created exclusively for this one extraordinarily important pastoral phenomenon. In the future it will surely be applied to other organizations as well. As long as it existed only in theory, this juridical form had a rather vague character. But once it was applied to a particularly strong and viable body within the Church, it proved itself to be a very useful and effective instrument of the Holy See.

According to canons 294 and 296 of the new Code of Canon Law, the Holy See (that is, the pope together with the Curia, the administrative organ of the universal Church) may establish as a personal prelature an existing organization composed of deacons and priests of the secular clergy, and lay people who dedicate themselves to its apostolic work. When it does so, the Holy See creates, in accordance with the will of the Council fathers and the documents that were the fruit of the Council, an instrument for the pastoral and apostolic service of the successor of St. Peter, the bishops, and the local churches.

The possible purposes of personal prelatures are defined very broadly in canon law and leave room for ample and varied development. Canon 294 states: "Their purpose is to promote a proper distribution of priests, or to carry out special pastoral or missionary enterprises in different regions or for different social groups." This formulation covers a wide range of pastoral and apostolic objectives: goals that are limited by time, area, or society, as well as those that are universal; goals that may be achievable primarily, or even exclusively, by the clergy, as well as those that are the province of the laity. The reality of Opus Dei fits within the parameters of canon 294 if "special pastoral enterprise" can mean a specific spiritual formation of ordinary lay Christians for the radical exercise of their universal mission of sanctification in the midst of the world; if "different regions" can encompass the whole world; and if "different social groups" can include all sectors of human society. That this broad interpretation is so clearly justified makes it evident that the personal prelature was not the result of some special legislation brought about exclusively for Opus Dei. It is, rather, a testimony to the foresight of the pope and the Curia, to their envisioning of a broader range of possibilities for serving the particular churches and, through them, the universal Church.

At times, the statement of canon 294 that a personal prelature consists of "priests and deacons" has led to erroneous conclusions, even on the part of canon lawyers. It is important to see this in conjunction with the provision in canon 296 for the involvement of the laity ("Lay people can dedicate themselves to the apostolic work of a personal prelature"). It is also important to bear in mind what Pope Paul VI said in his motu proprio *Ecclesiae Sanctae:* "There is no reason why lay people, whether celibate or married, should not dedicate their professional service, through contracts with the prelature, to its works and enterprises." A personal prelature is not designed to cater to certain associative tendencies within the Church, nor is it merely an association of the clergy. Rather, it is an integral part of the hierarchical structure of the Catholic Church.

The Personal Prelature of the Holy Cross and Opus Dei (this is Opus Dei's full, official name) consists — both de jure and de facto — of the prelate, the clergy incardinated into the prelature, and the lay people who have dedicated themselves to the apostolic works of the prelature. But this specific prelature would never have been established as such had it not already existed (though under a different canonical form) as the spiritual family of Opus Dei, whose principle of internal unity is a spiritual filiation with the Father (until 1975 the founder, and afterwards his successors), along with a spiritual fraternity among those whom God has also called to follow this way. It would, therefore, be an act of idle speculation to try to imagine whether and how this prelature would exist if no lay people were connected to it. If it consisted of only the prelate and his clergy, it would still exist theoretically; but Opus Dei, as founded by Josemaría Escrivá, would no longer exist.

The spiritual family of Opus Dei — the family which, by God's will, saw the light of day in 1928 — has not experienced the slightest qualitative change in its mission, spirituality, internal structure, direction, or unity with this new canonical form. Now, as before, those who come to Opus Dei perceive within themselves the calling to a lay dedication to God in the midst of the world and then follow this calling by requesting admission to the Work. If this request is granted, they become members — temporarily at first, and then permanently. From a theological point of view, this membership is based on the commitment, made before God, to seek personal sanctity and the sanctification of the world by being faithful to Opus Dei and to its spirit and norms, as an alive and active child of this family.

The men and women who, by means of a specific vocation, unite themselves to Opus Dei do so without at all renouncing their radical lay status; their lay status, in fact, forms the very basis for their vocation. The joining takes place by means of a contract. (From time immemorial, this has been considered the normal, legitimate way to take on a commitment.)[15] In essence, it has been done this way from the first days of Opus Dei. The bond holding together this spiritual family has always had the character, both in theory and in practice, of a mutual agreement. The founder and his successor spent years working for the creation and recognition of a juridical form that would provide for the unrestricted acceptance of Opus Dei's unique way and allow its unequivocally lay nature to become a permanent part of the general schema of the Church. With the establishment of Opus Dei as a personal prelature, the long search finally came to an end.

V

In 1943, it will be recalled, Escrivá founded the Priestly Society of the Holy Cross, for the purpose of providing Opus Dei with priests from its own ranks. When members of the Work were ordained, they were incardinated into this society. Once Opus Dei was approved as a secular institute, under the name "The Priestly Society of the Holy Cross and Opus Dei," diocesan priests could also associate themselves with it; but they had to have a different legal status. While priests chosen from among the lay members of Opus Dei were under the full and exclusive disposition of the president general (as the head of Opus Dei was then known), and he held full jurisdiction over them, this could not very well be the case with the diocesan priests who joined Opus Dei. This rather

muddled situation was clarified with the establishment of the
Prelature of the Holy Cross and Opus Dei. Diocesan priests (incardinated into their respective dioceses) who joined Opus Dei would
become members of the Priestly Society of the Holy Cross. This is
not a part of the prelature itself, but rather, in the words of *Ut Sit*,
"a clerical association intrinsically united to the prelature." A
diocesan priest who joins it does not become a member of the
clergy of the prelature. He remains under the authority of the
bishop of his diocese in every respect, and he must inform the
bishop of his membership in the Society. Thus, the Priestly Society
of the Holy Cross remains distinct from, but inseparably united
with, Opus Dei; the prelate of Opus Dei serves as its president general. And for all Opus Dei members — the clergy and the laity of
the prelature and the diocesan priests in the Society — the prelate
continues to be what he has always been: a father.

Clergy of the prelature are educated and prepared for the
priesthood by the prelature itself, and are subject to the prelate.
He exercises over them the full authority of an ordinary and is
charged with the care of their spiritual and material needs. The
priests of the prelature carry out their priestly activity both
internally, by participating in the spiritual, ascetical, theological,
and doctrinal formation of the members of Opus Dei, and exter-
nally, by supporting the various apostolic initiatives of their lay
brothers and sisters. They administer the sacraments to the faithful of the prelature and serve in an advisory capacity on the
local governmental boards of the Work; in both ways they help
the members of the Work to live their vocation and to persevere
in their struggle for sanctity. At the same time, the priests of the
Work naturally seek to build friendships with their brothers in
the diocesan clergy. They also participate in the apostolate of the
lay members of Opus Dei by preaching evenings of recollection
and retreats, by teaching classes in doctrine and theology, and
by giving spiritual direction not only to the cooperators and
friends of the Work, but also to other individuals who earnestly
seek such direction.

In being converted into a personal prelature, Opus Dei was in
effect transformed from an institute of papal law *approved* by the

Church into an apostolic instrument *created* by the Holy See within the hierarchical structure of the Church. This instrument was to be governed by its own statutes, as established in Article II of the apostolic constitution *Ut Sit*. Through the Sacred Congregation for Bishops, the prelate would present to the Roman pontiff every five years a report on the state of the prelature and its apostolic work. In addition, the Sacred Congregation for Bishops established practical norms regarding pastoral coordination with local ordinaries and the fruitful insertion of the prelature of Opus Dei in the local churches. Article V of *The Declaration of the Congregation of Bishops Concerning Opus Dei* states, "First, the prior permission of the competent diocesan bishop is required for the establishment of each center of the prelature; the diocesan bishop is informed regularly about the activities of those centers and has the right to visit them. Second, as regards parishes, chaplaincies, and other ecclesiastical offices which the local ordinary may entrust to the prelature, or to the priests incardinated in the prelature, an agreement will be drawn up in each case between the local ordinary and the prelate of Opus Dei or his vicars. Third, in each country the prelature will maintain regular contact with the president and with the organisms of the episcopal conference, and have frequent contact with the bishops of the dioceses in which the prelature is established."

Between 1928 and 1982, tens of thousands of normal, everyday lay Catholics — all of them active members of their own dioceses and parishes — had already dedicated themselves in Opus Dei to the radical following of Christ in order to sanctify the world through the sanctification of their ordinary work. From the very beginning, this created a truly profound and existential bond with the episcopacy. True, this bond had not always and everywhere been viewed as a natural thing. But to be a member of Opus Dei is to be a spiritual child of Msgr. Escrivá, who passionately loved the Church. Therefore, a member's striving for sanctity must include life as a faithful parishioner and faithful member of a diocese. No bishop or pastor can really know just how many of the sheep in his flock are sincerely and perseveringly striving to follow Christ. He can, however, be assured that those of his flock who are members of Opus Dei are attempting this with all fortitude and honesty. For all members of the prelature of Opus Dei, this bond of genuine loyalty to the local church — their own parish and diocese — has been from the beginning an integral part of their lay vocation, the vocation of an ordinary Christian.

Chronology

1902 *9th of January:* Josemaría Escrivá de Balaguer y Albás is born in Barbastro, in the province of Aragon, Spain.

1912-1915 First years at the school directed by the Piarists, in Barbastro.

1915 The Escrivá family moves to Logroño.

1918 Josemaría begins his studies of theology as a nonresident student at the seminary in Logroño.

1920 He transfers to the Pontifical University of San Valero and San Braulio, in Saragossa, and lives in the seminary of San Francisco de Paula.

1923 He takes up the study of law in addition to his other studies.

1924 *27th of November:* Death of his father, José Escrivá, in Logroño.

1925 *28th of March:* Josemaría is ordained priest in Saragossa.

1927 *April:* Escrivá moves to Madrid in order to complete his studies of law and to prepare his dissertation. He engages in welfare work and also teaches law courses, until 1931, at the Cicuéndez Academy.

1928 *2nd of October:* Founding of Opus Dei.

1930 *14th of February:* Founding of the women's branch of Opus Dei.

1933 *December:* The first corporate work of Opus Dei, the DYA Academy, begins its work in Madrid.

1934 Escrivá is appointed rector of the Santa Isabel convent. *September:* The first student residence of Opus Dei is established.

"Spiritual Considerations" is published: forerunner to *The Way*, published in its current form in 1939.

1936	*18th of July:* The Spanish Civil War begins.
1937	*March:* Escrivá is granted asylum in the Honduran Consulate.
	7th of October: He leaves Madrid to flee to the Nationalist Zone.
	2nd of December: His flight ends with his arrival in Andorra.
	12th of December: He reaches the Nationalist Zone.
1938	He sojourns in Burgos until the end of the war.
1939	*2nd of March:* Eugenio Pacelli is elected to the papacy and takes the name Pius XII.
	28th of March: Escrivá returns to Madrid.
	31st of March: The Civil War ends.
1939-1945	World War II. Spain remains neutral.
1939-1946	Opus Dei spreads in Spain.
1941	Opus Dei is granted recognition as a "pious union" for the diocese of Madrid.
	22nd of April : Josemaría's mother, Dolores Escrivá, passes away in Madrid.
1943	*14th of February:* Founding of the Priestly Society of the Holy Cross.
	11th of October: The Holy See hands down its first approbation of Opus Dei.
1944	*25th of June:* Ordination of the first three priests of Opus Dei: Alvaro del Portillo, José María Hernández de Garnica, and José Luis Múzquiz.
1945	End of World War II.
1946	Beginning of Opus Dei in Portugal, Italy, and England. Escrivá moves to Rome to establish there the headquarters of Opus Dei and to push for its final recognition.
1947	*2nd of February:* Pope Pius XII issues the apostolic constitution *Provida Mater*, which provides the framework for the temporary canonical approbation of Opus Dei as a secular institute.
	22nd of April: Escrivá is appointed monsignor. The site of the headquarters of Opus Dei is acquired.

1948   Establishment of the Collegium Romanum Sanctae
            Crucis, the international center for ecclesiastical studies
            of Opus Dei's men's branch.

1949   Opus Dei spreads overseas; it becomes established in
            Mexico and in the United States. Escrivá makes his first
            trips to Austria and to Germany, where he meets with
            Cardinal Faulhaber.

1950   *16th of June:* Opus Dei is granted final and complete
            approbation by the Holy See.

1952   Opus Dei starts its work in West Germany, beginning in
            Bonn. Construction of the current University of Navarre
            is begun in Pamplona. Between 1952 and 1960, Escrivá
            undertakes several trips to Spain, England, Ireland,
            France, Switzerland, Austria, and West Germany.

1953   Establishment of the Collegium Romanum Sanctae
            Mariae, the international center for theological studies
            of Opus Dei's women's branch.

1954   *27th of April:* Msgr. Escrivá, having suffered from a
            severe case of diabetes for ten years, goes into a death-
            like coma. Upon regaining consciousness later that day
            (the feast day of Our Lady of Montserrat), he is found to
            be completely cured of the diabetes; it never recurs.

1955   Beginning of Opus Dei in Vienna, Austria.

1956   General Congress of Opus Dei in Einsiedeln,
            Switzerland.

1957   *20th of June:* The founder's older sister, Carmen Escrivá,
            passes away in Rome.

1958   *9th of October:* Death of Pope Pius XII.
            28th of October: Angelo Roncalli becomes Pope John XXIII.

1960   *9th of January:* Completion of Villa Tevere, the
            headquarters of Opus Dei.
            The University of Saragossa bestows an honorary
            doctorate upon Escrivá.

1961   Pope John XXIII appoints him consultant to the Papal
            Committee for the Authentic Interpretation of the Code
            of Canon Law.

1962-1965   Second Vatican Council. The general secretary of Opus
            Dei, Alvaro del Portillo, participates in it as a consultant.

1963   *3rd of June:* Death of Pope John XXIII.
        21st of June: Giovanni Battista Montini becomes Pope
        Paul VI.

1970   Escrivá makes his first trip overseas, to Mexico.

1972   He undertakes a two-month catechetical trip through
        Spain and Portugal.

1974   *22nd of May - 31st of August:* Catechetical trip to Latin
        America (Brazil, Argentina, Chile, Peru, Ecuador,
        Venezuela).

1975   *4th - 23rd of February:* Continuation of the catechetical
        trip to Venezuela and Guatemala; return to Rome
        because of illness.
        28th of March: Msgr. Escrivá celebrates the fiftieth anni-
        versary of his priesthood.
        May: His last trip takes him to Spain, where he conse-
        crates the high altar of the newly erected church at the
        shrine of Our Lady of Torreciudad, in the province of
        Aragon.
        26th of June: Death of Msgr. Escrivá, by cardiac arrest.
        15th of September: Alvaro del Portillo is elected president
        general of Opus Dei.

1981   *12th of May:* Opening of the beatification and canoniza-
        tion process for the Servant of God Josemaría Escrivá, in
        Rome.

1982   *28th of November:* Establishment by Pope John Paul II of
        Opus Dei as a personal prelature.

1992   *17th of May:* Beatification of Josemaría Escrivá by Pope
        John Paul II.

Notes

[Note: The author was given access to a number of unpublished letters and other documents on the life of Josemaría Escrivá while doing research for this book. These are cited in the notes as *Registro Historico del Fundador (RHF)*, *Articoli*, *Alcune*, *Fama*, *Crónica*, *Noticias*, *Obras*, *Meditaciones*, *"Instruction of...,"* and *"Letter of...."*]

Tradition and Progress in the Life of the Church:
The Example of Opus Dei

1. *Conversations with Msgr. Escrivá de Balaguer* (London/New York, 1974), pp. 65-66.
2. *Conversations*, p. 65.
3. The Latin text can be found in *Acta Apostolicae Sedis* 58 (1966), pp. 991-1024; an English translation in *Vatican Council II: The Conciliar and Post Conciliar Documents*, ed. Austin Flannery, O.P. (Northport, NY, 1980), pp. 863-902.
4. The different parts of the Eastern Church are not differentiated so much by territory as by liturgical rite. Those faithful of the Eastern Church who were at one time in schism but have returned to union with the Church of Rome are sometimes called Uniates.
5. The head of Opus Dei was called the "president general" as long as Opus Dei had the canonical status of a secular institute; that is, until November 28, 1982.

    Opus Dei has been able to ordain and to incardinate its own priests since its establishment in 1947 as a secular institute subject to papal jurisdiction. As a personal prelature it keeps this right; in fact, this right is now anchored in canon law. As emphasized by the Congregation of Bishops in their declaration of August 23, 1982, the dioceses are thus not deprived of any potential candidates for the diocesan clergy. All the priests of the prelature's clergy were members of Opus Dei long before their ordination. At the time they were accepted into Opus Dei, they were practicing or preparing for secular professions and not thinking of becoming priests. For more on this subject, see Scepter Booklet no. 137, *Seeking God in the*

World, which contains two relevant press interviews with the current prelate of Opus Dei, Bishop Alvaro del Portillo.

6. Marcello Costalunga, "The Establishment of Opus Dei as a Personal Prelature," in the English edition of *L'Osservatore Romano,* December 6, 1982.

Footprints in the Snow

1. Hubert Jedin, K. S. Latourette, and Jochen Martin, *Atlas der Kirchengeschichte. Die christlichen Kirchen in Geschichte und Gegenwart* (Freiburg, 1979), pp. 58, 60, and 141.

2. Josemaría Escrivá's grandfathers, José Escrivá Zaydín and Pascual Albás, died before he was born, in 1894 and 1886 respectively. His paternal grandmother, Constancia Corzán, lived until 1912, and his maternal grandmother, Florencia Blanc, until 1925.

3. Salvador Bernal, *Josemaría Escrivá de Balaguer: A Profile of the Founder of Opus Dei* (London/New York, 1977), p. 23.

4. *Romana Postulazione della causa di Beatificazione e Canonizzazione del Servo di Dio Josemaría Escrivá de Balaguer y Albás, Sacerdote Fondatore dell'Opus Dei. Articoli del Postulatore* (Rome, 1979), section 7. (Henceforth referred to as *Articoli.*) A Spanish version was published alongside the Italian edition.

5. *Articoli,* section 5.

6. The person in question was Fr. Enrique Labrador. The Piarist Order, whose members are also called "Calasantians" or "Scolopi," was founded in 1617 by St. Joseph Calasanz, an Aragonese priest, as the Ordo Clericorum Regularium Pauperum Matris Dei Scholarum Piarum [Poor regular clergy of the Mother of God for pious schools].

7. Bernal, p. 116.

8. Bernal, p. 20.

9. Bernal, p. 24.

10. Georg von Rauch, *Lenin* (Göttingen, 1962), p. 12.

11. Bernal, p. 21.

12. *Articoli,* section 12.

13. Letter of March 28, 1971, to Manuel Gómez Padrós, Mayor of Barbastro. In *Articoli,* section 16. See Bernal, pp. 25-26.

14. *Articoli,* section 17.

15. Testimonial of Paula Royó, Bernal, p. 27.

16. The Carmelite Order grew out of a hermits' colony founded in 1155 by the crusader Berthold of Calabria. In 1238, members of this order began returning to the West, and in 1247 St. Simon Stock organized it into a mendicant order. The Ordo Fratrum Beatae Mariae Virginis de Monte Carmelo [Order of Our Lady of Mount Carmel] encompasses two branches of Carmelite monks and nuns. The more austere branch, popularly known as the "discalced" Carmelites, is based on the spirituality and teaching of Sts. Teresa of Avila and John of the Cross. However, the strictly contemplative

order also undertakes missionary work. ("Discalced" means "without shoes"; these monks and nuns, out of humility, go barefoot or wear only thin, open sandals.)

17. *Articoli,* section 18.
18. Bernal, p. 61.
19. Bernal, p. 62.
20. *Articoli,* section 20.

Prayer in the Night

1. The General Seminary of St. Charles Borromeo (San Carlos) was divided into smaller, individual seminaries named after different saints.
2. Bernal, pp. 65-66.
3. Bernal, p. 67. Recorded here is the young Escrivá's comment on the subject: "I don't think lack of cleanliness is a virtue."
4. The king's letter of July 21, 1978, is published in *Fama di Santità in vita,* vol. 1 of *Allegato Nr. 1 agli Articoli del Postulatore* (Rome, 1979), p. 225.
5. Specific callings to full, unrestricted dedication have been a constant element in the life of the Church. Sometimes there is the spur-of-the-moment realization of a specific vocation and the immediate decision to follow it. Sometimes there arises, without a specific vocation, a no less urgent desire to lead an intensified Christian life. On the wider spectrum, there is the conversion to faith in general or to a particular faith, the return to one's faith, or the radical renunciation of faith. Such are the possibilities inherent in personal freedom, which must take the responsibility for these decisions and which may never be infringed upon.
6. Josemaría Escrivá, *The Way* (New York, 1979), point 20.
7. *Articoli,* sections 26 and 27.
8. I was not able to find out if Escrivá ever accepted this invitation.
9. Escrivá received the four minor orders (as they were known then) — the ministries of porter, lector, exorcist, and acolyte — on the 17th and 21st of December 1922, from the suffragan bishop of Saragossa.
10. The tonsure, the shaving of the head as a sign of one's self-giving to God, was adopted for the diocesan clergy (from Eastern monks) in the fifth century, and was generally prescribed from the thirteenth century on. The requirement of the clerical, or minimal, tonsure remained in effect for the clergy until it was abolished in 1972 by Pope Paul VI.
11. See *Diccionario de Historia Eclesiástica de España,* vol. 4 (Madrid, 1975), p. 2499.
12. Conversation with Alvaro del Portillo on January 24, 1981, in Cologne.
13. Same conversation.
14. *Articoli,* section 29.
15. *Articoli,* section 29.
16. Escrivá's homily of April 13, 1973, *A Priest Forever* (New York, 1974), p. 8.
17. *Priest Forever,* p. 10.

18. *Priest Forever*, pp. 12-13.
19. *Articoli*, section 31.
20. *Articoli*, section 35.
21. Bernal, p. 32.
22. Bernal, p. 75.
23. *Articoli*, section 33.
24. Catechesis is the verbal teaching of religious doctrine. A distinction has traditionally been made between catechesis for adults and catechesis for children; the latter has generally been thought of as a subject to be taught in schools. But now, as in Escrivá's day, catechesis must be given to both adults and children outside of the schools.
25. Conversation with Dr. Juan Antonio Cremades Royó on June 19, 1981, in Saragossa. Cremades, who served several terms as the civil governor of the province of Lérida, was a lifelong friend of Escrivá and his family.
26. A "profesor mercantil" was the general equivalent of a business school professor.
27. The original title was "La forma de matrimonio en la actual legislación española" [Marriage in current Spanish law]. The article was published in the monthly publication *Alfa-Beta, Organo del Instituto Amado*, vol. 1, no. 3 (March 1927), pp. 10-12.
28. "Matrimonio," p. 12.
29. Testimonial of José López Ortiz, titular bishop of Grado, bishop of the Spanish armed forces, in an appendix to the postulation document, *Alcune Dichiarazioni a futura memoria* [Some declarations for future remembrance], vol. 1 (Rome, 1980). [English translation in *A Man of God*, vol. 2 (London/ New York, 1992), pp. 5-01 to 5-47.]
30. First edition: Burgos, 1944; second edition: Madrid, 1974. Using the source material and all the relevant literature (including several German books) as his point of departure, Escrivá describes the twelfth-century formation and subsequent development of Las Huelgas, a convent in the vicinity of Burgos, in light of the jurisdiction and governmental practices of a succession of abbesses who were able to defend a position approaching sovereignty. This book is an interesting and important contribution to Spanish ecclesiastical history which covers more than half a millennium. Chapter 11 is noteworthy for its comparisons between Las Huelgas and various royal European abbeys located outside of Spain — for example, Quedlinburg in Germany and Fontevrault in France.
31. Point 983.

The Bells

1. A distinction must always be made between expressions pertaining to formal political law and those describing the actual situation. In terms of political law, Spain was from December 9, 1931, until July 26, 1947, a republic; after that it became a monarchy. During the Civil War of 1936-1939, however, there existed de facto a Red Zone and a Nationalist Zone.

The Nationalist Zone developed into an authoritarian state during the war.

2. *Articoli,* section 44.

3. *Josemaría Escrivá de Balaguer, Founder of Opus Dei,* Bulletin no. 2 of the Office of Vice Postulation of Opus Dei (New York, 1977), pp. 6-7. [Subsequent "Bulletin" references are from this source.]

4. Editorial: "Life in Christ," in *Crónica* (the internal monthly magazine of the men's branch) 1963, no. 12. Cf. *Noticias* (that of the women's branch) 1967, no. 7.

5. Instruction of January 9, 1935. In *Meditaciones,* vol. 6 (Rome, 1972), section 461.

6. See note 4.

7. Yes, he was a kindred soul to Mother Teresa of Calcutta, who, when asked what earthly good she thought her nuns could do for beggars at death's door, responded simply, "First of all, we want to give them the feeling that they are wanted. We want them to know that there are people who really love them, who really want them, at least for the few remaining hours of their lives, so that they may learn of human and divine love. That they may experience that they are the children of God and have not been forgotten...." Malcolm Muggeridge, *Something Beautiful for God* (San Francisco, 1971), pp. 73-74.

8. *The Way,* point 194.

9. "Servant of God" is the term used in canon law to designate a person who was considered a saint while still on earth and whose cause for beatification has been opened.

10. In 1625, St. Vincent de Paul founded a congregation of priests, the Congregatio Missionis (hence the abbreviation C.M.), to be devoted to seminary and missionary activity. Usually called "Vincentians" in the United States, these priests are also sometimes referred to as "Lazarists," because their first motherhouse was St. Lazare in Paris.

11. *Articoli,* section 45.

12. *Articoli,* section 45.

13. Bulletin no. 1, p. 8. See also Escrivá's homily of October 12, 1947, "Living by Faith," in *Friends of God* (London/New York, 1981), pp. 171-182.

14. Bernal, p. 107; Bulletin no. 1, p. 8.

15. Bernal, p. 107.

16. Bulletin no. 1, p. 8.

17. Bernal, pp. 106-107.

18. *The Roman Catechism* (the catechism of the Council of Trent for pastors, published by order of Popes St. Pius V and Clement XIII), U.S. edition (South Bend, 1972).

19. *Roman Catechism,* p. 24.

20. *Roman Catechism,* p. 273.

21. *Roman Catechism,* p. 274.

22. Tb 5:6; 12:17.

23. Acts 12:7-9; 5:19.
24. Mt 18:10.
25. Homily of November 26, 1967, "Towards Holiness," in *Friends of God,* pp. 259-273.
26. Letter of March 24, 1930, section 20.
27. Letter of January 9, 1932, section 64.
28. With the establishment of Opus Dei as a personal prelature, its leader acquired a new title: that of "Prelate." But he is still addressed as "Father," and also referred to as such in the internal publications of Opus Dei. (That he is a father to all members of Opus Dei flows from its nature as a spiritual family.)
29. Since 1976 almost every edition of *Crónica* has included a section entitled "Recuerdos de nuestro Padre" [Remembrances of our Father]. This note is from *Crónica* 1977, no. 10.
30. Bulletin no. 1, p. 9.
31. *Articoli,* section 48.
32. Bernal, pp. 10 and 188.
33. Conversation with Dr. Amadeo de Fuenmayor on June 21, 1981, in Pamplona.
34. Same conversation.
35. Same conversation.
36. *Articoli,* section 45.
37. Statement to the press, June 26, 1976, *Crónica* 1976, no. 6, pp. 222-223.
38. *Conversations,* p. 82.
39. Letter of January 9, 1932, section 2.
40. Letter of March 11, 1940, section 35.
41. *Conversations,* p. 78.
42. However, it is important to note that Escrivá immediately notified the bishop of Madrid as to the occurrence of October 2, 1928.
43. Bulletin no. 1, p. 9.
44. Bernal, p. 114.
45. Bulletin no. 2, p. 8.
46. Bulletin no. 2, p. 8.
47. Bernal, pp. 115-117.
48. Bulletin no. 2, p. 8.
49. Bernal, pp. 205-206.
50. Bernal, p. 135.
51. *Articoli,* section 62.
52. Bernal, p. 135.
53. This was the mother of Luz Rodríguez Casanova, who founded the Damas Apostólicas.
54. Escrivá used the words "diferentes" (different) and "distintas" (separate).
55. Letter of July 29, 1965, section 2.
56. *Noticias* 1960, no. 5, p. 12.
57. *Noticias* 1960, no. 5, p. 12.
58. *Meditaciones,* vol. 5 (Rome, 1970), section 420.

59. Bulletin no. 1, p. 9.
60. The women's branch came into being on February 14, 1930; the Priestly Society of the Holy Cross, on February 14, 1943.
61. *Meditaciones*, vol. 5, section 393.
62. *Noticias* 1964, no. 9, p. 22.
63. "Women in the World and in the Church," Escrivá's interview with the magazine *Telva* (Madrid, February 1, 1968). In *Conversations*, pp. 101 - 102.
64. "Women," p. 103.
65. *Articoli*, section 65.
66. *Catequesis en América*, vol. 2 (Rome, 1974), pp. 399-400. (This is an internal publication analogous to *Crónica* or *Noticias*, but in book format.)
67. Letter of March 24, 1930, section 20.
68. Testimonial of Pedro Casciaro, *Articoli*, section 1041.
69. Testimonial of Francisco Botella, *Articoli*, section 1042.
70. Letter of May 31, 1954, section 22.
71. Letter of May 6, 1945, section 39.
72. Beyond that, wherever Opus Dei was active or hoping to become active, the founder always sought the approval of the local bishop.
73. *Articoli*, section 62.
74. Friedrich von Schiller, "Das Lied von der Glocke" [Song of the bell], 1799. The phrase "break the thunderbolts," which is inscribed on the bell alluded to in Schiller's poem, refers to an old popular belief in central Europe that the ringing of bells during storms would prevent lightning from striking in the vicinity.
75. Letter of March 24, 1930, section 1.
76. Letter of March 24, 1930, section 2.
77. Letter of March 24, 1930, section 5.
78. Letter of March 24, 1930, section 10.
79. Letter of March 24, 1930, section 12.
80. Letter of March 24, 1930, section 12.
81. See note 33.
82. The founder used this expression to refer to the meticulously punctual fulfillment of a duty prescribed in the plan for the day. The example he gave most often was the act of getting up in the morning "at the first sound of the alarm."
83. Letter of March 24, 1930, section 15.
84. Letter of March 24, 1930, section 17.
85. Letter of March 24, 1930, section 18.
86. Letter of March 24, 1930, section 22.
87. Letter of February 14, 1974, section 1.
88. For *Lumen Gentium* (Dogmatic Constitution on the Church), the English text can be found in *Vatican Council II: The Conciliar and Post Conciliar Documents*, pp. 350-427; for *Apostolicam Actuositatem* (Decree on the Apostolate of Lay People), in *Vatican Council II*, pp. 766-798; for *Gaudium et Spes* (Pastoral Constitution on the Church in Today's World), in *Vatican Council II*, pp. 903-1014; and for *Presbyterorum Ordinis* (Decree on

the Ministry and Life of Priests), in *Vatican Council II*, pp. 863-902.
89. Letter of February 14, 1974, section 9.
90. Letter of February 14, 1974, sections 28 and 29.

Conquistadors and Grains of Wheat

1. *Praktisches Bibelhandbuch Wortkonkordanz* [Practical guide to the Bible, concordance], 9th ed. (Stuttgart, 1968).
2. Letter of January 9, 1932, section 91.
3. *Conversations*, p. 137.
4. *Conversations*, pp. 137-138.
5. *Conversations*, pp. 137-138.
6. St. Francis de Sales (1567–1622) was bishop of Geneva, and one of the main proponents of the Catholic renewal movement in France after the Huguenot Wars. Together with St. Jane Frances de Chantal, he founded the Order of the Visitation of Mary. He was one of the most important theologians, preachers, and spiritual writers in Church history. His most important work, *Introduction to the Devout Life*, is at once a school of interior life and a guidebook for lay people who wish to seek Christian perfection within the framework of their familial and professional lives — that is, in the midst of everyday life. A doctor of the Church, Francis de Sales is the patron saint of authors and journalists.
7. Of the Roman priest St. Vincent Pallotti (1795–1850), Wilhelm Schamoni writes: "Following the iconoclasm of the Napoleonic Era, and during the decades of turmoil leading to the events of 1848, Palotti was the soul of reconstruction. His concern was not, however, to restore the past, but rather to find the path to a new future. In his keen enthusiasm for the kingdom of God, he dreamed of a renewal of the Church, and of society as a whole, by way of a rekindled apostolic movement comprised of priests and lay persons who would employ the weapons of prayer, penance, and charity to carry the truth of Christ's spirit into all aspects of life. Thus he became a forerunner of Catholic Action." In *Das wahre Gesicht des Heiligen* [The true face of the saint], 5th ed. (Würzburg/Hildesheim/New York, 1966).
8. John Henry Newman lived from 1801 to 1890. An Anglican clergyman and theologian, he was an important leader of the Oxford Movement, which aimed at reactivating the Catholic heritage of the Church of England. He converted to Catholicism in 1845 and was ordained in 1847, in Rome. He founded (in Birmingham) the first Oratory of St. Philip Neri in England. He was noted for combining frank criticism of opinionable matters with absolute loyalty to the dogmatic teachings of the Church. Pope Leo XIII elevated him to the rank of cardinal in 1879.
9. See the collection *Die kirchlichen Urkunden für die Weltgemeinschaften* [Church documents for the world communities] (Einsiedeln, 1963), especially "Instituta Saecularia."

10. Bernal, pp. 262-270.
11. *Meditaciones*, vol. 6, section 473.
12. *Meditaciones*, vol. 6, section 492.
13. Letter of October 24, 1942, section 41.
14. The social work with young people that is undertaken by the women's branch of Opus Dei is also placed under the protection of the archangel Raphael and is carried out in a manner analogous to that of the men's branch.
15. Letter of October 24, 1942, section 42.
16. Letter of October 24, 1942, section 41.
17. The text of the eulogy was given to me by the prelate of Opus Dei for research purposes.
18. Bernal, p. 119.
19. See note 17.
20. Bernal, p. 140.
21. Bernal, p. 140.
22. See note 17.
23. Alonso de Orozco (1500-1591) was an Augustinian monk and the court chaplain of Emperor Charles V. Working mostly in Madrid, he developed a life rich in pastoral activities, preaching and engaging in welfare work with the poor and the imprisoned. In his writings he combined mystical depth with a popular style.
24. *Articoli*, section 70. (The Italian text is as follows: "Egli avverti con singolare e vivissima chiarezza quel senso della filiazione divina che costituisce il fondamento della spiritualità dell'Opus Dei.")
25. Bernal, p. 214.
26. *Articoli*, section 70.
27. *Articoli*, section 72.
28. *The Way of the Cross* (London/New York, 1983), p. 23.
29. *Way of the Cross*, p. 71.
30. *Way of the Cross*, p. 87.
31. Editorial in *Crónica* 1962, no. 12.
32. The wall with the image of "La Virgen de la Almudena" is on a street called Cuesta de la Vega, not far from the royal cathedral La Almudena.
33. Letter of May 6, 1945, section 23.
34. *Crónica* 1961, no. 12.
35. This phrase comes from a prayer seeking the intercession of Blessed Josemaría Escrivá.
36. *Meditaciones*, vol. 1, section 46.
37. *Meditaciones*, vol. 1, section 46.
38. *Crónica* 1958, no. 9.
39. *Crónica* 1962, no. 7.
40. Instruction of May 1935 (communicated on September 14, 1950), footnote 179. Also *Meditaciones*, vol. 4, section 298.
41. Instruction of May 1935, section 18. Also *Meditaciones*, vol. 5, section 406.
42. Instruction of May 1935, section 24.

43. Rosa María Storti, "Isidoro Zorzano: La vida y el trabajo de un ingeniero" [Isidoro Zorzano: The life and work of an engineer], in *Cristianos corrientes. Textos sobre el Opus Dei*, collected by Francisco Martinelli (Madrid, 1970), p. 144.
44. Storti, p. 146.
45. Storti, p. 146.
46. St. John Bosco lived from 1815 until 1888. Ordained in 1841, he well deserved his title of "Apostle of Youth," because he spent his life looking after impoverished, homeless, and neglected adolescents. He was the founder of the Salesian Order (the Pious Society of St. Francis de Sales), which today has more than 22,000 members. He also founded the Society of Sisters of Mary.
47. Storti, pp. 147-148.
48. Conversation with Juan Jiménez Vargas on June 20, 1981, in Pamplona.
49. Testimonial of Jiménez Vargas for Escrivá's beatification, in *Registro Histórico del Fundador (RHF)*, 4152.
50. Testimonial of Jiménez Vargas, *RHF*, 4152; also, testimonial of José Antonio Palacios López, *RHF*, 2750.
51. *RHF*, 4152.
52. Regarding the following, also *Articoli*, section 83.
53. Letter of July 16, 1933, section 15.
54. Letter of July 16, 1933, section 1.
55. *Crónica* 1960, p. 881.
56. *Meditaciones*, vol. 6, section 475. The wide field of apostolate with adults (single and married, young and elderly) — the "work of St. Gabriel" — always forms a significant part of the rich harvest; this is not specifically mentioned here, but it is understood.
57. *Meditaciones*, vol. 6, section 475.
58. Instruction of March 19, 1934, section 20.
59. Instruction of January 9, 1935, section 25.
60. Some of the spiritual training and continuing education of the members of Opus Dei takes place in regularly convened short meetings (of no more than an hour's duration), in small groups called "circles."
61. The actual postulation document, which describes in concentrated form the saintly life of the Servant of God, is accompanied by the collected testimonials of witnesses — testimonials based on personal knowledge and experience. Msgr. Escrivá's postulation document is *Fama di Santità in vita*. (See "Prayer in the Night," note 4.)
62. Letter of September 3, 1976, from Bishop Castán Lacoma to Pope Paul VI, *Fama*, pp. 40-42.
63. Same letter.
64. Letter of August 14, 1931, in *Alcune*. And (also in *Alcune*) the testimonial of the archbishop of Saragossa, Pedro Cantero Cuadrado.
65. Same letter.
66. "Recuerdos," *Crónica* 1978, no. 1. See note 29 in "The Bells."

67. "Recuerdos," *Crónica* 1976, no. 12.
68. See note 66.
69. Bernal, p. 327.
70. *Diccionario de Historia Eclesiástica de España*, vol. 2 (Madrid, 1972), p. 1388.
71. Bishop Eijo y Garay was the president of the Instituto de España and of the Comisión de Educación Nacional de las Cortes Españolas. He also served as "Consejero del Reino" (counselor of the realm) and as director of the Francisco Suárez Institute of the Supreme Council for Research and Science.
72. Bernal, p. 122.
73. *Friends of God*, p. 36.
74. Letter of May 6, 1945, section 16.
75. Bernal, p. 215.
76. "Recuerdos," *Crónica* 1977, no. 10.

War in Spain

1. Spain is now a parliamentary democratic monarchy, and in this post-Franco era it seems to be opting for a synergetic federalism as a middle-road alternative between repressive centralism and self-destructive particularism or even separatism. It must be understood that the substantial economic, social, historical, and cultural differences among its various regions are some of the main obstacles on this otherwise solid path.

2. See Richard Konetzke, "Die iberischen Staaten von 1875 bis zum I. Weltkrieg (1875–1917)" [The Iberian states from 1875 until World War I (1875–1917)], in *Europa im Zeitalter der Nationalstaaten und europäische Weltpolitik bis zum Ersten Weltkrieg*, vol. 6 of *Handbuch der europäischen Geschichte*, ed. Theodor Schieder (Stuttgart, 1968), pp. 503-533. See also Ramón Menéndez Pidal, *Die Spanier in der Geschichte* [Spaniards in history] (Darmstadt, 1979).

3. In this context and with regard to the following, see Konetzke, *Die iberischen Staaten vom Ende des I. Weltkriegs bis zur Ära der autoritären Regime (1917-1960)* [The Iberian states from the end of World War I until the era of the authoritarian regimes (1917-1960)], vol. 7 of *Handbuch* (Stuttgart, 1979), partial vol. 1, pp. 651-693. See also Vicente Rodríguez Casado, *Conversaciones de historia de España*, vol. 3 (Barcelona, 1965).

4. *Weltmächte*, pp. 671-672.

5. *Weltmächte*, p. 676.

6. *Weltmächte*, pp. 677-678.

7. See Hellmuth Günther Dahms, *Der spanische Bürgerkrieg 1936-1939* [The Spanish Civil War 1936-1939] (Tübingen, 1962). This is one of the best German studies of this subject; Dahms gives an extraordinarily objective and just description of the conflict's complexities.

8. Conversation with Dr. Vicente Rodríguez Casado, professor of modern

history at the University of Madrid, on June 17, 1981. This was his explanation: "Spain did not experience any religious wars until the civil [Carlist] wars of the nineteenth century, in which the conservative Catholics and the Catholic liberals carried out their conflicts. The Spanish monarchy and the Spanish people, however, have always subjugated themselves to the idea of religious unity. Spain can always find the antidote to any poison — or, vice versa, the negative to every positive — and this always occurs in radical ways. Spain is a country where nothing remains in the realm of ideas, everything is immediately put into practice in a radical manner.... The Second Republic paved the way for Communism, though the Communists numbered only a few people. Being small in number has never prevented them from taking power; on the contrary, it encourages them. In Spain they were supported by a wide variety of socialists, as well as by the anarchists and syndicalists. The persecution of Christians and the Church was a program of action and a fact of life in the Second Republic long before the Civil War broke out."

9. *Weltmächte*, p. 685.
10. Letter of October 24, 1965, section 66.
11. Letter of June 16, 1960, sections 41 and 42.
12. Legislation passed in Spain on November 24, 1939, established the Consejo Superior de Investigaciones Científicas y Relaciones Culturale [Supreme Council of Scientific Research and Cultural Relations]. Albareda was appointed its general secretary.
13. See Enrique Gutiérrez Ríos, *José María Albareda, Una época de la cultura española* (Madrid, 1969).
14. Gutiérrez, p. 73.
15. Gutiérrez, p. 79.
16. Gutiérrez, p. 80.
17. Gutiérrez, pp. 80-81.
18. Gutiérrez, p. 81.
19. Gutiérrez, p. 81.
20. Gutiérrez, p. 94.
21. Gutiérrez, p. 94.
22. Gutiérrez, p. 94.
23. Gutiérrez, p. 95.
24. The notes of Pedro Casciaro Ramírez form a particularly important testimonial. Originally an architect, he has been working in Mexico for well over forty years as a priest. I had access to his reminiscences via *RHF*, 4197, 4198, 4200, 4201, and 4318.
25. Testimonial of Jiménez Vargas, *RHF*, 4152.
26. Testimonial of Jiménez Vargas, *RHF*, 4152.
27. Dahms, p. 72.
28. Gregorio Marañón y Posadillo (1887-1960) had a fascinating double career. He was both a well-known medical scientist who specialized in endocrinological research and a renowned author who dealt with a broad range of subjects. His biographies of the Duke of Olivares (1936) and of

Antonio Pérez (1947) have also been published in German translations.

29. José Ortega y Gasset (1883-1955), a philosopher influenced by Dilthey and Nietzsche, had studied in Berlin, Leipzig, and Marburg, and had maintained close ties with German culture. He wrote brilliant essays, but systematic thought was not his forte. Alienated from the Catholic faith, he substantially contributed to that alienation among Spanish intellectuals. As a dazzling writer, orator, and teacher, he wielded considerable influence over Spain's students and scholars. For decades he also used the newspapers *La Tribuna* and *El Sol* to manipulate Spanish public opinion into the mold of a libertarian individualistic spirit. From 1936 to 1949 he lived and taught in France, the Netherlands, Portugal, and South America.

30. Miguel de Unamuno (1864-1936) was an important scholar, philosopher, author, and poet. Under the dictatorship of Primo de Rivera, he went into voluntary exile in France after having been banned for one year to the Canary Islands. He returned to Spain and taught at the University of Salamanca, whose rector he was until 1936. Taking as his starting point the realization that no amount of "culture" can cancel out the conflicts of time and eternity, he theorized about the "tragic feeling of life" he saw as determining the character and destiny of the Spanish spirit. As a philosopher he was a spiritualist, and his religious point of view reflected a dogmatic individualism.

31. Ramón Menéndez Pidal (1889-1968), a philologist and historian, was one of the most important representatives of the Spanish humanities in the twentieth century. In 1910 he was appointed director of the Centro de Estudios Históricos. From 1925 to 1938, and again from 1947 on, he was the president of the Spanish Academy of Sciences. In 1940 he published a multivolume history of Spain.

32. Dahms, p. 69. On the 6th of June, the Communist Party transmitted to all functionaries precise orders for the opening fight. These orders regulated the armament and the actions of the raiding parties, as well as the cooperation between the Red cells working within the military barracks and those working in the towns that were to be taken. Furthermore, they specified which government officials, civil governors, security personnel, party members, and members of the bourgeoisie were to be executed, "incluso de sus familiares, sin exclusión de ninguno" [including all family members, without exception].

33. Dahms, pp. 81-82.

34. Testimonial of Jiménez Vargas, *RHF*, 4152.

35. *Articoli*, section 98.

36. Testimonial of Jiménez Vargas, *RHF*, 4152.

37. This term refers to the order one establishes, by way of a daily routine, to ensure the harmony of Mass attendance, prayer, Gospel reading, and so forth, on the one hand, and professional and other activities, as well as time for relaxation, on the other.

38. Escrivá encouraged his followers to enter a church at least once a day in order to pray before the Blessed Sacrament.

39. Testimonial of Pedro Casciaro, *RHF*, 4197.
40. Bernal, p. 232.
41. Bernal, p. 232.
42. Cf. *Crónica* 1976, no. 3. During a meeting with members of Opus Dei, Alvaro del Portillo recounted how one day the psychiatric clinic had been searched by the militia, an action that always spelled danger. On this occasion, one of the bona fide patients provided the life-saving distraction. He stepped up to one of the soldiers, pointed to his machine gun, and asked, "Is that a string instrument or a wind instrument?" "He was," said del Portillo, "really sent by God." (Also in "Recuerdos," *Crónica* 1979, no. 10.)
43. Testimonial of Jiménez Vargas, *RHF*, 4152 (section titled "La Legación de Honduras").
44. *RHF*, 4152 (section entitled "Cartas del Padre").
45. Bernal, p. 233; Gutiérrez, p. 109.
46. In this context and with regard to the following, testimonial of Jiménez Vargas, *RHF*, 4152.
47. Jiménez Vargas traveled under the name of Ricardo Vallespín, a member of Opus Dei who had fled into the Nationalist Zone.
48. Testimonial of Casciaro, *RHF*, 4197.
49. Testimonial of Casciaro, *RHF*, 4197.
50. Testimonial of Jiménez Vargas, *RHF*, 4152.
51. Testimonial of Casciaro, *RHF*, 4197.
52. In this context and with regard to the following, *Obras* 1982, no. 2, pp. 12-30, and no. 4, pp. 12-26. (*Obras* is an internal publication of Opus Dei similar to *Crónica* and *Noticias*, but issued less frequently and written for a somewhat wider audience.)
53. Gutiérrez, pp. 115-116.
54. In the time following his departure from Barcelona, he always said the Mass in honor of the Blessed Virgin. He had copied its liturgy onto small pieces of paper, and he carried with him the Mass kit necessary for its celebration.
55. Testimonial of Casciaro, *RHF*, 4197.
56. Testimonial of Jiménez Vargas (section titled "La rosa de Pallerols"), *RHF*, 4152.
57. Gutiérrez, pp. 123-134.
58. "Recuerdos," *Crónica* 1977, no. 12.
59. In German, "Konveniat" — a weekly meeting of clergy.
60. Regarding the following, see Gutiérrez, pp. 122-131.
61. Testimonial of Casciaro, *RHF*, 4197.
62. "Recuerdos," *Crónica* 1978, no. 6.
63. "Cid" was the Moorish name of the Spanish national hero Rodrigo (Ruy) Díaz, who lived from 1043 to 1099. Banned by his king, Alfonso VI of León, he occasionally served the prince of Saragossa. This, incidentally, included defending the prince against his Christian enemies. In 1094 he captured the Moorish empire of Valencia, and it was there that he died. He became a literary hero mainly as a symbol for the loyalty of a vassal

who is not discouraged by anything, not even by the ingratitude of his master. Menéndez Pidal (see note 31) researched his life and times.

64. Testimonial of Casciaro, *RHF*, 4197.
65. Testimonial of Casciaro, *RHF*, 4197.
66. Testimonial of Casciaro, *RHF*, 4197.
67. Testimonial of Casciaro, *RHF*, 4197.
68. *The Way*, point 976.
69. Testimonial of Casciaro, *RHF*, 4197.
70. This thought is expressed in point 811 (of *The Way*), which was written in Burgos: "Do you remember? You and I were praying silently as night was falling. From close by came the murmur of water.

   "And through the silence of the city, we also seemed to hear the voices of people from many lands, crying to us in anguish that they did not yet know Christ.

   "Unashamedly you kissed your crucifix and asked him to make you an apostle of apostles."
71. Testimonial of Casciaro, *RHF*, 4197.
72. Point 962 of *The Way* uses the same metaphor: "Unity. Unity and submission. What do I want with the loose parts of a clock — finely wrought as they may be — if they can't tell me the time?"
73. Testimonial of Casciaro, *RHF*, 4197.
74. Testimonial of Casciaro, *RHF*, 4197.
75. The last Republican cities to fall were Jaén, Ciudad Real, and Albacete on March 29th; Sagunto and Valencia on March 30th; and Almería, Cartagena, and Murcia on March 31, 1939.
76. *Articoli*, section 115.

The Miraculous Catch of Fishes

1. The only years in which Escrivá did not visit Spain were 1952, 1955-1957, 1965, and 1971.
2. *Crónica* 1961, no. 1, p. 44.
3. *Articoli*, section 140.
4. *Articoli*, section 117.
5. It was customary to publish a brief statement or bit of advice from Msgr. Escrivá at the beginning of every edition of *Crónica* and *Noticias*. These introductory remarks have now been compiled in a collection, *De nuestro Padre* [From our Father], which is intended for use within Opus Dei. In their entirety they represent a compendium of the spirit and the spirituality of Opus Dei. The collection includes quotes from the January 1954 through June 1976 issues of *Crónica* and *Noticias*. This one is point 4 (from *Noticias* 1966, no. 2) .
6. *De nuestro Padre*, point 40.
7. *Articoli*, section 120.
8. Letter of March 11, 1940, section 34.

9. Letter of October 24, 1942, section 9.

10. Letter of May 31, 1943, section 62.

11. Letter of February 14, 1944, section 18.

12. Letter of May 6, 1945, section 42.

13. The terms "co-redemption" and "co-redeemer" can easily be misinterpreted. In no way do they imply doubt that Jesus Christ is the one and only redeemer of the human race, or that the act of redemption occurred once and for all. But though it did take place in the past, the redemption did not abolish world history, the path of humankind on this earth. Rather, it continues to operate in the daily Christian celebration of the intimate union between Christ and his spouse, the Church, and in this sense it is permissible to speak of "co-salvation," a daily contribution to redemption. Those who are saved should not be passive and just wait, but instead should act with Christ and as Christ's representatives — as apostles, if you will. As del Portillo says in his introduction to *The Way of the Cross*, "Christians mature and become strong when they stand near the cross, in the very place where they also find Mary, his mother." It is there that we discover in the Holy Spirit that we ourselves are called upon to join in the great achievement that is redemption by partaking in the suffering of Christ in the midst of our daily endeavors. This link allows everyone who is called upon to become one with Christ on the cross to share in the graces of the secret of salvation. One thus becomes a "co-redeemer." Msgr. Escrivá was fond of using this strong expression in connection with the Church's doctrine of salvation. See *The Way of the Cross*, pp. 12-13. See also Peter Berglar, "Geschichte – Heil – Heilsgeschichte" [History – salvation – salvation history], in *Kultur als christlicher Auftrag heute* [Culture as a Christian mandate today] (Kevelaer/Graz/Vienna/Cologne, 1981), pp. 197-245.

14. Letter of May 6, 1945, section 40.

15. *Crónica* 1964, no. 9, p. 69.

16. Instruction of April 1, 1934, section 65.

17. Instruction of December 8, 1941, section 109.

18. Letter of May 6, 1945, section 68.

19. Letter of May 6, 1945, section 68.

20. The Spanish term is *operarias doctrineras*.

21. Testimonial of Encarnación Ortega, *RHF*, 5074.

22. Testimonial of Encarnación Ortega, *RHF*, 5074.

23. Testimonial of Encarnación Ortega, *RHF*, 5074.

24. *The Way of the Cross*, pp. 95-96.

25. Testimonial of Encarnación Ortega, *RHF*, 5074.

26. Testimonial of Encarnación Ortega, *RHF*, 5074.

27. Schamoni, *Jung und Heilig: Wahre Bildnisse* [Young and saintly: True portraits] (St. Augustin, 1980), p. 5.

28. Opus Dei has, of course, always adhered to the canonical norms regarding the age requirement for limited or final commitment.

29. *Meditaciones*, vol. 1, section 46.

30. Letter of January 9, 1959, section 53.
31. Testimonial of Encarnación Ortega, *RHF*, 5074.
32. Bernal, pp. 142-143.
33. *Conversations*, section 14, p. 26.
34. Testimonial of Encarnación Ortega, *RHF*, 5074.
35. There were also several household workers who were not members of Opus Dei, but employees under the supervision of these three young ladies.
36. "Recuerdos," *Crónica* 1976, no. 8.
37. *Conversations*, pp. 159-160.
38. *Articoli*, section 1160.
39. *Articoli*, section 1160. (The Spanish translates literally as: "for my sister, for my Father...," conveying the direct discourse of the person praying. The change to second person has been made to prevent misunderstandings.)
40. *Articoli*, section 1055.
41. The canonical regulations governing a priest's right to hear confessions must, of course, be taken into account.
42. Point 220 from *De nuestro Padre* (*Noticias* 1973, no. 7) is relevant in this context. "Love the holy sacrament of Penance," says Escrivá. "Prepare your weekly confession and make it with a sense of tact. As for me, partaking in this means of grace fills me with great joy, for I know that the Lord forgives me and imbues me with courage. And I am convinced that the pious practice of the sacrament of confession teaches one to feel deeper pain, and thus also deeper love."
43. Testimonial of Archbishop José María García Lahiguera, *Testimonies to a Man of God*, vol. 1 (London/New York, 1992).
44. Testimonial of García Lahiguera.
45. With respect to the general subject of this section, see Alvaro del Portillo, *Faithful and Laity in the Church* (Dublin, 1972).
46. The overarching unity of the calling to Opus Dei, which includes lay people and priests, celibate and married people, men and women, is an absolute novelty in the Church. In his letter of August 8, 1956, section 5, Escrivá addressed this novelty. "Opus Dei," he said, "has created many canonical and theological problems in the Church and has solved them. I say this with humility, for humility is truth. Once solved, the problems appeared simple — in particular, the fact that [Opus Dei] knows only one vocation, though it is intended for clergy and laity alike."
47. Bernal, p. 83.
48. He said this on October 19, 1972, in Madrid. See Bernal, p. 81.
49. This problem is discussed in Escrivá's letter of January 9, 1959.
50. Letter of January 9, 1959, section 15.
51. Bernal, p. 144.
52. Letter of February 2, 1945, 25.
53. *De nuestro Padre*, point 145 (*Noticias* 1969, no. 4).
54. Bernal, p. 145.
55. *Articoli*, section 995.

56. Dolores Escrivá died on April 22, 1941, of heart failure. She was at home, in the house at 14 Diego de León St. in Madrid.

57. Cf. Bernal, pp. 145-148. Also pertinent is footnote 103 to the Instruction of December 8, 1941, in which del Portillo speaks of Escrivá's readiness to entrust the direction of Opus Dei to others and to create a new society for diocesan priests. "God permitted our founder," he says, "to make the sacrifice that Abraham made. The Father agreed to make this sacrifice, and in doing so he was presented by the Lord with the solution [of the problem]. It was clear that secular priests also had a place in Opus Dei, since all members of Opus Dei strive for sanctity by hallowing their own professional work, as dictated by personal circumstances."

58. Conversation with the Rev. Florencio Sánchez Bella on June 17, 1981, in Madrid.

59. See *The Life of the Holy Mother Teresa of Jesus*, vol. 1 of *The Complete Works of St. Teresa of Jesus* (London, 1978), pp. 254-255.

60. Conversation with the Rev. Gonzalo Redondo on June 20, 1981, in Pamplona.

61. Joseph Cardinal Frings, *Für die Menschen bestellt: Erinnerungen des Alterzbischofs von Köln* [Appointed for the people: Reminiscences of the former archbishop of Cologne] (Cologne, 1973), pp. 149-150.

62. See Rafael Gómez Pérez, *Política y religión en el régimen de Franco* [Politics and religion under Franco] (Barcelona, 1976), especially pp. 250-267.

63. *Articoli*, section 882.

64. *De nuestro Padre*, point 12 (*Noticias* 1970, no. 11).

65. The enmity against Escrivá and Opus Dei found its most violent expression in Barcelona, where a convent held a ceremonial book-burning of *The Way*. On the advice of the nuncio, Bishop Cicognani (who later became a cardinal), airplane tickets for Escrivá were ordered under the name "E. de Balaguer," because it would have been too dangerous for him to use the name "Escrivá." *Articoli*, sections 126, 127, and 129.

66. Testimonial of Bishop José López Ortiz, *RHF*, 3870. Also instructive on this subject is Antonio Fontán, *Los católicos en la universidad española actual* [Catholics in today's Spanish university] (Madrid, 1961).

67. Testimonial of López Ortiz, *RHF*, 3870.

68. See Fontán, pp. 60-65.

69. Fontán, p. 64.

70. Fontán, p. 64.

71. Testimonial of Laureano Castán Lacoma, *RHF*, 751. See also *Un Hombre de Dios: Testimonios sobre el Fundador del Opus Dei* [A Man of God: Testimonies about the Founder of Opus Dei], vol. 8 (Madrid, 1992).

72. Testimonial of Castán Lacoma, *RHF*, 751. "The reality of Church doctrine," the bishop writes, "and the truth of Msgr. Escrivá's teaching, which the Church ceremonially adopted at the Second Vatican Council, have proved and still prove, in the midst of the crisis the Church is currently experiencing, the exact opposite. The work of the sons and daughters of Msgr. Escrivá, wherever they may be in this world, spiritually

enlivens their environment, which leads to callings for all. Through his sons who are incardinated in the dioceses, Msgr. Escrivá is in the process of saving and rendering fruitful many diocesan seminaries."

73. Testimonial of López Ortiz, *RHF, 3870.* See also *A Man of God,* vol 2 (London–New York, 1992). "I know for sure," writes the bishop, "that Josemaría sent them vocations which were awakened as a result of his spiritual direction."

74. Testimonial of López Ortiz, *A Man of God.*

75. Testimonial of López Ortiz.*A Man of God.*

76. Testimonial of López Ortiz.*A Man of God.*

77. See the remarkably objective biography by the British historian Brian Crozier, *Franco* (Boston, 1967).

78. See Arnold Gehlen, *Moral und Hypermoral: Eine pluralistische Ethik* (Frankfurt/Bonn, 1969).

79. *Articoli,* section 802.

Roman and Marian

1. Letter of August 21, 1975. In *Fama,* p. 17.

2. *Fama,* p. 8.

3. *Articoli,* sections 57 and 58. See also *AAS* 39 (1947), p. 245.

4. *Provida Mater* is the apostolic constitution on the canonical states of life and international communities for the attainment of Christian perfection. In *AAS* 39 (1947), pp. 114-124.

5. *Provida Mater,* article 3, p. 121.

6. *Provida Mater,* article 4, p. 122.

7. Though Spain and Mexico should be mentioned first, all of Latin America has been rich in supernumerary vocations. Since the mid-sixties, so have such countries as Italy and the Philippines.

8. Letter of January 9, 1959, section 10.

9. Letter of January 9, 1959, section 54.

10. Letter of January 9, 1959, section 4. Also *Obras* (June 1962), pp. 11-12.

11. Letter of January 9, 1959, section 6.

12. Letter of January 9, 1959, section 6.

13. "En el orden religioso...."

14. Letter of January 9, 1959, section 11.

15. "...organización desorganizada...."

16. Letter of January 9, 1959, section 11.

17. Letter of January 9, 1959, sections 38 and 41.

18. Letter of January 9, 1959, section 42.

19. Letter of January 9, 1959, section 51.

20. Letter of January 9, 1959, section 51.

21. Letter of January 9, 1959, section 59.

22. Instruction of May 1935/September 14, 1950. In *Meditaciones,* vol. 5, section 405.

23. Interview with Jacques Guillemé-Brûlon in the May 16, 1966, issue of *Le Figaro* (Paris), in *Conversations*, p. 57. See also the interview with Pedro Rodríguez in the October 1967 issue of *Palabra* (Madrid), in *Conversations*, p. 35.

24. Interview with Peter Forbath of *Time* (New York) on April 15, 1967. In *Conversations*, section 29.

25. *Meditaciones*, vol. 5, sections 380-386.

26. *Meditaciones*, vol. 5, section 380.

27. Nowadays it is sometimes said that in terms of content the words "universal" and "catholic" are the same, the only difference being that one word is Latin, the other Greek. That is not quite the way it is. The principle of universality is something innerworldly; it does not have a laid-down content, but rather refers to general expectations within space and time. Thus we have expressions like "universal history" and "universal state." The principle of catholicity, however, represents the general expectation of the truth, especially the truth of Christ. This principle would remain in force even if only a few people in some obscure village continued to adhere to it.

28. *Meditaciones*, vol. 5, section 385.

29. *Meditaciones*, vol. 5, section 387.

30. *Meditaciones*, vol. 5, section 382.

31. *Conversations*, p. 57.

32. Msgr. Escrivá had important private audiences with Pope Pius XII on December 8, 1946, and on January 28, 1949; with Pope John XXIII on March 5, 1960, and on June 27, 1962; with Pope Paul VI on October 10, 1964, and on July 15, 1967.

33. *Articoli*, section 645. This prayer ("Let us pray for our Holy Father") forms part of the daily prayer said by members of Opus Dei.

34. *Articoli*, section 648. (It was in 1971 that he said this.)

35. *Articoli*, sections 649 and 650.

36. We know this from the account given by Alvaro del Portillo of his audiences with Pope Paul VI on February 5, 1976, and on June 19, 1978. In *Fama*, p. 8.

37. Letter of May 24, 1978, from Loris Capovilla, titular archbishop of Mesembria, prelate of Loreto, to Pope Paul VI. In *Fama*, pp. 7-8.

38. Berglar, "Pius XII," in *Personen und Stationen* (Bonn, 1966), especially pp. 171-179.

39. Testimonial of Encarnación Ortega, *RHF*, 5074.

40. *Articoli*, section 207.

41. *Articoli*, section 161.

42. *Articoli*, section 146.

43. *Articoli*, section 207.

44. *Articoli*, section 207.

45. *Articoli*, section 677.

46. *Articoli*, section 728.

47. February is a special month for Opus Dei: the women's branch was founded on February 14, 1930, and the Priestly Society of the Holy Cross was

founded on February 14, 1943. May has always been the month most particularly consecrated to the Virgin Mary; special prayers and pilgrimages during this month are a staple of popular Catholic devotion. October has been the "month of the rosary" ever since Pope Gregory XIII, in 1573, designated October 7th as the Feast of the Holy Rosary. (He determined that it be held on that day as an expression of eternal gratitude for the victory over the Turks in the sea battle of Lepanto; this victory, attributed to the recitation of the rosary, took place on October 7, 1571.)

48. See especially the homilies "To Jesus through Mary" and "Mary, Cause of our Joy," in *Christ is Passing By* (London/Chicago, 1971), pp. 189-200 and pp. 227-238. See also the homily "Mother of God, and our Mother," in *Friends of God*, pp. 243-258.

49. Escrivá, *Holy Rosary* (Chicago, 1972), introduction.

50. *Articoli*, section 963.

51. *Articoli*, section 964.

52. Letter of March 24, 1931, section 26.

53. *Articoli*, section 1031.

54. *Articoli*, section 1031.

55. *Articoli*, section 1056.

56. *Articoli*, section 1058.

57. Testimonial of Rosalía López, *Articoli*, section 966.

58. Testimonial of José Miguel Ibáñez Langlois, *Articoli*, section 970.

59. *Articoli*, section 1014.

60. The invitation came by way of Don Cruz Laplana, bishop of Cuenca, a relative of Escrivá's, in 1955. Also *Articoli*, section 1015.

61. *Articoli*, section 1015.

62. *Articoli*, section 1015.

63. *Articoli*, section 1002.

64. Alvaro del Portillo, at that time the general secretary of Opus Dei, helped to overcome Escrivá's inhibitions by convincing him that as an apostle he must use all the means available to him. Future generations had a right to see and hear their founder and spiritual father through this marvelous medium which, despite all its susceptibility to abuse, was a gift of God to human inventiveness. Escrivá recognized the truth of what del Portillo was saying, and he gave in, but a little bit of internal opposition (which he did his best to smooth over with a sense of humor) remained to the end.

65. *Articoli*, section 1016.

66. *Articoli*, section 1016.

67. *Articoli*, section 1017.

68. Although the women's branch works completely independently of the men's branch, not only sacramental care but part of the women's religious and spiritual instruction is the responsibility of the priests of Opus Dei.

69. *Conversations*, pp. 75-76 (section 63).

70. *Conversations*, p. 35 (section 19); and p. 6 (section 35).

71. "Currently" — as of 1966.

72. *Conversations*, pp. 64-65 (section 53).

73. See points 59, 60, and 63 of *The Way*.
74. Letter of September 19, 1957, section 53.
75. Letter of September 19, 1957, section 53.
76. Testimonial of Encarnación Ortega, *RHF*, 5074.
77. Bernal, p. 302.
78. *Articoli*, section 152.
79. *Articoli*, section 152.
80. *Articoli*, section 193. On February 14, 1963, Msgr. Escrivá consecrated the altar of the chapel of the Villa delle Rose.
81. Letter of January 25, 1961, sections 43 and 44.
82. Apart from a short trip to Portugal, Msgr. Escrivá had been in Spain from December 12, 1950, until January 23, 1951. On April 28 he again traveled to Madrid, where he stayed until the 12th of May. He was in Florence on the 6th and 7th of July. During October he again traveled in Spain and in Portugal, with a brief stop in Lourdes.
83. This was Ildefonso Cardinal Schuster, who at that time was archbishop of Milan. (He is mentioned in Escrivá's letter of January 25, 1961, section 44.)

   The testimonials of Juan Udaondo, a priest and a member of Opus Dei, are very informative. Written in 1975 and 1978, these reminiscences deal with events that had happened more than two decades before. As reflections of personal experience, they constitute reliable and highly valuable source material. They illuminate the founder's behavior in a situation that was obviously very threatening to the survival of Opus Dei.

   Once the archbishop had granted his approval, the first center of Opus Dei in Milan took up its apostolic work, in December 1949. Then the archbishop was made a cardinal. A Benedictine monk, Cardinal Schuster had a deep understanding of, and a lot of affection for, Opus Dei. From 1950 to 1954, Udaonda often met with this high prince of the Church. According to Udaonda, the cardinal always spoke of Msgr. Escrivá with deep admiration and respect. He saw Escrivá as being one of those rare individuals who from time to time are presented to the Church by the Holy Spirit so that they may leave an indestructible trace in the life of the Church. "I am," he said, "a Benedictine monk, formed by the rules of St. Benedict, and I have my way of living my poverty. You, however, have to live yours in the manner taught to you by your founder. I do not want to set up any obstacles against the Holy Spirit." Udaonda also says that upon being presented with a beautifully bound edition of *The Way*, the cardinal informed them that he had already read it and was using it in his personal prayer. (Testimonial of August 27, 1978. *RHF*, 3360).

   Near the end of September 1951, says Udaonda, Cardinal Schuster warned them that certain "high, very high officials" had told him unfavorable things about Opus Dei. "I do not believe them, I do not believe them," he said. "I am very pleased that Opus Dei is working in my diocese." But he emphasized again the high position of the officials who had told him these negative things about Opus Dei.

When the founder learned of this, he asked Udaondo and some of his other sons in Milan to clarify matters to the cardinal. After they had done so, the cardinal's good will towards Opus Dei was not only still intact, it was augmented and solidified. (Testimonial of August 22, 1975. *RHF*, 3360.)

In the beginning of March 1952, in a conversation with Udaonda and Juan Masía, the cardinal once again repeated his warning, this time giving it a historical context. The founder should think, he said, of Sts. Joseph Calasanz and Alphonsus Liguori, and be on his guard. Both of these saints had founded orders and had encountered extreme difficulties within the Church. Joseph Calasanz was even removed from the order he himself had founded.... Deeply concerned, Udaonda immediately wrote to Escrivá about this conversation. A few days later he met him in Rome. He tells us of the enormous sense of internal peace, cheerfulness, and courage that emanated from the Father — an attitude that did not, however, exclude deep concern and sadness. "I had just finished saying Mass," writes Udaonda, "and had finished the ten minutes of thanksgiving, when the Father stepped into the chapel. Here, in the presence of the Almighty, he told me certain things that will forever be engraved on my heart and mind. 'My son,' he said, 'how often have you heard me tell you that I would be happy to leave Opus Dei — only to apply immediately for membership in it and to obey all in all matters and be in last place. You know that I never wanted to be the founder of anything; it was God's wish. Do you see how they are trying to destroy Opus Dei, and how they are attacking me? They want to throw me out of Opus Dei: *strike the shepherd and the flock will scatter.*' Tears welled up in the Father's eyes, and I started to cry too when he said, 'My son, if they throw me out, they will kill me; if they dismiss me, they will kill me. They should put me in last place, but not throw me out. They have already been told that they will be committing a murder if they throw me out.'"

Udaonda writes that Escrivá was forced to bear this cross, the constant threat of the destruction of Opus Dei, almost all by himself. He did this with joy. In fact, he made every effort to make sure no one else had to share the burden, with the one exception of Alvaro del Portillo. "At this very moment," the founder said, "the entire weight of Opus Dei rests upon my shoulders and on the shoulders of this son of mine." (Testimonial of December 8, 1975. *RHF*, 3360).

84. Escrivá had already made a pilgrimage to Loreto in January 1948.
85. *Articoli*, section 68.
86. "Recuerdos," *Crónica* 1979, no. 7. (Also *Noticias* 1956, no. 3.)
87. For this and the following, *Noticias* 1968, pp. 652-653.
88. As human beings, we are subject to conditions inherent in our nature. With no amount of force can we shed these limitations, and we should not even try to do so. It is expected of us, instead, to accept them in the humble recognition of our frailty and dependence — without, however, enslaving ourselves to them.

Escrivá's Day-To-Day Life

1. See *Dudens Das grosse Wörterbuch der deutschen Sprache in sechs Bänden*, vol. 1 (Mannheim/Vienna/Zürich, 1976), p. 108. See also *Trübners Deutsches Wörterbuch*, vol. 7 (Berlin, 1939), p. 4.
2. Escrivá says this in point 301 of *The Way*: "A secret, an open secret: These world crises are crises of saints. God wishes to see a handful of "his" people in every human endeavor. Then, *pax Christi in regno Christi* — the peace of Christ in the kingdom of Christ." [The German translation of *The Way* used by the author says *Es gibt Weltkrisen weil es an Heiligen fehlt.* "There are world crises because of the lack of saints." — Ed.]
3. To love only the materially poor and to want to exclude the wealthy from one's love is just another form of prejudice. As we know from the Gospel, the rich may be more in need of God's grace and our spiritual help than the poor, since they have more opportunities to fail in God's sight.
4. *Articoli*, section 170.
5. *Articoli*, sections 165-180: "A Day in the Life of the Servant of God, Josemaría Escrivá de Balaguer."
6. Point 179 of *The Way* is: "Choose mortifications that do not mortify others."
7. For example, Rm 8:13, 2 Cor 4:10, and Col 3:5.
8. This is point 173 of *The Way*.
9. *De nuestro Padre*, point 205.
10. Psalm 50 (51).
11. *Articoli*, section 163.
12. *Articoli*, section 184. Also "Recuerdos," *Crónica* 1977, no. 7.
13. *Die Stunde des Thomas Morus: Einer gegen die Macht* [The hour of Thomas More: One man against power], 3rd ed. (Freiburg, 1981).
14. Early on in the history of Opus Dei, the founder entrusted certain areas of its life and activity to the protection of saints who during their lives had been involved in similar spheres and pursuits. Thus, for example, St. Thomas More is called upon in all matters concerning Opus Dei's relationship to the state and other temporal powers; Pope St. Pius X in affairs connected with the Holy See; St. John Vianney in concerns involving the local bishops; St. Nicholas of Myra in times of material need; and St. Catherine of Siena in everything relating to the apostolate of Christianizing public opinion.
15. This is from a letter I received from the president general, Alvaro del Portillo, dated June 8, 1977. Villa Tevere has a relic of St. Thomas More.
16. See *Die Kirche zwischen Revolution und Restauration* [The Church between revolution and restoration], vol. 6 of *Handbuch der Kirchengeschichte*, ed. Hubert Jedin (Freiburg/Basel/Vienna, 1962-1979), pp. 180-185 and pp. 551-560.
17. See note 8 in "Conquistadors and Grains of Wheat."
18. In this context and with respect to the following, "Recuerdos," *Crónica* 1981, no. 3.

19. *Crónica* 1981, no. 3. (This was in Rome, on November 2, 1958.)
20. Coming from Belgium, Msgr. Escrivá spent July 1-3, 1956, in Cologne and Bonn. Coming from Switzerland, he again visited these two cities for three days in August. In 1959 he was at the Rhine from September 15th to 17th, and in 1960, on the 4th and 5th of May.
21. Conversation with del Portillo on January 24, 1981, in Cologne.
22. Taking Kant as his point of departure, Karl Christian Friedrich Krause (1781-1832) developed a doctrine of "Kategorienlehre des reinen Seins" (categories of pure being). He became influential in Spain and indirectly imparted a broad spectrum of the idealistic school of German philosophy, especially its philosophy of law.
23. I received from the directors of Opus Dei in Rome a precise enumeration of the founder's travels. This itinerary contains a description by Ignacio Sallent of the first trip to Central Europe in which he participated. Also, "Recuerdos," *Crónica* 1980, no. 11.
24. This letter was written on November 25, 1949.
25. "Recuerdos," *Crónica* 1980, no. 11.
26. The particular place is not known with certainty. It may have been the Church of the Holy Trinity.
27. Such conversations were very important in terms of laying the ground-work for the establishment of Opus Dei in new cities and dioceses, and instrumental in obtaining the good will of the local bishops. They were a matter of principle to the founder, and thus a reflection of his wisdom and loyalty.
28. With respect to the following, "Recuerdos," *Crónica* 1979, section 9.
29. In 1955, Escrivá was at Althaus three days in May, one day in November, and two days in December. He went there again on July 2, 1956; August 23, 1957; September 22, 1958; and September 16, 1959. His sojourns in Cologne during his trips to the Rhineland were even more numerous.
30. This prayer was answered in 1956. The first German center of the women's branch was in Cologne, in the vicinity of the Eigelstein-Tor. The founder paid it a visit on August 23, 1957.
31. The bare-bones itinerary for just one year, 1960, should give some idea of the intensity of Msgr. Escrivá's travel:
    April 5, Rome – Perugia – Assisi – Spoleto – Rome; April 25, depar-ture from Rome to northern Italy; April 27-29, travel to San Sebastián via Marseilles and along the Spanish-French border; April 30, Bordeaux; May 1-2, Paris; May 4-5, Cologne; May 8, Loreto; May 9, back to Rome. (These trips were by car.)
    July 7, depart again for northern Italy; July 7, Marseilles. July 8, travel through southern France; July 9, Lourdes and on to Bayonne; July 10, to Spain via Irún; July 11, Molinoviejo (a conference center near Segovia). July 12, to France via Irún and Hendaye; July 13-15, travel through France, with a brief stop in Paris, to Boulogne. July 16, Boulogne – Dover – London; July 17 - September 3, third sojourn in England. September 4, London – Southend – Calais. September 5, travel through France without

stopover in Paris. September 6-9, Biarritz – San Sebastián – Bilbao – Pamplona. September 10, Molinoviejo. September 11, Molinoviejo – La Pililla (a conference center to the southwest of Madrid). September 12, La Pililla. September 13, La Pililla – Los Rosales (study center of the women's branch) – Madrid – France (via Irún, Hendaye). September 19 to 21, Castello di Urio (conference center on Lake Como in Italy). September 22, back to Rome.

October 10, depart again for northern Italy. October 11-13, through France to Spain. October 14, to Madrid via Irún and Burgos. October 14-19, Madrid. October 20, Madrid – Saragossa. October 21, Saragossa. October 22, Saragossa – Pamplona. October 24, Biarritz – Pamplona. October 25-26, Pamplona. October 27, Pamplona – France. October 28-31, travel through France with stopover in Paris. November 1, Lyons – Ars – Milan. November 2, back in Rome. December 4, Milan; December 7, back to Rome.

32. With regard to the following, "Recuerdos," Crónica 1981, no. 7.

33. Meeting with members of Opus Dei on January 1, 1974, in Rome.

34. The miraculous image of Maria Pötsch dates back to the year 1676. It is located in the last bay of the side aisle, under a sixteenth-century altar baldaquin.

35. "Recuerdos," Crónica 1979, no. 10; Noticias 1960, no. 6.

36. Once they have made, in a true spirit of repentance, a good examination of conscience and a sincere confession of their sins, Catholics are expected to do penance not only for their own sins but also for the sins of others. The principle of representation, something very much in accord with the mind of Christ, includes the ability of a Christian to atone for sins committed by others, especially those committed on a massive scale — abortion, racial and religious persecution, economic injustice, terrorism, etc. One way to do this is to make a pilgrimage of atonement. Throughout the Middle Ages, this was a common form of expiation.

37. Articoli, section 223.

38. In December 1531, on a hillside near Mexico City, the Virgin Mary appeared to an Indian peasant named Juan Diego. As authenticating evidence for the bishop, she provided Juan Diego with roses that would normally be found only in Castile. But as soon as he opened his cloak to give the bishop these roses, a miraculous image of the Virgin appeared on his cloak. To this day, the cloth (which would normally have lasted only about twenty years) has remained intact. (This is only one of several facts about this phenomenon that have baffled scientists.) The image is now enshrined in the new basilica in Mexico City. Pope John Paul II prayed before it during his 1979 pilgrimage to Mexico. [And in 1991 he beatified Juan Diego. – Ed.]

39. RHF, 20760-1.

40. RHF, 20770-1 and 20775-6.

41. This may no longer be the case. Ignorance about the moral teaching of the Church is growing at an alarming rate. However, the conscious determi-

nation to ignore Church teaching seems to be growing at an even more alarming rate.

42. Prepared at the direction of Pope St. Pius X in the early part of this century, this catechism is a question-and-answer summary of Catholic doctrine. It is considerably shorter than the catechism published after the Council of Trent at the direction of Pope St. Pius V.

43. Filmed documentation of the meeting on June 16, 1974, in the General San Martín Convention Hall in Buenos Aires.

44. From the standpoint of the Catholic Church, the pope is not a mere "honorary chairman" of the college of bishops, but is in fact the real leader of the Church universal. Endowed with complete religious and canonical powers of jurisdiction, he is, by the will of Christ, the leader of all Christians, whether or not they accept him as such.

45. A prelate nullius is a dignitary who presides over the clergy and lay people of a certain territory not belonging to an established diocese — a mission territory, for example. However, prelates nullius exercise the right of consecration only if they have special papal permission to use the pontificals (liturgical books containing rites normally reserved to bishops) or, as in the case of titular bishops, if they have been ordained as bishops.

46. See vol. 1 of *Summa Pontificia. Lehren und Weisungen der Päpste durch zwei Jahrtausende: Eine Dokumentation* [Two millennia of papal teachings and instructions: A documentation], ed. P. Amand Reuter O.M.I. (Abensberg, 1978), pp. 480-482.

47. *Summa Pontificia*, vol. 1, pp. 474-480.

48. Karol Wojtyla (John Paul II), *Von der Königswürde des Menschen* [On the royal dignity of the human being] (Stuttgart, 1980), pp. 155-176.

49. Wojtyla, p. 176.

50. See Mt 25:14-30.

51. These three were Ignacio María de Orbegozo y Goicoechea, then prelate of the Yauyos (Peru) prelature, currently bishop of Chiclayo (Peru); Luis Sánchez Moreno Lira, then suffragan bishop and vicar general of Chiclayo, currently prelate of the Yauyos prelature; Alberto Cosme do Amaral, then suffragan bishop of Oporto (Portugal), recently retired as bishop of Leiria/Fatima (Portugal).

52. *Articoli*, section 209.

53. *Articoli*, section 210.

54. *Articoli*, section 212.

55. *Articoli*, section 212.

56. See *Lexikon für Theologie und Kirche. Das Zweite Vatikanische Konzil. Konstitutionen, Dekrete und Erklärungen*, 3 vols. (Freiburg/Basel/Vienna), 1966-1968.

57. No matter where authority originates or how it is justified and defined, it is inherent to its nature that it be accepted and followed. Authority has a legitimate claim to obedience. Where obedience is denied, it is probable that authority has been at least undermined, if not shattered.

58. Letter of February 14, 1964, section 12 .
59. Letter of October 24, 1965, section 73.
60. "Thomism," in its original sense, is the philosophical and theological system of thought set forth by St. Thomas Aquinas and his school. In a narrower sense, the term is used to distinguish St. Thomas' theology of grace from that of Luis de Molina (1535-1600). With the encouragement of the popes, Thomism has seen a strong revival since the middle of the nineteenth century.
61. See James Weisheipl, *Thomas von Aquin. Sein Leben und seine Theologie* [Thomas Aquinas: his life and theology] (Graz/Cologne, 1980). The book closes with this inviting challenge: "Thomas is not locked into the chambers of history; he is accessible to all generations who know how to read."
62. Letter dated February 14, 1974, section 26.
63. Letter dated February 14, 1974, section 26.
64. Letter dated February 14, 1974, section 26.
65. *Articoli*, section 215. See Franz Cardinal König, "Il significato dell'Opus Dei," in the November 9, 1969, issue of *Corriere della Sera* (Milan); Giacomo Cardinal Lercaro, "Significato della presenza dei cristiani nel mondo," in the June 25, 1976, issue of *Corriere della Sera*; and Joseph Cardinal Frings, *Für die Menschen bestellt* (Cologne, 1973), pp. 149-150.
66. In this encyclical (dated March 4, 1979), see especially chapter 3, section 13.
67. *Gaudium et Spes*, 91, in *AAS* 58 (1966), 1113.
68. *Gaudium et Spes*, 38 (p. 1056).
69. *Gaudium et Spes*, 76 (p. 1099).
70. See Gn 1:27.
71. *Gaudium et Spes*, 24, *AAS* 58 (1966), 1045.
72. All of these excerpts are from chapter 3, section 13, of *Redemptor Hominis*.
73. From a speech given on November 25, 1970. In *Articoli*, section 217.
74. Joaquín Mestre Palacios served for many years as secretary to the archbishop of Valencia, Marcelino Olaechea; he became canon at the cathedral of Valencia after Olaechea's death in 1972, *RHF*, 181.
75. [Berglar used the word "malochen," from the Yiddish word "maloche," meaning heavy, usually physical work.]
76. See Pope John Paul II's encyclical *Laborem Exercens* (September 14, 1981). See also Germán Rovira, *Das Persönlichkeitsrecht auf Arbeit* [The right of the individual to work] (Salzburg/München, 1978); and José Luis Illanes, *La santificación del trabajo* [The sanctification of work], 6th ed. (Madrid, 1980).
77. "Work" should be understood here in the general sense of purposeful performance — by human beings, yes, but also by horses, cattle, elephants, ... and even machines. Birds building their nests perform work by following their instincts. So do hamsters, ants, bees, beavers, and so forth.
78. *Articoli*, section 253.
79. Here he refers to extraordinary experiences of a mystical type.
80. "Work" cannot be equated with "action." An invisible, purely internal

process such as penance or prayer can be work, while an action such as eating is not considered work.

81. Letter of January 9, 1932, sections 5 and 6.
82. Letter of October 15, 1948, section 15.
83. Letter of October 15, 1948, section 10.
84. Letter of October 15, 1948, section 10.
85. Letter of May 6, 1945, section 25.
86. *Meditaciones*, vol. 2, section 96.
87. *Meditaciones*, vol. 3, section 225.

"For centuries," wrote Escrivá, "this doctrine sounded new, and even now the school of thought that everyone should seek Christian completeness within their profession and class through the observance of their daily work has a newness to it. For centuries, work was considered something humiliating. Even great theologians started with the premise that it was an obstacle to personal sanctity.

"My daughters and sons, I tell you that you should assure each and every person who rejects honorable, human work, be it significant or unimportant, on the assumption that it is neither sanctifying nor sanctifiable, that God has not called that person to Opus Dei. We must pray, and suffer too, so that this error may be erased from people's minds — so many good people are afflicted with it. However, the day will come when work performed by people on all levels, both intellectual and manual labors, will make everyone call to the heavens with one voice: *Cantate Domino canticum novum, cantate Domino, omnis terra* [Sing a new song to the Lord; sing to the Lord, all the earth..."] (Ps 95:1).

88. Letter of October 15, 1948.
89. Letter of October 15, 1948, section 33.
90. Letter of October 15, 1948, section 34.
91. Instruction of April 1, 1934, section 1.
92. Letter of April 30, 1946, section 46.
93. Letter of March 11, 1940, section 12.
94. *De nuestro Padre*, point 14.
95. *De nuestro Padre*, point 21.
96. Letter of March 11, 1940, section 49.
97. *Meditaciones*, vol. 1, section 88.
98. This expression denotes the transcendent, provident, and planning "reason" of God by which he sustains and guides our salvation. Human endeavor fulfills a decisive cooperating function in this sequence of events that is willed by his unfathomable wisdom.
99. Letter of February 14, 1950, section 17.
100. Letter of October 15, 1948, section 26.
101. *Way of the Cross*, p. 53.
102. *Articoli*, section 974.
103. *Articoli*, section 976.

Portrait of a Man and a Priest

1. Conversation with Alvaro del Portillo on January 24, 1981, in Cologne.
2. Paul Claudel and Reinhold Schneider, among others, reflect on the problem of whether there is such a thing as Christian tragedy. For Schneider, history shows that the consistent following of Christ is incompatible with political action and creation; history is one great, everlasting crucifixion of Christ. But even if one were to agree with this interpretation of history, would it be justifiable to see in it a tragedy? In the final analysis, only if there were no resurrection and beatitude at the end.
3. *The Way*, point 404.
4. Bernal, p. 338.
5. *Articoli*, section 429.
6. *Articoli*, section 241.
7. On this subject, see Schamoni, *Das wahre Gesicht der Heiligen*, pp. 23-75.
8. Testimonial of Thomas Muldoon, suffragan bishop of Sydney. *Fama*, p. 7. Also *Articoli*, section 1249.
9. Audience of Alvaro del Portillo with Pope Paul VI, March 5, 1976. In *Articoli*, section 1249.
10. Letter from Bishop Leopoldo Eijo y Garay to Dom Aurelio M. Escarré, dated March 10, 1942. In *Articoli*, section 1251.
11. With respect to the following, see note 74 of "Escrivá's Day-to-Day Life."
12. While the canonization of Pope Pius X took place only forty years after his death in 1914, Thomas More was canonized in 1935, four hundred years after his death.
13. *Articoli*, section 243.
14. *Articoli*, section 100.
15. The party that put up the banner was very likely the Communist Party, which might well be included among the "sowers of hatred" referred to in the first point of *The Way*.
16. *Articoli*, section 324.
17. *Articoli*, section 313.
18. *Articoli*, section 356.
19. *Articoli*, section 374.
20. *Articoli*, section 470.
21. *Articoli*, section 483.
22. Relevant in this context is point 201 of *De nuestro Padre*: "The magnanimous love that gives happiness to the soul comes out of pain, the fulfillment of one's duties, and the joy of overcoming oneself."
23. *Articoli*, section 525.
24. "Tengo que avistar el futuro...."
25. *Articoli*, section 526.
26. *Articoli*, section 779.
27. The prevention of evil is one of the most difficult problems facing any individual or society. On the one hand, in any diagnosis or prognosis of

an evil there is the possibility of error, and therefore a risk that the preventive measure may itself turn out to be an act of injustice. On the other hand, there is the basic human responsibility not to be passive about impending evil, not to just sit back and let it happen, but to make every effort to forestall it. And for one entrusted with authority, this responsibility is even greater: the faithful shepherd must protect the flock from the wolf. But that duty carries with it some thorny questions. May that faithful shepherd kill a wolf before it has done any actual harm? Is it not possible that what looks like a wolf may not be one at all? Or even if it is, might it not have a plentiful supply of food elsewhere and not be on the prowl? The problem with any preventive measure is that it is an action based on prediction; underlying assumptions have to be taken as certain when they are really not certain.

The legitimacy of preventive defense is a question with which historians and jurists have been wrestling from time immemorial. Moral theologians have also tried to find an answer. On the one hand, they deny the legitimacy of trying to forestall a bad thing by resorting to one that is equally bad, or by committing a smaller (even much smaller) evil. On the other hand, they concede justified defense. And therein lies the rub. Apart from the fact that *defendere* and *praevenire* in many situations cannot be clearly differentiated, experience shows that it is almost impossible, at least in the realms of society and politics, to defend oneself effectively without dirtying one's hands.

28. *Articoli*, section 784.
29. On August 14, 1838, King Ludwig I of Bavaria issued a decree whereby all Bavarian soldiers, including those who were Protestant, were ordered not only to attend Mass but also to genuflect before the Blessed Sacrament, whether inside a church or during a procession. This decree remained in force until December 1845.
30. *RHF*, section 181.
31. In fact, neither the region of Navarre as a whole nor its university has been spared the activities of the Basque terrorists. In June 1980, and again in June 1981, bomb attacks occurred in the area of the university's main building. In July 1982, the bookstore of the university press in Pamplona was destroyed by explosives.
32. This was the "Convenio entre la Santa Sede y el Estado Español sobre el reconocimiento, a efectos civiles, de los estudios de ciencias no eclesiásticas realizados en España en Universidades erigidas por la Iglesia" [Agreement between the Holy See and the Spanish government concerning the civil recognition of nonecclesiastical studies completed in Spain, in universities established by the Church]. In this connection, see Amadeo de Fuenmayor, *El Convenio entre la Santa Sede y España sobre Universidades de estudios civiles* (Pamplona, 1966).
33. By virtue of this agreement, other church-owned institutions of higher learning also came to be recognized by the state.
34. Letter of January 9, 1951, section 6.

35. "Ansprache an Wissenschaftler und Studenten im Kölner Dom am 15. November 1980" [Speech to scientists and students in the Cologne cathedral on November 15, 1980], *Announcements of the Holy See* (published by the Secretariat of the German Conference of Bishops), no. 25A: "Pope John Paul II in Germany, November 15 to 19, 1980."

36. Conversation with Professor Francisco Ponz on June 20, 1981, in Pamplona.

37. Same conversation.

38. Same conversation.

39. Gutiérrez, pp. 277-278.

40. Special edition of the university newspaper, *Redacción* (Pamplona, November 1976), on the occasion of the ninth conference of delegates of the Society of Friends of the University of Navarre.

41. "... manos que se divinicen ..."

42. *Redacción*, p. 20.

43. *Redacción*, p. 21.

44. *Redacción*, p. 21.

45. Testimonial of Bishop Thomas Muldoon, *Fama*, p. 33.

46. Testimonial of Encarnación Ortega, *RHF*, 5074, p. 43.

47. Testimonial of Encarnación Ortega, *RHF*, 5074, p. 43.

48. Testimonial of Encarnación Ortega, *RHF*, 5074, p. 158.

49. Testimonial of Encarnación Ortega, *RHF*, 5074, p. 190.

50. *The Way*, point 331.

51. According to the legend, Sisyphus was the founder and first king of Corinth. Because of his cruelty and trickery, he was condemned in the underworld to roll a huge stone up a mountain. But each time he comes close to success, just before he reaches the peak, the stone thunders back down into the depths.

52. Having become "Christ" in baptism, an individual is included in the reconciliation of God with the human race that was brought about by Jesus Christ, is included in the restoration of the original bonds of love, and is in that sense saved. This salvation, however, is not something that automatically endures; it can be lost. Human freedom is such that it is possible to destroy one's salvation by deliberately turning away from God and holding fast to that renunciation.

53. Escrivá used the Italian word *pochezza*, which can be translated as "meagerness," "sparseness," "littleness."

54. *Articoli*, section 235.

55. Bernal, p. 269.

56. Bernal, p. 269.

57. Bernal, p. 73.

58. Bernal, p. 216.

59. Bernal, pp. 311-312.

60. Letter of August 7, 1931.

61. A collection of polemic essays written in 1873-1876: for example, "Vom Nutzen und Nachteil der Historie für das Leben" [On the advantages and

disadvantages of history for life] and "Schopenhauer als Erzieher" [Schopenhauer as educator].

62. Von Hoffmannsthal's *Jedermann*, written in 1911, is subtitled "Das Spiel vom Sterben des reichen Mannes" [A play on the death of the rich man].

63. *Conversations*, pp. 119-120.

64. The papers of Josemaría Escrivá included a collection of more than two thousand aphorisms. These were later published in two books (similar in format to *The Way*) under the titles *Surco* [Furrow] and *Forja* [The forge]. [The English editions were published in 1987 and 1988—Ed.]

65. In 1956, the Spanish Commission of Opus Dei received from Rome a picture of Our Lady of Torreciudad. Escrivá had written on the back that in 1904 his parents had taken him there and placed him under her protection. But no one on the Commission knew the location of Torreciudad, and it could not be located on any current map. Finally, it was discovered on an old map dating back to the eighteenth century. Several members of Opus Dei reached Torreciudad on October 2nd. There they found the family that was looking after the little church, which had been built in the twelfth century. The miraculous image had been hidden during the Civil War, but regional veneration, the visitors learned, had never quite broken off. Torreciudad was mentioned in 1908 in a recommendation issued by the bishop regarding places of pilgrimage to the Virgin Mary. As a result, in that year approximately one thousand pilgrims came to the chapel.

In 1962, the bishop in charge of the chapel transferred to Opus Dei the caretaking responsibilities for this place of pilgrimage. Ambitious, long-term plans for its renovation were then developed. Rendered possible only by extraordinary efforts (material and apostolic) on the part of the entire Spanish branch of Opus Dei, this undertaking was completed in a little over a decade.

66. Mercedes Eguíbar, "Montserrat Grases: Una Vida sencilla" [Montserrat Grases: A simple life], in *Cristianos Corrientes* ... (See note 43 of "Conquistadors and Grains of Wheat"), pp. 154-202.

67. *Articoli*, section 238.

68. *Articoli*, section 1263.

69. *Articoli*, section 1264.

70. *Articoli*, section 1264.

71. According to the letter "Nuestro Padre, en el Cielo" (dated June 29, 1975), which general secretary Alvaro del Portillo addressed to all the members of Opus Dei, the fight for the founder's life continued for one and a half hours, though death had probably occurred shortly after his collapse. (*Crónica* 1975, no. 7.)

72. The complete text (in the Neovulgate) reads as follows: "Melior est finis negotii quam principium." ("The end of a task is better than its beginning.")

Epilogue: Opus Dei as a Personal Prelature

1. For a further understanding of the personal prelature, and of what this designation means to Opus Dei, see Pedro Rodríguez, *Particular Churches and Personal Prelatures* (Dublin, 1988); Amadeo de Fuenmayor, "La erección del Opus Dei in Prelatura Personal," in *Ius Canonicum*, Revista del Instituto Martín de Azpilcueta, vol. 23 (University of Navarre, 1983), pp. 9-55; *Primatial Power and Personal Prelatures* (Communication to the Fiftieth International Congress of Canon Law: Ottawa, August 1984); José Luis Gutiérrez, "De Praelatura personali iuxta leges eius constitutivas et Codicis Iuris Canonici normas," in *Periodica de re moralia, canonica liturgica* 72 (1983), pp. 71-111; Rafael Navarro-Vals, "Las Prelaturas personales en el Derecho conciliar y codicial," in *Estudios eclesiásticos* 59 (1984); Rudolf Schunck, "Die Errichtung der Personalprälatur Opus Dei," in *Theologie und Glaube* 73 (1983), pp 91-107; A. de Fuenmayor, V. Gómez-Iglesias, and J. L. Illanes, *El itinerario juridico del Opus Dei: Historia y defensa de un carisma* (Pamplona, 1985), an English translation of which is currently in preparation.

2. *RHF*, 20160, p. 312.

3. *RHF*, 20171, p. 1259.

4. *RHF*, 4197.

5. What the founder was hinting at was the necessity of seeking a canonical figure for Opus Dei within the hierarchical structure of the Church, but one not based on the territorial principle proper to a diocese. This was the situation exemplified by these two men buried beneath the church: each of them was a bishop who had exercised jurisdiction over a group of Christians united by particular circumstances, not by territory. The comparison refers to this point, and to it alone.

6. A basic work on this theme is Alvaro del Portillo's *Faithful and Laity in the Church* (Dublin, 1972).

7. See *Apostolicam Actuositatem*, 7.

8. *Lumen Gentium*, 31.

9. Letter of February 2, 1945.

10. Letter of January 25, 1961.

11. Preamble to *Ut Sit*, Latin text in *AAS* 85 (1983), pp. 757-787.

12. Letter of May 25, 1962.

13. *RHF*, 20171, p. 1265.

14. *RHF*, 20171, p. 1266.

15. A contract is constituted by the entering of a plurality of parties (at least two) into a determined relationship involving certain rights and obligations. For the validity of a contract, it is of no importance whether the parties are equal or unequal in terms of position, power, or even ontological nature. With regard to a prelature, any commitment has to be made with full freedom in order to be valid. The lay member and the prelature enter into a relationship of mutual commitment. The prelature undertakes, with

respect to this person, to make possible the fulfillment of his or her divine vocation, placing at the member's disposition the necessary spiritual assistance. The members, in return, commit themselves to living according to the spirit and internal law of the prelature.

Bibliography

1. *English translations of the writings of Josemaría Escrivá de Balaguer*

Christ is Passing By. Dublin/New York/Sydney, 1974 and 1985.
Conversations with Msgr. Escrivá. Dublin, 1974. (This book contains interviews which the founder of Opus Dei granted to journalists of the international press, as well as a homily titled "Passionately Loving the World," which he gave at the University of Navarre.)
Friends of God. 2nd ed.: London/New York, 1980.
Furrow. London/New York, 1987.
Holy Rosary. 3rd ed.: London, 1978.
In Love with the Church. London/New York, 1991.
La Abadesa de Las Huelgas: Estudio teológico jurídico [The Abbess of Las Huelgas. A theological and juridical study]. 2nd ed.: Madrid, 1974. (This book has not been translated into English.)
The Forge. London/New York, 1988.
The Way. Revised ed.: New Rochelle, 1985. (This book was first published in 1934, under the title *Consideraciones Espirituales.* It received its final title and was published in its entirety in the new edition that appeared in 1939 in Valencia.)
The Way of the Cross. London/New York/Dublin, 1983.

2. *Selected bibliography on Josemaría Escrivá and Opus Dei*

A Man of God. Testimonies by various authors. London/New York, 1992.
Bernal, Salvador. *Msgr. Josemaría Escrivá de Balaguer: A Profile of the Founder of Opus Dei.* London/New York, 1977.
Blank, W. and R. Gómez Pérez. *Doctrina y vida.* Madrid, 1970.
Gómez Pérez, R. *La fe y los días.* Madrid, 1973.
Gondrand, F. *At God's Pace: Josemaría Escrivá, Founder of Opus Dei.* New York/London, 1988. (Original French edition: *Au pas de Dieu,* Paris, 1982.)
Helming, Dennis M. *Footprints in the Snow: A Pictorial Biography of Josemaría Escrivá, the Founder of Opus Dei.* New York, 1986.
Herrán, L. M. "La devoción a San José en la vida y enseñanzas de Mons. Josemaría Escrivá de Balaguer, Fundador del Opus Dei (1902-1975)." *Estudios Josefinos* 68 (1980): 147-189.

Herranz, G. *Sin miedo a la vida y sin miedo a la muerte. Palabras de Mons. Josemaría Escrivá de Balaguer y Albás a médicos y enfermos. En memoria de Mons. Josemaría Escrivá de Balaguer.* Pamplona, 1976. (See especially pp. 133-173.)

Hervada, J. "Vita mutatur, non tollitur." *Recuerdo de Mons. Josemaría Escrivá de Balaguer y Albás, Fundador y Primer Gran Canciller de la Universidad de Navarra (1902-1975), Persona y Derecho* 2 (1975): 12-70.

Illanes, J. L. *La santificación del trabajo.* 6th ed.: Madrid, 1980.

Le Tourneau, Dominique. *What is Opus Dei?* Cork/Dublin, 1989.

Martinelli, F. *Cristianos corrientes. Textos sobre el Opus Dei.* Madrid, 1970.

Monseñor Josemaría Escrivá de Balaguer y el Opus Dei. En el 50 Aniversario de su Fundación. Pamplona, 1982. (This collection contains, apart from contributions by Escrivá and Alvaro del Portillo, additional descriptions and studies by M. González Cardinal Martin and Franz Cardinal König, as well as by Luis Alonso, Peter Berglar, Cormac Burke, José María Casciaro, Cornelio Fabro, José Luis Illanes, and others.)

Msgr. Josemaría Escrivá de Balaguer. Bulletin published by the vice postulator for the process of beatification. U.S. address of publication: 330 Riverside Drive, New York, NY 10025. To date, ten editions have been published in English.

O'Connor, William. *Opus Dei: An Open Book.* Cork/Dublin, 1991.

Roegele, Otto B., Albrecht Bekel, and Hugo Reiring. *Opus Dei - Für und Wider.* Osnabrück, 1967.

Seco, Luis I. *La herencia de Mons. Josemaría Escrivá de Balaguer.* Madrid, 1976.

West, William. *Opus Dei: Exploding a Myth.* Sydney, 1987.

3. **Documentation on Msgr. Escrivá's beatification and canonization process that is not readily and publicly available**

Romana Postulazione della Causa di Beatificazione e Canonizzazione del Servo di Dio Josemaría Escrivá de Balaguer y Albás. Sacerdote, Fondatore dell'Opus Dei. See especially *Articoli del Postulatore*, Rome, 1979 (1980 also, in Spanish translation); *Fama di Santità*, vol. 1, *Fama di Santità in vita* (Rome, 1979); and *Alcune Dichiarazioni a futura memoria I.* These are important testimonials regarding the life and work of Josemaría Escrivá. Some have been published in English, in two volumes, under the title *A Man of God* (London/New York, 1992). A larger collection has been published in Spanish in a multivolume series entitled *Josemaría Escrivá de Balaguer: Un Hombre de Dios* (Madrid, 1992).

Régistro Histórico del Fundador (RHF). This is the catalogued collection of material pertaining to the life and work of Msgr. Escrivá preserved in the archives of the prelature in Rome.

Index